Clinical Applications of Biofeedback: Appraisal and Status
(PGPS-75)

Pergamon Titles of Related Interest

Clinical Applications of Biofeedback: Appraisal and Status

Edited by
Robert J. Gatchel
Kenneth P. Price

Pergamon Press

NEW YORK • OXFORD • TORONTO • SYDNEY • FRANKFURT • PARIS

Pergamon Press Offices:

U.S.A.   Pergamon Press Inc., Maxwell House, Fairview Park,
                     Elmsford, New York 10523, U.S.A.

U.K.   Pergamon Press Ltd., Headington Hill Hall,
                     Oxford OX3 0BW, England

CANADA   Pergamon of Canada Ltd., 150 Consumers Road,
                     Willowdale, Ontario M2J 1P9, Canada

AUSTRALIA   Pergamon Press (Aust) Pty. Ltd., P O Box 544,
                     Potts Point, NSW 2011, Australia

FRANCE   Pergamon Press SARL, 24 rue des Ecoles,
                     75240 Paris, Cedex 05, France

FEDERAL REPUBLIC Pergamon Press GmbH, 6242 Kronberg/Taunus,
OF GERMANY   Pferdstrasse 1, Federal Republic of Germany

Library of Congress Cataloging in Publication Data
Main entry under title:

Clinical applications of biofeedback.

  (Pergamon general psychology series ; v. 75)
  1. Biofeedback training. I. Gatchel, Robert J.,
1947-   II. Price, Kenneth P., 1947-
(DNLM: 1. Biofeedback (Psychology) WL103 C641)
RC489.B53C55 1979   615'.851   78-26959
ISBN 0-08-022978-6
ISBN 0-08-022977-8 pbk.

Printed in the United States of America

To Our Loving Parents
Who Contributed So
Much To Our Lives

CONTENTS

FOREWORD

This important book neatly summarizes our present-day scientific knowledge pertaining to the usefulness of biofeedback in clinical practice. While biofeedback has been and will continue to be a valuable research tool for determining under what conditions individuals can learn to control seemingly involuntary physiological processes, the preliminary results of biofeedback research have often been prematurely applied in the clinic. It is becoming strikingly clear that effects attributed to biofeedback in clinical settings are often due to confounded variables such as the teaching of relaxation and self-management skills. Also, the modern equipment and impressive milieu of the biofeedback clinic may catalyze therapeutic processes by leading clients to believe that a scientific or "physical" approach to their problems is being implemented and by arousing their interest in the treatment and motivating them to carry out their part of the therapeutic regimen. The chapters in this book discuss these and many other kinds of "placebo" effects, and they indicate that much more research is needed to delineate the types of biofeedback procedures that can have specific effects on specific kinds of clients.

The text also points to other neglected clinical problems that need serious consideration. It appears that biofeedback training may be the least effective with individuals who need it the most; for example, learned control of vasomotor functions may be more difficult with migraine patients than with normal controls. Along similar lines, Robert Gatchel notes that heart rate biofeedback for the management of anxiety may be helpful only for those few clients who are capable of learning to voluntarily control heart rate and for whom heart rate change is the dominant component of their anxiety response. The concerns of this text are representative of the second wave of biofeedback research, which focuses on delineating biofeedback procedures that can play a limited but useful role as part of a broad-spectrum therapy.

Theodore X. Barber, Ph.D.
Medfield Foundation, Inc.
Medfield, Massachusetts

PREFACE

In recent years, a great amount of interest has been generated by the potential treatment applications of biofeedback techniques. It is unfortunately the case that, for many, biofeedback is still very much at the "cult" stage, with many proponents suggesting that biofeedback is a "cure-all" therapeutic technique largely on the basis of poorly controlled research studies or uncontrolled case studies. It became apparent to us that a critical evaluation of the field was sorely needed. We believe that this text makes a significant first step in such an evaluation. The contributors to the text were specifically chosen because of their broad expertise in the area of biofeedback, and for their past demonstrated ability to provide a critical and comprehensive evaluation of specific areas of biofeedback applications. The text as a whole will provide the reader with a better understanding of the areas where biofeedback has been unequivocally shown to be clinically effective, and those areas in which it has not yet been objectively validated as clinically useful. Chapters 2, 3, 4, 6, 12 and 13 are partially based upon papers delivered at a biofeedback symposium held in the spring of 1977 at the University of Texas at Arlington. The remaining chapters were written specifically for this text.

In Chapter 2, Peter J. Lang discusses two other potential uses of biofeedback in addition to that of treatment technique. They are biofeedback as a clinical-assessment tool and as a means of analyzing emotional imagery. Lang reviews methods for manipulating imagery through instructions and biofeedback, and discusses their use in behavioral therapy and fear reduction. The potential use of biofeedback techniques in the diagnosis of various forms of psychopathology, such as psychosomatic disorders, is also discussed. To date, applications of biofeedback methods to the above two areas have been almost totally neglected. To our best knowledge, this unique chapter is the first to formally present these potentially new uses of biofeedback technology.

In 1974, Edward B. Blanchard and L.D. Young published a very influential review article which critically evaluated the clinical significance of cardiovascular biofeedback techniques. It has become a widely cited article. In his chapter, Blanchard updates and substantially extends this review by critically evaluating the evidence for the efficacy of biofeedback treatment of cardiovascular diseases. He discusses the bases for evaluating clinical research and considers seven different dimensions that should be considered in evaluating clinical applications of biofeedback. Using those dimensions, he then reviews research on the clinical effectiveness of biofeedback in treating hypertension, cardiac arrhythmias, and peripheral circulatory disease.

In Chapter 4, James H. Geer reviews the literature relating to biofeedback and sexual responses. Geer discusses the role of cognitive factors in sexual arousal, and presents a very worthwhile set of suggestions as to how biofeedback can be utilized in the treatment of sexual dysfunctions. The chapter makes a novel and substantial contribution to this literature.

Chapter 5, written by William N. Kuhlman and Bonnie J. Kaplan, reviews the use of biofeedback in the treatment of epilepsy, hyperkinesis, insomnia, and in the induction of "altered states of consciousness." The extensive alpha conditioning literature is reviewed. An evaluation is made of the current state of knowledge, taking into account methodological differences between studies, conflicting results, and the importance of suggestion effects. Chapter 5 is the best updated summary of the EEG literature currently available. Moreover, it holds a great deal of theoretical significance.

In Chapter 6, John V. Basmajian and John P. Hatch discuss the use of biofeedback as a tool for skeletal muscular reeducation and as an improvement of many forms of therapeutic exercise. Both for reeducation of weak muscles and for relaxation of hyperactive muscles (either local or general), biofeedback techniques are shown to be the natural accompaniment of many clinical procedures. This chapter is an excellent up-to-date summary and a practical guide to neuromuscular reeducation by means of biofeedback.

A. Barney Alexander and Deborah Dimmick Smith review the literature pertaining to the use of biofeedback as a relaxation training technique in Chapter 7. They discuss the relationship of EMG biofeedback to relaxation and to such clinical disorders as tension headache and asthma. They also evaluate the generalization of training at specific muscle sites. In Chapter 8, Kenneth P. Price discusses migraine headaches and critically evaluates the use of biofeedback for the treatment of this disorder, presenting a balanced statement about biofeedback and relaxation for migraine problems.

Robert J. Gatchel reviews research on the use of biofeedback in the treatment of fear and anxiety in Chapter 9. Some recent research is discusssd which demonstrates that biofeedback methods are therapeutically effective in reducing anxiety by inhibiting the physiological component of this aversive emotional state. Along with the review of this recent research, the theory, measurement, and psychophysiology of anxiety and fear is discussed.

In Chapter 10, Edward S. Katkin and Steve Goldband discuss the role of placebo factors in biofeedback therapy. They point out that, unfortunately, the great bulk of research assessing the effectiveness of biofeedback therapy has failed to include appropriate controls for the contribution of nonspecific or placebo effects to therapeutic outcome. They present several worthwhile placebo-control conditions that may be of some value in future biofeedback therapy research.

Chapter 11, written by John D. Rugh, provides a discussion and illustration of the bioengineering principles involved in biofeedback and of things to look for in commonly available commercial hardware. This chapter will be of great practical value to clinicians and/or researchers planning to purchase biofeedback equipment.

The theme of Chapter 12 is somewhat different from that of the preceding chapters in that Bernard Tursky presents a review and assessment of the general theory and practice underlying biofeedback methodology including, for example, a discussion of biofeedback as reinforcement or information. The use of stimuli external to the subject such as tones or visual displays is discussed in the context of a proposal for a new methodology for biofeedback utilizing proprioceptive feedback. A new kind of positive feedback loop is proposed. It is a very interesting and novel contribution to the literature.

In Chapter 13, Neal E. Miller provides a general discussion of the chapters by Lang, Blanchard, Geer, Basmajian and Hatch, and Tursky. He provides an interesting commentary on the current status of the field and also reviews some of his recent biofeedback research with paralyzed patients. Finally, the last chapter by Price and Gatchel presents a general discussion of the content of the text. It also provides a final perspective and summary of the clinical effectiveness of biofeedback, and enumerates some of the issues that ought to be considered in future biofeedback research.

This text is intended for investigators, clinicians, teachers, and both graduate and advanced undergraduate students. It will provide the reader with a comprehensive and critical evaluation of the clinical effectiveness of biofeedback as a treatment modality, as well as a practical guide to effective clinical use of biofeedback. The book also presents future directions of biofeedback research and clinical utilization.

We would like to acknowledge a grant from the University of Texas at Arlington Organized Research Fund, sponsored through the Graduate School, which supported a biofeedback symposium held in the spring of 1977. This symposium contributed significantly to the inception and subsequent development of this text. Special thanks are also expressed to Mary Johnson, who provided secretarial help, and to Anita Taunton-Blackwood, who provided editorial assistance in organizing and reviewing the contents of the book. Finally, we express appreciation to the staff of Pergamon and, in particular, the consulting psychology co-editor, Leonard Krasner, who has helped greatly in the publication of this volume.

Chapter 1
Biofeedback: An Introduction and Historical Overview

Robert J. Gatchel and Kenneth P. Price

Before Harry Houdini performed one of his famous escapes, a skeptical committee would search his clothes and body. When the members of the committee were satisfied that the Great Houdini was concealing no keys, they would put chains, padlocks and handcuffs on him. . . . Of course, not even Houdini could open a padlock without a key, and when he was safely behind the curtain he would cough one up. He could hold a key suspended in his throat and regurgitate it when he was unobserved. . . . The trick behind many of Houdini's escapes was in some ways just as amazing as the escape itself. Ordinarily when an object is stuck in a person's throat he will start to gag. He can't help it — it's an unlearned, automatic reflex. But Houdini had learned to control his gag reflex by practicing for hour after hour with a small piece of potato tied to a string. (Lang, 1970).

EARLY HISTORY OF BIOFEEDBACK

Through the years, there have been unusual instances of the exercise of voluntary control over physiological functions noted in the scientific literature, such as the case of a middle-aged male who had the ability to control the erection of hairs over the entire surface of his body (Lindsley & Sassaman, 1938), or the case of an individual who could willfully produce complete cardiac arrest for periods of several seconds at a time (McClure, 1959). Numerous instances of voluntary acceleration of pulse rate were reported by Ogden and Shock (1939). The Russian psychologist Luria (1958) described a mnemonist who had attained remarkable control of his heart rate and skin temperature. This individual could abruptly alter his heart rate by 40 beats per minute. He could also raise the skin temperature of one hand while simultaneously lowering the temperature of the other hand.

1

The modification of physiological activities has been the subject of practice and investigation by mystics and scientists for a considerable period of time. The goal of control of physiological functions has been pursued for at least three reasons. These include: One, to achieve spiritual enlightenment. Yogis and other mystics of the Eastern tradition have shown that through certain physical exercises or by sheer act of will they are capable of producing tremendous physiochemical changes in their bodies resulting in perceived pleasant states of consciousness (Bagchi, 1969; Bagchi & Wenger, 1957). Two, to test theories of learning. Later in this chapter, we will review some of the early research in this area. Three, as a clinical treatment procedure for modifying psychological and medical disorders. The purpose of the present chapter is to evaluate the current status and effectiveness of biofeedback as a clinical treatment modality.

THE BIOFEEDBACK TECHNIQUE

The biofeedback technique is based on the fundamental learning principle that we learn to perform a particular response when we receive feedback or information about the consequences of that response and then make the appropriate compensatory behavioral adjustments. This is how we have learned to perform the wide variety of skills and behaviors utilized in everyday life. For instance, we learn how to drive a car by receiving continuous feedback concerning how much we need to rotate the steering wheel in order to turn the car a certain distance and how much pressure we must apply to the accelerator in order to make the car move at a certain speed. If we are denied this feedback, for example by being blindfolded, we would never receive information about the consequences of our driving responses. We would therefore never be able to learn the appropriate adjustments needed in order to perform a successful driving maneuver. Accurate information feedback is thus fundamental to the learning of visual-motor skills. Indeed, Annent (1969) has reviewed numerous experimental studies demonstrating the importance of feedback in the learning and performance of a wide variety of motor skills.

The ANS and CNS

The autonomic nervous system (ANS), which is sometimes referred to as the visceral or vegetative system, modulates the activity of the internal organs, glands, heart, lungs, and all the smooth muscles of the body. It serves to regulate the internal ''milieu'' and homeostasis of the body. Its activities are usually involuntary, and they most often occur automatically without our conscious awareness. This system has traditionally been viewed as strictly an ''involuntary'' system over which an individual could exert no voluntary control. Commonly recorded physiological measures such as heart rate, blood pressure, electrodermal (sweat gland) activity, and skin temperature are neurally innervated responses that are controlled by the ANS.

The ANS is further divided into the sympathetic nervous system (SNS) and parasympathetic nervous system (PNS) components. The SNS component generally involves "emergency" responses that prepare the organism for sudden activity or stress. For example, the heart beats faster and increases the amount of blood pumped out with each heart beat, the arteries innervating the large muscles dilate so that more blood is supplied to these muscles, and the pupils dilate to facilitate perception. The PNS component is usually active during states of quiescence, such as sleep, when physiological functions including cardiovascular activity are reduced and metabolism is slowed down. It should be pointed out that both of these branches of the ANS are always active, so that even during an emergency stress reaction when the sympathetic component dominates, the parasympathetic component is not completely dormant.

The cerebrospinal or central nervous system (CNS) includes the brain and the spinal cord. This system controls behaviors such as moving our limbs, which are normally under our voluntary control. Two commonly recorded physiological measures — striate muscular activity (recorded by the electromyogram or EMG) and brain wave activity (recorded by electroencephalogram or EEG) are neurally innervated and controlled by the CNS.

Difference Between Pavlovian Conditioning and Instrumental Conditioning

Traditionally, human responses have been divided into two distinct types, voluntary and involuntary, corresponding to the CNS and ANS respectively. It was assumed that any new learning of responses controlled by the ANS could only be accomplished by classical conditioning. In this type of learning, first described by Pavlov, an initially neutral, *conditioned stimulus* (such as a bell) is presented along with an *unconditioned stimulus* (such as food) that normally elicits an innate *unconditioned* reflexive *response* (salivation). After a number of pairings of the conditioned stimulus with the unconditioned stimulus, the conditioned stimulus starts to elicit a similar response (salivation) by itself. Every time the bell is presented, salivation occurs. This process was viewed as strictly an involuntary type of learning. It was assumed that internal visceral responses could only be modified by classical, involuntary conditioning.

CNS-innervated responses have always been thought modifiable via instrumental (operant) conditioning. This type of conditioning, described by Skinner, occurs by reinforcing whatever desired response is emitted. For example, every time a hungry rat presses a lever in its cage, a food pellet is given. The rat eats the food and soon presses the lever again. The food reinforces the lever-pressing response, and the rat becomes operantly conditioned to press the lever whenever hungry.

It was assumed that internal physiological events could not be operantly conditioned. After all, it was argued, how can this type of conditioning occur if the organism cannot voluntarily control and emit an internal response in order to receive reinforcement? If you tell a hungry man that he will receive food (reinforcement) if he decreases his blood pressure to a certain level, chances are he will remain hungry. Most people cannot voluntarily control this internal response when requested, and therefore operant conditioning of the response does not have a chance to occur. In contrast, if you tell that same hungry man that he must perform a skeletal-muscular response such as jumping up and down three times in order to receive food, he will eat to his heart's content. The man has voluntary control over this somatic response, and it would be a safe bet to assume he would continue to perform the response as long as you continue to supply the food reinforcer.

The belief that involuntary responses mediated by the ANS could only be modified by classical conditioning, and that operant conditioning is only possible for voluntary responses mediated by the CNS, was used as the major argument for the notion that the two types of conditioning are different phenomena with different neurophysiological underpinnings. However, starting in the 1960s, a number of studies began to appear in the scientific literature which discredited this notion with the demonstration that visceral responses can be instrumentally conditioned. These demonstrations were accomplished by providing human subjects with biofeedback of the internal response that was being conditioned. The biofeedback allowed subjects to learn how to exert control over these "involuntary" responses. Also, research employing laboratory animals by Neal E. Miller and his colleagues provided convincing evidence that the ANS *can* be brought under voluntary control through instrumental conditioning (Miller, 1969).

HISTORICAL DEVELOPMENT OF BIOFEEDBACK

Although the prevailing *zeitgeist* argued against the possibility of operant control of internal physiological events, as early as 1938 Skinner tried (and failed) to condition vasoconstriction through positive reinforcement. One of the first experiments successfully demonstrating that human subjects could learn to voluntarily control a visceral response was conducted by the Russian psychologist Lisina (1958). She initially tried to train subjects how to constrict or dilate blood vessels in their arms in order to avoid electric shock (avoidance of shock was used as the reinforcement). Her initial efforts to condition these vascular changes were unsuccessful. However, control of constriction and dilation was obtained when subjects were permitted to watch their vascular changes displayed on a recording device, that is, they were given biofeedback.

With regard to striate-muscular activity, an early study by Hefferline, Keenan, and Harford (1959) demonstrated operant shaping of a virtually imperceptible thumb-muscle twitch using avoidance and escape conditioning procedures. Using needle electrodes and providing feedback over an oscilloscope and loudspeaker, Basmajian (1963) demonstrated that subjects could even learn to control the activity of *single* motor units. Subjects could also learn to produce various firing rhythms of these single units (Basmajian, Baeza, & Fabugar, 1965).

Shearn (1962) was the first investigator to demonstrate the operant conditioning of heart rate. He trained subjects to control their heart rates by allowing them to listen to amplified feedback of their heartbeats while learning how to avoid a mild electric shock by increasing their heart rate to a specified level during different parts of the experiment.

Lang and colleagues (Hnatiow & Lang, 1962; Lang, Sroufe, & Hastings, 1967) were the first American investigators to provide a visual type of continuous feedback in training subjects how to stabilize their heart rates. A cardiac display apparatus was utilized in which a pointer, which moved on a white field (with a center red stripe and a blue stripe positioned on each side) paralleled changes in heart rate recorded on a polygraph. Subjects were requested to try to maintain the pointer near the red stripe (which was their resting base-level heart rate), and to try to keep the variability within as small a range around the stripe as possible. The investigators found that subjects learned to significantly decrease the amount of heart rate variability while performing the task, and that this ability improved with practice.

In the above studies, Lang and his coworkers did not use shock avoidance or positive rewards such as money in order to motivate performance (many previous investigators had used these incentives). They found that the biofeedback task itself was intrinsically rewarding and that subjects learned a considerable degree of heart rate control without special incentives.

At about this time, when various investigators were demonstrating the voluntary control of heart rate, Kamiya (1962, 1968) reported that human subjects could learn to control the appearance of alpha rhythms in brain-wave activity, by providing them with biofeedback (subjects were given external feedback such as brief lights or tones when alpha rhythms were produced). The maintenance of a high level of alpha was said to be related to relaxation, pleasant affect, and "letting go."

Another investigator who had a great influence on the field was Kimmel. In a series of studies (Kimmel & Kimmel, 1963; Fowler & Kimmel, 1962; Kimmel & Hill, 1960), he and his colleagues showed that the number of spontaneous fluctuations of skin resistance (SRR) could be conditioned to increase or decrease by means of operant procedures using odors and light as reinforcements. Sweat-gland activity is an especially interesting response to study because it is innervated only by the autonomic nervous system and within that, only by the sympathetic branch of the ANS. Thus, in conditioning SRR activity, one need not confront the issue of which of the two branches of the ANS is dominant or inhibited.

Of all the modalities, blood-pressure control has, perhaps, the most potential for clinical significance. The first study of blood-pressure control via biofeedback in humans was reported by the Harvard group (Shapiro, Tursky, Gershon, & Stern, 1969). They reported that normal subjects were able to decrease (and to a lesser extent increase) their systolic blood pressure as a consequence of being provided with beat-to-beat feedback of Korotkoff sounds (and additional reinforcement for blocks of successful trials). The amount of change during the one session study was small, not exceeding an average of 5mm. Hg. This study provided impetus for subsequent studies that attempted to increase the amount of change to clinically significant levels and to induce such changes in clinical hypertensives.

The finding in this study by Shapiro *et al.* (1969) that heart rate declined both when blood pressure decreased and increased led Schwartz (1972) to propose that biological systems ought not to be considered in isolation but rather as patterns of activity. Thus, heart rate and blood pressure can operate in an *integrated* fashion or in a *differentiated* manner. Schwartz conducted a number of experiments in which he trained subjects to increase heart rate and blood pressure simultaneously, to decrease them simultaneously, or to increase one while decreasing the other. He found that it was easier for subjects to learn to change blood pressure and heart rate in the same direction (integration) than in opposite directions (differentiation). Schwartz suggested that these findings had two implications. First, they demonstrated how biofeedback methodology could be used to clarify biological constraints on learning in the ANS; second, they suggested that multiple-response training (for instance, conditioning desired responses in blood pressure and heart-rate activity) may be more effective than single-system conditioning in altering pathophysiological autonomic activity.

Since the time of these pioneering experiments, there have been demonstrations of the learned control by human subjects of a wide variety of "involuntary responses": cardiac ventricular rate (Engel, 1971); systolic and diastolic blood pressure (Brener & Kleinman, 1970; Shapiro, Schwartz, & Tursky, 1972); peripheral vascular responses (Snyder & Noble, 1966); electrodermal activity (Crider, Shapiro, & Tursky, 1968; Klinge, 1972); gastric motility (Deckner, Hill, & Bourne, 1972); salivation (Frezza & Holland, 1971); skin temperature (Roberts, Kewman, & MacDonald, 1973); and penile erection (Rosen, 1973). A series of annual volumes published by Aldine contains reprints of much of the work that has been done in the field of biofeedback during the last decade (Kamiya, Barber, Miller, Shapiro, Stoyva, eds.). A journal, *Biofeedback and Self-Regulation*, which publishes research in the field, is also available.

THE QUESTION OF MEDIATION

Although a host of studies reported that human subjects could learn how to control various visceral responses, the results did not necessarily mean that direct learning in the autonomic nervous system had been demonstrated. One can, for example, make one's heart rate go faster by breathing deeply or by tensing muscles that are already under voluntary control. Most visceral responses can be modified by the voluntary manipulation of skeletal-muscular events. Many investigators have contended (for example, Katkin & Murray, 1968) that what may have been happening in the studies purporting to show direct learning in the autonomic nervous system was that subjects merely learned to modify skeletal-muscular responses over which they already had voluntary control to produce (mediate) the visceral response change. As a case in point, Wenger and Baggchi (1961) took polygraph recordings of yogis in India who performed well-known feats of controlling normally involuntary visceral events. They concluded that the yogis accomplished these feats by manipulating voluntary muscular responses, such as retention of breath and increased muscle tension in the abdomen and thorax, which in turn mediated the visceral control. It should also be noted that Wenger and his coworkers found no evidence for the alleged claim that yogis can make the heart stop completely (Wenger, Baggchi, & Anand, 1961). A skilled performer of yoga can give the *appearance* of stopping his heart by making heart and radial pulse sounds weaken or disappear. This can be done by manipulating rib cage and diaphragm muscles in such a way that pressure within the chest is increased to a point where venous return of the blood to the heart is retarded.

In the initial biofeedback experiments, it was difficult to rule out the possibility that individuals learned to control autonomic responses via skeletal-muscular mediation. Attempts were made to control for this possibility. For example, Sroufe (1969) trained subjects to breathe at specified rates and depths. After they had learned this, he trained them to control their heart rates. Results indicated that subjects were able to achieve good heart-rate control with respiration experimentally controlled. Thus, control of heart rate can be achieved without the use of breath-control mediation.

Studies like the above still did not conclusively rule out the possibility of mediational effects. The manipulation of any of a large number of muscle groups can alter a visceral response such as heart rate, and it is extremely difficult to control for all the potential muscle mediators available to an intact human subject. It was not until a series of studies, using animal subjects, were performed by Neal Miller and colleagues (Miller, 1969) that evidence was presented indicating direct learning of visceral responses can occur without peripheral mediation.

The Miller Experiments

One way to insure that learning effects are not due to skeletal-muscular mediation is to completely eliminate the potential mediators. One can achieve this with injections of the drug curare. This blocks acetylcholine, which is the chemical transmitter by which cerebrospinal nerve impulses are delivered to skeletal muscles. When injected into an animal, it eliminates skeletal-muscular activity and causes the animal to lie limp and motionless. The animal cannot breathe, and therefore must be artifically respirated with a mechanical device. The drug does not, however, interfere with consciousness or with the activity of the brain and internal organs. Miller and coworkers administered curare to rats and then operantly conditioned visceral responses in these animals.

It is difficult to reward curarized rats for performance with commonly used reinforcers such as food because the animals can neither eat nor drink. The reinforcer utilized in many of these studies was direct electrical stimulation of the ''pleasure center'' of the brain, which is located in the medial forebrain bundle of the hypothalamus. Such stimulation has been found to be a powerful positive reinforcer.

In their first study, rats were rewarded for certain heart-rate changes with this reinforcing stimulation. One group of rats was rewarded for heart-rate increases and another for decreases. It was found that the animals would make their hearts beat at the rate which would produce the most stimulation. As the animals learned, the amount of rate change required to receive reinforcement was made progressively more difficult, so that the animal was ''shaped'' to give larger and larger responses. Final results indicated the average increases or decreases were approximately 20 percent of the normal baseline. In subsequent studies of this kind, Miller noted that some rats rewarded for decreasing heart rate slowed it down drastically and died, thus testifying to the extremely powerful effect of this particular operant conditioning procedure.

Miller and colleagues went on to demonstrate the operant conditioning of a variety of visceral and glandular responses, including contractions of intestinal muscles, blood pressure, the amount of blood flow to stomach walls, the amount of blood flow in the ears and tail, and even the rate of urine formation in the kidneys. As a demonstration of how specific this learning can be, they had rats learn to simultaneously dilate the blood vessels in one ear but not the other.

The Miller experiments were believed to convincingly demonstrate that internal visceral events can be instrumentally conducted in a manner analogous to instrumental conditioning skeletal-muscular responses. The method of using curarized animals eliminated the possibilities of respiration and muscular-response artifacts as mediating events.

Subsequent to his early experiments, Miller reported difficulty in replicating the large-magnitude heart-rate changes reported in earlier studies. At first, unlike the 20 percent change from baseline originally reported, only between 5 and 10 percent changes were found by Miller as well as other investigators (Hothersall & Brener, 1973; Slaughter, Hahn, & Rinaldi, 1973). Later results continued to decline progressively in magnitude so that it was difficult to produce any effect at all (see Miller, 1978). Miller and Dworkin (1974) discussed possible reasons for these vanishing effects, suggesting that they may lie in subtle changes through the years in experimental variables, such as type of rats used, chemical makeup of curare, and artificial respiration technique. Although there is some better evidence for again producing the effect with better controlled procedures, Miller (1978) points out that it is currently "prudent not to rely on any of the experiments on curarized animals for evidence on the instrumental learning of visceral responses" (p. 376).

Some Human Evidence of Direct Visceral Learning

Miller and Dworkin (1974) have reported some strong evidence for direct human visceral learning. As these authors note, the urethral sphincters involved in urination are innervated exclusively by the autonomic nervous system. Most individuals have learned to control urination as a result of early toilet training reinforcement experiences. Many investigators had assumed that skeletal-muscular responses (for instance, tensing the abdominal muscles, increasing pressure on the bladder) were involved in this control; that is, they mediated the urethral sphincter events. However, Miller and Dworkin review a study conducted by Lapides, Sweet, and Lewis (1957) which argues against this assumption.

Lapides and his coinvestigators paralyzed 16 human subjects by either curare or succinylcholine (which produces the same effects as curare). The paralysis was so complete that the subjects had to be maintained on artificial respiration. Results indicated that these subjects could initiate urination on command about as fast as during a nonparalyzed state. Moveover, they could stop urination twice as fast as during a nonparalyzed state, even if a large amount of fluid still remained in the bladder. These data demonstrate that human subjects can exercise learned voluntary control of a visceral event when potential skeletal-muscular mediators are blocked.

Mediation and Clinical Implications

The just reviewed human and animal studies provide evidence for the direct operant conditioning of visceral responses. A chief goal of the investigators who presented these findings was to demonstrate the invalidity of the traditional distinction between voluntary responses of the cerebrospinal nervous system and "involuntary" responses of the autonomic nervous system. These results have profound implications for learning theory. However, the question of mediation in many ways becomes a moot point when viewing the potential clinical applications of learned visceral control. Human subjects will learn this control with an intact skeletal-muscular system, which they may consciously or unconsciously use to produce the desired visceral changes.

A clinician may not be concerned with obtaining a "pure," unmediated control effect, but only in producing a large, long-lasting effect that will transfer outside the laboratory setting. Thus, for a given patient who must learn to stabilize his heart rate, if it were found that muscle relaxation and breath control produced the greatest and most rapid stabilization of heart rate, these methods would be utilized. In this instance, somatic mediation would be helpful. In fact, Sroufe (1971) has shown that a greater degree of heart-rate control can be obtained by subjects who are taught to breathe at a certain rate and depth. One reason why yogis have such precise control of various visceral responses is because breath and muscular control are vital components of their training technique.

Lisina (1958) has also suggested that the use of somatic mediators early in training can facilitate learned control of autonomic events. These somatic responses then drop out when control is well learned. Kimble and Perlmuter (1970) describe a similar process through which self-control over any response may be acquired. After reviewing a number of studies which investigated how new responses are learned, these authors conclude that:

> such studies . . . suggest that acquisition of control over involuntary responses is always accomplished with the aid of supporting responses already under voluntary control. The desired response is elicited initially as a part of a larger pattern of reactions. With practice, the supporting responses gradually drop out, an accomplishment that required careful paying attention to the desired behavior and a simultaneous ignoring of the others. With still further practice the now voluntary reaction becomes capable of being performed without deliberate intent. What was once involuntary and later became voluntary is now involuntary again, in the sense of being out of awareness and free of previous motivational control.

One last point should be made before we leave this discussion of mediation. Schwartz (1973) has appropriately noted that the question of mediation is more complex than originally envisioned. The curare experiments conducted by Miller and colleagues eliminated potential peripheral skeletal-muscular mediators. However, as pointed out by Schwartz, the curare procedure does not stop the animal from using skeletal mediators "in its head." He cites some evidence indicating that potential mediators at the level of the brain may affect visceral learning. For example, Goesling and Brener (1972) reported that training a rat to tense or relax muscles *prior to* the administration of curare greatly influenced its later ability to raise or lower heart rate while under curare. Thus, mediation at the level of the brain ("in the head") can affect visceral responding even when potential peripheral skeletal-muscular mediators are eliminated by curare.

CLINICAL APPLICATIONS OF BIOFEEDBACK

The clinical studies reviewed in this volume drew their inspiration and methodology from the seminal experiments described above. These clinical studies vary greatly in experimental rigor and sophistication. Some of them revolve around important questions, use adequate experimental designs, and report the analyzed data fully. Many studies, unfortunately, are only at the demonstrational level and/or suffer from serious methodological inadequacies, making the drawing of general conclusions about clinical biofeedback extremely risky. Throughout this book and especially in the concluding chapter, the reader's attention is called to the conceptual and methodological requirements of acceptable research in clinical biofeedback. We hope that this brief review has set the stage for the discussion of clinical biofeedback that follows.

Chapter 2
Emotional Imagery and Visceral Control*

Peter J. Lang

In the course of human development, we learn to follow instructions that control a host of simple and complex bodily functions. Thus, the average adult has no difficulty in raising his hand when told and can generally respond appropriately to a request to smile, solve a mathematical problem, or even void his bladder; he can also tell himself to do these things. Instructional control over the effector system is indeed a fundamental characteristic of human beings. The practical goal of much biofeedback research can be seen as an effort to extend the range of this control. Prompted by clinical need, investigators hope to augment the language-mediated response repertoire of human beings to include less usual feats, such as increasing or decreasing heart rate, blood pressure, and stomach motility, and the modulation of general tension level or specific tonicity in various recondite muscle groups.

There are two broad paths along which clinical and research work in biofeedback proceed: (1) Attempts to develop a new tonic level of system activity in the patient such that the habitual functioning of a viscus or muscle will be permanently altered and (2) Efforts to increase control over phasic patterns of somatovisceral responding, which may be related to specific stimulus circumstances (often defined as stressful). Considerable biofeedback research is directed towards the first goal. For example, researchers and clinicians in the area of hypertension are interested in training afflicted patients in the general reduction of blood pressure (Elder & Eustis, 1975). Thus, the aim of their efforts is a modification of tonic levels of activity, such that an individual who has a high resting diastolic blood pressure of 110 mm. of mercury would, after treatment, have a resting blood pressure of 80 mm. of mercury. The role of language mediation in effecting fundamental changes in

*The writing of this paper was supported in part by a grant to the author from the National Institute of Mental Health (Grant No. MN 10993).

organ functioning is moot (if such basic alterations are indeed possible), and it may be more reasonable to formulate these experiments within the conceptual systems of operant or classical conditioning. However, it is difficult to ignore the role of language mediation and instructions if we follow the second path. In this case, we require that the subject detect a specific circumstance, either in the external environment or in his own response pattern, and that he then initiate specific alternative behaviors. This second approach is particularly relevant to the treatment of psychophysiological stress reactions such as fear or anxiety, and to the treatment of medical illnesses which are characterized by episodes of acute distress with a return to more moderate levels of functioning. This latter situation is typical of many chronic illnesses (migraine headache, arthritis, or colitis), and it is hypothesized to be typical of the early stages of illnesses later characterized by egregious organ tonicity such as high blood pressure or heart disease.

The focus of this chapter is on the second approach, aimed at controlling stimulus-related episodes of somatovisceral dysfunction. This is clearly a practical goal and, given the relative success of researchers in promoting phasic rather than tonic visceral change, it is one that we may reasonably hope to achieve. However, an issue to be faced at the outset of this enterprise concerns the individual's specific capacity for instructional control over somatovisceral systems. I have suggested elsewhere that there are broad individual differences in underlying capacity for phasic visceral control (Lang, 1975). Furthermore, it has been noted that individuals who develop functional diseases of the viscera may be less capable of learning to control these systems than are normal, healthy human beings. In a recent experiment (Lang, Troyer, Twentyman, & Gatchel, 1975), young college students, patients with a history of ischemic heart disease, and a group of age-matched controls were trained, using instructions and organ feedback, to increase and decrease heart rate on command. We discovered that both the latter groups were inferior in this ability to the college students (who learned the task quite quickly) and, furthermore, that the patient sample performed least well of all subjects. It is clear that we need to know much more about the basis for such differences. Does control deteriorate with organ dysfunction? Is there a differential learning deficit or is the degree of relationship between intentional language and behavior an individual trait?

IMAGINATION AND VISCERAL AROUSAL

The fact that some subjects have difficulty in generating visceral responses on demand (with or without biofeedback) strikes few people as surprising. Indeed the biofeedback enterprise is founded on the presumption that such verbal control over autonomically mediated organs is beyond the normal range of human abilities without special exteroceptive prosthetics. However, the ties between an individual's language behavior and visceral systems are not as tenuous as it would first appear. While such events as an increase in blood pressure or decrease in gastric activity are generally recalcitrant to direct command, it would be incorrect to say that they are wholly independent of a client's verbal behavior or of the instructions of others. Research and lay observations agree that to be informed by a superior that one has been fired without just cause, or that the building is on fire, are both communications which prompt significant visceral and somatomotor changes in the average individual. These examples describe contexts in which language has evoked affective expression, resulting in patterns of somatovisceral change which include responses often considered involuntary or outside of verbal control.

It is significant that this emotive power of linguistic communication is not limited to the relaying of information about imminent stressful circumstances. In all known cultures, artists, poets, and storytellers have generated the full gamut of affective expression through the evocation of emotional images, that is, through the artful description of selected scenes or situations to an audience that was prepared to process these images as if they were real. In other words, if we invite someone to imagine that he has lost his job or that he is trapped in a burning building, we may generate a somatovisceral pattern which in many ways apes that of the real circumstance.

A number of investigators have suggested that image manipulation may be fundamental to the effectiveness of biofeedback methods with human beings (Katkin & Murray, 1968; Schwartz, 1975). This process is further implicated as a basic mechanism underlying many other behavioral and dynamic psychotherapies. The purpose of this paper is to examine emotional imagery as a specific vehicle for the control of visceral organs and muscular tension, and to consider the implications of our knowledge for clinical uses of this phenomena in contemporary treatment of anxiety and fear.

IMAGERY IN THERAPY

The evocation of emotional imagery is a fundamental part of many behavioral and dynamic therapies. It is basic to such diverse techniques as systematic desensitization, psychodrama, various hypnotherapies, "flooding," and transactional analysis. In the practical clinical context, emotional imagery is generally evoked through instructions. These instructions may be reduced to three primary elements: the *image cue,* an *image orthesis,* and *a behavioral set of participant engagement* in the scene. The *image cue* is a simple instruction to image a particular scene or event. For example, a patient might be told to imagine that he was speaking before a large group or to imagine himself as a child talking to his mother. The *image orthesis* is usually a script, although it can be a film, a slide, or a stage with other actors. In an imagery therapy like "flooding" or in the generation of emotional catharsis in hypnotherapy, the script may be very elaborate, with the therapist describing the stimulus situation in great detail as well as the responses expected of the patient. In all imagery therapies, patients are also given a *behavioral set*, vis-à-vis the image, which is usually one of involvement as an active participant in the scene. The patient is instructed to experience the events as if they are real, as he would live through the situation in reality. Imagery that is generated by subjects without this active, participant set, engendering comments such as, "It was like I was watching a movie," or "I was outside myself, seeing myself doing things in the scene," is considered to be therapeutically ineffective (Wolberg, 1948; Wolpe, 1958).

In most imagery therapies, patients are instructed to visualize emotionally arousing scenes related to their focal fears or conflicts. There is ample anecdotal evidence to indicate that such instructions do evoke verbal reports, overt motor behavior, and physiological reactivity similar to that occasioned by the actual stimulating events. Figure 2.1 compares the heart-rate responses of a patient to three different imagery scripts, one describing material that most individuals find somewhat arousing, one based on relaxing, neutral material, and one describing an incident central to the subject's problem. It is readily seen that patients respond with greater cardiovascular reactivity to material based on their own distress than to the other contents. Nevertheless, there is considerable variation in this response between individuals, and some subjects do not respond physiologically at all to relevant imagery instructions. This may be due to a refusal to be cued, an inadequacy in the image orthesis employed by the therapist, or a failure to take the set of participant involvement in the scene. In any event, some apparently cooperative subjects fail to respond to even the most artfully conceived scripts. They appear to have an imagery deficit, at least to the extent that affective imagery instructions do not mobilize their physiological reactivity. In fact, research suggests that imagery ability may covary with specific kinds of psychological distress.

PHOBIC TYPE AND IMAGERY VIVIDNESS

In a study of desensitization (Lang, Melamed, & Hart, 1970), we compared the responses to fear imagery of two groups of subjects — one whose primary fear concerned live snakes and a second group with public-speaking anxiety. The two groups were selected for similar intensities of distress relative to the distribution of these fears in the normal population. After training in relaxation and imagery practice, they were presented with materials from their own individual anxiety hierarchies (scenes previously scaled from minimum to maximum fear, as described by Wolpe[1958]) in random order, while physiological responses were recorded. In Fig. 2.2 the subjects' heart-rate

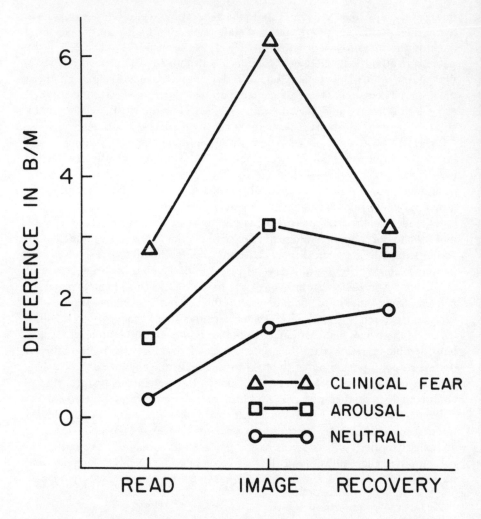

Fig. 2.1. Heart-rate responses of anxiety patients to neutral, treatment-relevant, and treatment-irrelevant but potentially arousing imagery (a description of an auto accident). Changes in beats per minute (estimated from heart period data) are noted on the ordinate as deviations from a preceding resting rate. On the abscissa are recorded the time when the script was read (50 secs.), the imagery period (30 secs.), and a postvisualization recovery period (30 secs.).

responses to the scenes and their verbal reports of fear intensity are compared. In will be noted that the snake phobics tended to show a monotonic increase in heart rate and verbal report of fear with increasing elevation of the hierarchy item. Although their hierarchies were created in the same way, the socially anxious subjects showed fear responses which leveled off and were considera-

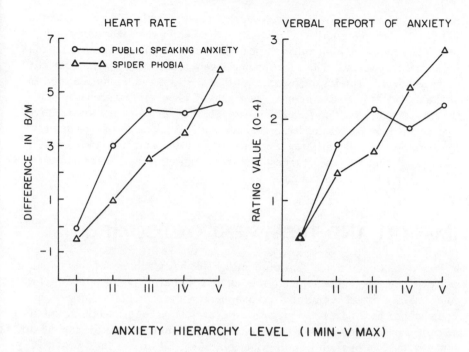

HEART RATE   VERBAL REPORT OF ANXIETY

ANXIETY HIERARCHY LEVEL (I MIN-V MAX)

Fig. 2.2. Results for spider-phobic and public-speaking-anxious subjects are presented for increasing levels of the anxiety hierarchy (Scales I-V). On the left side of this figure, heart rate during scene imagery is expressed as deviation from rate during the preceding neutral scene. Mean verbal report of anxiety during the same visualized scenes (Scales I-V) are presented on the right side.

bly below those of the snake phobics at the upper end of the hierarchy. Furthermore, the snake phobics reported that their imagery was significantly more vivid than was reported by the public-speaking anxious subjects.

We recently undertook an experiment designed to cross-validate this phenomenon (Weerts & Lang, in press). In the first group, subjects were selected who were both high in a focal phobia (fear of spiders) and low in social-performance anxiety. A second group were high in social anxiety and low in spider phobia. In this experiment, the subjects visualized several different kinds of scenes, including scenes relevant either to their own distress or to the other group's fear, as well as scenes that were simply generally arousing, and other scenes that involved only neutral, relaxing contexts. Again we found that subjects with focal phobias reported their imagery experiences to be more vivid than did the socially anxious subjects. Furthermore, the higher vividness reports were not limited to the fear material but appeared to be a general characteristic of the response of focal phobics to all types of imagery material. When the two groups were compared to their verbal reports and physiological reactivity to both fear-relevant and fear-irrelevant scenes, similar differences were observed. That is to say, the spider phobics' fear rating of their own fear scenes were higher than those of the socially anxious reporting on their individual fear scenes. The focal phobics again tended to be physiologically more responsive to relevant fear scenes than the speech-anxious subjects. In addition, they projected more movement activity into their fear scenes than did the anxious subjects. To summarize, focal phobics appear to be more reactive to relevant fear scenes than are subjects with social-performance anxiety. Furthermore, imagery differences between fear groups are not limited to fear contents. Rather, the data suggest that these subject groups differ in a basic quality of their emotional imagery.

IMAGERY AND TREATMENT OUTCOME

We have already noted that clinicians hold that a successful therapeutic outcome depends on the generation in treatment of affective responses to the image. Since Freud, emotional involvement in the therapeutic process has been held to be a necessary precursor to cure. Translated into the terms of empirical measurement, this means that subjects are expected to respond to imagery instructions with appropriate physiological arousal and postscene verbal reports of emotional reactivity. Despite the wealth of clinical lore, the relationship between these imagery responses in therapeutic process and the outcome of treatment has seldom been formally assessed. Nevertheless, in an earlier study of systematic desensitization therapy we did obtain preliminary data relevant to this issue (Lang, Melamed, & Hart, 1970). Subjects were treated using an automated desensitization procedure, which permitted the careful assessment of physiological reactivity to scene presentation. A specific analysis was made of scenes which subjects reported to be maximally frightening (that is, scenes that were so affectively disturbing that the subjects requested that the treatment process be temporarily discontinued). Such scenes are rare in properly conducted desensitization; however, they will occur for nearly all subjects a few times in the course of therapy. These scenes are of particular interest from a "three systems" point of view (Lang, 1977) because, while there was clear behavioral and verbal-report evidence that the scenes generated a high level of fear, these same scenes produced a broad distribution of intensities of physiological reactivity. For example, some subjects responded to the material with large heart-rate increases while others showed no cardiovascular change at all. Correlational statistics were used to study the relationship between scene arousal and therapeutic outcome, the latter variable being assessed through behavioral testing, questionnaires, and verbal scales. The results showed a close relationship between heart-rate reactivity to the fear images and therapeutic success. That is to say, subjects who improved after therapy were physiologically responsive to affective scene presentation during therapy, and their response covaried positively with the other affective dimensions measured. Subjects who were not helped by the treatment reported just as many high fear scenes, and, like successful patients, stopped the progress of therapy temporarily because of them. However, unlike the reactions of successfully treated subjects, these scenes did not produce objective evidence of physiological arousal.

THE INSTRUCTIONAL CONTROL OF AFFECTIVE IMAGERY

The research described above emphasizes the importance of assessing subjects' response to affective imagery prior to beginning treatment, and also the need to develop methods for improving the reactivity of patients who show a specific deficit in generating the visceral components of emotional imagery. We have recently undertaken a program of investigation designed to meet these goals. We are trying to determine the specific relationship between imagery scripts and the affective response of the patient. For purposes of this research, the imagery script is considered to be a propositional structure which potentially bears a one-to-one relationship with the evoked image in the subject's brain (Lang, 1977). The elements of the script/image may be roughly divided into two classes: stimulus propositions and response propositions. Stimulus propositions are those descriptive details which establish the context and designate specific stimuli. The response propositions are the things the subject does in the scene. As we are talking about emotional images, the response-propositional content may include events occurring in all three response systems — overt motor acts, verbal behaviors, and physiological responses. A sample script is presented in Fig. 2.3, with some of the categories of propositional content appropriately labeled. A more elaborate image taxonomy is available in Lang (1977).

The point of view proposed here is that the script, with attendant training and instruction presented by the therapist, constitutes an important determinant of the image ultimately generated in the subject's brain. Furthermore, such images are not merely shadow perceptual experiences; the emotional image is understood to be a response set. That is to say, the image is a kind of template for overt responding, and it is for this reason that modification of the image can be presumed to be a vehicle for broad change in the affective behavior of the patient.

The role of image scripts has rarely been studied in investigations of imagery therapies. Indeed, there are few published examples of scripts actually used by therapists in treating their patients. However, important differences in style and content appear to exist for different treatment methods. For

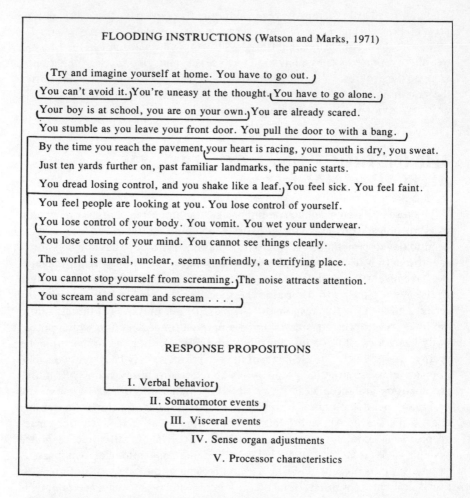

FLOODING INSTRUCTIONS (Watson and Marks, 1971)

Try and imagine yourself at home. You have to go out.

You can't avoid it. You're uneasy at the thought. You have to go alone.

Your boy is at school, you are on your own. You are already scared.

You stumble as you leave your front door. You pull the door to with a bang.

By the time you reach the pavement, your heart is racing, your mouth is dry, you sweat.

Just ten yards further on, past familiar landmarks, the panic starts.

You dread losing control, and you shake like a leaf. You feel sick. You feel faint.

You feel people are looking at you. You lose control of yourself.

You lose control of your body. You vomit. You wet your underwear.

You lose control of your mind. You cannot see things clearly.

The world is unreal, unclear, seems unfriendly, a terrifying place.

You cannot stop yourself from screaming. The noise attracts attention.

You scream and scream and scream . . . .

RESPONSE PROPOSITIONS

I. Verbal behavior

II. Somatomotor events

III. Visceral events

IV. Sense organ adjustments

V. Processor characteristics

Fig. 2.3. The material underlined at the top of the figure includes the major stimulus propositions that describe the physical situation to be represented in the image and define the stimulus context in which the subject is to behave. The major categories of response propositions are listed at the bottom. The script was employed by Watson and Marks (1971) in actual treatment as part of an investigation of the clinical effectiveness of primary phobia-relevant and phobia-irrelevant flooding.

example, it is clear that scripts used in desensitization and in flooding differ greatly in propositional structure. Desensitization scripts generally involve no more than an image cue and very cursory stimulus elaboration. Scripts used in flooding (see Fig. 2.3), on the other hand, are often elaborate, literary efforts, which include detailed stimulus material and, perhaps more important, an extended catalog of responses and exhortations from the therapist to the patient to experience the stimuli he or she would in reality. These responses generally include self-referent statements about experienced fear or anxiety, visceral events such as heart palpitations, stomach distress, flushing, trembling, and muscle tension, as well as such overt behaviors as gross avoidance or panic. It is not unreasonable to suppose that differences that have been found between these two treatments may be attributed, at least in part, to differences in the imagery scripts.

It is suggested that, given proper training, the emotional image in the brain of a cooperative patient comes to be more or less consonant with the propositional structure of the administered instructional set. "Furthermore, if the image is indeed a preparatory set, we should observe partial responses in imaging subjects which are consistent with the response elements of the script. In point of fact, in many experimental situations no methodological distinction need be made between the imagery instructions and the hypothesized image in the brain. While this may not be expedient for individuals who idiosyncratically add or subtract from the suggested propositional structure, the instructions will be very close to the image for groups of subjects whose numbers improve the signal to noise ratio. Thus, if elaborate response propositions are part of the instructional set given to one group of subjects and not to another then the premotor, verbal, and visceral responses during imaging will be relatively augmented for the group so instructed" (Lang, 1977).

IMAGE CONTENT AND VISCERAL AROUSAL: AN EXPERIMENT

In a recently completed experiment, Michael Kozak and I examined this general hypothesis for fear images, for other-arousing (nonfearful) images, and for affectively neutral contents. Forty normal college students participated in the experiment. They were randomly assigned to one of three independent groups, each with equal representation of both sexes. The three groups differed in that one group was trained in imagery and was administered scripts with a response orientation ($N = 16$); the training of the second group emphasized attention to stimulus propositions, and their scripts included only stimulus material ($N = 16$); and a third group was also administered stimulus scripts but with no prior training ($N = 8$). It was expected that response-trained subjects would show the largest visceral and somatomotor responses during imagery, that they would find fear images to be more fearful than did stimulus-trained subjects, and that the pattern of visceral responding would parallel the pattern of response propositions in the script.

Subjects in the stimulus group were trained in imagery, using a method developed by Lang and Lazovik (1963). The subject was first given an image cue with brief stimulus elaboration. After a period of visualization, the subject was asked to describe the experienced scene in as much detail as he was able to recall. The experimenter reinforced, through interest and praise, each detail provided by the subject. Over the course of many image trials in two practice sessions, subjects came to give very elaborate descriptions of their imagery experiences. The assumption of the earlier research on desensitization was that this ability to describe elaborately was representative of more detailed and thus more vivid cognitive images in the brain of the patient.

The response group was similarly trained; however, reports of responses received special attention from the experimenter while stimulus detail was ignored. Subjects in this group received encouragement for all reports of actual behavior experienced in a scene. If a subject said that during the image he had a feeling of his body moving, of breathing hard, or of his heart racing, such reports of experienced behavior were rewarded. Thus, these response-trained subjects came to describe their affective images in very different terms from the stimulus-trained group. Their imagery reports stressed such active participation as walking, running, sweating, and jumping; unlike their co-subjects in the other training group, their reports included only cursory descriptions of external stimuli. The third, untrained group of 8 subjects was included as a control condition and received no preimagery test training.

Following imagery training, in the final session of the experiment, subjects were presented with one of two types of test imagery scripts. Stimulus-trained subjects were administered scripts including an image cue elaborated only by stimulus propositions (see Fig. 2.4). These scripts were essentially detailed descriptions of the physical context to be imagined. The untrained subjects were read these same scripts. The response-trained subjects were presented with scripts that provided a description of the stimulus context, but also included response propositions. As in catharsis or flooding therapies, the specific, appropriate affective behaviors were included in the fear scenes (see Fig. 2.5). Scripts were matched for length between groups.

The presentation of the imagery scripts was by tape recorder, and the sequencing and timing of all procedures were under the control of an on-line computer. Heart rate, skin conductance, eye movement, muscle tension in the head and neck area, and respiration were monitored by a Beckman polygraph throughout the experimental session.

The results clearly indicated that response training in combination with response-oriented scripts produce imagery with a pronounced physiological component. As may be seen in Fig. 2.6, the heart-rate response of stimulus-trained and untrained subjects is roughly similar. However, the response-trained subjects show an increase in heart rate with the presentation of a scene and a pronounced further acceleration during scene imagery. The fact that these responses are cued by the specific script is indicated by the reduced reaction of the response-trained group (indeed no different from untrained or stimulus-trained subjects) to the neutral scripts.

The results obtained for heart rate were replicated in other physiological systems. Furthermore, there appears to be a close covariation between the

FEAR SCRIPT — STIMULUS PROPOSITIONS ONLY

You are alone, taking a steam bath, and the temperature of the sauna starts to become unbearable. Thick clouds of white mist swirl around you, while droplets of the condensed steam accumulate on the walls, mingling in small rivulets of moisture which stream down the wooden walls and onto the floor. The heavy fog blankets the room with an almost impenetrable whiteness. The large wooden door is tightly closed, swollen from all the steam and jammed shut. The wooden walls of the small room surround you, closing you in with the oppressive steam.

NO-FEAR SCRIPT — STIMULUS PROPOSITIONS ONLY

You are flying a kite on the beach on a bright, sunny day. Your red kite shows clearly against the cloudless blue sky, and whips quickly up and down in spirals with the wind. The sun glares at you from behind the kite and makes the white sandy beach sparkle with reflection. The long white tail dances from side to side beneath the soaring kite. A strong gust of wind catches the kite, sending it higher and higher into the sky.

Fig. 2.4. Fear and no-fear arousal imagery scripts, which include only stimulus propositions.

FEAR SCRIPT — STIMULUS AND RESPONSE PROPOSITIONS

You are alone, taking a steam bath, and the temperature of the sauna becomes unbearable. You sweat great buckets of perspiration, which roll down your skin and mingle with the condensed moisture from the swirling clouds of steam. The heavy fog hampers your breathing and you take deep rapid gulps of the seemingly liquid air. You tense all the muscles of your forehead, squinting to exclude the burning steam from your eyes, as they dart left and right to glimpse the exit. Your heart pounds wildly as you pull with all your strength on the door, which is jammed shut.

NO-FEAR SCRIPT — STIMULUS AND RESPONSE PROPOSITIONS

You breathe deeply as you run along the beach flying a kite. Your eyes trace its path as it whips up and down in spirals with the wind. The sun glares into your eyes from behind the kite and you tense the muscles in your forehead and around your eyes, squinting to block out the bright sunlight. You follow with your eyes the long white tail, which dances from side to side beneath the soaring kite.

Fig. 2.5. Fear and no-fear arousal scripts, which contain both stimulus and response propositions. The response propositions are underlined.

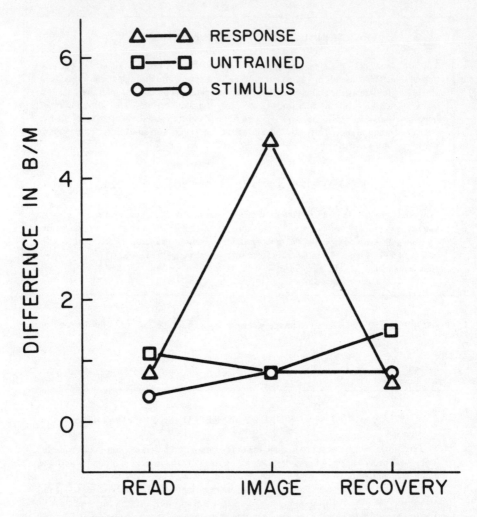

Fig. 2.6. Heart-rate changes from rest occasioned by fearful imagery. Three groups are represented: (1) subjects who were trained in a response orientation and were administered scripts that included response propositions; (2) subjects trained in a stimulus orientation, reacting to scripts with stimulus propositions only; (3) untrained subjects, reacting to stimulus scripts.

response propositions of a script and the specific physiological reactions in imagery of response-trained subjects. Thus, in Fig. 2.7 it may be observed that larger muscle-tension responses were occasioned by no-fear arousing scenes (which included muscle response propositions) while responding in the muscle system was less elevated for the fear scene (which did not include these specific propositions). This was not indicative of a general difference between the two scene types in overall arousal, but instead highlights the differentiated

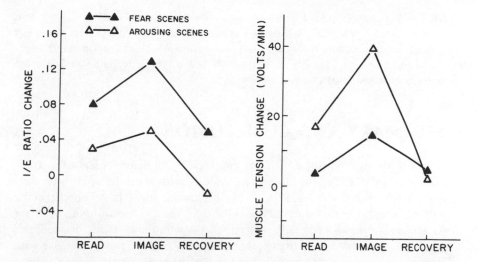

Fig. 2.7. Muscle tension and inspiration/expiration ratio changes from rest in reaction to fearful and no-fear-arousing imagery. All subjects were trained in a response orientation and were administered stimulus *plus* response scripts.

patterns of image psychophysiology. As may also be noted in Fig. 2.7, fear scenes occasioned a greater response than did no-fear arousing scenes when respiratory rather than muscle-tension response was examined.

The verbal report data were consistent with the results of the physiological analysis. That is to say, response-trained subjects reported greater feelings of fear to the fear scenes than did the stimulus-trained subjects. However, this was not accompanied by a significant difference in reports of imagery vividness. Despite the fact that response-trained subjects experienced their scenes as more frightening they did not report them to be more real or more vivid than did stimulus-trained subjects. All subjects reported fear scenes to be less vivid than nonaffective material, a tendency which has been observed in several previous experiments (Lang, 1977).

The overall results clearly indicate that the physiological reactivity of subjects in the context of their cognitive imagery may be augmented through appropriate instructions and training. In the present research studies, this was accomplished through the manipulation of script material and by modification of the subject's verbal descriptions of their imagery experience. It is possible that this could be further augmented through the use of biofeedback technology. Subjects' physiological reactivity can be monitored during visualization and subjects subsequently reinforced not just for verbal report, but for a recorded differential arousal in the relevant physiological systems. Through this methodology, subjects may be trained to increase their imagery-mediated verbal control over the arousal system. It is possible that such training may be used as a preparation for therapy to overcome the visceral control deficits that appear in some patients to which we have already alluded. The effectiveness of imagery therapies and the size of the population which is responsive to them could then be considerably increased. A test of these hypotheses is on the immediate agenda of our research group.

SUMMARY AND CONCLUSIONS

A significant goal of biofeedback research is the achievement of instructional control over the somatovisceral system, with special emphasis on control of those organs active in patterns of emotional arousal. It was noted that the native capacity for such authority over the body (and/or the ability to augment it) appears to be an unequally distributed human talent. Thus, biofeedback studies suggest that the ability to learn control of heart rate may decrease with age and is least manifest among subjects with a history of heart disease. These data raise questions about the effectiveness of biofeedback therapies, which may be designed for the very populations that are least able to profit from them.

We have suggested that some degree of verbal control over visceral systems is in the behavioral repertoire of most individuals. It is clearly manifest in the psychophysiological response to emotional imagery, in which changes in a person's cardiovascular responses, muscle tension, skin conductance, and respiratory activity normally accompany verbal descriptions of stressful experience, particularly when supplemented by instructions to imagine the described situation "as if" it were a real experience.

As in the studies of biofeedback, individual differences in instructed visceral arousal are apparent. We have shown that focal phobics appear to generate more vivid emotional images, as indexed by verbal report and physiological reactivity, than do subjects equally concerned about social-performance anxiety. Furthermore, some data suggest that the degree to which patients are able to generate the physiological covariates of an emotional image may determine their prognosis for imagery therapies, such as desensitization or flooding.

A psychophysiological model of emotional imagery is proposed, which implies that the response components measurable during and after imagery (physiological reactivity and verbal report of anxiety and arousal) can be controlled through pretraining and the manipulation of imagery script structure. An experiment is described which supports this general hypothesis. It is shown that when the response elements in subjects' verbal reports of images are systematically reinforced, and when scripts emphasize the behaviors in emotion (muscle tension, heart-rate increase, sweating, etc.), subsequent test images yield both greater physiological arousal and elevated subjective reports of feeling.

The results are seen as supporting a conception of the image as a response set and as a propositional cognitive structure which is at least in part controlled by the propositional structure of the image instruction script. It is further suggested that the pattern of imagery training described here might be employed to augment the emotional imagery of patients and thus to improve their prognosis for treatments that are dependent upon image manipulation and control.

Chapter 3
Biofeedback and the Modification of Cardiovascular Dysfunctions

Edward B. Blanchard

The theme of this chapter is one which is dear to me, namely, taking a long, hard, objective look at biofeedback as a treatment modality. The particular aspect of clinical biofeedback research with which this chapter is concerned is cardiovascular problems.

It has long been known that mental and emotional factors can affect a patient's cardiovascular system (MacKenzie, 1916; Pickering, 1968). Moreover, within the area of psychosomatic medicine, it has long been speculated that specific psychological factors are indicated in the etiology of various kinds of cardiovascular disease. This theorizing, primarily from a psychoanalytic viewpoint (Alexander, 1950), has led to psychological treatment, primarily verbal psychotherapy, for patients suffering from cardiovascular diseases. The late 1960s and the 1970s have witnessed a large upsurge of interest in psychological treatment of cardiovascular diseases, spearheaded by work in the area of biofeedback. This work has raised the possibility of psychological treatment of cardiovascular diseases as either an adjunct to standard pharmacological or surgical treatment or even as an *alternative* to them. The present paper will summarize this recent work, the vast majority of which has been published since 1970, and will critically evaluate the evidence for the efficacy of biofeedback treatment of cardiovascular diseases.

BASES FOR EVALUATION

Before tackling the main purpose of this paper, however, I would like to discuss the bases for evaluating clinical research. In an earlier review of the field of clinical biofeedback (Blanchard & Young, 1974a), we stated: "We believe biofeedback should be evaluated in the same manner as one would evaluate a new drug or new form of psychotherapy." We then proceeded to make the experimental design used in each particular study the *sole* criterion by which to evaluate studies of clinical biofeedback.

Since then, my thinking has changed (and hopefully matured) somewhat; I believe there are at least seven different dimensions one should consider in evaluating clinical applications of biofeedback, the first six of which probably apply to evaluations of any treatment procedure. Briefly these are:

1. the degree of clinical meaningfulness of the changes obtained;
2. the experimental design used in gathering or reporting the data;
3. the extent of follow-up data obtained and reported;
4. the fraction of the treated patient sample which improved significantly;
5. the degree of transfer of changes obtained in the laboratory to the patient's environment;
6. the degree of replicability of the results;

and, especially for biofeedback studies,

7. the degree of change in the biological response for which feedback training was supplied.

I would like to spend a few moments amplifying and justifying each of these points before proceeding to the formal evaluative review.

Clinical Effects. The *most* important dimension for evaluating clinical biofeedback research is the extent to which the results obtained represent clinically meaningful changes. A few years ago Bernie Engel and I exchanged views in *Psychological Bulletin* about this issue. In an earlier review (Blanchard & Young, 1973) we arbitrarily defined a response as *clinically significant* if it was of a certain magnitude. Engel (1974) very appropriately criticized us on this issue and made the point that a change can only be clinically significant if it is obtained in a clinical problem. We later (Blanchard & Young, 1974b) acknowledged the wisdom of Engel's comment.

Thus, unless a response is a clinical problem, changes in it cannot constitute clinically meaningful results. Moreover, it is possible to obtain statistically significant but clinically trivial changes in clinically meaningful responses. For example, reducing the blood pressure of a hypertensive patient by 2 or 3 mm. of mercury, while possibly leading to a statistically significant effect on a group basis, is hardly clinically meaningful. Likewise, reducing the average rate of premature ventricular contractions in a patient from 15 to 12, again while possibly leading to a statistical effect on a group basis, is not a clinically meaningful change. Unless a clinically meaningful change is obtained, all the other features of research, elegant experimental design, or long-term follow-up become trivial.

Experimental Design. I have described in some detail elsewhere (Blanchard & Young, 1974a; Blanchard & Epstein, 1977) five categories of experimental designs which have been used in clinical biofeedback research. To my mind, these five categories can be ordered in terms of the degree of confidence one has that the results obtained are attributable to the biofeedback training. Thus, as a more rigorous design is used, one can put more credence in the conclusions.

Probably the important aspects of experimental designs are the factors which the various designs control so that one can *rule out* these factors as explanations for the observed changes. The five classes of designs in ascending order are: anecdotal case reports; systematic case studies and multiple systematic case studies; single-group outcome studies; single-subject experiments and replicated single-subject experiments; and controlled-group outcome studies.

In the anecdotal case report, little or nothing is controlled. In particular, there are no controls for aspects of treatment not mentioned in the description, or for other events taking place in the patient's life in the course of the treatment.

In the systematic case study, there are data available both from baseline and during the course of treatment. It is possible to observe the time course of change in the response of interest if such data are provided. However, it is not possible to rule out other events which have taken place in the patient's life as responsible for the observed changes nor other aspects of the treatment situation which are not specified.

In the single-group outcome study, the results are presented on a group basis rather than on an individual basis; thus it is possible to say with what percentage of patients a given technique works. However, in this type of study there are no controls for other events taking place in the patient's life which could be responsible for the observed treatment effects nor for such things as the nonspecific effects of being in treatment.

In the single-subject experiment, it is possible to isolate a particular treatment or aspect of treatment which is responsible for the change. However, without systematic replications of the experiment, it is not possible to rule out the possibility that the observed effects are idiosyncratic to the particular patient. It is also not possible to rule out sequence effects. The use of a reversal design does rule out other events taking place in the patient's life as being responsible for change.

In the controlled-group outcome study, the control group enables one to rule out the other events that may be taking place in the patient's life as being responsible for the change observed in the experimental group. Moreover, if an attention-placebo condition is used in the control group, it is possible to rule out these nonspecific effects as being responsible for the observed change.

Follow-up Data. Although obtaining a change by the end of treatment is certainly important, the long-term effects of treatment are probably more clinically relevant. One is interested not only in short-term treatment effects but also in how these effects hold up over time. One would hope that the follow-up period would be long enough to determine that the observed change was not due solely to the natural recurring or fluctuating course of the disorder. If the treatment effects hold up over a very long period of time, this natural fluctuation can be ruled out.

Fraction Improved. In group studies it is possible to find significant results when the number of subjects who changed are few but who manifested large-scale changes; the majority of patients obtained only a small, but not clinically meaningful, change. One thus needs to know what percent of patients who are given treatment will show a clinically meaningful change. In this way, one could begin to advise patients ahead of time as to the likelihood of their improving as a result of receiving treatment. Of course, the higher the percentage of patients who show a clinically meaningful change, the greater the utility of the treatment.

Transfer to the Natural Environment. Most of the data reported in clinical biofeedback studies relate to changes in responses measured in the laboratory. Although it is certainly important to be able to obtain change in the laboratory, the ultimate utility of the procedure lies in transferring changes obtained in the laboratory to the patient's natural environment. Ideally we would like to obtain measures of the clinical response both in the laboratory and in the patient's natural environment. At a minimum, we would like some type of independent, outside verification that the observed changes held up, such as examination by an independent physician.

Replicability. A very important dimension in evaluating biofeedback treatments is their replicability, or the ability of independent investigators working at other locations to obtain the same effects as those who initially report them. When one finds that independent investigators can obtain results comparable to those initially reported, one's faith or credence in the data rises immensely. Unfortunately for our literature, the journal editors do not especially reward replications. However, these are certainly greatly needed in order to be sure that the effect is more than the result of nonspecific relationship factors between one particular investigator and the patient population.

Change in Biological Response. In much of biofeedback work, biofeedback training is given for one biological response while the response of interest, or of clinical interest, is another physiological response or even possibly a self-report, as in headache work. At a minimum, one would want to see a change in the response for which feedback was given as a result of training. To find an improvement in the clinical response of interest, such as headaches, with no concomitant change in the response for which feedback was provided, would lead one to suspect that the changes were due to attention-placebo factors rather than anything having to do with biofeedback treatment. Thus, in the case where feedback is given for one response and the clinical response of interest is another, data on both responses should certainly be reported.

This review is limited to published reports or reports presented at national meetings. The attempt has been made to be comprehensive without being exhaustive. The review is organized around three broad categories of cardiovascular disease: (1) hypertension; (2) cardiac arrhythmias; (3) peripheral vascular disease. Deliberately excluded from this chapter is work on the biofeedback treatment of vascular, or migraine, headaches. For each category, all of the studies will be briefly described, chiefly in tabular form. Then the experimental procedures used and the subsequent conclusions drawn from the data will be critically evaluated on the previously described bases to determine the "state of the art."

HYPERTENSION

It is not surprising, given the large-scale health problem which hypertension represents in this country (Stambler, Stambler, Riedlinger, Algera, & Roberts, 1976), that a great number of studies have dealt with hypertension. Moreover, it has long been held that "factors operating through the mind" play a role in the genesis of essential hypertension (Pickering, 1968) and this postulate has been supported by biochemical measurements (DeQuattro & Miura, 1974).

Biofeedback of Blood Pressure

Shapiro and his colleagues at Harvard developed a procedure for giving direct feedback of blood pressure on a beat-by-beat basis for short durations (approximately one minute). The system, described in some detail by Tursky, Shapiro, & Schwartz (1972), utilizes a cuff which is automatically held near systolic or diastolic blood pressure and has come to be the "standard" apparatus in the field. It is even available commercially.

With this device, Shapiro and his colleagues (Shapiro, Tursky, Gershon, & Stern, 1969; Shapiro, Tursky, & Schwartz, 1970; Shapiro, Schwartz, & Tursky, 1972) have demonstrated that direct feedback of blood pressure could enable normotensive volunteers to gain some degree of control over their blood pressure. These reports led to a fairly widespread effort to apply biofeedback of blood pressure to the treatment of hypertension.

In Table 3.1 are summarized the eight studies which have used direct biofeedback of blood pressure in the treatment for hypertension.

Examining the studies summarized in Table 3.1 in terms of the previously listed evaluation criteria, one finds that with but one exception (Schwartz & Shapiro, 1973), clinically and/or statistically significant decreases in blood pressure have been obtained through the use of biofeedback training. Changes in both systolic and diastolic blood pressure have been observed. In several studies, the magnitude of change is probably of only borderline clinical meaningfulness, such as the changes of 6 to 8 mm mercury in Elder and Eustis (1975) and of 6 mm. mercury systolic in Goldman, Kleinman, Snow, Bedus, and Korol (1975).

Studies of several levels of sophistication have been conducted, including one controlled-group outcome study (Elder, Ruiz, Deabler, & Dillenkoffer, 1973). This latter study, however, presents problems, including a very short baseline (one session) and very small groups (N = 6).

Good follow-up data have been conspicuously absent in the studies of the biofeedback treatment of hypertension. In four studies, there was no follow-up data. In the well-designed study by Elder et al. (1973), follow-up was for only one week and differential dropout rates precluded drawing any definite conclusions from the data. In two other studies there was either no maintenance of treatment effects (Elder & Eustis, 1975) at 2 months or the beginnings of a loss of treatment effects by 1 to 4 weeks (Blanchard et al., 1975). Informal follow-up (Benson, personal communication) of the patients in the study by Benson, Shapiro, Tursky, and Schwartz (1971) revealed that their blood pressure tended to return to pretreatment levels over a few months' time.

The only study with good follow-up data is that of Kristt and Engel (1975). They obtained systematic data over 2 to 3 months after treatment. Moreover, in 3 of the 4 patients, the reductions in blood pressure obtained through biofeedback training in the hospital held up over the follow-up period. Interestingly, Kristt and Engel (1975) had instructed the patients in certain self-management skills such as regular monitoring of blood pressure and regular practice of the blood-pressure lowering learned with biofeedback training. The regular utilization of these self-management skills is probably responsible for the good follow-up results and is a policy which should certainly be instituted on a clinical basis.

In most of the studies with adequate clinical effects, a majority of patients showed clinically meaningful changes. Only in the studies by Schwartz and Shapiro (1973) and Elder and Eustis (1975) did fewer than half of the patients show a clinically meaningful response.

In this particular area of research there is a marked deficit of data on transfer of training effects from the biofeedback laboratory to the patient's natural environment. Only one study has reported data on this point (Kristt & Engel, 1975). There was informal reporting of transfer in Miller's (1972) systematic case study and in the results of Benson et al. (1971). Kristt and Engel (1975) obtained regular, and probably very reliable, data on patients' blood pressures as measured by the patients at home. Certainly more work of this kind is needed. One would hope that independent assessment of the patient's blood pressure by his or her personal physician could also be obtained.

The dimension of replicability presents some interesting findings. The initial clinical study of blood-pressure biofeedback training for hypertension used the Harvard group's constant cuff pressure technique and obtained good results. A later attempt to replicate these results by part of the same research

TABLE 3.1: Biofeedback Treatment of Hypertension/Direct Feedback of Blood Pressure

STUDY	TYPE OF TREATMENT (LOCATION)	DURATION OF BASELINE (B) AND TREATMENT (T)	NUMBER OF PATIENTS	TYPE OF STUDY	RESULTS	FOLLOW-UP
Miller, 1972	Biofeedback of BP (Inpatient and Outpatient)	B: 26 sessions in 6 weeks T: 37 sessions in 3 months	1	Systematic case study	Diastolic BP decreased from 97 to 76 mm., antihypertensive medications stopped.	None
Benson, Shapiro, Tursky, & Schwartz, 1971	Biofeedback of BP (Outpatient)	B: 5-16 daily sessions, $\bar{x}=11$ T: 8-34 daily sessions, $\bar{x}=22$	7	Single-group outcome	Average decrease in systolic BP was 16.5 mm., 5 out of 7 patients showed significant response.	None
Schwartz & Shapiro, 1973	Relaxation instructions + biofeedback of BP (Outpatient)	B: 5 daily sessions T: 15 daily sessions	7	Single-group outcome	No overall change in diastolic BP; 1 out of 7 patients showed reduction of 14 mm.	None
Goldman, Kleinman, Snow, Bidus, & Koral, 1975	Biofeedback of BP (Outpatient)	B: none T: 9 sessions	7	Single-group outcome	Average decrease in systolic BP was 6 mm.; in diastolic BP, 15 mm.	None
Kristt & Engel, 1975	Biofeedback of BP + home monitoring of BP and home practice (Inpatient)	B: 5 weeks 4/day measures at home T: 3 weeks	5 (baseline data on 4)	Single-group outcome	Average decrease in systolic BP was 18 mm.; in diastolic BP, 7.5 mm. All 4 patients showed decreases in systolic or diastolic BP. All 5 patients showed ability to lower BP at home.	2 or 3 months, 3 out of 4 patients maintained gains.

TABLE 3.1 (Cont'd)

STUDY	TYPE OF TREATMENT (LOCATION)	DURATION OF BASELINE (B) AND TREATMENT (T)	NUMBER OF PATIENTS	TYPE OF STUDY	RESULTS	FOLLOW-UP
Elder, Ruiz, Deabler, & Dillenkoffer, 1973	E: Biofeedback of BP + social reinforcement for lowering C-1: Biofeedback of BP C-2: Monitoring BP (Inpatient)	B: 1 session T: 7 sessions in 4 days	18 (6 per condition)	Controlled-group outcome	Systolic BP: E = C-1 = C-2 Diastolic BP: E < C-1 < C-2 E: Diastolic BP = 80% of baseline C-1: Diastolic BP = 93% of baseline 4 out of 6 patients in E showed significant response.	1 week, differential dropout rate, E group apparently maintained gains.
Elder & Eustis, 1975	Biofeedback of BP (Outpatient)	B: 1 session T: 20 sessions in 12 or 82 days	22	Single-group outcome	Average decrease in systolic BP was 7.8 mm; in diastolic BP, 6.5 mm. 9 out of 22 patients showed significant decrease.	2 months on 4 patients, no maintenance of gains.
Blanchard, Young, & Haynes, 1975	Biofeedback of BP (Outpatient)	B: 4 sessions T: 5-13 sessions	4	Single-subject experiments	All 4 patients showed decreases in BP during feedback training, ranging from 9-51 mm. Average decrease: 26 mm.	1-4 weeks, 3 out of 4 patients maintained 65 percent plus of gains.
Shoemaker & Tasto, 1975	E-1: Biofeedback of BP E-2: Progressive relaxation C: Monitoring (Outpatient)	B: 3 sessions T: 6 sessions of 80 min. each in 2 weeks	15 (5 per condition)	Controlled-group outcome study	Average change in Systolic Diastolic Relaxation: 7 mm. 8 mm. Biofeedback: 0 mm. 1 mm. Control: 2 mm. 0 mm. 4 out of 5 Relaxation subjects showed improvement.	None

team (Schwartz & Shapiro, 1973) failed. In fact, this failure along with others (Shapiro, 1974) seemed to have led to the Harvard group's abandoning clinical work with biofeedback and blood pressure. Goldman et al. (1975) were able to obtain fairly good results using the constant cuff pressure technique, providing an outside replication. However, their failure to use any baseline session calls into question whether the changes they reported are due to biofeedback training or merely to adaptation effects. One must remember that it took an average of 11 sessions for Benson et al.'s (1971) subjects to fully adapt and show baseline stability.

Kristt and Engel (1975) also used the constant cuff pressure technique with good results. However, their training program was radically different from that of Benson et al. (1971). Thus, at this point there is some evidence, admittedly contradictory, which shows the replicability of the effectiveness of constant cuff pressure technique.

Miller, after his initial glowing success (1972), has reported on more tnan 20 successive failures to obtain clinically meaningful changes in the blood pressure of hypertensives with his feedback system (Miller, 1975). In fact, he, too, seems to have abandoned this line of research.

The study of Elder et al. (1973), despite some of its faults, produced substantial (20 percent) changes in diastolic blood pressure with very brief training. It continues to amaze me that the addition of mere verbal social reinforcement could have so powerful an effect over the instructions and biofeedback received by one control group. Nevertheless, the attempted replication (Elder & Eustis, 1975) on an outpatient basis yielded much poorer results. Average decreases in blood pressure were less than 10 percent and only 9 of 22 patients showed significant decreases.

My own work on the biofeedback treatment of hypertension has fallen prey to that demon, lack of replicability. After our (Blanchard et al., 1975) initial success with an open-loop, intermittent feedback system for the treatment of hypertension, we embarked upon a controlled-group outcome evaluation of this technique.

In an attempt to rectify some of the mistakes committed by others, we (Blanchard, Miller, Abel, Haynes, & Wicker, 1977) have recently completed the following unpublished study. Thirty hypertensive patients were independently evaluated by a collaborating physician and then given four baseline sessions of 40 minutes (15 mins. adaptation, 5 mins. in-session baseline, 20 mins. treatment) during which they were asked to relax. The patients were then randomly assigned to one of three conditions: (1) direct biofeedback of blood pressure using the open-loop, intermittent (once per minute) feedback described by Blanchard et al. (1975); (2) analogue auditory feedback of frontalis EMG to aid in relaxation; or (3) instructions to try to relax on their own and try to reduce blood pressure. Treatment lasted for 12 sessions spread over 6 to 10 weeks. Patients were asked to practice at home lowering their blood pressure on a daily basis in the same manner they used in the laboratory.

Patients were followed up in the equivalent of baseline (instructions but no feedback) sessions, twice per week for 2 weeks and then at 6, 10, and 14 weeks posttreatment. During the first two weeks of follow-up, the patients were reevaluated by a physician who was blind to treatment condition.

Results show *no* significant differential effects of treatment and very small treatment effects per se. Average reduction of systolic blood pressure from pretreatment baseline to the first 2 weeks of follow-up was 6.5 mm. mercury; for diastolic blood pressure it was 2.0 mm. mercury. Thus blood-pressure feedback and frontalis EMG feedback were no more effective than mere instructions to relax and try to lower blood pressure in the laboratory.

At this point we have abandoned direct biofeedback of blood pressure as a psychological treatment strategy for hypertension and have moved to the exploring of some of the different relaxation techniques.

The last study listed in Table 3.1, Shoemaker and Tasto (1975), has not been discussed above, since the biofeedback condition was ineffective. In fact, it was such a crude system of feedback, allowing patients to view the polygraph record by a set of mirrors, that it is unlikely that patients could tell if their blood pressure had changed. Certainly it was ineffective. At best it seems to have provided a good attention-placebo condition against which to compare the effects of progressive relaxation. The latter condition was marginally effective, resulting in a drop of 7 to 8 mm. mercury. A further problem with this study is that the subjects were probably not hypertensive; blood pressures were in the range of 132-136 over 90.

Conclusions

At this point, the evidence for the utility or even efficacy of direct biofeedback of blood pressure in treating hypertension is marginal at best. Promising results obtained in one study fail to hold up on replication, or the replication is so poorly controlled that the results are of little value.

Only one study using the Tursky, Shapiro, and Schwartz (1972) constant cuff pressure technique has obtained meaningful clinical results, after an adequate baseline, which held up during follow-up: Kristt and Engel (1975). Even this study is problematic since it is a small-scale single-group study at best. However, the data do seem to support the notion that the patients really learned to control their blood pressure.

In fact, it is the training procedures and follow-up procedures which mark this study as different. Patients were hospitalized for three weeks and given approximately two training sessions per day. They were taught to raise, lower, and alternately raise and lower blood pressure. This is in contrast to all other studies, which gave training only in lowering blood pressure.

My own speculation (admittedly without supporting data) is that the key to the success of Kristt and Engel's approach lay in training patients in the hospital "to use a BP cuff to perform a BP lowering maneuver" (p. 372), which they then used at home during follow-up. This self-control and self-management training probably enabled patients to maintain lowered blood pressures. Epstein and I (Epstein & Blanchard, in press; Blanchard & Epstein, in press) have argued elsewhere that such self-control training followed by self-management techniques is probably the optimum strategy for controlling a tonic physiologic response.

Biofeedback of Other Responses to Reduce Blood Pressure

In addition to the studies of direct feedback of blood pressure, there have been several other attempts to treat hypertension through the use of biofeedback training with other responses. In all of this work, summarized in Table 3.2. the rationale seems to have been to reduce blood pressure through either reducing sympathetic nervous system activity or reducing overall level of muscle tension.

The work by Patel and her associates, summarized in Table 3.2, is one of the most outstanding sets of studies in the whole field of clinical biofeedback. She has reported three separate studies on groups of 17 to 20 patients in each. All the patients were clearly hypertensive and the vast majority were on antihypertensive medications. Treatment in the first two studies was a combination of biofeedback of galvanic skin response (GSR) and a set of yoga exercises which involve passive relaxation training and meditation. In the first study (Patel, 1973) systolic blood pressure was reduced by 25 mm. mercury and diastolic by 14 mm. mercury on the average, with 16 of 20 patients showing a significant degree of improvement. In the second study (Patel, 1975), a controlled-group outcome study, similar levels of change in blood pressure were found in the experimental subjects. More importantly, at a 12 months' follow-up, the blood pressure of the experimental subjects was maintained at its low end of treatment level.

In the third study (Patel & North, 1975), more rigorous controls were imposed and treatment was shortened from 36 sessions over 3 months to 12 sessions over 6 weeks. All blood pressure measurements in this last study were made by a "blind examiner." Decreases in blood pressure were again comparable to the levels seen before. An interesting feature of this study was that 4 months after the completion of a treatment, the subjects in the control condition were given a similar treatment and also showed significant decreases in blood pressure, 28 mm. mercury systolic and 16 mm. mercury diastolic. This use of half cross-over design, in which the untreated controls are now treated and show a response similar to the treated subjects, is a very powerful demonstration of effects because it answers the possibility that the treatment effect was specific to the experimental group even with random assignment of subjects. The replication of effects on the controls rules out this possibility. Follow-up data on these subjects at 4 months and 7 months showed a maintenance of the gains obtained during treatment.

TABLE 3.2: Biofeedback Treatment of Hypertension/Biofeedback of Other Responses

STUDY	TYPE OF TREATMENT (LOCATION)	DURATION OF BASELINE (B) AND TREATMENT (T)	NUMBER OF PATIENTS	TYPE OF STUDY	RESULTS	FOLLOW-UP
Patel, 1973	Biofeedback of GSR + passive relaxation training + meditation (Outpatient)	B: variable, at least 3 sessions; T: 36 half-hour sessions over 3 months	20	Single-group outcome	Average decrease in BP: Systolic: 25 mm. Diastolic: 14 mm. 16 of 20 patients showed significant response; 12 out of 20 also had reduction in medication.	None
Patel, 1975	E: same as above; C: resting quietly for 30 minutes (Outpatient)	B: 3 sessions; T: 36 half-hour sessions over 3 months	E = 20 C = 20	Controlled-group outcome study	Average decrease in BP: E C. Systolic 20 mm. 1 mm. Diastolic 14 mm. 2 mm. 12 out of 20 patients in E had reduced medication.	12 months, E: 5 months rise in systolic BP; C was unchanged.
Patel & North, 1975	E: same as above; C: same as above (Outpatient) (BP's taken by "blind" examiner)	B: 3; T: 12 half-hour sessions over 6 weeks	E = 17 C = 17	Controlled-group outcome study with crossover (controls treated at end of experiment)	Average decrease in BP: E C. Systolic: 26 mm. 9mm. Diastolic: 15mm. 4mm. C after treatment 28 mm. 16 mm.	4 months for C, E: 7 months. A 4 mm. rise in systolic BP.
Moeller & Love, 1974	Biofeedback of frontalis EMG + autogenic training (Outpatient)	B: 2 sessions; T: 17 (once per week	6	Single-group outcome	Average decrease in systolic BP was 18 mm; in diastolic BP, 12 mm. 5 out of 6 patients showed significant decreases.	None
Love, Montgomery, & Moeller, 1974	Biofeedback of frontalis EMG + various relaxation trainings C: Monitoring of BP for 4 weeks (Outpatient)	B: 1 session; T: 16 weeks (one or two sessions per week)	40 (27 completed treatment); 10 controls	Single-group outcome	Average decrease in systolic BP was 15 mm. In diastolic BP, 13 mm. Control group showed essentially no change in 4 weeks.	8 months. $n = 23$ further decreases in BP: systolic– 6.5 mm., diastolic– 4 mm.

It would certainly seem that Patel has developed a "treatment package" which has very beneficial effects on hypertensive patients. Whether biofeedback plays any important role in their treatment is not known. Personal communication from Patel indicates that the biofeedback is a minor part of treatment and that the passive relaxation training and meditation are probably the more important aspects. She also introduces regular practice of this relaxation and seeks to teach her patients other ways of adopting a more relaxed attitude towards life, especially in her last study (Patel & North, 1975). Whatever the components of her treatment, it would certainly seem that the package is well worth investigation by others as it has very strong, and more importantly, very consistent effects upon replication.

In terms of our evaluation dimensions, the most important missing feature is replication of the effectiveness of the treatment package by independent investigators. There are also no data on the response for which feedback was given. Independent assessment of the treatment effects is provided to some extent by the use of a "blind examiner" to take the blood pressure measurements in the last (Patel & North, 1975) study.

The studies by Love and his associates (Moeller & Love, 1974; Love, Montgomery, & Moeller, 1974), while not as elegant as those of Patel, do seem to show that a combination of frontalis EMG biofeedback training and various other relaxation training procedures leads to moderate reductions in blood pressure. One interesting finding in the study by Love et al. (1974) was that at an eight months' follow-up, there had been further decreases in blood pressure in the treated subjects who continued to regularly practice their relaxation, and no relapses had occurred among the 79 percent of subjects still available.

In terms of clinical effectiveness, the treatment package described by Love seems to be useful in the treatment of hypertension. Evidence for this efficacy is somewhat weak, unfortunately, since only single-group outcome studies have been reported and relatively short baselines obtained. The follow-up data are impressive for the second study; however, no confirmation of generalization or transfer of treatment effects has been obtained. In the first study, 5 out of 6 patients responded significantly; no data were available on the second. Finally, no explicit data on EMG changes has been presented. Some autocorrelation data were given in the second study, which purports to show that the changes in blood pressure *lag behind* changes (decreases) in frontalis EMG by 1 to 2 weeks. Overall, it does seem that relaxation training utilizing biofeedback training is a reasonable way to try to help patients lower their blood pressure. Of course, Shoemaker and Tasto (1975) found reasonably good results without the addition of biofeedback.

Conclusions

As mentioned above, the systematic work by Patel certainly seems to show that the combination of GSR biofeedback, passive relaxation training, and meditation is consistently effective in producing significant reductions in blood pressure in a hypertensive. Along many of the evaluative dimensions, this work stands up exceedingly well. There is still the need for independent replication of the effects by other investigators using her treatment package, as well as the need to determine which parts of the total "treatment package" are necessary to this success and which parts are not.

With regard to the other studies, it would appear that relaxation training, either of an active, Jacobsonian, progressive relaxation nature or of a passive, meditative form, combined with frontalis EMG biofeedback can lead to some improvement in hypertensive patients (a reduction in blood pressure of about 10 to 15 mm. of mercury). Furthermore, recent work by Benson and his associates (Benson, 1975; Benson, Rosner, & Marzetta, 1973; Benson, Rosner, Marzetta, & Klemchuk, 1974a, 1974b) has shown that "regular elicitation of the relaxation response," or a passive, meditative form of relaxation training alone, can lead to significant reductions in the blood pressure of hypertensive patients.

Interestingly, regardless of the method of psychological treatment, a consistent finding seems to be that the relaxation training or biofeedback training must be regularly practiced (on almost a daily basis) for the benefits of treatment to be maintained. Discontinuation of practice at the end of treatment leads to a gradual return to the elevated level of blood pressure. Thus, psychological treatment of hypertension has some of the same problems present in pharmacological treatment, that is, the treatment must be maintained over the rest of the patient's life in order to give him the benefit of the reduced blood pressure. Similar compliance problems may be found in the psychological approach as are found in the pharmacological approach.

However, while the side effects of antihypertensive medications are well known and are usually indicated as part of the reason for poor compliance, (Podell, Kent, & Keller, 1976) the side effects of these various "relaxation" procedures seem to be of a positive nature (Patel & North, 1975). Patients in several studies as well as our own (Blanchard et al., 1977) reported improvement in other spheres of their lives, such as feeling less tense and anxious and sleeping better. It may be that these "positive" side effects would enhance compliance with this regimen. Certainly, at this point, there have been no reported deleterious effects of psychological interventions with hypertensive patients. As an adjunct to pharmacological intervention, they could be recommended. However, the evidence is not clear at present if they could be considered as an alternative to pharmacological intervention.

At the present time, no large-scale series of patients has been run so that one can begin to predict which patients among the hypertension population are more amenable to psychological intervention. The work by Stone and DeLeo (1976) seems to indicate that autonomic arousal and biogenic amines are implicated in the process by which blood pressure was lowered.

CARDIAC ARRHYTHMIAS

Cardiac rate, or heart rate, was one of the first responses used in biofeedback research; and if one judged the clinical importance of a response by the number of reports concerning it, control of heart rate, and particularly control of heart-rate acceleration, would be the clear-cut nominee for most important. More is probably known about the parameters of biofeedback of heart rate than any other response. By my count, over 70 articles have been published on this topic. When one turns to the clinical application literature, however, the size of the literature is much reduced. Most of the clinical applications of biofeedback training of heart rate are in the treatment of cardiac arrhythmias. This work is summarized in Table 3.3

Looking at the studies reported in Table 3.3, one can see that, with one exception, the reports have been concerned with only one or two patients. Moreover, the overall level of sophistication of the studies is lower than that in the area of hypertension; for the most part, studies have been at the level of the systematic case study, with two examples of single-subject experiments and possibly one single-group outcome study.

There are probably at least two reasons for the smaller number of subjects and less sophisticated studies: there are probably fewer patients available with diagnosed arrhythmias than with hypertension and these disorders tend to be viewed as more serious than hypertension and thus are more likely to be treated strictly through pharmacological intervention.

Premature Ventricular Contractions (PVCs)

By far the best study in this area is the series of systematic case studies on the treatment of PVCs by Weiss and Engel (1971). Eight patients with well-documented and frequent PVCs were given essentially the same training although the number of patients who completed the various phases of the program varied. The purpose of the training seemed to be to teach patients to control heart rate; hopefully, if they mastered heart-rate control, this mastery would lead to a decrease in PVCs.

All training was conducted while the patients were hospitalized. Each phase of training lasted approximately 10 sessions. Patients were taught to increase heart rate, then to decrease heart rate, and then alternately to increase and decrease heart rate for 1 to 3 minute periods. Next the patient was taught to reduce heart rate variability by holding it within a specified range. An important aspect of this phase was that the arrangement of the feedback apparatus was such that patients received direct feedback of the occurrence of PVCs in this phase.

In the last phase, training in true self-control, as contrasted with feedback-assisted control, was begun. While the patient was keeping heart rate within the specified range, feedback was systematically "faded out" — first 1 minute of feedback on followed by 1 minute with feedback off, then 1 minute on and 3 minutes off, and finally 1 minute on and 7 minutes off.

Three patients completed the entire training program; one more completed all but the final step of the fading out of feedback; and a final patient completed the initial step of feedback fade out.

In terms of the evaluative criteria, 5 of the 8 patients treated by Weiss and Engel (1971) showed marked reductions of PVCs in the laboratory, thus confirming the clinical efficacy of the training on a group basis. The experimental design is a bit problematic in that it represents a series of systematic case studies. Unfortunately, no baseline data on rate of PVCs were obtained in the laboratory although all of the patients had well-documented histories of PVCs. Moreover, improvement seemed to be related to length of treatment: if one divides the patient sample into those receiving 47 or more training sessions and those receiving fewer than 47 sessions, then by Fisher's Exact Probability Test there is a significant ($p < .05$) relation between treatment length and treatment outcome.

Because Weiss and Engel presented session-by-session data on both the response for which feedback was given (heart rate) as well as for the clinical response of interest, it is possible to determine in which training phase the major improvement occurred. For 2 patients, the major improvement was during alternation training; for 2 more patients, the major reduction occurred during range training. However, 1 patient, who eventually improved, did worse during range training. The final patient improved during heart slowing and also improved further during alternation training. Thus, there did not seem to be a consistent relationship between training phase and decrease in PVC rate.

Despite these negative features, this study is excellent in many regards: follow-up data of 3 to 21 months were obtained on all patients and showed that 4 of the 5 patients who improved in the laboratory maintained the improvement at home; the degree of transfer of the changes was masured by telemetry in the hospital but outside of the laboratory and was also confirmed by independent assessment after discharge.

Engel and Bleecker (1974) were able to replicate these results with another patient. In this case, baseline data were obtained in the laboratory. Improvement occurred during range training. Independent confirmation of her improvement was obtained several times during a lengthy follow-up.

Very important independent confirmation of the efficacy of heart rate biofeedback in the treatment of PVCs was provided by Pickering and Gorham (1975). Even though the experimental design used in their report was at the level of anecdotal case report, this confirmation is important. They treated a woman whose PVCs were rate dependent, that is PVCs started at certain fairly low cardiac rates. As a result of the biofeedback treatment, the heart rate at which the PVCs began was raised by about 30 beats per minute. This change

TABLE 3.3: Biofeedback Treatment of Cardiac Arrhythmias

STUDY	CLINICAL PROBLEM	TYPE OF TREATMENT (LOCATION)	DURATION OF BASELINE (B) AND TREATMENT (T)	NUMBER OF PATIENTS	TYPE OF STUDY	RESULTS	FOLLOW-UP
Weiss & Engel, 1971	Premature ventricular contractions (PVCs) 10-20/min.	Biofeedback of heart rate (Inpatient)	Baseline: by history Treatment: 22 to 53 sessions (1-3/day)	8	Multiple systematic case studies	Decreases in PVCs to less than 1 min. in 5 of 8 patients in the laboratory; confirmed decrease at independent check in 4 of 8 patients.	3-21 months, improvement maintained; patients continue to have self-control.
Engel & Bleecker, 1974	Various cardiac arrhythmias 1. PVC (15/min)	Biofeedback of heart rate (Inpatient)	B: by history and 2 sessions T: 16 days of 3-5 sessions	1	Systematic case study	Decrease in PVCs to less than 1 min.	Continued improvement independently confirmed. Time span not given.
	2. Supra-ventricular tachycardia plus paroxysmal atrial tachycardia (PAT); Baseline HR 116 BPM	(Inpatient & Outpatient)	B: by history and 1 session T: 25 sessions	1	Systematic case study	Final session HR: 105 BPM Independent confirmation of improvement.	5 months, improvement maintained.

TABLE 3.3: (Cont'd)

STUDY	CLINICAL PROBLEM	TYPE OF TREATMENT (LOCATION)	DURATION OF BASELINE (B) AND TREATMENT (T)	NUMBER OF PATIENTS	TYPE OF STUDY	RESULTS	FOLLOW-UP
	3. Sinus tachycardia; Baseline HR by history 106 BPM	(?)	B: by history T: 21 daily sessions	1	Systematic case study	1st session HR: 86 BPM Final session HR: 68 BPM Independent confirmation of 30 BPM decrease in HR.	?
	4. PAT and episodic sinus tachycardia	(Inpatient)	B: by history T: 40 daily sessions	1	Anecdotal case report	No intreatment data provided.	6 months, no PATs during follow-up.
Pickering & Gorham, 1975	Ventricular parasystolic rhythm; (0-15 PVCs/min depending on HR)	Biofeedback of heart rate (Outpatient)	B: not specified T: 16 sessions over 6 weeks	1	Anecdotal case report	Patient learned to raise HR by up to 25 BPM; threshold HR at which PVCs began increased from 78 BPM to 106 BPM.	None
Scott, Blanchard, Edmundson, & Young, 1973	Sinus tachycardia	Biofeedback of heart rate (Outpatient)	B: 4 sessions T: S-1: 53 sessions, 1-2/day; S-2: 30 sessions, 1-2 day	2	Single-subject experiment	S-1: lowered HR to normal range; returned to work. S-2: lowered HR by 18 BPM; less anxious.	S-1: 18 months; S-2: 3 months.
Blanchard & Abel, 1976	Episodic sinus tachycardia and "blackouts"	Biofeedback of heart rate (Outpatient)	B: 10 sessions T: 44 sessions	1	Single-subject experiment	Patient learned to lower HR in the absence of feedback while listening to "rape cues." Blackout spells disappeared.	4 months, improvement maintained.

enabled the patient to engage in many nonstrenous activities without having PVCs.

Sinus Tachycardia

The second arrhythmia which has been treated by biofeedback training is sinus tachycardia, or an abnormally high cardiac rate in which the rhythm is still controlled by the sino-atrial pacemaker. Blanchard and his associates (Scott, Blanchard, Edmundson, & Young, 1973; Blanchard & Abel, 1976) have reported on 3 cases of sinus tachycardia treated by biofeedback of heart rate. In each instance, a single-subject experimental design has been used. Although the results led to clinically meaningful changes, that is, to reductions in heart rate to the normal range, the experimental design aspects were problematic. There was a failure to obtain a reversal when baseline conditions were reinstated to complete the A-B-A design. While clinically this is a highly desirable result, experimentally it casts doubts on whether the treatment per se was responsible for the improvement. The replicability of the finding helps in this area, however. Formal follow-up data were reported in only one case; in that one case, the improvement had held up for at least 4 months. Informal follow-up revealed maintenance of improvements for 12 to 18 months in 2 of the 3 cases (Scott et al., 1973).

In terms of transfer of improvement to the patients' natural environment, no formal data were gathered. However, there were informal reports from the patients of marked improvement in certain areas. For example, S-1 in the report by Soctt et al. (1973) sought and obtained a job after being on disability benefits for his arrhythmia, decreased his use of minor tranquilizers, and reported being more calm and relaxed during the treatment phase in which his heart rate declined. The patient treated by Blanchard and Abel (1976) reported the cessation of her ''blackout spells'' and an overall improvement in functioning as a result of treatment.

Engel and Bleecker (1974) report an independent confirmation of the value of heart-rate biofeedback training in the treatment of sinus tachycardia. In this systematic case report, heart-rate lowering training was given and resulted in a decrease in heart rate to the low end of the normal range after a history of years of elevated cardiac rate. Very importantly, the improvement noted in laboratory was confirmed by independent assessment by the patient's personal physician. Training started with trials in heart-rate slowing and then progressed to Engel's fade-out of feedback technique to build in a high level of self-control.

Other Arrhythmias

Engel and Bleecker (1974), as noted in Table 3.3, have reported on the successful treatment of several other arrhythmias in either systematic case studies or anecdotal case reports. The disorders include paroxysmal atrial tachycardia (PAT) and supraventricular tachycardia.

Conclusions

The work on the treatment of cardiac arrhythmias by biofeedback training, despite beginning at about the same time as the work on hypertension, is at a less advanced level of development. The initial work seems promising, especially for patients suffering from PVCs and sinus tachycardia. There have been successful replications of systematic case reports and/or single subject experiments in both of these areas. Moreover, the work by Engel and his colleagues in treating PVCs is in many ways excellent by many of the evaluative criteria, since good follow-up data and independent confirmation of treatment successes have been obtained.

However, given the limited number of patients who have been treated (a total of 16 patients are reported in Table 3.3), this work is far from conclusive. It would certainly seem that small-scale controlled-group outcome studies are needed. With the problems of side effects of the various arrhythmia-arresting drugs, and hence problems in patient compliance, this area would certainly seem to warrant further exploration. Finally, for arrhythmias other than PVCs and sinus tachycardia, the level of data is so sketchy as to be enticingly suggestive at best.

PERIPHERAL CIRCULATORY DISEASE

The third category of cardiovascular problems which has been treated with biofeedback is the peripheral circulatory diseases. In particular there has been much work on Raynaud's disease over the past five years. Raynaud's disease is a functional disorder of the peripheral vascular system in which the patient suffers painful episodes of vasoconstriction in the hands and sometimes the feet. During an attack, the skin blanches and is cold to the touch. Attacks are usually precipitated either by exposure to cold, such as touching a cold object, or by emotional upset.

Treatment has traditionally consisted of keeping the extremities warm and well protected in cold weather as well as by supplying external warmth during an attack. Drugs sometimes help. In some cases surgery, in the form of a sympathectomy is performed.

In Table 3.4 are listed reports on the treatment of 19 patients with either Raynaud's disease or Raynaud's phenomena. Most of the biofeedback treatment has been biofeedback of surface skin temperature, although feedback of the vasomotor response has also been used. Furthermore, there has been EMG biofeedback for relaxation training frequently included, as well as other psychological treatment such as autogenic training or hypnosis.

Length of treatment has varied from 8 sessions to as many as 70 sessions. Improvement, in terms of reduction of painful vasospasm episodes, does not seem to be related to length of treatment. A feature which seems to be

TABLE 3.4: Biofeedback Treatment of Raynaud's Disease

STUDY	TYPE OF TREATMENT (LOCATION)	DURATION OF BASELINE (B) AND TREATMENT (T)	NUMBER OF PATIENTS	TYPE OF STUDY	RESULTS	FOLLOW-UP
Schwartz, 1972	Biofeedback of vasodilation (Outpatient)	No data on baseline; Treatment for case 1 (male) > 10 sessions; for case 2 (female) < 10 sessions	2	Anecdotal case reports	Case 1: complete relief of symptoms (in feet) for 1½ years; then symptoms returned and booster treatment given. Case 2: no improvement.	1½ years
Pepper, 1973	Biofeedback of skin temperature	Not given	1	Anecdotal case report	Patient learned ''hand warming'' but had no improvement in Raynaud's.	None
Surwit, 1973	Biofeedback of skin temperature, autogenic training, and psychotherapy	Patient had disease for 5 years; had had sypathectomy 70 sessions over one year	1	Anecdotal case report	Patient had symptomatic relief for 1 year during treatment; basal skin temperature increased 3.6°C; marked decrease in frequency of attacks.	1 year, patient relapsed to pretreatment level at follow-up.
Jacobson, Hackett, Surman, & Silverberg, 1973	Hypnosis and biofeedback of skin temperature (Outpatient)	Patient was symptomatic for 3 years 8 sessions	1	Systematic case study	Patient showed no improvement with hypnosis; with biofeedback he could reliably increase hand temperature by 3.9 to 4.6°C; much symptomatic improvement.	7½ months, patient continued in much improved state.

TABLE 3.4: (Cont'd)

STUDY	TYPE OF TREATMENT (LOCATION)	DURATION OF BASELINE (B) AND TREATMENT (T)	NUMBER OF PATIENTS	TYPE OF STUDY	RESULTS	FOLLOW-UP
Blanchard & Haynes, 1975	Biofeedback of skin temperature	B: 4 sessions T: 24 sessions over 2 months	1	Single-subject experiment	Patient showed approximately 5°F increase in hand temperature due to biofeedback over effect of instruction; overall hand temperature increased by 12°F. Clinical improvement also.	7 months, patient continued much improved with increased hand temperature.
May & Weber, 1976	Biofeedback of skin temperature	No baseline data T: 16 sessions over 8 weeks	8 (4 primary Raynaud's; 4 secondary)	Multiple systematic case studies	All patients showed at least 2°C increase in temperature. For severe cases, vasospastic episodes reduced from 5/week to 1/week. All patients reported some transfer and some clinical improvement.	None
Sedlacek, 1976	Biofeedback of skin temperature and EMG biofeedback for relaxation	No baseline data T: 9-16 sessions plus regular home practice	3	Anecdotal case reports	All patients could produce 5°F increase in hand temperature in 5 min. by end of treatment. All patients report clinical improvement.	None
Stephenson, 1976	Relaxation training, autogenic training, temperature biofeedback from hands, EMG biofeedback for relaxation	No baseline T: 64 sessions and 19 sessions	2	Systematic case studies	Both patients could raise hand temperature by at least 10°F with final temperature 94°F. Complete remission of symptoms.	16 months and 2 months, continued remission of symptoms.

necessary for continued improvement is regular home practice and a continuation of practice after the cessation of formal treatment.

In terms of the evaluative criteria, treatment has been at least somewhat successful in 17 of the 19 reported cases, or 89 percent. This is probably an inflated percentage because it is easier to publish reports of successful treatment than reports of treatment failure. However, in most of the reports, there is at least anecdotal evidence of clinically meaningful improvement in the successful cases. Although most of the reports are at the level of anecdotal case reports, there have been a few systematic case studies and one single-subject experiment (Blanchard and Haynes, 1975). All of these different levels of reports support the conclusion that biofeedback is an efficacious treatment for Raynaud's disease. Fortunately, there have been a few reports in which biofeedback of one response alone was used effectively so as to help isolate the critical ingredients. The reports with multiple-treatment intervention, although yielding clinical success, sometimes cloud the issue. In this respect, the work here is much like that on cardiac arrhythmias, and like that work is in need of some small-scale, controlled-group outcome study. The relative rarity of the disorder has probably prevented such a study to date.

Follow-up data have been reported for up to a year and a half. Within this area, there are several reports of temporary relapses which respond fairly well to booster treatment sessions. Although there have been no formal assessments of the degree of transfer of the improvement from laboratory to the patient's environment, the anecdotal report of patients seems to confirm that transfer occurs. It would be good in the future to obtain frequency data on number of vasospastic episodes before and after treatment as well as independent assessment of improved state.

Certainly the replicability dimension is well handled. Table 3.4 lists successful reports from six different investigators. In all but one report, the response for which feedback was given was surface skin temperature. In most reports there has been a statement about ability to raise surface temperature by the end of treatment, with reports ranging from 2.8 to 5.6°C. Furthermore, basal skin temperature has also been reported to have become appreciably warmer (Blanchard & Haynes, 1975; Stephenson, 1976).

Although one might suspect that direct feedback of the vasomotor response would be better than feedback of surface skin temperature, since the former is the real response of interest, this has not yet been put to any real test. Schwartz (1972) did report success using feedback of vasomotor response, however. Because of the difficulty in quantifying and giving feedback of the vasomotor response, it has not been used widely.

Conclusions

Overall it would seem that temperature biofeedback is a viable alternative treatment for Raynaud's disease. Certainly, since surgical treatment by means of a sympathectomy is permanent, irreversible, and not always effective (Baddeley, 1965), it would seem that biofeedback treatment might well be recommended before resorting to surgical intervention; this idea seems even more compelling since some authorities (Porter, Snider, Bardana, Rosch, & Eidemiller, 1975) no longer recommend the operation. Another conclusion which comes from the various case reports is that a fairly motivated patient is required, that is, one who is willing to come to treatment sessions regularly and to practice on his or her own regularly. Finally, a controlled-group outcome study in which the nonspecific effects of being in treatment can be assessed and controlled and in which the percent of subjects who respond positively can be determined, is much needed in this area.

SUMMARY AND CONCLUSIONS

This section will contain some very brief summary statements which seem justified by this review. Many of the qualifications which might be attached to these statements have been omitted in favor of brevity, but are available in the individual section summaries.

1. There is no clear-cut evidence from a well-controlled study that direct biofeedback of blood pressure has any utility in the treatment of hypertension. Initial effects reported in relatively uncontrolled studies fail to hold up upon systematic replication. Many studies are inadequate in terms of length of baseline or follow-up.

2. There is very strong evidence from the work of Patel that a treatment combining GSR feedback to reduce autonomic arousal, passive relaxation training and meditation, and regular practice of these techniques is very efficacious in the treatment of hypertension. The key elements in Patel's work as well as that of Kristt and Engel (1975) may be: (1) teaching patients some techniques which they can use to relax and lower blood pressure; and (2) instructing them in self-management techniques to obtain a high degree of use of the techniques in the natural environment.

3. In the treatment of PVCs and sinus tachycardia by biofeedback of heart rate, there is very suggestive evidence of efficacy and utility. There is a lack of well-controlled studies and definite conclusions must wait for such work. For other arrhythmias, it is too early to say.

4. In Raynaud's disease there is highly suggestive evidence that a biofeedback treatment based on surface skin temperature is efficacious. Again, no well-controlled group outcome studies have been performed, but the evidence to date certainly seems to warrant such a study. In fact, a clinical trial of thermal biofeedback would certainly seem to be indicated before the patient undergoes surgical treatment.

Chapter 4

Biofeedback and the Modification of Sexual Dysfunctions

James H. Geer*

It is common to see discussions of research and issues in biofeedback begin with an apology (for example, Blanchard & Young, 1973). These apologies usually refer to two kinds of problems. One is the difficulty that has been encountered in replicating some of the original research. The second problem is the difficulty that is being experienced in fulfilling the often-speculated-upon promise of dramatic and substantial application of biofeedback to practical concerns. Many papers seem aimed at explaining away the difficulties while continuing to pursue the seemingly evanescent yet fascinating phenomena reported in the biofeedback literature. This chapter differs from the type alluded to above in that it is my contention that in the field of sexuality, biofeedback may very well prove to be of substantial and practical importance. In order to support that position, I will endeavor to marshall arguments from several seemingly divergent lines of research and then to suggest why biofeedback procedures and sex therapy may have a bright future. We shall begin this task by reviewing those studies that report the effect of biofeedback techniques upon sexual responses.

BIOFEEDBACK AND GENITAL RESPONSE

Thus far, we have found only a few reports that directly evaluate biofeed-

*The author wishes to thank Francine Rugendorf, who assisted in gathering the material for this paper.

back and genital response. In a clinical setting, Quinn, Harbison, and McAllister (1970) presented a slide of an attractive female to a 28-year-old client with a homosexual history. The patient was instructed to fantasize about the slide's content, while penile tumescence was monitored by a penile plethysmograph. The patient was placed on a water-deprivation schedule and informed that increases in tumescence would be rewarded with a drink of cold lime juice. The reinforcement was signaled by means of a light which was turned on when penile circumference increases were observed. Throughout the course of treatment, there was an increase in penile response to reports of heterosexual fantasy.

Rosen and Kopel (1977) reported a case study using biofeedback in the treatment of transvestite exhibitionism. Using the sound of an alarm clock as the response-contingent stimulus, they reported reduction in penile tumescence to a videotape that included stimuli associated with the client's sexual preference. Since the volume of the alarm clock was controlled by the amplitude of the genital response, this study might have been conceptualized as an aversive procedure. It also should be noted that they reported a loss of short-term therapeutic gain.

Herman and Prewett (1974) also reported a case study in which they treated an instance of erectile dysfunction. They reported an increase in tumescence to contingent feedback followed by a decrease and subsequent increase when using noncontingent and contingent feedback. They noted that sexuality outside the laboratory also changed. However, as with Rosen and Kopel's case, therapeutic gains were lost over the follow-up period.

Csillag (1976) described using biofeedback to treat impotent males. While there was a suggestion that the overall procedure may have been effective, there was no evidence that biofeedback played a central role. The report does not satisfy even weakly stated criteria for demonstrating effectiveness of biofeedback in treatment of sexual disorders.

Rosen (1973) studied the effect of contingent feedback upon suppression of penile tumescence. One of the four groups (the contingent feedback group) was provided with instructions to suppress their penile tumescence when presented with a red light, which was to be turned off when their circumference increase exceeded the criterion level. The three other groups were a yoked feedback group, an instructions only group, and a no treatment group. The results indicated that only the contingent feedback group showed a significant suppression of penile tumescence ($p < 0.01$) over 3 treatment sessions.

Rosen, Shapiro, and Schwartz (1975) reported a study on facilitation of fantasy-produced erection via biofeedback procedures. They reported fantasy alone produced erections and, further, that the contingent reward group "obtained a greater and more consistent change" (p. 191) than a fantasy only group.

Price and Geer (1973) reported a study that found evidence that feedback resulted in subjects maintaining an erection longer to erotic tapes than did "listening only" controls.

Hoon, Wincze, and Hoon (1977) used a single-subject design with 2 subjects to try to determine the effects of fantasy and biofeedback on vaginal
engorgement contingent upon a TV monitor which displayed the subjects'
vaginal blood volume (VBV). The subjects were initially presented with
feedback of VBV without their knowledge of what measure was presented.
Secondly, they were told to fantasize as a means of increasing vaginal engorgement. Finally, the subjects were presented with the feedback and told
that it was a measure of VBV and that the use of fantasy could help them
increase their vaginal engorgement. The results indicate that biofeedback
alone was not sufficient to increase vaginal engorgement. Erotic fantasy was
effective for 1 subject. However, the combination of biofeedback and erotic
fantasy produced the highest reliable changes of vaginal engorgement in both
subjects. These reports, when taken together, provide initial support for the
suggestion that biofeedback results in the modification of genital response. In
fact, Laws and Pawlowski (1976) have published a description of a penile
biofeedback system even though they reported no data on its utility, and
Reynolds (1977) has noted that biofeedback may prove effective in treatment
of erectile dysfunctions. Caution is well advised, however, as suggested by the
follow-up problems noted by Rosen and Kopel, and Herman and Prewett.
Also, we should note that Barlow, Agras, Abel, Blanchard, and Young (1975)
report that they found no evidence that biofeedback facilitated tumescence
increases.

Biofeedback and Aversive Conditioning

There have been reports that, while typically not having been conceptualized as biofeedback, may very well be so viewed. These are the reports of
attempts to change clinical behaviors through the direct application of aversive
procedures to genital responses. When genital responses are used to determine
the timing and occurrence of stimuli, the procedure qualifies as an instance of
biofeedback. These reports differ from laboratory studies of biofeedback in
important ways. That is, the clients are often exposed to many other conditions, such as reassurance; there is motivation for change other than provided
in the procedures; and there is the complicated yet powerful effect of viewing
oneself as "sick" or "disturbed." Nevertheless, these reports use genital
responses as the criterion for delivery of response-contingent stimuli and thus
qualify as a form of biofeedback.

What are the findings from these clinical reports and studies? Two studies
have been reported that used genital responses as the behavior to be punished.
In these procedures, shock was administered contingent upon penile circumference increases to "deviant" stimuli. Shock levels were set by the individual
clients and were set anywhere from painful to maximum shock level that could
be tolerated. Bancroft (1969) used the procedure to treat 10 homosexual
clients. The clients were shown slides that were related to their sexual interests

and were instructed to imagine a sexually arousing situation involving themselves and the individual in the slide. Tumescent changes were monitored by a penile plethysmograph. When penile circumference increase exceeded a criterion level, shock was delivered. Three additional shocks were administered after 15 seconds if the circumference measure had not fallen or was not below the criterion level. Subjects were exposed to this procedure from between 30 to 40 sessions. The sessions varied from 1 to 2 daily for the 3 subjects that were treated on an inpatient basis to 2 to 3 sessions per week for the remaining seven subjects. The author reported no objective data concerning penile responding of his patients to the treatment procedure. It was stated, "In most cases, suppression of erection occurred early in treatment and the erection tended to return as treatment continued. In only one case (A) did the suppression continue and generalize outside of treatment" (p. 1425). Further, in his discussion of the treatment, it was said that the changes that result "cannot be adequately explained in S-R learning theory terms, and a more profitable approach is to consider the treatment as a method of changing attitudes . . ." (p. 1430).

Callahan and Leitenberg (1973) used a similar punishment procedure. Slides were projected, and their 6 clients were instructed to imagine a sexually arousing situation involving themselves and the individual in the slide. Penile circumference was monitored by means of a penile transducer. Shocks were delivered if the circumference exceeded a criterion level at any time. The study reports primarily case history results of these procedures. The authors do state, "Contingent shock was used during eight treatment phases, and it produced a suppression of erection from levels established in the preceding phase in three of these applications. It continued previous produced suppression in three other phases and produced an increase in erection to deviant stimuli in two phases" (p. 70). The reports of Bancroft and Callahan and Leitenberg provide some tentative evidence that response-contingent shock procedures decrease genital response. Since it is possible to conceptualize these procedures as a form of biofeedback, these studies provide some additional minimal evidence for effectiveness of biofeedback. We should note carefully that the effects are often transitory and that the reports do not follow patterns that could be expected on the basis of S-R learning theory. Using the criteria Blanchard has described elsewhere in this book, the effectiveness of biofeedback on genital response is still open to question.

Instructional Control of Genital Response

In order to present the reasons why I feel biofeedback procedures may play an important role in altering sexual behavior, we need to examine several lines of research that do not directly relate to biofeedback. The first of these are the investigations of the effect of instructing subjects to change genital responses. These studies have been conceptualized by their investigators as addressing the problem of voluntary control of genital responses. Laws and Rubin (1969) reported that males watching an erotic film were able to inhibit penile responses when instructed to do so. Hensen and Rubin (1971), in a follow-up, replicated that study while assuring that subjects were attending to the erotic film. Barlow (1977) reports that in a study of volunteer homosexuals, subjects were able to suppress erections to erotic movies and slides but not to audio tapes. Rosen (1973) in his study that included biofeedback also had one group that showed suppression of penile response to instructions alone. Finally, Quinsey and Bergersen (1976) reported that some males were able to modify penile response contingent upon instructions. These studies have demonstrated that when males were presented with erotic stimuli and were given instructions to inhibit their genital responses they were able to do so; there is tentative evidence of facilitation of responding via instructions. They do not, however, clarify the mechanism by which subjects inhibit responses. The authors of these studies speak of voluntary control but do not identify the nature of the control. I shall argue, on the basis of work reported later in this chapter, that the mechanism is a cognitive one. It is likely that subjects are employing cognitive strategies that distract them from the erotic stimulus and loss of tumescence results and that to increase genital responding, they use erotic fantasy.

To follow up on the notion of cognitive factors in sexuality, I would like to argue that cognitive factors play a central and important role in human sexual behavior. We begin by examining the data that leads to such a position. Many of us can attest to having experienced genital responses as a result of having sexually oriented ''daydreams'' or fantasies. Several recent studies have provided empirical support for those informal observations. In addition, there has been the beginning of experimental research into exploring the complex processes that are involved in fantasy. Elsewhere (Geer, 1976) I have argued that the field of experimental cognitive psychology holds the promise of helping clarify problems in human sexuality. The following is a review of the research that has been generated thus far on these issues.

Self-Regulated Fantasy. As I noted, many of us can attest to how self-regulated fantasy can elicit genital responses. There now have been a series of studies that have provided empirical verification of that report. Julia Heiman (1977), among other procedures, instructed both men and women to fantasize sexual scenes on four separate occasions. The subjects were seated comfortably in a laboratory with no erotic stimuli present during the fantasy periods. Vaginal vasocongestive responses and changes in penile circumference were measured. There was clear and unequivocal evidence of genital responses, often of considerable magnitude, occurring to self-generated sexual fantasies. Robert Fuhr (1976), replicated Heiman's results on males. Rosen (1976) instructed subjects to increase penile size, and he noted that there was "significant voluntary control of penile tumescence in the absence of any external erotic stimulus" (p. 191). These studies provide unequivocal evidence that self-generated fantasy can produce extensive genital changes in the complete absence of an external stimulus other than instructions to fantasize. Perhaps it should be noted that simple resting or baseline conditions did not result in genital changes, and we have considerable unpublished data that nonerotic fantasy fails to yield genital changes. On a less formal, yet highly provocative level, Kinsey and colleagues reported that 2 percent of women can achieve orgasm on the basis of fantasy alone, without any physical stimulation (Kinsey, Pomeroy, Marin, & Gebhard, 1953).

The Role of Imagery

We have begun research employing the procedures and concepts of experimental cognitive psychology to issues and problems in sexuality. The focus of Robert Fuhr's dissertation (1976) was upon the role of imagery in fantasy-based sexual arousal. He found several very interesting results that have encouraged us to further consider cognitive factors. First, he found that measures of individual's differences in imagery were related to physiological measures of sexual arousal to fantasy. That is, individuals who score high on certain imagery measures tend to yield larger genital responses to self-initiated fantasy. Secondly, he found experimental procedures that have been used to block visualization were effective in reducing sexual arousal in subjects who were listening to an erotic tape recording. Those findings were taken as support for assigning importance to the role of visual images in the production of sexual arousal to audio tapes.

In an earlier study, we (Geer & Fuhr, 1976) were able to manipulate the degree of distraction, using a strictly cognitive task, from listening to an erotic tape. That study revealed that as time available for attending to the erotic stimuli decreased, sexual arousal decreased. What was crucial in that study was that: (1) the erotic tape was loudly and clearly presented to all subjects, and (2) the distractions were different difficulty levels in mental arithmetic, a strictly cognitive task.

My point is that there now exists a body of experimental literature that documents that cognitive activity affects genital responses. Further, there is an experimental methodology developing that allows empirical research on the subject. The question is no longer "do cognitive processes affect sexual arousal?" but the nature of those processes and the role that they play. One might speculate that to the degree in which clinical procedures emphasizing fantasy, such as in "masturbatory conditioning" therapies, are successful, we are seeing the powerful effect of cognitive factors. Lang (1977) has offered a conceptual framework for examining some of the issues relating imagery to therapeutic change.

Estimates of Sexual Arousal and Measures of Genital Change

The next series of investigations to be considered are those that report the relationship between genital responses and the subjective estimate of the intensity of sexual arousal. As will be seen, the correlations between judgments or estimates of sexual arousal and measures of genital change are quite high. I wish to emphasize that these are correlations between genital responses and cognitive events. The correlations regularly exceed those reported between other autonomic responses and estimates of emotional arousal. In another paper (Geer, 1977), I surveyed that literature and noted that, for women, the correlations ran between .50 to .60. There is tentative evidence (Heiman, 1976; Hoon, Wincze, & Hoon, 1977) that sexually dysfunctional women yield lower correlations or lower arousal levels, points we shall pursue later. For males, the correlations reach into the .70s, with specialized scaling techniques extending the correlations to as high as .87 (Spiess, 1977). The correlations are substantially greater than is typically found between autonomic measures and estimates of emotional arousal. It should be noted, parenthetically, that there are substantial individual differences. We shall speculate upon the reasons for the high correlation later in this paper and suggest that they have implications for the application of biofeedback procedures. I might also note that this finding has research implications for Lang's (1977) recent work on the analysis of imagery. Since the relationship between genital responding and the experience of sexual arousal is higher than found for most emotional states, sexual behavior may well provide an arena for the testing of Lang's propositional model.

COGNITIVE FACTORS AND SEXUAL RESPONDING

The various studies that we have reported provide the background from which we can approach an understanding of the potential use of biofeedback procedures in sexual responding. The model that we shall propose is not fundamentally different from other formulations. It is, however, based upon more substantial evidence than is the case in other autonomic response systems. First, recall that we noted several studies and reports that yielded evidence, albeit sometimes rather tentative, that biofeedback procedures do affect genital responses. Secondly, there is considerable evidence that reductions in genital responses can be found by instructing subjects to inhibit penile responding to erotic stimuli. While the mechanism behind this phenomena is not clear, it is our contention that it must be a cognitive procedure. The notion of voluntary control proposed by the investigators in the "instructions" research, as well as some of the biofeedback research, sound like cognitive processes. Rosen (1976) in his review of biofeedback and sexual responses notes that, "Genital blood flow should not be viewed as a completely *reflexive* response to external stimuli" (p. 195). Certainly, his view leaves open the door to cognitive processes.

The second line of research that we presented established that cognitive mechanisms can result in sexual arousal and that experimental study of the phenomena is possible. High levels of sexual arousal up to and reportedly including orgasm can be attained in the absence of external erotic stimuli. Individuals report the use of imagery, particularly visual, as the mechanism underlying these phenomena. I have noted some experimental research that supports those reports and demonstrates that manipulation of the phenomena is possible. The now almost classical arguments (Katkin & Murray, 1968; Crider, Schwartz, & Shnidman, 1969) concerning the possible role of mediation no longer seems relevant, at least in sexual responding. At the time those arguments were conducted, genital responses had not been studied extensively and, since they were "out of sight," they were "out of mind." For our purposes we need not be concerned with whether or not cognitive processes are necessary for genital responding; it is enough that they are sufficient. Finally, we wish to recall to your attention the relationship between genital responses and judgments of level of sexual arousal. Those reports reflect one aspect of the importance of cognitive factors in sexual behavior. The correlations between genital responding and subjective feelings of arousal do not, of course, indicate any causal relationship. Taken, however, in the context of clear demonstrations of the effect of cognitive factors, a causal relationship is strongly suggested. Why do cognitive events so powerfully affect sexual arousal is a question to which we have no answer. It does, however, reflect the general trend in evolution away from hormonal controls over sexual behavior. Taken together, results on biofeedback, instructions research, and research on cognitive processes can be viewed as providing the background for conceptualizing how biofeedback procedures may be employed to alter genital responses.

Before discussing how biofeedback could be used, I would like to offer to you some considerations as to why genital responses may be more amenable to biofeedback procedures than is true in other aspects of the autonomic nervous system. Ellmore and Tursky (1976) have suggested that part of the reason for disappointments in biofeedback research is that many of the studies may have used inappropriate afferent feedback. That suggestion would appear to have considerable merit in many instances; but in sexual responding those issues appear to be less important. The reason is that genital responding has more "naturally effective" afferent feedback than is true for most other components of the autonomic nervous system. The naturally effective afferent feedback, I would argue, is, in part, founded in biological roots. It is easy to conceptualize the penis as a natural biofeedback device. While for females the feedback may not be as obvious as in males, it may very well be much more effective than other components of the autonomic response system. Most women can report the occurrence of genital sensations with little difficulty. We note that sensory nerve endings are more densely packed in the genitals than in other parts of the human anatomy. Perhaps they detect vascular changes and provide natural feedback more readily than other components of the autonomic response system. For both sexes, the very high correlations between genital change and judgment of level of sexual arousal may result from this biologically effective feedback system. I recognize that this view has strong overtones of James-Lange theorizing. I also recognize the fact that Schachter's (1964) theories on emotion are consistent with the viewpoint suggested above.

While the biological substrate of sexual responding influences the effectiveness of biofeedback procedures, there is an experiential base as well. Likely, the two act synergistically and insure a close association between cognitive events and physiological responses. The experiential base is well proposed in Gagnon and Simon's (1973) theory of social scripting. In that view, we are all trained by society as to the nature of things sexual. We learn, according to their model, scripts which are cognitive structures that provide directions for behavior. These scripts resemble Tolman's cognitive maps described so many years ago. In the scripting model, the cognitive representations are used to guide actions, to identify sexual situations, and to provide the individual with information about what is sexuality. From that model, Gagnon and Simon suggest that parts of the script in our society are representations that sexual arousal is associated with genital changes. We may be taught that if certain changes have occurred, we are sexually aroused. Indeed, it is very difficult for a male under most conditions to deny sexual arousal if he has an erect penis. Thus, the acquisition of societal standards guarantees that to greater or lesser degrees we all will associate genital changes with judgments of arousal. In fact, Spiess' finding of correlations in the .80s suggests the possibility that some males may use genital responses as an index of arousal. While the Gagnon and Simon model eschews biological factors, in my view they likely act to complement the social learning dimension.

Gagnon and Simon feel that the cognitive-physiological relationship differs for the sexes. In their formulation, they suggest that, in our culture, males are taught that sex is physical whereas females see sex more in a relationship context. The male sexual ethic emphasizes physical gratification and body sensations to a greater extent than is true for females. That formulation would lead to the expectation that males would be more likely to use genital responses as part of their evaluation of sexual arousal. Further, the theory predicts that the correlation between genital responses and judgments of level of sexual arousal will differ for the sexes. Males' correlations should be higher than for females, and the evidence accumulated thus far supports the prediction. To reiterate, the correlation differences between the sexes should result from both increased genital cues (for example, clothing pressure, visual cues) and increased societal emphasis upon the physical aspect of sex for males.

I have suggested that both biological factors and societal factors have led to genital responses being "naturals" for biofeedback. I would like to suggest that these factors are reflecting aspects of the nature of things sexual. First, sexual behavior is reinforcing. Selection pressures guaranteed that reproductive acts would occur at sufficient frequency to ensure specie survival. Apparently, this was accomplished by assuring that sexual behavior, arousal, and stimuli are powerfully rewarding. While one could argue whether or not the reinforcing effect is learned versus innate, that it is rewarding is not in serious doubt. So strong is this association that individuals who report sex as being unpleasant are often considered to be experiencing a psychological disorder. This means that if biofeedback procedures are effective, they may be so in part because there is a built-in reinforcing system. One doesn't have as much need for external rewards if the response itself has positive reinforcing characteristics. It also means that there is, via the reward, additional information concerning the state of the genitals.

A second aspect of the nature of sexual behavior that differentiates it from most other autonomic nervous system functions is the fact that the response in question interfaces with the environment. Genital responses play a crucial role in sexual behavior whereas for most autonomic responses the environmental interface is much more indirect at best. For heterosexual intercourse to occur an erect penis is necessary and a lubricated vagina is desirable. Similar statements for other emotional states and other autonomic responses are not as obvious nor as direct. The implication of these considerations needs elaboration. It follows that if the response is the interface with the environment, its manipulation has more direct impact upon the behavior sequence. If there is an absence of genital responding, certain sexual acts could not occur or would be painful. It would seem reasonable that since genital responses are often the interface with the environment, they would be more directly affected by the environment and its consequences. Thus, I would expect that manipulation of environmental events, perhaps such as biofeedback procedures provide, would be particularly effective in the alteration of genital responses. Given a rationale, let us turn our attention to possible application.

THERAPEUTIC APPLICATION OF BIOFEEDBACK

I anticipate that there are two principal effects that biofeedback procedures would have upon dysfunctional sexual behavior. It should be made very clear from the start that neither of these are the gradual shaping or direct instrumental conditioning of the genital response. While response shaping may be possible, it would be an inefficient procedure. The first potential therapeutic goal would be an attack upon dissociation between cognitive and physiological events. To the extent that a given sexual dysfunction has its roots in or is in part based upon a relative dissociation between genital responses and level of experienced arousal, biofeedback procedures may have therapeutic value. If a part of the dysfunction is based upon being "out of touch" with the body, biofeedback provides a natural therapeutic tool. It should be possible to institute training procedures using biofeedback that will enhance the individual's sensitivity to genital changes. At Stony Brook we have some preliminary evidence that is consistent with this suggestion. Lang's (1974) notions of the model of skills training I would find quite acceptable as a description of the process that might actually bring about increased correlations.

There have been numerous suggestions by sex therapists that lack of an association between cognitive and physiological events is the basis of some sexual dysfunctions. For example, Kaplan (1974) feels that premature ejaculation results from the individual not discriminating arousal levels and thus reaching a stage of orgasmic inevitability too rapidly. Since it has been speculated that over one half of all men are premature ejaculators, the potential gain from developing increased awareness of genital sensations, if Kaplan is correct, is considerable. Spiess (1977) in our lab did not find that premature ejaculators were less aware of genital sensations, thus the issue is in doubt. In women, a lack of awareness of their own sexual nature has been held (Dodson, 1974) to be the basis of many female sexual dysfunctions. Women, so this view holds, may suffer from not recognizing their own sexuality (Heiman, 1976; Hoon, Wincze, & Hoon, 1977). Barlow (1977) has noted that many sexually dysfunctional individuals have difficulty, sometimes intentionally, in defining the nature of idiosyncratic erotic stimuli. My point is that biofeedback may have powerful therapeutic gain by increasing the individual's awareness of and thus perhaps the degree of association between genital responding and the experience and judgment of arousal. To some degree, this use of biofeedback may be allowing the individual to conform to society's scripts. The message may be that you are now sexually O.K. since we have put you back in touch with your body.

The second therapeutic use of biofeedback has been explored clinically. That is the use of biofeedback to identify erotic cognitions and to use genital responses as guides to the development of effective erotic fantasies. Also, the procedures have been used to provide assessment of the nature of dysfunctions and the assessment of change (Barlow, 1977; Geer, 1977). It should be noted that this application assumes that the cognitive-physiological association is sufficiently high to allow genital responses to track erotic cognitions. Thus, we might well find that in a given instance there would be a need to first sharpen the cognitive-physiological relationship before the present use could be attempted. To return to the point, biofeedback could be used to identify effective erotic cognitions. In the application setting, the role of the clinician would be to provide the client with material upon which the client can operate to form erotic thoughts. The therapist would provide cues and aids to the client along with encouragement and support in his or her endeavor. The biofeedback procedures would help the client and clinician identify cognitive activities that are most effective in producing desired changes. Also, the procedures would encourage the client to recognize his or her own sexual responsiveness and, thus, perhaps to modify their self-perceptions. This latter point may be particularly helpful for women who question their own sexuality.

As was noted, this procedure has been attempted with some success. Bancroft (1974) reporting his own work described a variant of the procedure by saying, "Bancroft (1971) has made use of the erectile response to deviant fantasies act both as a reinforcer of the preceding fantasy and as an indicator of its erotic effect" (p. 45). Barlow (1977) reports using audiotapes as erotic stimuli and then:

> These audio tapes are then played back to the patient. While he listens to this recording, the erection responses on the readout are observed. We then make new audio tapes, based on and enlarging the content which was correlated with the penile responses. This new tape, in turn, will elicit erections, usually larger than those noted on the first tape. Finally, the content of the tape correlated with the larger erection is once again elaborated on after considerable discussion with the patient. What emerges is an audio tape which is highly erotic to the particular patient undergoing assessment. (pp. 7-8)

The procedure, developed originally by Abel, Blanchard, Barlow, and Mavissahalian (1975), can be viewed as using genital responses to provide information used in modifying subsequent environmental events. It can be viewed as a variant of biofeedback and certainly resembles the procedure that I have outlined.

Other procedures for modifying sexual fantasies, while not using genital responses to help direct and guide the treatment, have been reported with varying degrees of success (Bancroft & Marks, 1968; Davison, 1968; Gold & Neufeld, 1965; Lobitz & LoPiccolo, 1972; McGuire & Vallance, 1964; and Marks & Gelder, 1969). The use of the objective data from genital responses may provide the conditions that optimize the likelihood of success in these techniques. Those studies do add support to the position taken here that cognitive events have powerful influences upon sexual behavior.

Let me restate, I am not suggesting the use of biofeedback for the shaping or gradual conditioning of the genital response per se. I do not see that biofeedback procedures will be powerfully effective by direct operation upon the genital response. Rather, I am suggesting that the procedures may be quite valuable when viewed as techniques to modify cognitive operations that in turn have powerful effects upon sexual behavior. Hopefully, this paper will stimulate research on the issues. The outcome would have significant impact upon both theoretical and practical issues in human sexuality.

SUMMARY

In brief summary, I have presented data from several different lines of research. These data were interpreted as indicating that sexuality may well become an area in which biofeedback may have important practical and theoretical contributions. It is my contention that the effectiveness will not be based upon a model that looks to gradually shape or instrumentally condition increases or decreases in genital responses. Rather, the procedures should act to increase the association between cognitive and physiological responses and should act as a guide for the development of effective erotic cognitions. I would argue that the data point in these directions, and I would urge research to verify or reject the proposals that I have offered.

Chapter 5
Clinical Applications of EEG Feedback Training*

William N. Kuhlman and Bonnie J. Kaplan

The general rationale in electroencephalographic (EEG) feedback training** as a therapy is, first, that there is an orderly relationship between some aspect of brain electrical activity and a clinical condition or associated behavioral state, and, second, that feedback training is effective in the modification or control of that EEG pattern. If these two premises are true, it is logical to investigate whether feedback training can be used to modify the EEG in such a way as to change a clinical condition. The studies reviewed in this chapter follow this general logic. It goes without saying, however, that training may be ineffective no matter how logical the rationale, or that therapeutic benefits may occur for reasons other than those originally proposed. Without the proper control procedures, the observation of a clinical effect alone does not validate the original premises.

In the clinical application of EEG feedback training, one is immediately faced with several problems. First, the human brain is one of the most complex and least understood structures in existence, and the electrical activity of the brain is correspondingly complex. Known orderly relationships between EEG activity and behavior are few. It is beyond the scope of this chapter to review the great variety of electrical patterns which can be recorded from the human scalp; the reader is referred to Rémond (1976) for a comprehensive summary of this information. A second problem is that because of this complexity, EEG feedback training is the most demanding of all the feedback training modalities, often requiring elaborate (and expensive) equipment for adequate analysis and interpretation. The third problem is that regardless of what clinical benefit EEG feedback training

---

*We thank Drs. Truett Allison and William R. Goff for comments on the manuscript.

**The term *training* will be used to refer to feedback combined with appropriate instructions to enhance or suppress EEG activity. It has been considered synonymous with *reinforcement* by some investigators.

may have, the scientific evidence for effective modification of human EEG rhythms is scarce. Johnson's recent (1977) review of EEG feedback training concluded that EEG conditioning has yet to be demonstrated. If the evidence is insufficient to demonstrate this modification, then training strategies designed to have therapeutic effects contingent upon learned EEG changes can be (and have been) easily questioned.

As a result of these three problems, the clinical applications of feedback training of other physiological variables such as electromyographic (EMG) activity, cardiovascular functions, and peripheral skin temperature have greatly outnumbered EEG, even though EEG feedback training provided the initial impetus for the current widespread interest in biofeedback. Nevertheless, the number of studies involving EEG feedback for clinical application has increased considerably since Blanchard and Young's (1974) review.

Following a brief introduction to the modification of central nervous system activity, this chapter will review the application of EEG biofeedback techniques to the control of epileptic seizures. Next, we will evaluate the status of alpha feedback training as a therapeutic technique. Finally, the few studies on the disorders of hyperkinesis and insomnia will be reviewed.

MODIFICATION OF CENTRAL NERVOUS SYSTEM ACTIVITY

Because this chapter focuses on the *therapeutic* application of EEG feedback training, several important areas of central nervous system (CNS) conditioning and feedback training will be treated only insofar as they pertain to clinical questions.

CNS Operant Conditioning in Animals

Investigations demonstrating conditioning of CNS activity in animals have paralleled the development of human EEG feedback training. Spontaneous EEG activity has been conditioned in cats who were given food reinforcement for the occurrence of sensorimotor cortical activity (Wyrwicka & Sterman, 1968; Chase & Harper, 1971). Hippocampal slow waves have been conditioned in several species by Black and his colleagues (see Black, 1972, for a review). Cortical evoked activity has been conditioned in a series of studies by Rudell, Fox, and Rosenfeld. Using control procedures to rule out mediation by extraneous variables, these investigators have demonstrated specific learning effects on single components of visual evoked potentials (see Rosenfeld & Rudell, 1976, for a review).

Investigators have also used operant techniques to alter firing rates of single neurons since the first demonstration of the phenomenon by Olds in 1965. Single units in monkey motor cortex (Fetz, 1969; Schmidt, Bak, MacIntosh, &

Thomas, 1977) and feline visual cortex (Shinkman, Bruce, & Pfingst, 1974) have been trained to increase or decrease firing rates. This control has also been demonstrated in monkey motor cortex previously made epileptic by the application of alumina cream (Wyler & Fetz, 1974), and subsequent changes in seizure activity have been reported (Wyler, Fetz, & Ward, 1974). The relevance of these studies for EEG feedback training in humans is that they may clarify the mechanisms by which neural activity may be modified and the limits and behavioral correlates of such modification.

Nontherapeutic Applications of EEG Feedback

The largest body of literature in the area of human EEG feedback training is certainly the research on the alpha rhythm, the topic which provided much of the impetus for the popularity of feedback training in the early 1970s. Most of this research has centered on basic issues in normal subjects, investigating whether alpha can be increased above baseline, and if so, under what conditions (Travis, Kondo, & Knott, 1975; Johnson, 1977). The interested reader can find a comprehensive review of the methodological issues in Ancoli and Kamiya (1978). A subset of this literature has focused on subjective correlates of alpha occurrence, and whether the "alpha experience" is valid (Plotkin, 1977). These issues are discussed later in relation to clinical applications of alpha feedback training.

A related area is the topic of alpha feedback as a research and diagnostic tool. Although EEG evaluation is routinely used for neurological diagnosis, EEG feedback has been used for this purpose by only one group of investigators. Since the early 1960s Mulholland and his colleagues have been using a control systems approach to EEG alpha in order to analyze the normal range of responsivity of this activity to various kinds of stimuli (Mulholland, 1977). Using a time series analysis of alpha presence and absence during feedback stimulation, they have characterized orienting and habituation processes as minifest in the EEG (Eberlin & Mulholland, 1976; Mulholland, McLaughlin, & Benson, 1976) and have used the method to provide EEG feedback assessment of psychiatric disorders (McLaughlin & Lewis, 1975) and brain lesions (Mulholland & Benson, 1976).

EEG FEEDBACK TRAINING AS A TREATMENT FOR EPILEPTIC SEIZURES

Background and Rationale

Many consider that there is no single disease entity called "epilepsy," but that there are many neurological conditions which include seizures as one manifestation (Gaustaut & Broughton, 1972). Some refer to "the epilepsies" to emphasize this heterogeneity. In this review, we shall simply use the term "epilepsy" and shall seldom provide clinical descriptions of the patients studied. Investigators should, of course, include seizure classification in their reports, since an important unanswered question is whether a particular type of seizure disorder is more "susceptible" to EEG feedback training than other types. However, clinical descriptions, while crucial for the long-term assessment of this technique, are beyond the scope of this review.

Occurrence of seizures is frequently influenced by emotions, expectations, environmental factors, and a number of placebo factors (Mattson, Heninger, Gallagher, & Glaser, 1970). The reactivity of seizure occurrence to behavioral variables has resulted in the success of some behavior modification approaches with certain types of patients (for a review, see Mostofsky & Balaschak, 1977). Definitions of placebo effects vary. Some include primarily the variable of expectation or "faith" (Peek, 1977), while others consider a placebo effect to be any effect which "is independent of or minimally related to the pharmacological effect of the medication or to the specific effects of the procedure, and which operates through a psychological mechanism" (Shapiro, 1960). No matter whether one accepts a narrow or broad interpretation of placebo effects, it is clear that for many epileptic patients seizures are very responsive to such factors. For example, it is well known that some patients will show a decrease in seizures simply with admission to a hospital or during EEG monitoring.

It is often estimated that 25 percent of epileptic patients have poorly controlled seizures despite maximal anticonvulsant therapy. It is these patients who have been involved in studies with EEG feedback training. The use of EEG feedback training to reduce the incidence of epileptic seizures has largely stemmed from the work of Sterman and his colleagues. The rationale was derived from behavioral and neurophysiological studies in cats. Roth, Sterman, and Clemente (1967) noted the occurrence of a 12–16 cycle per second (c/sec.) EEG rhythm in cats given food reinforcement to inhibit a previously learned bar-pressing response. This EEG activity, previously described by Brazier (1963), was termed the "sensorimotor rhythm" (SMR), because it tended to occur over the sensorimotor area of the cortex. The relationship between feline SMR and behavior was investigated by Wyrwicka and Sterman (1968), who utilized SMR occurrence as an instrumental response. Food-deprived animals were given milk reinforcement when they produced SMR at 13–17 c/sec. With training, this rhythm increased in occurrence and was associated with stereotyped postures, all of which involved a cessation of movement. When low-voltage desynchronized activity was reinforced, SMR disappeared and behavior was characterized by restlessness and frequent movement.

Howe and Sterman (1972) sought to localize the origin of SMR by recording from a variety of cortical and subcortical locations in cats. A 12–16 c/sec. SMR rhythm was observed predominantly over the postcruciate gyrus of the sensorimotor cortex, the primary receiving area for somatosensory afferent input. Subcortically, this activity was largest in the nucleus *Ventralis Posterolateralis*, a major thalamic relay station in the somatosensory system. At both locations, SMR was observed during the absence of phasic motor activity. In a dose-response study of monomethylhydrazine, a powerful convulsant, Sterman, LoPresti, and Fairchild (1969) found that in cats previously trained to enhance SMR activity, seizure onset was significantly delayed compared to untrained cats.

In summary, these studies demonstrated that feline SMR: (1) is correlated with the absence of phasic movement; (2) is blocked by movement; (3) is localized cortically to the sensorimotor area; (4) can be enhanced by training; and (5) is somehow associated with increased seizure threshold.

Clinical Research

The studies to be reviewed in this section have involved feedback and instructions designed to enhance selected EEG frequencies recorded from the central area of the scalp overlying the sensorimotor area of the cortex. The principal features of these studies are summarized in Table 5.1.

The seizure resistance exhibited by SMR-trained cats led Sterman and his colleagues to employ feedback training techniques first in one patient (Sterman & Friar, 1972) and then in three others (Sterman, Macdonald, & Stone, 1974). Feedback and instructions for enhancement were given for 12–14 c/sec. activity recorded from the central area of scalp, overlying the Rolandic area, which is the human analog of cat cruciate area. With three training sessions per week over a period of 6–18 months, seizure rates declined by an average of 66 percent, compared to two-year pretraining levels. During extended interruptions in training, however, seizure rates rose to pretraining levels after 4–6 weeks.

It is worth noting at this point that training interruptions may be an adequate control for seizure decreases which are due to chance or maturational changes, but they are not an adequate control for placebo factors, since removal of the patient from the feedback environment automatically removes many of the variables which might exert placebo effects. For placebo effects due to expectancy of treatment benefit, training interruptions should result in patients' expectancy of no benefit.

To account for the decreased seizure rates which occurred during feedback training, Sterman (1973) proposed that human "SMR" provided a "bioelectric label for the process of motor inhibition" such that long term training of "SMR" resulted in "selective overstimulation of motor inhibitory pathways," leading to "neutral reorganization" and increased seizure thresholds. Whatever the value of this hypothesis for the results in cats given monomethylhydrazine, its relevance for human epileptics is more speculative, since Sterman et al. (1974) were unable to document a systematic change in

TABLE 5.1: Biofeedback Training of Central EEG Activity/Applications to Epilepsy

STUDY	NUMBER OF PATIENTS	CONCOMITANT EEG CONTINGENCIES (c/sec.) ENHANCE	SUPPRESS	TRAINING DURATION[a]	EXPERIMENTAL DESIGN	NUMBER WITH DECREASED SEIZURES[b]	EEG RESULTS
Sterman et al., 1974	4	12–14	slow waves and high voltage	6–18 months	Pre/post; treatment interruptions for 3 patients; no statistical analysis	4 66 percent average reduction; seizures increased with training breaks.	Reduction in abnormal slow activity; no increase in 12–14 c/sec. SMR.
Kaplan, 1975	2 3[c]	12–14 7–9.5	none none	4–6.5 months	Systematic case studies	2 52 percent average reduction; no effect with 12–14 c/sec. feedback.	No change in 12–14 c/sec.; other EEG change in 1 patient was not due to training.
Finley et al., 1975; Finley, 1976, 1977	2	11–13	4–7 and high voltage	6.5–8 months	Systematic case studies; switch to noncontingent feedback in 1 patient	1 No reversal with noncontingent feedback.	Increased 11–13 c/sec.; decreased 4–7 c/sec.
Lubar & Bahler, 1976	8	12–14	4–7 and high voltage	6–8 months	Systematic case studies; treatment interruption in 3 patients	5 Seizures increased with training breaks.	Increase in amount of feedback obtained.
Kuhlman, 1976	5	9–14	none	4–10 months	Controlled systematic case studies; random feedback preceded contingent	3 60 percent average reduction; no effect of random feedback.	Increased alpha, EEG frequency, and decreased abnormal activity in separate patients; no increase in SMR.

TABLE 5.1: (Cont'd)

STUDY	NUMBER OF PATIENTS	CONCOMITANT EEG CONTINGENCIES (c/sec.) ENHANCE	SUPPRESS	TRAINING DURATION[a]	EXPERIMENTAL DESIGN	NUMBER WITH DECREASED SEIZURES[b]	EEG RESULTS
Wyler et al., 1976	4	14–30 26 18	activity below 14 and high voltage	4–7 months	Systematic case studies; an additional patient showed no effect with EMG feedback	3 Results not dependent on EEG frequency.	Could not be determined.
Quy, 1976	3	12–16 8–10	high voltage	12 months	Systematic case studies; sequential training on all contingencies	3 56 percent average (max.) reduction; not dependent on EEG frequency.	Increase in 8–10 c/sec. activity.
Sterman & Macdonald, 1978	4 4	12–15 18–23	6–9 6–9 high voltage[d]	9–12 months (home training)	Controlled systematic case studies; contingency reversal design	6 74 percent average (max.) reduction, specific to 12–15 condition in 3; others decreased across time.	Decreases in abnormal activity without increases in 12–23 c/sec.

[a]2–5 sessions per week.

[b]Does not include patients in whom there is experimental evidence for placebo or medication effects.

[c]Includes 1 patient previously given 12–14 c/sec. feedback training.

[d]High-voltage suppression was constant across experimental conditions.

12–14 c/sec. activity in epileptic patients. On the other hand, abnormal high voltage EEG discharges at low frequencies (e.g., 1–7 c/sec.) and polyspike and spike-wave abnormalities (patterns typical of epileptic EEGs) were said to be attenuated in all patients. These changes all have the effect of "normalizing" an EEG, as will be discussed later.

Attempting to replicate Sterman and Friar's report, Kaplan (1975) gave two patients feedback training for central 12–14 c/sec. activity. No changes in seizures or in EEG activity occurred. Questioning the existence of a human SMR rhythm, she then gave feedback to 3 patients to enhance their dominant rhythmic EEG activity, which in these patients ranged from 7–9.5 c/sec. In 2 patients in whom medication changes did not occur, seizure rates decreased; however, in no patient could a significant change in the EEG be linked to feedback training. Since no EEG change could be detected which might have been responsible for clinical improvement, and since the improved patients were ones who often experienced seizures associated with stress, Kaplan suggested that these patients may have learned relaxation skills in the quiet feedback setting.

Finley, Smith, and Etherton (1975) and Lubar and Bahler (1976) essentially replicated Sterman's results when epileptic patients were given feedback for EEG activity in the frequency range of the feline SMR. In the patient of Finley et al., seizure rate decreased from 7 to 1 per hour over the first 10 sessions of training (according to parents' home report from a daily observation hour). In addition, the amount of feedback for 11–13 c/sec. activity increased and was negatively correlated with seizure frequency across a 3-month period. Finley et al. interpreted this correlation as indicating that SMR was involved in the inhibition of epileptogenic activity. In a second patient studied by Finley (1977), seizure decreases were primarily attributable to placebo effects and medication changes. In the study by Lubar and Bahler (1976) seizure decreases occurred in 5 of 8 patients, with the other 3 showing either no change or a decrease coinciding with medication changes. As in Sterman's patients, increases in seizures occurred during interruptions in training. Increases in amount of feedback were noted for several patients across training sessions.

As a control for the placebo factor of expectancy of treatment benefit, Finley (1976) switched the patient to noncontingent (sham) feedback after seizure reduction had occurred. This control procedure was superior to that of Sterman et al. and Lubar and Bahler, since the patient was not removed from the setting which would be responsible for producing positive expectancies. However, no significant increase in seizure rate was observed during the noncontingent feedback period.

In addition to the issue of placebo effects, another variable merits consideration. Sterman et al., Finley et al., and Lubar and Bahler employed "inhibit" circuits which prevented the delivery of feedback for 12–14 c/sec. "SMR" activity when it occurred in the presence of epileptiform EEG activity. These investigators were using analog filter systems which were set to detect the very low voltage 12–14 c/sec. activity, but systems of this type have a tendency to "ring" or emit the frequency to which they are maximally responsive, due to the presence of high-voltage activity in frequencies outside the specified frequency band. Since the EEGs of epileptic patients are often characterized by such high-voltage discharges, the inhibit circuits were employed to avoid accidentally reinforcing epileptiform activity. The inhibit circuits were useful in preventing erroneous feedback, but they also added an additional experimental contingency such that patients may have been trained to suppress certain EEG activity. Finley et al. and Lubar and Bahler, in addition to providing feedback for 12–14 c/sec. activity (which the patient was instructed to increase), also gave feedback for low frequency activity (which the patient was told to decrease). Thus, interpretation of these studies is difficult due to the confounding of experimental variables; seizure decreases may have been due to suppressing abnormal EEG activity in addition to, or instead of, increasing "SMR" activity.

An evaluation of the studies reviewed thus far suggests two important questions: (1) Does a human sensorimotor rhythm exist which is functionally equivalent to feline SMR, and if so, (2) Can this activity be increased by EEG feedback training?

Kuhlman (1978a) conducted a topographic study to determine if a sensorimotor rhythm could be identified in the EEG of normal subjects and epileptic patients. Criteria for identification of the rhythm were based on the characteristics of the feline SMR: the activity should be rhythmic, localized to the sensorimotor area (Howe & Sterman, 1972), and functionally related to the absence of movement (Roth et al., 1967). EEG was recorded from medial-lateral and anterior-posterior chains of peri-Rolandic and occipital electrodes (Fig. 5.1) and quantified by power spectral analysis. The reactivity of the EEG to movement and to opening or closing the eyes was analyzed to functionally separate a sensorimotor rhythm from the alpha rhythm. The rhythmic activity which was dominant posteriorly when subjects' eyes were closed, and which was not significantly affected by movement, met the criteria of the classic definition of occipital alpha (Rémond, 1976). In contrast, rhythmic activity which was dominant over the central area, was attenuated by movement, but was not affected by opening or closing the eyes, matched the characteristics of the mu rhythm or *rhythme en arceau* described by Gastaut (1952) and Chatrian, Petersen, and Lazarte (1959). As shown in Fig. 5.2, the frequencies of both mu and alpha activity were in the nominal alpha range, but were separable by spectral analysis. Mu rhythm was identifiable in 5 out of 8 normal subjects and in 2 out of 6 epileptic patients.

These data indicate that the mu rhythm is a human analog of the feline SMR: both are rhythmic activities localized to the sensorimotor area, both occur in the absence of movement and are attenuated by movement, and neither is significantly attenuated by visual stimulation. The major difference is in terms of frequency: mu ranged from 8–13 c/sec. (mean of 10.1) in Kuhlman's study,

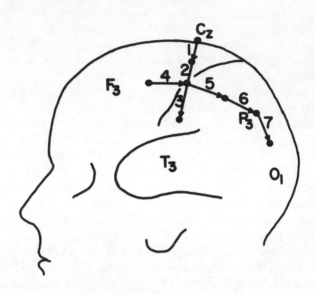

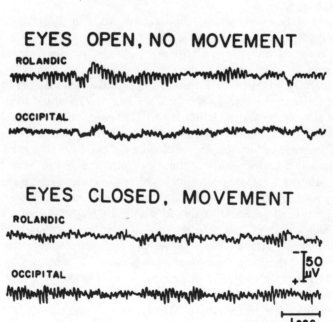

Fig. 5.1. Mu rhythm activity at 9.75 c/sec. is shown in the Rolandic EEG recorded from bipolar pair 5 (top) in the absence of movement. With eyes open the occipital EEG (bioplar pair 7) is desynchronized. With contralateral hand movement and eyes closed, mu activity is attenuated and an 11 c/sec. alpha rhythm appears in the occipital EEG.

REST   HAND MOVEMENT

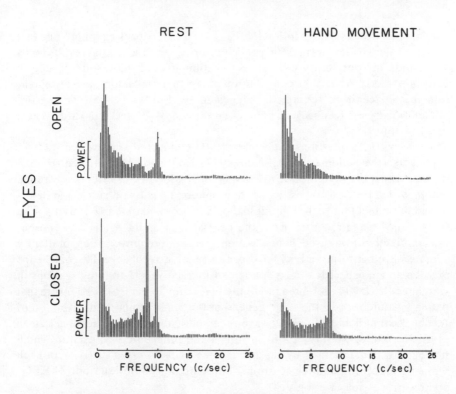

Fig. 5.2. EEG power spectra recorded from bipolar pair 5 (see Fig. 5.1) in another subject, illustrating the independent variation of alpha activity (peak at 8.0 c/sec. with eyes closed) and mu activity (peak at 9.5 c/sec. with no movement).

while feline SMR ranges from 12–16 c/sec. In no human subject was there a rhythm in the 12–16 c/sec. range which was separable from mu and which had characteristics similar to feline SMR.

To determine if long-term feedback training was effective in modifying the mu rhythm, Kuhlman (1978b) gave fifty 20-minute sessions of enhancement training to 3 normal subjects who exhibited a mu rhythm in the 9–11 c/sec. range. All 3 subjects showed an increase in this activity which was linearly related to cumulative feedback experience. Central EEG activity outside the 9–11 c/sec. band did not significantly change, nor did occipital activity at 9–11 c/sec. In contrast, neither of 2 subjects given an equivalent amount of training to enhance central 12–14 c/sec. activity showed a reliable change in this activity as a function of feedback experience.

By demonstrating that the mu rhythm is a human analog of feline SMR and that mu can be enhanced by feedback training, these studies answer the two questions posed above. The data also raise a third question: If a human sensorimotor rhythm at 12–14 c/sec. does not exist, why have some epileptic patients had fewer seizures following 12–14 c/sec. feedback training? The fact that several investigators in different laboratories reported similar results tends to exclude the possibility of chance variation. Could the results be due to placebo effects? What is the contribution of nonspecific factors such as relaxation in the feedback setting, as suggested by Kaplan (1975), or sensory stimulation by the feedback signals, as suggested by Wyler, Lockard, Ward, and Finch (1976)?

To assess these questions, Kuhlman (1976) conducted a controlled study in 5 patients (see Kuhlman & Allison, 1977; Kuhlman, 1978c). Rather than training a specific rhythm, he provided feedback for an EEG frequency range within which previous investigators had obtained positive results, and determined the effect that such training had on seizures and on EEG activity. The 9–14 c/sec. range recorded from the central area of the scalp was chosen. No inhibit circuit was used; hence, patients were not required to concomitantly suppress epileptiform activity in order to receive feedback. To control for placebo and nonspecific effects, patients first received 12 training sessions in which feedback was presented randomly in relation to the EEG. To insure that patients would receive the same general amount and temporal distribution of feedback stimuli as they would have received had contingent feedback been given (Katkin & Murray, 1968), a self-yoked procedure was used in which feedback was determined by the occurrence of 9–14 c/sec. activity in each patient's preceding training session. Following this control period, 24 EEG-contingent sessions were given.

Significant seizure reductions occurred in 3 of 5 patients, averaging 60 percent below pretraining levels. Figure 5.3 illustrates the results of this experiment in one patient. For the 3 patients who improved, no significant reduction in seizure frequency was observed during the initial, noncontingent phase of the study. This lack of effect during a period of time in which others have observed clinical improvement with contingent feedback tends to argue against a placebo effect, at least in these patients. An interpretation of a nonspecific effect due to relaxation or sensory stimulation is similarly difficult to support, since all conditions during random feedback were identical to subsequent contingent training. When feedback was made contingent upon 9–14 c/sec. EEG activity, seizures decreased rapidly within 4–6 sessions. Blood serum levels of anticonvulsant medications, determined every 6 sessions, were generally stable and were statistically unrelated to seizure rate.

EEG spectral analysis showed no significant change in 12–14 c/sec. activity, similar to previous findings in normal subjects (Kuhlman, 1978b) and epileptics (Kaplan, 1975). Although feedback was given for enhancement of 9–14 c/sec. EEG, no general increase occurred across this broad band of activity. Rather, three separate EEG changes were observed upon the initiation of contingent feedback, coinciding with a reduction in seizures. In one patient there was a shift in dominant EEG frequency from lower to higher frequencies (Fig. 5.3); in another, there was a significant increase in occipital

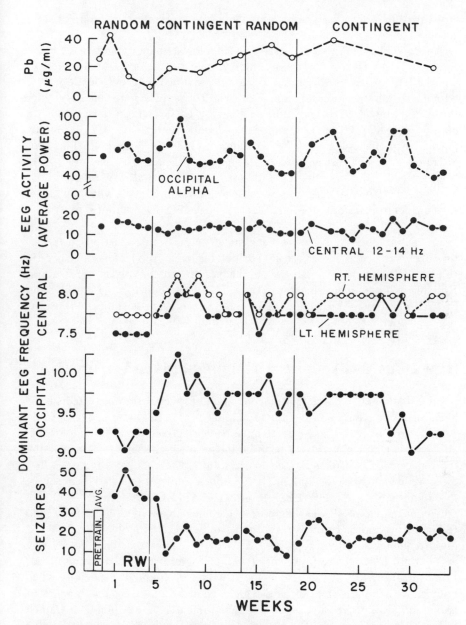

Fig. 5.3. Clinical and EEG results in one epileptic patient. Seizures (bottom) decreased below pretraining and noncontingent (random) feedback levels when contingent feedback training was given and the reduction was maintained across a replication of the procedures. In this patient upward shifts in dominant EEG frequency of occipital alpha activity and central slow activity were associated with seizure reduction during contingent training. Power of occipital alpha and central 12–14 c/sec. activity did not change. Variation in blood concentration of phenobarbital (Pb, top) was unrelated to changes in seizure rate.

alpha rhythm, and in a third patient, there was a decrease in abnormal slow activity.

A second phase of this study involved the reinstatement of random feedback for 12 sessions. During this phase, there was no change in seizure frequency, and the EEG changes which had occurred previously did not "extinguish" with the withdrawal of contingent feedback. These results are consistent with those of Finley (1976) and indicate that the EEG changes observed with contingent feedback were not simply an unconditioned effect of EEG-stimulus pairing. Kuhlman suggested that subsequent random feedback sessions provided patients with a structured opportunity to practice what had previously been learned. Consistent with the reports of Sterman et al. (1974) and Lubar and Bahler (1976), seizures did increase to pretraining levels when 2 patients took breaks from training for 9–15 weeks, suggesting that continued practice is necessary.

In summary, this study shows that clinically significant reductions in epileptic seizures can occur which are not attributable to placebo factors, nonspecific relaxation, sensory stimulation, or changes in anticonvulsant medication. Reliable within-subject changes in the EEG were specific to the introduction of EEG-contingent feedback but were not the same across subjects, illustrating the inadequacy of any theory which attributes all clinical improvement to a specific EEG frequency.

How Does EEG Feedback Training Reduce Seizures?

First, it should be noted that placebo and nonspecific training effects have been ruled out in only a few of the total number of patients studied (see Table 5.1). In cases where these effects have been discounted and in which EEG changes were systematically measured, the term which seems best to describe the reported EEG effects is "normalization." The changes have been in a direction which made the epileptic EEG appear, at least in a statistical sense, more similar to a "normal" EEG: upward shifts in EEG frequencies (which in epileptics tend to be slower than normal), enhancement of alpha activity, and reduction in abnormal slow waves. In the studies which involved feedback for high frequency activity, including "SMR," we can assume that this activity was of the "low-voltage-fast" variety which represents EEG desynchronization. Seizure reductions which occurred with such training, especially when coupled with the "inhibit" circuits which added the additional contingency of spike and slow wave suppression, might logically be attributed to trained reduction of abnormal EEG activity. Consistent with this hypothesis is the study which investigated specific training of 12–14 c/sec. activity without concomitant suppression training and found no clinical improvement (Kaplan, 1975). Although increases in 12–14 c/sec. activity have been reported (Finley et al., 1975), it has not been shown that this activity has the spatial or functional properties of the feline SMR. Evidence for reduction in abnormal slow activity has been more compelling than evidence for enhancement of 12–14 c/sec., to which the clinical effects have been attributed. However, some seizure reductions have occurred without any apparent decrease in epileptiform activity (Kaplan, 1975; Kuhlman, 1976).

A partial test of the normalization hypothesis was the study by Wyler et al. (1976). Based on his conditioning studies of single neurons in monkey cortex (Wyler et al., 1974), Wyler hypothesized that a "critical mass" of neurons discharging in synchrony was needed for the development of an epileptic seizure. He suggested that EEG feedback training might be used to reinforce desynchronization of neural activity, hence effectively preventing the development of a critical mass. This idea is consistent with the often-reported phenomenon that some epileptic patients can abort their seizures by alerting to some environmental stimulus. Such alerting is often accompanied by low-voltage fast, or "desynchronized" EEG activity. Wyler et al. (1976) compared the effects of feedback training of three different EEG frequency bands between 14 and 30 c/sec. in 4 patients. Significant reductions in seizures were observed in 3 of the patients, whereas 1 additional patient given feedback to reduce EMG activity (recorded from the scalp) showed no change in seizures. Although these investigators were unable to reliably measure EEG changes, "the tendency was for all frequencies to be equally effective" in reducing seizures. Here also, as in most of the studies previously mentioned, a concomitant contingency was employed such that feedback was withheld in the presence of low-frequency, high-voltage activity. Wyler et al. suggested that the effects were due to EEG desynchronization, perhaps as a nonspecific effect of patients' "alerting" or attending to sensory stimuli.

Additional support for the normalization hypothesis was provided by Quy (1976), who studied 3 inpatient epileptics across 12 months of feedback training. Seizure rates were determined by nursing staff observations. For the first 6 months, training was given for 12–16 c/sec. activity, with an inhibit circuit and additional feedback for high voltage abnormal activity. Seizure reduction was seen in 1 patient during this period. The consistent EEG change seen in all patients was an increase in 8–10 c/sec. activity. Increases in 12–16 c/sec. occurred in 2 patients, but not in the 1 patient who experienced reduced seizures. In the next 3 months the patients received feedback for 8–10 c/sec. activity. One patient who had not improved during feedback for 12–16 c/sec. exhibited an increase in 8–10 c/sec. and a decrease in seizure rate. During the final 3 months of the study, the 2 patients who had previously shown clinical improvement received training only for suppression of high-voltage activity: both experienced fewer seizures. In one of these, however, seizures appeared to be progressively declining across the full 12 months, from .44/week to .2/week. Quy concluded that "the therapeutic effect is not dependent on the training of any specific EEG component" and suggested that enhancement of a broad band of activity in the middle range of EEG frequencies, coupled with suppression training of abnormal activity, might be the most appropriate general procedure in the application of feedback training to epilepsy.

A recent study from Sterman's laboratory (Sterman & Macdonald, 1978) used a contingency-reversal experimental design to test whether clinical effects were specific to the contingency between feedback and EEG frequency. Two groups of 4 patients each received training for enhancement of either 12–15 or 18–23 c/sec. activity, both with concomitant feedback and inhibit circuits for 6–9 c/sec. EEG. When contingencies were reversed, feedback was for enhancement of 6–9 c/sec. and suppression of the higher frequencies. The procedure was then repeated; each condition lasted 3 months and the order of conditions was counterbalanced among patients. During all training phases, feedback for high voltage abnormal EEG activity was provided, and feedback for the activity to be enhanced was withheld during abnormal high voltage activity. Significant seizure reductions were reported in 6 patients. In 3, the decrease appeared to be specific to feedback for 12–15 c/sec. activity, while in the other 3, seizures progressively declined across time, regardless of the experimental contingency. Changes in the EEG, recorded at 2-week intervals because the patients trained at home with portable units, were to be reported later. However, preliminary analysis indicated that seizure reductions were associated with reductions in high-voltage abnormal slow-wave patterns, independent of any change in higher frequencies. Sterman and Macdonald concluded that the clinical effects may best be attributed to EEG normalization, rather than to changes in a sensorimotor rhythm.

At this point in the discussion, the results of EEG feedback training of epileptic patients may seem divergent. There are, however, many common elements and also the beginning of a consensus with respect to the machanisms hypothesized to be responsible for clinical improvement. All studies have reported seizure reductions of 50 percent or greater in over half of the patients studied. The common procedures employed have included generally three training sessions per week for a long time period, and visual feedback for some range of EEG frequencies. Most important from the standpoint of future progress, there now appears to be a consensus that EEG normalization rather than selective enhancement of any specific frequency range of EEG activity is most clearly associated with reduced seizures. Table 5.1 shows a total of 38 patients studied with EEG feedback, with 27 (71 percent) experiencing seizure reductions. Effects have been reported during training of EEG frequencies from 6 to 30 c/sec., which in itself argues against a frequency specific mechanism.

EEG feedback training of epileptics is often thought to be an attempt to train patients to voluntarily control their seizures. It is clear that clinical improvement has not been limited to the laboratory sessions or to the two or three days each week on which feedback training was conducted. Patients in the studies in Table 5.1 have reported overall seizure decreases not limited to training days, although one study (Wyler et al., 1976) noted that there were fewer seizures on training days.

What Explains Seizure Reductions Outside the Laboratory?

Two theoretical models to explain reduced seizures outside the laboratory are: (1) the neural exercise model and (2) the voluntary control model.*

The Neural Exercise Model. The approach taken by most of the EEG feedback studies of epilepsy can be explained in terms of this model, which predicts that a relatively permanent EEG change will occur as a function of practice. The underlying assumption is that this tonic change in the EEG will be sustained outside the laboratory, and that the effect is in some manner incompatible with seizures. Sterman (1973) specifically proposed that long-term laboratory training might result in "neural reorganization" through "directed exercise of specific functional pathways."

What evidence exists to support this model? One of its implications is that EEG effects acquired as a function of contingent feedback training should not only be present during actual training sessions but should also be visible in the EEG in the absence of feedback. In the Kuhlman (1976) study the changes seen in the training EEGs of patients were also reflected in recordings made in the absence of feedback (Fig. 5.4). These recordings were obtained before the start of each training session and patients were given no instructions to attempt to control their EEGs. While one might assume that this was the EEG activity which patients "brought to the laboratory," telemetric recordings in the home are necessary to confirm the interpretation that similar EEG changes were sustained outside the laboratory setting.

More evidence for the neural exercise model is that during extended inter-ruptions in training, seizure rates increased (Sterman et al., 1974; Kuhlman, 1976; Lubar & Bahler, 1976). In the Kuhlman study, no patient reported learning the ability to prevent or shorten a seizure, an ability which they could then have used during the training breaks. In fact, none of the studies reviewed in Table 5.1 reported that subjects were asked to attempt to control seizures outside the laboratory.

---

*The term *voluntary control* has been variously and vaguely defined in the literature. These semantic difficulties have been discussed by Black, Cott, and Pavloski (1977), who argued that all effects of feedback training are best described in an operant conditioning framework. Epstein and Blanchard (1977) employed the label *self-management* in much the same way we have used *voluntary control*. In any case, both *neutral exercise* and the acquisition of *voluntary control* can be described in terms of operant learning theory and it is not our intention to suggest otherwise. We use these terms to distinguish between two interpretations of how clinical effects occur outside the feedback training environment.

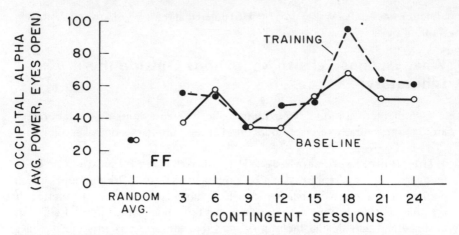

Fig. 5.4. EEG changes observed during feedback training were seen also in recordings without feedback (baseline). In this patient (FF) power of occipital alpha activity increased across contingent feedback sessions but there was no significant change across the previous 12 sessions of random feedback (random avg).

The Voluntary Control Model. In contrast to the neural exercise model, this approach involves an attempt on the part of the patient to prevent or shorten a seizure outside the feedback setting, using a strategy or behavior acquired during training. A necessary component of this model is discrimination or "awareness" (Black et al., 1977) of the onset of an attack in time for it to be aborted. In contrast to the neural exercise model, evidence for voluntary control requires phasic rather than tonic changes in the EEG. Thus, the EEG should change in the desired direction in the absence of external feedback only when the patient performs the acquired skill (Epstein & Blanchard, 1977).

This approach has often been used in feedback with modalities other than EEG, for example, in training tension-headache patients to reduce EMG levels at the onset of muscle tension to avoid the pain, or in training migraine patients to warm their hands to abort an impending headache. In the treatment of epilepsy, however, this model has not been involved in the rationale behind most of the studies, in spite of the fact that it was the model for one of the earliest attempts to use EEG feedback with seizure patients. Stevens (1962) tried to provide 5 patients with subjective awareness of their EEGs by signaling to them the occurrence of abnormal spike activity. She found that the association between the feedback signals and the EEG spikes was not learned easily and was unable to demonstrate the clinical value of this method.

The following studies have employed the voluntary control approach and/or alpha feedback training in the treatment of epilepsy. The principal features of these studies are summarized in Table 5.2.

A recent application of techniques designed to train patients to voluntarily

TABLE 5.2: Voluntary Control and Alpha Feedback Training/Applications to Epilepsy

STUDY	NUMBER OF PATIENTS	EEG CONTINGENCY	OTHER TREATMENT	TRAINING DURATION	EXPERIMENTAL DESIGN	NUMBER WITH DECREASED SEIZURES	EEG RESULTS
Green, 1976	4	10–13 or 12–25 c/sec. "good"; 5.5 c/sec. and high voltage "bad"	EMG and temperature feedback training preceded EEG	12 months	Voluntary control model; systematic case studies; no statistical analyses	0 Voluntary control not demonstrated; no effect of any treatment.	No EEG change could be demonstrated.
Upton & Longmire, 1975	13	Focal spike abnormalities (increase and decrease)	None	1–11 sessions over 3 years	Voluntary control model; systematic EEG data; Anecdotal seizure reports	5	8 patients reduced spike abnormalities.
Johnson & Meyer, 1974	1	Alpha and theta enhancement	Relaxation exercises (concurrent)	36 sessions across 1 year	Voluntary control model; pre/post	1 46 percent reduction, maintained at 3 months follow-up.	Not reported
Cabral & Scott, 1976	3	Alpha enhancement	Jacobson relaxation (sequential)	6 months	Pre/post; estimated seizure rates	3 92 percent average reduction with both treatments.	3 patients increased alpha; 2 reduced abnormal EEG activity.
Rouse et al., 1975	1	Stabilization of alpha frequency	Placebo instructions	1 session per week for 4 months	Anecdotal case report	1 Patient reported no seizures.	Increase of alpha at 10 c/sec.

control their seizures was the study by Green (1976). She provided auditory feedback to 4 patients for 10–13 c/sec. alpha activity or 12–25 c/sec. activity, termed the "good brainwaves," as well as for abnormal high-voltage slow activity, termed the "bad brainwaves." The goal was to teach the patients to discriminate the occurrence of abnormal EEG activity and thus to acquire an "aura" preceding seizure onset, and also to identify a "mental state" associated with the "good brainwaves" which could subsequently be used to abort seizures. The purpose, therefore, was not primarily to effect a unidirectional long-lasting change in the EEG (as is true with the neural exercise approach) but rather to provide the ability to discriminate and control EEG activity on a seizure-contingent basis (which characterizes the voluntary control model).

Throughout the feedback sessions, the experimenter was present to assist and direct the acquisition of this ability. Prior to EEG feedback training, no effect on seizure rates was found with training to increase hand temperature or to reduce EMG activity. The results of EEG feedback were also negative: no effect could be demonstrated either in seizure rates or in EEG variables. Despite systematic questioning, patients reported "few consistent mental/emotional experiences that clearly correlated with the presence of the 'good' brainwaves, nor could they identify subjectively the presence of the 'bad' brainwaves." Only one patient reported being able to discriminate between "good" and "bad" brainwaves without feedback and to abort seizures by invoking the mental state related to the "good" ones; however, this ability was not effective in reducing overall seizure rate.

The value of the voluntary control approach has also been investigated by Upton and Longmire (1975). They quantified and signaled to 13 patients the occurrence of focal epileptic spike discharges in 1–11 sessions over a 3-year period. The goal was to make patients aware of abnormal EEG activity which, when recognized, could serve as a discriminative cue for attempts to inhibit further seizure activity. Patients practiced both decreasing and increasing spike activity. Consistent with a voluntary control model, reductions in spike activity (which occurred in 8 patients) were apparent during and following feedback when compared to daily baseline levels, and there was no change in spike activity in the baseline EEG across sessions. Five of the 13 patients reported reduced seizure rates. The authors acknowledged that the effect on seizures outside the laboratory may not be reliable. They suggested the development of miniaturized portable feedback units to monitor ongoing EEG activity and to warn patients of impending seizures.

Johnson and Meyer (1974) gave feedback for EEG activity in alpha and theta frequencies to one patient over a 1-year period, together with daily relaxation exercises (Wolpe, 1969) in order to "develop a low arousal anti-stress response." The patient was instructed to "stay calm as if she were in the feedback situation" when she experienced an aura. Over the training period, the patient reported an average of 1.5 seizures per month, compared with 2.8

per month over the 2 years prior to training. Although the patient could not suppress seizures which did occur, she reported the ability to voluntarily prevent a seizure by producing an "alpha state" when experiencing an aura preceding seizure onset. In contrast to studies using the neural exercise approach (see Table 5.1), the seizure decrease was maintained at a 3-month follow-up after laboratory training ended.

Cabral and Scott (1976) used 3 months of alpha feedback training and 3 months of relaxation training (Jacobson, 1938) to reduce anxiety in 3 patients whose seizures were associated with anxiety and phobic reactions. All exhibited increases in alpha activity and 2 reduced abnormal epileptiform activity. For all patients, seizures were similarly reduced during both training procedures.

Rouse, Peterson, and Shapiro (1975), in a study predominantly directed toward EEG feedback of alpha rhythm activity in normal subjects, anecdotally noted the case of 1 epileptic patient who reported a complete cessation of seizures when given training to stabilize the frequency of alpha activity. "The strong possibility of a placebo reaction" was suggested.

With the exception of the study by Green, which found no experimental effect, none of the studies cited in Table 5.2 employed any control procedures. It is a common phenomenon that patients who experience stress-related seizures can occasionally abort them by relaxing. It is perhaps even more common that alerting, talking, or some kind of sensory stimulation can effectively abort seizures in other patients. Epileptic patients who fit into these two categories often discover these techniques by themselves and need no feedback for their EEG to learn them. On the other hand, since most epileptics do not have reliable auras preceding seizures, it is a reasonable hypothesis that feedback training may have value in training patients to recognize certain abnormal EEG patterns which could serve as discriminative stimuli for attempts to prevent seizures (as suggested by Upton & Longmire, 1975). However, the evidence to date is not particularly encouraging in this regard (Stevens, 1962; Green, 1976). It appears that the acquisition of voluntary control can account for the improvement of relatively few of the patients given EEG feedback training. The neural exercise approach, emphasizing long-term normalization of the EEG, appears to explain the benefit for most epileptic patients studied to date.

Future Research

Obviously, the use of control procedures is imperative. Although it appears that seizure reductions that are not due to placebo or nonspecific variables can occur with training, this does not imply that placebo effects cannot occur, or did not occur in the uncontrolled studies reviewed. With regard to types of control procedures appropriate for within-subject designs, it appears that starting training with random feedback (Kuhlman, 1976) is the method most likely to yield interpretable data, since a placebo effect is most likely to occur upon initiation of a new treatment, and since the most noticeable changes in seizures have occurred within the first few weeks of training. Use of a random feedback period subsequent to a seizure reduction may yield ambiguous results. The absence of a reversal during noncontingent feedback may be due to a real experimental effect which was resistant to extinction. Thorough EEG analysis is imperative also, since a reliable change in the EEG should be demonstrable if a clinical effect is to be attributed to EEG modification.

All the studies to date have been case studies utilizing within-subject designs. This is a reasonable approach when months of training are required and only a few patients can feasibly be studied. When statistics have been applied, they have necessarily been done on individual patients. Ultimately, in order to be able to generalize to the larger population, group outcome studies with group statistical procedures will be necessary, and eventually double-blind experiments should be conducted (Cohen, Graham, Fotopoulos, & Cook, 1977). This will require large numbers of patients. Fortunately, clinical improvement (when it does occur) appears to occur rapidly. However, there is evidence that continued practice is necessary to maintain the effect. The efficacy of home practice, which has recently been demonstrated by Sterman and Macdonald (1978), will have to be explored further, since the procedure will have little practical clinical value if the effect can be maintained only with uninterrupted laboratory training.

Summary

At the present time, there is no evidence for the existence of a sensorimotor rhythm specifically in the range of 11–15 c/sec. in humans, corresponding to the SMR at similar frequencies in cats. Rather, the human mu rhythm, although not seen in all subjects, exhibits the spatial and functional characteristics of feline SMR and occurs at a mean of 10 c/sec., with a range approximating that of the alpha rhythm. There is also no evidence that training of the mu rhythm or of "SMR" at 11–15 c/sec. can account for the effects of EEG feedback in human epileptics. "SMR training," as previously applied to epileptics, may be considered a misleading label for a method of training, and should not refer to the functional identity of the activity trained, or to the mechanism responsible for seizure reduction. It is a frequent occurrence in research that an experiment may produce results for reasons other than those originally proposed. Based upon the evidence to date, plus progress made in their own laboratory, Sterman and his colleagues no longer advocate the position that the clinical efficacy of EEG feedback training is specific to any one frequency of the EEG.

Our assessment at the present time is that clinical improvement in epileptics can occur as a result of EEG feedback training. It is most likely that the neural exercise model, rather than direct voluntary control over seizures, best describes the way in which clinical improvement occurs: with repeated practice, EEG changes are sustained outside the laboratory setting. More important, it appears that the most effective approach for training is becoming clear: "normalizing" the EEG by suppressing epileptiform discharges and by enhancing "normal" EEG activity. We emphasize that this is still an hypothesis, but it is the one which we think best describes the data reported thus far. There is still much research to be done before EEG feedback can make a significant contribution to the treatment of epilepsy.

THERAPEUTIC APPLICATIONS OF ALPHA ENHANCEMENT

The studies summarized in Table 5.3 involve feedback training to increase the occipital alpha rhythm. Epilepsy research involving alpha feedback training (reviewed in the previous section) is not included. The alpha rhythm is demonstrably present in 90 percent of individuals and its frequency varies among subjects, occurring predominantly in the 8–12 c/sec. range. Alpha activity is dominant over the occipital region, the cortical area involved in visual processing.

Rationale

Since the original recording of alpha activity from the human scalp in 1929, it has repeatedly been shown that alpha is maximal in a quiet, relaxed, nondrowsy state when the eyes are closed, and that it is attenuated or blocked when the eyes are open. Alpha is also attenuated by mental activity such as arithmetic calculations and visual imagery. Alpha feedback training was first reported by Kamiya (1962, 1969), and was later investigated by Nowlis and Kamiya (1970) and Brown (1970). These investigations were directed toward understanding subjective experience associated with EEG activity. When subjects were given alpha feedback and instructed to increase it, they reported feelings of relaxed alertness, passive attention, and mental relaxation. These subjective reports subsequently came to be termed the "alpha state." The reports were similar to those associated with autogenic training (Luthe, 1963) and meditation. Studies in experienced yoga meditators reported predominant alpha activity during meditation and no alpha blocking even when the hands were maintained in ice water for extended periods (Anand, Chhina, & Singh, 1961). Zen meditators also showed enhanced alpha activity (Kasamatsu & Hirai, 1966).

In the early studies of subjective experience associated with alpha feedback training, it was assumed that the "alpha experience" arose as a consequence of enhancing alpha by training. The rationale behind the clinical application of

TABLE 5.3: Alpha Feedback Training/Applications Other than Epilepsy

STUDY	CLINICAL CONDITION	NUMBER OF SUBJECTS	OTHER TREATMENT (CONCURRENT)	TRAINING DURATION (SESSIONS)	EXPERIMENTAL DESIGN	CLINICAL RESULTS	EEG RESULTS
Gannon & Sternbach, 1971	Vascular headache	1	None	67	Anecdotal case report	No change in duration or frequency; latency increased.	Increased alpha by session 40.
Andreychuck & Skriver, 1975	Migraine headache	28	Placebo instructions	10	Controlled group outcome: Alpha, temperature feedback, and hypnosis	Similar decrease in headache in all groups; greater decrease in highly suggestible patients.	Not reported
Wargin & Fahrion, 1977	Headache	1	Hand-warming feedback training	8 at week 129	Uncontrolled case study	Fewer headaches and less medication after alpha training.	Shift from 18 c/sec. to 11 c/sec.
Melzack & Perry, 1975	Chronic pain (organic origin)	24	Placebo instructions	6–8 alpha; 2–4 hypnosis	Controlled group outcome: alpha, hypnosis, and alpha plus hypnosis	Decreased pain during alpha plus hypnosis; no effect of either alone.	Comparable alpha increases in all groups.
Mills & Solyom, 1974	Obsessive thoughts	5	Relaxation instructions	7–20	Anecdotal case reports	4 reported no obsessive thoughts during sessions.	2 increased alpha across sessions.
Weber & Fehmi, 1974	Various psychiatric disturbances	10	Home practice of alpha/theta state	20	Anecdotal case reports	"Good" response in 6 patients.	Not reported

TABLE 5.3: (Cont'd)

STUDY	CLINICAL CONDITION	NUMBER OF SUBJECTS	OTHER TREATMENT (CONCURRENT)	TRAINING DURATION (SESSIONS)	EXPERIMENTAL DESIGN	CLINICAL RESULTS	EEG RESULTS
Glueck & Stroebel, 1975	Various psychiatric disturbances	146	Psychotherapy	20 alpha; 8 weeks TM; 4 weeks autogenic	Controlled group outcome: alpha, TM, autogenic training, and controls	No effect of alpha or autogenic training; TM patients improved compared to controls.	Alpha increased in alpha and TM groups.
Murphy et al., 1977	Learning disabilities	40	EMG reduction preceded alpha training	5 EMG 10 alpha	Controlled group outcome: alpha, beta, and control	Improvement in math achievement in alpha group.	.2 c/sec. increase with alpha feedback and .1 c/sec. decrease with beta.
Benjamins, 1976	Snake phobia	50	Systematic desensitization	7	Controlled group outcome: alpha, relaxation, and control.	Both treatment groups reduced fear more than controls.	Unspecified
Hardt & Kamiya, 1978	Anxiety	16	None	7	Group outcome; Bidirectional design	State anxiety decreased in highly anxious subjects.	Trait anxiety reductions correlated with alpha increases.
Cohen et al, 1977	Methadone withdrawal	21	EMG decrease	14	Uncontrolled group outcome;	67 percent detoxified.	Both studies: no conclusive learning effect on the EEG.
		29	EMG decrease	14	double-blind study: contingent vs. non-contingent feedback	34 percent detoxified; no difference between groups.	

alpha enhancement training is that the subjective experiences of mental relaxation associated with increased alpha would be incompatible with the experience of pain, anxiety, depression, and other clinical problems with psychogenic components.

Paskewitz, Lynch, Orne, and Costello (1970) have argued that subjects enhance alpha activity with feedback training by the process of "disinhibition" (ignoring stimuli which normally inhibit alpha) rather than by learning to increase alpha above maximal pretraining levels. Paskewitz and Orne (1973) found it impossible for subjects to increase alpha above the level exhibited simply by closing the eyes in the dark. Although not explicitly stated, the implication of this finding was that such training had no unique physiological significance. However, the rationale of clinical applications of alpha feedback training has not involved an assumption of physiological benefit from the occurrence of synchronous neural activity in occipital regions. Rather, the subjective experience associated with training is considered to be of main importance.

Clinical Research

One of the first published reports of the clinical use of alpha feedback training was that of Gannon and Sternbach (1971), working with a patient with vascular headache pain. Across 67 sessions of alpha feedback there was no effect on the duration and frequency of headaches which could be separated from spontaneous variation. Although there was no alleviation of pain during feedback, the patient did report that by producing an "alpha state" there was a delayed onset of pain outside the laboratory in situations which normally precipitated headache occurrence.

Andreychuck and Skriver (1975) studied the effects of feedback training on migraine headache in 28 patients. Three groups received either alpha enhancement training, feedback training for hand warming, or self-hypnosis training for 10 weekly sessions. A positive expectancy of benefit from treatment was encouraged for all patients. All three groups showed significant reductions in migraine headache during the last 5 weeks of training compared with 6 weeks of baseline data before training. However, there were no differences in improvement among the three treatment groups. Across groups, subjects scoring high on the Hypnotic Induction Profile tended to show greater improvement in headache (71 percent reduction) than subjects scoring lower (41 percent reduction). The greater response of highly suggestible subjects regardless of treatment supported a placebo explanation for the results.

Wargin and Fahrion (1977) reported improvement when "synchronized alpha training" was added to a temperature (hand warming) training program to reduce headaches. One patient with tension and migraine headaches, anxiety, depression, and obsessive thought disturbances showed minor improvement across 129 weeks of hand-temperature training, relaxation exercises, autogenic phrases, and analgesic medication. When 8 sessions of training to simultaneously enhance alpha recorded from both hemispheres was then given (by a different therapist), there was a greater reduction in headaches, obsessive thoughts, and amount of drugs used. The authors suggested that alpha feedback training combined with temperature or EMG feedback training may be more effective than these procedures alone.

Melzack and Perry (1975) compared the effects of alpha feedback training, hypnotic training, and a combination of these two procedures in the treatment of chronic pain of known organic origin in three groups of patients (total number = 24). All groups received positive placebo instructions to the effect that the procedures could reduce pain. The combination of hypnotic training and alpha training led to a 33 percent or greater pain reduction in 58 percent of the patients. However, no significant change could be demonstrated with either of the procedures alone. Alpha training alone had the least effect on pain. Pain was assessed during the training sessions, although 10 patients reported a carryover effect from 15 minutes to 4 hours following the sessions. The authors concluded that the effects were not due to increased alpha, but to "distraction, suggestion, relaxation and a sense of control." While emphasizing placebo effects, it was suggested that "multiple approaches are more effective in treating problems with multiple determinants" such as pain.

Mills and Solyom (1974) studied 5 neurotic patients with obsessive thought disturbances. It was thought that increased alpha activity with feedback training, if associated with a state of "mental relaxation," would be incompatible with obsessive ruminations. Reports of the frequency of obsessive thoughts were obtained during 7–20 sessions of feedback for alpha activity. Four subjects reported no ruminations, and one reported only a few during the feedback. Since no control procedures were employed, we do not know if simply listening to a noncontingent tone would be similarly incompatible with obsessive thoughts. However, since 3 of the 5 subjects showed no change in alpha, an increase in the quantity of alpha was clearly unnecessary for therapeutic benefit.

Weber and Fehmi (1974) reported 10 cases with various neurotic disturbances who were given 20 sessions to enhance alpha activity recorded separately or simultaneously from five scalp locations. Therapeutic response in 6 patients was considered "good." The rationale for this approach was based on reported similarities between subjective states associated with alpha feedback training and those associated with therapeutic effects of autogenic training. It was suggested that the value of EEG feedback training over autogenic training would be to "simplify and shorten the training."

Glueck and Stroebel (1975) compared the effects of alpha feedback (26 patients), Transcendental Meditation (54 patients), and autogenic training (12 patients) as general relaxation procedures for lowering tension in psychiatric inpatients. All patients given autogenic training asked to withdraw from the exercises after 4 weeks. Although patients learned discriminative control over alpha density with 20 one-hour sessions of alpha feedback, "this experience . . . did not prove to be an effective means for improving these patients' ability to relax, nor did it have a significant impact on their anxiety symptoms." By comparison, patients who completed 8 weeks of Transcendental Meditation showed significantly greater improvement than a matched comparison group of untrained patients.

EEG feedback training in 9 adolescent students with learning disabilities was reported by Murphy, Darwin, and Murphy (1977). With alpha training (feedback for dominant occipital EEG frequency lower than daily baseline) students showed improvement in arithmetic achievement tests compared to students given feedback training to enhance higher frequency ("beta") activity and no-treatment controls. The difference in math grades was also significant between subjects given alpha feedback and 31 no-feedback control subjects, although there was not a significant difference between alpha and beta feedback subjects. It was suggested that alpha training produced "reductions in anxiety, leading to better attention and concentration to aid arithmetic."

Benjamins (1976) reported that alpha feedback training and Jacobsonian progressive relaxation facilitated systematic desensitization in student volunteer subjects assessed as being fearful of snakes. Following 3 training sessions, 50 snake phobics were given 4 sessions in which a hierarchy of aversive scenes was presented in ascending order. Both the muscle-relaxation group and the "mental relaxation" alpha feedback group showed significant reduction in snake-avoidance behavior from pretraining levels compared to controls. However, the alpha feedback group did show a greater decrease in trait anxiety than other groups. Subsequently, Benjamins (1978) reported no significant difference in training effects between eyes-open and eyes-closed conditions.

In a recent report, Hardt and Kamiya (1978) provided 7 sessions of alpha feedback training to 16 student volunteer subjects. In each session, both enhancement and suppression training were given. For those in whom trait anxiety was reduced from pretraining levels, the decreases correlated with increases in alpha activity. State anxiety decreased following enhancement and increased following suppression, but only in subjects with high trait anxiety. Although no EMG control group was run, a lack of change in forehead EMG levels suggested to the authors that alpha feedback may be more effective than EMG feedback training in treating high anxiety.

The therapeutic effectiveness of EEG plus EMG feedback training in the detoxification of methadone addicts has been evaluated in a thorough study by Cohen et al. (1977). In an initial study, the daily dose of methadone was reduced to zero over a 2-week period in 21 patients. During this period and the following week, 14 training sessions were provided for concomitant enhancement of alpha amplitude and reduction of forehead EMG activity, in order to facilitate detoxification by reduction of withdrawal symptoms. Detoxification, as verified by urinalysis, was successful in 67 percent of the subjects and a large reduction in withdrawal symptoms was reported. Of these 14 successes however, there was no conclusive evidence of a learning effect on EMG activity in 8, and in no subject was there evidence of a learned increase in alpha activity. It was noted that as the study progressed, both the patient population and the experimenters developed positive expectations regarding the impressive therapeutic effectiveness of the treatment, compared to previous attempts at detoxification.

To evaluate the influence of expectancy and nonspecific factors in the training effects, Cohen et al. then compared noncontingent (taped) feedback signals versus contingent feedback for EEG/EMG activity in a second group of 29 addicts. A clever double/blind procedure was developed such that both contingent and noncontingent subjects were treated identically in all respects other than the contingency, and such that the experimenters were unaware of the form of feedback being given. At the end of the experiment, it was determined that 14 subjects received contingent feedback and 15 noncontingent. Analyses were adequate to show that the integrity of the double-blind procedure was maintained. In comparison to the uncontrolled study reviewed above, detoxification was achieved in only 34 percent of the subjects. As in the previous study, there was no evidence for a training effect on alpha activity. Only the subjects who received contingent feedback and who succeeded at detoxification showed evidence of a learned reduction in EMG activity. However, in terms of therapeutic outcome, there was no difference in the number of subjects detoxified between the contingent "active treatment" group and the noncontingent control group.

Summary

The study of Cohen et al. illustrates that placebo and nonspecific factors can account for a large component of therapeutic effectiveness. The authors correctly point out that these results should not be generalized to other clinical applications of feedback training. However, the influence of these effects in studies involving alpha feedback thus far seems rather consistent.

In a recent study by Plotkin and Cohen (1976) investigating the extent to which occipital alpha during training is related to the subjective phenomena of the "alpha state" in normal subjects, it was concluded that "the three most definitive attributes of the 'alpha experience' (body relaxation, 'mental relaxation,' and tranquillity) are not induced by alpha per se. Thus it appears that the major contribution that alpha feedback makes to the attainment of meditative-like experiences is to supply a setting which is conducive to . . . such states." We may also conclude from the clinical studies reviewed that whatever therapeutic value the "alpha state" may have, it does not necessarily include the alpha rhythm.

OTHER CLINICAL APPLICATIONS OF EEG FEEDBACK TRAINING

Studies involving the application of EEG feedback training to insomnia and hyperkinesis are few. "SMR training" has been applied to hyperkinesis with the rationale based on Sterman's work in cats (discussed previously in this chapter) showing that SMR enhancement is associated with the absence of movement.

Lubar and Shouse (1976) reported results in one eleven-year-old child diagnosed as hyperkinetic. During the study, the child's classroom behavior was rated by observers on 13 categories relating to overactivity and short attention span. Initial improvement was observed during three weeks of treatment with Ritalin. Across 6 weeks of feedback training for 12–14 c/sec. enhancement and 4–7 c/sec. suppression (and during continued administration of Ritalin), further improvement was noted in 8 of 13 categories. When the feedback contingencies were then reversed (12–14 c/sec. suppression and 4–7 c/sec. enhancement) for 3 weeks, a reversal in these behaviors was observed. Similar changes in the amount of feedback, indicating a training effect and subsequent reversal, were reported. Baseline (no feedback) EEG also changed coincident with training EEG, and chin EMG activity was inversely related to increases in 12–14 c/sec. activity. Behavioral and EEG changes returned following reinstatement of the original contingencies. Lubar and Shouse interpreted the data as indicating that "SMR is correlated with motor inhibition." These results were subsequently extended to 3 other patients (Shouse & Lubar, 1977) and improvement was maintained after Ritalin withdrawal. Despite the lack of evidence for a human SMR at these frequencies (discussed previously), and indications that such training can best be described as EEG activation or desynchronization, this report deserves a follow-up study. In particular, it should be feasible to have the observers of the children's behavior "blind" to the experimental contingency.

Patmon and Murphy (1978) compared the effects of EEG and EMG feedback training in 28 hyperactive adolescents. One group received training to decrease dominant EEG frequency: over 8 sessions of feedback, a decrease of 0.7 c/sec. was reported but there was no effect on hyperactive behavior. Another group received training to increase dominant EEG frequency: an increase of 0.9 c/sec. was reported, but again there was no effect on hyperactive behavior. A third group which received training to reduce forehead EMG levels did exhibit improved classroom behavior, although this was the only group which did not show a reliable reduction in EMG activity during the training sessions.

The rationale behind the application of feedback training to insomnia stems from the observation by Sterman, Howe, and Macdonald (1970) that cats trained to enhance SMR activity while awake exhibited increased spindle burst activity during sleep and improvements in sleep quality (defined as longer durations of quiet sleep and reduction of movements). Feinstein and Sterman (1974) attempted to train insomniacs to enhance SMR. Preliminary results from laboratory sleep recordings before and after 12 weeks of training indicated "significant improvement in sleep EEG and subjective sleep quality."

Previously, Budzynski (1973) had noted a decrease in sleep-onset latency in 2 of 3 patients given feedback training to enhance theta activity. Theta waves occur at a frequency of 3–7 c/sec. during drowsiness and several stages of sleep, but are rarely seen in the normal waking EEG (see review by Schacter, 1977). The rationale for theta training was to facilitate deep relaxation and drowsiness to induce sleep. Stoyva, Budzinski, Sittenfeld, and Yaroush (1974) applied theta training to 12 patients with sleep-onset insomnia. Training was combined with feedback to reduce forehead EMG activity, because Sittenfeld (1973) had found that relaxation of muscle activity was necessary for enhancement of theta with training. Of the 12 patients, 6 showed improvement in sleep onset time, as measured by home sleep logs.

Hauri (in press) compared the effects of feedback training for EMG reductions, "SMR" enhancement, and theta/EMG combination training in three groups of 10 insomniacs each, while a control group of 7 patients received the "best current treatment" such as medication or psychotherapy. For the feedback subjects, 15 to 60 sessions were given, occasionally interspersed with progressive relaxation exercises. Sleep was evaluated by night-laboratory EEG recordings before and after the experiment, as well as by home sleep logs. Subjects who received EMG feedback training showed significant reduction in sleep onset latency (30 minutes) assessed in sleep logs, but no improvement in laboratory recordings. The "SMR" feedback group showed similar reduction in sleep latency in home logs (32-minute decrease) as well as improvement in percentage of time asleep in the laboratory. The EMG/theta group and the no-feedback control group did not show statistically significant changes in these parameters, although there was an average reduction in sleep-onset latency of 33 minutes in the EMG/theta group. The lack of significant effect with the EMG/theta combination training compared to the apparent effectiveness of EMG feedback alone was attributed to less thorough EMG training in the EMG/theta group. Hauri concluded that "if relief from the complaint of insomnia at home is the primary purpose, EMG biofeedback seems most appropriate" compared to EEG feedback training, if only because "SMR training is technically much more difficult to administer than EMG feedback."

In a recent study by Besner (1978), 43 subjects with sleep-onset insomnia received 16 sessions of feedback training either to enhance theta activity or to reduce forehead EMG, or 8 sessions of each. All experimental groups received 4 sessions of baseline recordings prior to training. Individuals assigned to three control conditions received an equivalent number of physiological monitoring sessions without feedback, discussions of insomnia, or no treatment. All groups showed a reduction in sleep-onset time as assessed by home sleep logs and there was no difference in therapeutic effect between groups.

Besner concluded that "just monitoring sleep patterns and an attention effect reduces onset insomnia."

Although the results with insomnia are preliminary, the evidence for EEG feedback training effectiveness is not particularly encouraging, when compared to placebo effects or the effects of training of other physiological variables which are less technically demanding or more easily learned.

CONCLUSIONS

The best evidence for effective clinical application of EEG fedback training is in the area of epilepsy. Several studies using the same or similar procedures have obtained similar results. In terms of rationale, there is no evidence that the effect is due to specific enhancement of an SMR, but the results reported thus far are clinically significant and relatively long lasting. The consensus now is that the EEG phenomenon most clearly associated with the clinical improvement of epileptic patients is the normalization of EEG activity rather than the enhancement of any specific frequency range. It should be emphasized that larger groups of patients are needed in order to generalize to the population. Also needed are improvements in the efficiency of training for potential clinical use. The procedure may eventually have value as an adjunctive therapy in patients whose seizures are poorly controlled by medication.

Alpha feedback training has generally been used for problems with large psychogenic components, such as pain and anxiety. Controlled studies have emphasized the large contribution of placebo related effects. However, this need not discourage future investigations in this area. Perhaps more research is indicated to determine if feedback training has value in *systematically* exploiting these powerful placebo effects. Also needed is evidence for clinical changes outside the laboratory, as opposed to an effect demonstrable only during training sessions.

The data on EEG feedback training for hyperkinesis and insomnia are very preliminary, although for insomnia, EEG feedback training appears to have little unique value at the present time. Hyperkinesis requires more investigation.

We conclude that EEG feedback training applied to clinical problems is still very much in the research stage and is not ready for uncontrolled routine use. Progress has been made in the past few years, and we hope that the value of this technique will become clearer in the not-too-distant future with continued, carefully controlled research.

Chapter 6
Biofeedback and the Modification of Skeletal Muscular Dysfunctions

John V. Basmajian and John P. Hatch

Teaching patients to control a wide range of physiological processes can have amazing therapeutic results, but legitimate clinical use of biofeedback must be differentiated from its faddish popular image. In this era of exotic nonpharmaceutical treatments, therapists are rightly suspicious of novelties that they first read about in the public press. Biofeedback may appear at first to be just another fad, and it is true that its popularity has been promoted by self-serving as well as sincere adherents.

However, biofeedback's popular image masks its significance as a new tool in medicine, especially in rehabilitation of physically handicapped patients and in psychotherapy. Certain types of clinical biofeedback — almost wholly unrelated to the popular variety — have been proved at the scientific and practical level to be useful for alleviating serious neurologic symptoms, particularly in patients with upper motor-neuron paresis and spasticity. The unfortunate and apparently unbreakable link of clinical biofeedback with the fad of the same name should not alienate ethical therapists.

Biofeedback is the technique of using equipment (usually electronic) to reveal to human beings some of their internal physiologic events, normal and abnormal, in the form of visual and auditory signals and of teaching subjects to manipulate these otherwise involuntary events by altering displayed signals. As we shall see, biofeedback has been successfully used in the treatment of a broad range of neuromuscular disorders resulting from both central and peripheral pathology.

Furthermore, certain kinds of pain are being treated by psychotherapists with one form or another of biofeedback which has been proved useful in the rehabilitation setting. The placebo caution must be sounded, yet one cannot dismiss the success some clinics have achieved with biofeedback for achieving deep relaxation of muscles that are in spasm or are hyperactive in the treatment of severe chronic tension headache (Budzynski, Stoyva, Adler, & Mullaney, 1973). The results seem to go far beyond placebo effects, and they persist. Of course, deep relaxation strikes directly at the cause of muscle-tension headache. Good psychotherapists quickly wean their patients from the biofeedback instruments and teach them self-control for long-term treatment.

In the rehabilitation clinic, total body relaxation has been used along with exercise to reduce muscle spasms and associated pain in patients with cerebral palsy and cervical spasms. Training patients with cerebral palsy and stroke in biofeedback relaxation may enhance subsequent training of motor performance.

In rehabilitation and therapeutic exercise, the most useful biofeedback approach is electromyography. A premise of the technique has always been that patients can respond to a physician's request to alter the coarse level of activity of individual muscles that they could see as spikes on the cathode-ray oscilloscope and hear as popping noises on a loudspeaker (Basmajian, 1974). Basmajian's demonstrations in the 1950s and 1960s of the possible application of EMG to myoelectric prostheses led to more intense studies of how this control is exerted and how fine it can be.

Before discussing some of the most recent results obtained by Basmajian and colleagues, a brief general review of the use of biofeedback in the treatment of neuromuscular disorders is in order.

PARALYSIS

Marinacci and Horande (1960) were the first to report having succeeded in using biofeedback of the EMG signal in the therapy of neuromuscular disorders. They succeeded in restoring some degree of motor control to patients with several different dysfunctions. Shortly thereafter, Andrews (1964) provided visual and auditory feedback to 20 hemiplegics, all of whom had become static in their condition on conventional therapy. Whereas none of these patients could produce any recordable EMG activity in the biceps or triceps muscles before training, 17 were able to produce voluntary EMG activity within the first 5 minutes of biofeedback training.

Another demonstration on the effective use of biofeedback in physical rehabilitation was provided by Johnson and Garton (1973). These investigators treated 10 hemiplegic patients, all of whom showed residual tibialis anterior paralysis. All of the patients had suffered their lesion at least a year prior to the study, and their conditions had become stable. By using stabilized patients, some attempt was made to minimize the probability of spontaneous improvement, even though no control group was used. Three of the patients showed gross clinical improvement in ankle dorsiflexion and gait, to the point where they were able to do without their short leg braces. This represents a functional gain of a truly clinically significant magnitude. It was also noted that the patients who showed poor motivation for therapy dropped out of the program early and received little benefit.

Amato, Hermsmeyer, and Kleinman (1973) reported a single case study in which they treated a patient who had suffered a traumatic head injury resulting in left hemiparesis with spasticity. Using EMG biofeedback, this patient was trained to dorsiflex the ankle while inhibiting the activity of the spastic gastrocnemium muscle. Improvement was reported in strength, gait, and range of motion of the ankle joint.

Brudny, Korein, Levidow, Grynbaum, Leiberman, and Friedman (1974) described a training program which they used on a sample of 36 patients suffering from quadriparesis and hemiparesis as well as torticollis, dystonia, and facial spasms. Several different types of auditory and visual biofeedback were applied to this wide variety of disorders. The authors reported that good results were obtained in many of the patients. An encouraging point revealed by the study was that at a 2-year follow-up examination, it was found that the motor improvement had been incorporated into the tasks of daily living in some of the patients.

In another study, Brudny, Korein, Grynbaum, Friedman, Weinstein, Sachs-Frankel, and Belandres (1976) reported on their use of EMG biofeedback on 114 patients again suffering from a wide variety of disorders. All of these patients had failed to respond to conventional therapy, and all but 1 of them had some residual motor control. The feedback used consisted of simultaneously presented proportional auditory and visual integrated EMG. An interesting feature of the training procedure was that in some cases, biofeedback was provided from two muscles simultaneously. For example, auditory feedback was provided for flexor activity while visual feedback was provided for activity in the corresponding extensor. This procedure nicely allowed for the shaping of the proper pattern of muscular activity needed for voluntary movement. Clinicians examined the patients before treatment, again following 8 to 12 weeks of therapy, and again at a follow-up examination 3 months to 3 years following termination of therapy. It was reported that improvement (as rated by clinicians on a four-point scale) occurred in many of the patients during biofeedback training.

Teng, McNeal, Kralj, and Walters (1976) attempted to compare biofeedback training with electrical perioneal nerve stimulation during the swing phase of gait, on foot dorsiflexion in nine hemiplegic patients. Unfortunately, their primary measure of improvement, isometric torque of foot dorsiflexion, was judged to be inadequate in that it showed wide individual variations in the patients' responses to treatment. No conclusions regarding the relative efficacy of the two treatment modes were drawn from the experiment.

In an experiment designed to compare true EMG biofeedback with noncontingent "placebo" feedback and conventional physical therapy without biofeedback, Lee, Hill, Johnston, and Smiehorowski (1976) tested 18 hemiplegic patients, all showing residual deltoid weakness. Each patient served as his or her own control, and received one of the above three therapies in each of 3 sessions. Although surface electrodes were used, these investigators took the trouble to mark the exact electrode placement sites with dye so that they could be replicated across sessions. The data consisted of the peak recorded myoelectric signal produced during 20 instructed 5-second contractions in each session. No significant differences were found among the three treatments. However, when a post-hoc grouping of the patients was performed based upon the experimenters' judgments of motivational level and age, it was found that the older and more poorly motivated patients improved with feedback and with conventional therapy, whereas the younger and more highly motivated patients performed more poorly under these conditions. With placebo feedback, all three subgroups displayed a decrement in performance. These curious results, which are inconsistent with other reports of the effects of age and motivational level on performance, are not readily explicable.

The only reported studies of biofeedback as a therapeutic intervention in neuromuscular paralysis in which a separate control group was included were performed by Basmajian and colleagues. In the first study (Takebe & Basmajian, 1976) 12 subjects showing residual foot dorsiflexion paresis following stroke received either 40 minutes of conventional therapeutic exercise or 20 minutes of exercise followed by 20 minutes of combined auditory and visual biofeedback from the tibialis anterior muscle. The respective treatments were given 3 times per week for 5 weeks. The biofeedback patients showed good improvement in the strength of the tibialis anterior as well as in gait. The group given physical therapy alone showed only a slight improvement in gait.

In a second study, Basmajian, Kukulka, Narayan, and Takebe (1975) used the same type of design but included 20 patients in each treatment group. Prior to treatment a neurological examination was given, and each patient's gait was evaluated on a 0 to 5 scale. Strength was measured by means of a dynomometer, and range of motion was also evaluated clinically. Both groups showed good progress in range of motion and strength of ankle dorsiflexion; however, the biofeedback group improved approximately twice as much as did the group given only therapeutic exercise. Four patients in the biofeedback group achieved and retained conscious control of dorsiflexion. Three of these patients could walk without the use of their short leg brace at follow-up. There were no differences, however, between the two groups in terms of nerve-conduction velocity or spasticity (Takebe, Kukulka, Narayan, & Basmajian, 1976).

Another application of biofeedback which has recently been shown to be clinically useful with paralyzed individuals is in the treatment of postural hypotension. Many patients with cervical cord lesions have impaired reflex vasoconstriction when in an upright position. Recently it has been shown experimentally (Pickering, Brucker, Frankel, Mathias, Dworkin, & Miller, 1977) that large magnitude increases in systolic blood pressure can be voluntarily achieved in patients with complete cervical-cord transection through the use of biofeedback. In addition, Brucker and Ince (1977) have reported a case study in which they treated a patient with a high cervical-cord lesion for severe postural hypotension using biofeedback. The technique used was to provide the patient with verbal feedback of both systolic and diastolic blood pressure every 60 seconds during the training sessions. At the end of training, the patient was able to voluntarily raise mean blood pressure by 17 mm. mercury. When seen one month later, during which time the patient had practiced at home, voluntary increases of 48 mm. mercury were recorded for both systolic and diastolic pressure. It is also clinically relevant that the patient was able to sit up and stand on braces without severe postural hypotension after treatment.

SPASTICITY AND OTHER UNDESIRED MOTOR ACTIVITY

In cases in which there is an excess of motor activity, voluntary control can be impaired as much as in cases in which motor paralysis is the problem. This has recently been emphasized (Basmajian, 1977), and the working hypothesis has been put forward that motor learning consists of a steady inhibition of motoneurons whose activation is superfluous to the best performance of the peripheral musculature. Work on the training of single motor units (Smith, Basmajian, & Vanderstoep, 1974) has shown that as a specific motor unit comes under voluntary control, other surrounding units become electrically silent. These findings have also been extended to a grosser level of muscular control in both humans and animals (Basmajian, 1974). It has been found that in the execution of most trained movements, the so-called antagonist muscle relaxes completely. It seems as if the brain learns to excite only those fibers needed for the execution of a voluntary act while inhibiting the rest. Thus, there is a minimal expenditure of energy consistent with the ends to be achieved. Truly voluntary skills, therefore, require the learning of patterns of specific activity within the musculature. Any superfluous motor activity is an impediment to voluntary control, and its elimination is desirable if possible. It is to this end that EMG biofeedback has been applied.

An extreme example of tonic excessive motor activity is the condition known as spasmodic torticollis. In this condition, chronic unilateral muscle spasms of the neck and shoulder result in distorted head posture and reduced mobility.

Cleeland (1973) successfully treated nine torticollis patients and one retrocollis patient with a combination of EMG feedback and aversive electric shock therapy. Proportional auditory feedback from the spasmodic sternocleidomastoid was provided from surface electrodes. In addition, whenever EMG activity exceeded a set threshold level, a painful shock was automatically delivered to the hand for the duration of the spasm. Eight of the 10 patients showed reduced spasmodic neck activity during treatment, and 6 showed continued therapeutic benefit after 19 months. This study gave suggestive evidence that the observed improvement was due, at least in part, to the biofeedback training; however, the independent roles of biofeedback and shock were not evaluated.

Brudny and coworkers (Brudny, Grynbaum, & Korein, 1974; Brudny et al., 1974, 1976) have also reported success in treating spasmodic torticollis with EMG biofeedback. The technique used by these investigators involved teaching patients to relax the spasmodic trapezius and sternocleidomastoid while contracting the corresponding contralateral muscles. The feedback consisted of auditory proportional and visual integrated EMG activity. Again, many of the treated patients were reported to have made clinically meaningful improvements.

Undesired choreiform movements in a patient suffering from Huntington's chorea were treated by MacPherson (1967) in a three-stage treatment program. In the first stage of therapy, the patient was taught progressive deep muscular relaxation. In the second phase, auditory feedback from the muscle under training was given. In the final phase, training involved teaching the patient to voluntarily relax at the very first sign of involuntary movement. Movies were taken of the patient's movements throughout various stages of therapy. These reportedly showed much improvement, although they were not quantified in any way. At a 1-year follow-up examination, involuntary movements were almost absent.

Peck (1977) reported on the treatment of a severe case of blepharospasm, or spasmodic blinking, with a biofeedback approach. First, baseline recordings of EMG level and spasm frequency were recorded from surface electrodes placed over the frontalis and obicularis oculi muscles. Next, a "placebo" session was provided in which white noise was presented as a control for any distraction effect of an auditory stimulus. Thereafter, contingent auditory feedback of the involved muscle activity was provided. Blink frequency was reduced from 1600 to 15 in 20 minutes in the 3 sessions of treatment. EMG amplitude also showed a reduction. The improvement was maintained at a 4-month follow-up.

Undesired contractions of the peroneus longus muscle during knee extension was treated by Swaan, Van Wieringer, and Fokkema (1974) in 7 patients. The patients were trained to contract the quadriceps, while inhibiting auditory feedback from the peroneus longus.

Netsell and Cleeland (1973) employed auditory EMG feedback to reduce undesired hypertonicity of the upper lip and severe lip retraction in a patient suffering from Parkinson's disease. This patient was able to learn to relax the lip during speech, which produced improvement in both the lip retraction and speech. It should also be noted that there was a significant cosmetic effect as well as a functional improvement in this patient's condition following biofeed-back therapy.

CEREBRAL PALSY

Yet another area of rehabilitative medicine which has attempted to utilize biofeedback technology is in the treatment of inappropriate movements involved in cerebral palsy. For example, Harris, Spelman, and Hymer (1974) have viewed athetoid movements in cerebral palsy as due to "inapproprioception" (faulty operation of the muscle stretch receptors). Biofeedback is viewed as an artificial sense organ which can be used to substitute for the faulty proprioceptors. In an experiment, these investigators mounted motion transducers on pendulums suspended within a helmet worn by the patient, whose task it was to maintain a steady erect head posture. An auditory signal was presented contingent upon the production of an inappropriate head movement, defined in terms of a set threshold angle. In addition, visual feedback from 4 lights provided information as to the direction of the error in space. The children who served as subjects in this investigation were not highly motivated to work for feedback information alone. Therefore, a system was devised in which a movie projector was allowed to run as long as erect head posture was maintained, but which was immediately shut off whenever head position deviated into the error range.

Stability of limb position was trained in a similar manner, except that the angle of rotation of the elbow and wrist joints defined the target response. The output of the motion transducers was recorded on strip charts for analysis. The results showed that some of the treated patients did show improvement during therapy both in terms of the number of position errors made and in the duration of periods of stability.

Wooldridge and Russel (1976) also attempted to train cerebral palsied children to maintain an erect head position using a combination of auditory and visual feedback. By placing a mercury switch in a helmet worn by the children, they were able to transduce head movements into a feedback signal. Inappropriate movements to the left produced a tone in the left ear, and movements to the right produced a tone in the right ear. Anterior and posterior movements produced tones in both ears. A visual pointer was also used on which accumulated errors were continuously displayed. In addition to the feedback of sensory information, tangible reinforcers such as the operation of a toy cable car, record player, TV, or radio were also provided during periods of appropriate head posture. The data, collected as the frequency and cumulative duration of inappropriate head movements, showed that 3 of the 12 subjects showed improvement which was maintained once the feedback was removed, and another 6 showed improvement with feedback which did not transfer to the no-feedback condition. The remaining 3 children evidenced a sensitivity to the feedback in that their performance with feedback was superior to their performance without it; however, they did not show regular improvement during training. An autocorrelational analysis of 1 child's behavior showed successive systematic decreases in both frequency and duration of inappropriate movements from session to session. There was also, however, a deterioration of performance over time following the discontinuation of therapy.

Using a markedly different biofeedback technique, Finley, Ninman, Standly, and Ender (1976) trained 6 athetoid cerebral palsied patients to relax the forehead muscles using proportional auditory and visual feedback of integrated EMG activity. Apparently, the forehead relaxation training showed a considerable amount of generalization since all but 2 of the patients improved in speech production, and all improved in both fine and gross motor control. Also, all but 1 of the patients showed a decrease in forehead EMG activity across sessions, suggesting that the feedback did have a measurable effect on the target muscle group.

In a second study, Finley and collaborators (Finley, Ninman, Standly, & Wansley, 1977) applied auditory and visual forehead biofeedback training to the treatment of 4 cerebral palsied children showing primarily a spastic component in their illness. In this study, a tangible reinforcer such as candy, a toy, or money was also provided if the frontal EMG signal remained below threshold for at least 60 seconds. The study formed a complete ABAB design. During the pretest baseline period speech and fine-motor control were clinically evaluated. This was followed by 6 weeks of biofeedback training. Following this course of therapy, performance was reevaluated. At this point, it was found that all of the children showed a reduction in forehead EMG activity as well as improved speech production. All but 1 showed improved fine-motor control as well. Evaluation at 6 weeks following completion of therapy revealed that all of the children had deteriorated. However, their former improvement was regained during a subsequent 4-week retraining period.

Spearing and Poppen (1974) reported a case study of a university student suffering from athetoid cerebral palsy who was successfully treated for a foot-dragging problem. Switches attached to the patient's shoes produced an auditory signal whenever foot-dragging occurred. There was a reduction in the problem behavior during the biofeedback treatment period, but foot-dragging returned to near original baseline level after a 3-month period of no treatment.

MYOFACIAL PAIN

Two studies (Carlsson, Gale, & Ohman, 1975; Carlsson & Gale, 1977) have been reported in which EMG biofeedback has been applied to the treatment of temporomandibular joint syndrome. The treatment procedure in both studies involved providing digital EMG activity feedback from the masseter muscle while the patient attempted to relax the jaw. Following some initial relaxation training, the patients were requested to attempt to produce a specific low EMG reading in microvolts with the biofeedback meter covered. Training was also given in relaxing the masseters as rapidly as possible. Finally, the patients were asked to rate their masseter muscle tension in microvolts every hour on the hour during their normal day. This phase of the training program was designed to help the patients develop an awareness of masseter-muscle tension outside the therapy situation. The procedure was successful in reducing facial pain in 11 patients treated.

INJURY TO THE PERIPHERAL NEUROMUSCULAR SYSTEM

Biofeedback presentation of the EMG signal has also been applied in rehabilitation following injuries to the periphery. Kukulka, Brown, and Basmajian (1975) reported three case studies in which biofeedback was used to increase range of motion in the hand following surgery. These patients received therapy consisting of whirlpool treatments and supervised exercise followed by 20 minutes of biofeedback 3 times per week for 3 weeks. Range of hand motion, measured before and after treatment, revealed that all 3 patients made gains during the treatment program.

Another interesting case study has been provided by Booker, Rubow, and Coleman (1969). The patient, who had suffered a severed left facial nerve in an auto accident, underwent surgical anastomosis of the facial nerve periphery with a major peripheral bundle of the left spinal accessory nerve. Thus, fibers which originally innervated the trapezius and sternocleidomastoid now served the muscles of facial expression. This allowed the patient to mediate changes in facial expression through shoulder movements. Initially this patient practiced producing facial expressions before a mirror, but it was largely unsuccessful. EMG feedback was then instituted in which a target spot moved across an oscilloscope screen in a sine-wave pattern. The patient was required to track this target with a second cursor spot which was controlled by facial EMG. Later in training, two targets were tracked with two separate cursors, one controlled by facial EMG. Later in training, two targets were tracked with two separate cursors, one controlled by the right facial muscles and the other by the left facial muscles. Eventually, the two targets were removed entirely, and the patient practiced coordinating the movement of the two cursors with respect to each other. This phase of the training was intended to teach the patient to produce a symmetrical response in the two sides of the face. Initially, shoulder movement was required for the production of facial expression, but later on only isometric shoulder contraction was required. The authors reported a marked improvement in the patient's ability to produce facial expression as well as an elevation of her mood and an improvement in her self-image. The latter gains are highly significant clinically, and they should not be overlooked in evaluating the therapeutic outcome. These clever therapists deserve much credit for their ingenuity.

In another study, Jacobs and Felton (1969) tested 10 normal subjects and 10 who had suffered injury to the trapezius for their ability to relax the trapezius with visual feedback of the raw and integrated EMG signal. Both the normal and injured groups were able to demonstrate decreased trapezium EMG output during the biofeedback to a greater degree than they were during instructed relaxation alone. Following biofeedback training there was not significant difference in trapezius activity between the two groups, whereas the injured group had shown more tension than the normal group prior to training. This study indicated that, although the injured subjects found it more difficult to relax their injured muscle using only proprioceptive cues, they were able to perform as well as normals when provided with sensory biofeedback.

EVALUATION

Quite naturally, the studies reviewed above have been guided to a major extent by the clinical needs of the patients being tested, and this principle will hopefully never be subordinated. However, the paucity of controlled group-outcome studies with a sound scientific experimental design is conspicuous. There is a preponderance of single- and multiple-case studies in this literature, which although very creative and encouraging in many instances, must be viewed with a healthy dose of scientific skepticism until replicated on larger samples with the appropriate controls. Even where control groups or control treatments in the case of within-subject designs have been employed, only a few outcome measures (sometimes of questionable reliability) have been used. Samples sizes have been small, and statistical handling of the data has been weak or nonexistent. Clearly more well-controlled group-outcome studies are needed which compare different types of biofeedback, different training techniques, and different types of patients with treatment conditions standardized within a given experiment. Another area of research that should be encouraged is the comparison of biofeedback therapy with other accepted and more conventional treatment modalities such as physical therapy, exercise, electronic nerve stimulation, chemotherapy, and behavior modification. Yet another area of relatively virgin territory is in comparing different combinations and different sequences of therapies. Another question regards the effects of pairing tangible reinforcers with biofeedback training. With children, this procedure seems to have worked well. But what about the frequently mentioned adult patient who was ''judged to be poorly motivated'' and who dropped out of the study? Can we devise motivational systems which will allow these patients too to be included in our success column? It is felt that these necessary experiments can be designed by thoughtful investigators without in any way subordinating the patients' needs. But where this is deemed a problem, research should continue on normal populations with the aim of refining our therapeutic techniques.

With this brief review as frame of reference, we will now turn to a consideration of some recent results obtained by the senior author and his colleagues in their use of EMG biofeedback in a variety of rehabilitative applications.

FOOT DROP

In our routine clinic, 39 patients have been treated with varying success for foot drop. About two-thirds had short leg braces (Basmajian, Regenos, & Baker, 1977). Our results follow.

Patients Previously Treated with Short Leg Brace

Twenty-five patients had been treated up to the time of biofeedback with a short leg brace which appeared to be reasonably efficient. All but one of these patients (who was age 70) fell into the age range of 31 to 64 years with a good spread among the various ages. The shortest duration since the time of stroke was 3 months, but almost all of the patients had suffered their strokes many months or several years prior to biofeedback treatment, so that the condition of their foot drop had stabilized. Of these 25 patients, 16 were able to discard their short leg brace entirely following 3 to 25 sessions (approximately one-half hour) of biofeedback rehabilitation training. The remaining 9 patients showed little or no improvement, sometimes due to obvious reasons such as poor motivation, severe spasticity, early discontinuance of treatment, and intercurrent illnesses. Some of the patients were even able to discard their canes for the activities of daily living; several use their short leg brace intermittently when they are working for long periods of time on their feet.

Patients Previously Untreated with Short Leg Brace

Fourteen patients with foot drop had reasonably good function at the ankle and had not been treated with braces. After 3 to 17 sessions of biofeedback training, only 2 had no improvement of ankle function, while 6 had moderate to excellent improvement of strength and range of ankle motion, greatly improving their gait.

Effects of Age, Sex, and Duration of Foot Drop

No apparent direct relationship could be demonstrated for the effectiveness of biofeedback when it was compared (both successes and failures) with the age of the patient and the duration of the foot-drop condition. Both patients who were in their thirties and in their sixties were among those who discarded short leg braces. The successful cases included males and females in the same population as the general population of our cases. The duration of foot drop seems to have no relationship with successes among patients many years or 3 months after stroke; the failures included both recent and nonrecent stroke victims.

SUBLUXATION OF SHOULDER

Our experience with shoulder subluxation has been uniformly good. Basing our approach on the hypothesis that subluxation is due to an unlocking mechanism (Basmajian, 1974), we have concentrated on improving the mobility of the scapula with the emphasis on restoring the proper glenoid-cavity orientation. When the glenoid cavity is facing upwards as well as forwards and laterally as in normal shoulders, the subluxation is eliminated. This is due to a tightening corachohumeral ligament and adjacent superior capsule of the glenohumeral joint.

Thirteen patients with subluxation in our early series (Basmajian, et al., 1977) received muscle reeducation with biofeedback of the shoulder region. Clinical results have ranged from moderate to excellent reduction of the subluxation (including radiographic evidence) and an accompanying improvement of scapular and glenohumeral mobility.

IMPAIRED HAND FUNCTION

Both relaxation techniques for spastic muscles and muscle reeducation of paretic muscles are employed for the forearm musculature for intrinsic hand muscles. Severe spasticity can be moderately modified by targeted relaxation techniques where electrodes placed over the spastic group of muscles provide the patient through the biofeedback apparatus with instant feedback of his hyperactivity. A growing number of patients can be trained to relax spastic muscles by direct conscious effort. This in turn permits the voluntary use of the hand and the strengthening of grip and pinch without exuberant flexor synergies being evoked. Approximately a dozen sessions of personally tailored biofeedback rehabilitation therapy are needed. Perhaps a great part of the effectiveness of this therapy arises from the improved body image and motivation that the patient gains from the therapists. However, we have gained the impression that another part of the improvement is due to a restoration of motor controls through new or indolent cognitive and motor pathways. Postsurgical patients have had their exercise regimen greatly shortened by intensive biofeedback (EMG and electrogoniometry) in our hand clinic (Kukulka, et al., 1975; Brown, 1976). Biofeedback permits a closer cooperation between the patient and the therapist also with posttraumatic hand-retraining programs.

OTHER DEVICES

In common with other rehabilitation centers, we also use various forms of force and motion analysis that measure and display changes in the body, such as pressure transducers, joint-angle devices, electrogoniometers, accelerometers, electronic "spirit levels," and others (Brown, 1976). The readout of these devices is fed back to the patient and therapist visually and acoustically. This permits them to work together to manipulate the readout by an effort of the patient's will to restore body balance or to achieve a desired pressure, angle, or motion. My occupational-therapy colleagues have devised a host of instruments that patients respond to with enthusiasm.

To motivate younger patients, some of the feedback is provided in the form of a desirable response, for example, turning on and maintaining a TV or radio program only by giving the desired performance. It certainly works in the Hand Clinic of Grady Memorial Hospital, where youngsters must move or squeeze their hands in order to play their transistor radios.

Of course, there are many conditions, such as complete spinal transection, in which biofeedback can only act on the obviously normal residuum of the patient's body. It would be folly to attempt to retrain muscles that are completely cut off along the control pathway from the brain. Yet even here there is a ray of hope. The patient with a spinal-cord injury may not have a complete lesion, and may also be trained to raise blood pressure voluntarily to prevent postural hypotension.

GENERAL RELAXATION THERAPY

We feel that there is a major application of *generalized relaxation therapy* to the stroke patient and the cerebral palsy patient who obviously are under great emotional stress. A patient who is apprehensive and tense cannot cooperate to the fullest in therapeutic exercises. Thus, the therapist should not concentrate only on local relaxation (Fair & Basmajian, 1976).

STRATEGIES

In the selection of strategies for applying biofeedback in the therapeutic exercise setting, the judgment of the supervising therapist and the realities of the situation result in great variation. Our actual management of patients has been described elsewhere (Baker, Regenos, Wolf, & Basmajian, 1978). Outpatients are generally seen as often as possible, not less than twice a week being highly recommended. Sessions are of necessity rather short (30 to 60 minutes).

In EMG biofeedback, electrodes are invariably "skin" or surface electrodes. For monitoring very weak muscles or for control of spasticity, large electrodes are used. Smaller Beckman silver-silver chloride electrodes are used for the control of finer movements or the training of larger muscles. For general relaxation therapy, standard forehead leads widely used and described are effective.

Initiating Contractions

Often a muscle will appear inactive, and the patient will seem to have no means of knowing what he has to think or do to make the muscle contract. We have been using a very simple technique to help the patient initiate a contraction. The therapist supports the joint involved. As the patient thinks hard about the desired motion, the movement is passively performed. As the limb is returned to the initial position, the patient concentrates on relaxing and for maximal concentration, does so with eyes closed. After 5 to 10 passive motions, the motion is attempted unassisted. In the majority of cases, this procedure has been successful in eliciting a voluntary contraction in the appropriate muscle, often with some visible joint motion. If, after several attempts, a voluntary response cannot be elicited, a repetition of the procedure may be of some benefit (Baker, et al., 1978).

Gaining Control over Specific Muscles

After applying the electrodes, the patient is asked to contract the muscles and try to perform the desired joint motion. Once the concentration is initiated, he is urged to work harder for a higher meter reading and to attempt a maximal effort for approximately 5 seconds. Rest periods of 15 to 30 seconds between contractions are important, because once the patient learns to reuse his paralyzed muscle, complete relaxation often is impossible. Therefore, maximal electrical activity during a contraction and minimal activity during the rest periods is stressed. The therapist should play a very active role during the session by: (1) adding constant verbal feedback and encouragement; (2) setting slightly higher meter readings as the goal of the subsequent contraction; (3) making sure the motion produced is the appropriate one; (4) discouraging excessive muscle activity in the rest of the limb; (5) changing the position of the limb for better results; and (6) checking the electrodes to ascertain that they have not been displaced or pulled loose.

In the early training sessions, the stroke patient will very likely elicit the entire flexion synergy in both the upper and lower extremities as he attempts to dorsiflex the ankle. The therapist must decide whether to allow this pattern to continue. In the earliest sessions, this may well be the only way the patient can contract the desired muscle. As strength increases, the associated muscle involvement must be discouraged by having the patient dorsiflex only to the point where the heel begins to move. The therapist must explain the importance of being able to dorsiflex without involving the other muscles (Baker, et al., 1978).

Control of Spasticity During Movements

Instead of working for a high EMG meter reading and a loud acoustic feedback signal, the patient is instructed to work on attaining silence and a null meter reading. The joint is positioned so that the muscle is electrically silent. The limb is then carried passively through a range which stretches the spastic muscle. The patient is instructed to relax completely. The verbal reinforcement is carefully administered throughout the session.

Once the control of spasticity through passive stretch has been learned, the patient is asked to contract the antagonist muscle(s), while keeping the spastic muscle relaxed and quiet. A slow contraction of the antagonist(s) lends itself to easier control of the spastic muscle. The main objective of the session is to help the patient become aware of the feeling of a tight, contracted muscle compared to a relaxed muscle. Awareness of this difference may take several sessions, but once the patient has mastered this concept he is often able to relax the spastic muscle upon command without the biofeedback reinforcement (Baker, et al., 1978).

Sometimes the patient must learn to relax a spastic muscle before successful attempts can be made at strengthening the antagonist muscle, as in the case of a spastic gastrocnemius overpowering any attempts at dorsiflexion. Here again, emphasis is placed on the patient's recognition and control of the spasticity in the gastrocnemius. Once the relaxation of spasticity through passive stretch is learned, the electrodes are placed over the tibialis anterior to elicit dorsiflexion, as the therapist encourages dorsiflexion and reminds the patient to keep the gastrocnemius relaxed (Baker, et al., 1978).

CONCLUSION

Biofeedback, especially EMG biofeedback, is a tool that may be used by physicians and therapists to improve many forms of therapeutic exercise. Both to reeducate weak muscles and to relax hyperactive muscles (either local or general), the technique is the natural accompaniment of many procedures in the clinic aimed at improving cognitive and sensorimotor performance.

Chapter 7
Clinical Applications of EMG Biofeedback

A. Barney Alexander and Deborah Dimmick Smith

In this chapter we will critically evaluate the use of electromyographic (EMG) biofeedback as a relaxation training technique. We will also assess the scientific status of EMG biofeedback as a therapeutic method through a review of reported clinical applications. Specifically excluded from this review will be the uses of EMG feedback technology in the rehabilitation of neuromuscular disorders, which is covered elsewhere in this volume.

THE HISTORY OF EMG BIOFEEDBACK

The possibility of employing EMG biofeedback methods to produce generalized muscular relaxation was first suggested by Budzynski and Stoyva (1969) in a study demonstrating the feasibility of biofeedback-assisted, learned relaxation of a specific muscle (in this case, the frontalis) because it was thought to be a very difficult muscle to relax (Balshan, 1962). These authors anecdotally reported that when subjects successfully reduced tension in the frontalis muscle, a generalized relaxation effect was produced which was characterized by a corresponding relaxation of other skeletal muscles in the body and by a subjective feeling of calmness and relaxation. In what came to be known as "cultivated low-arousal training" (Soyva & Budzynski, 1974), it was subsequently claimed that presumed autonomic correlates of relaxation (for example, heart rate) manifested the same function-lowered relationship to decreased tension in the frontalis.

The promise of an efficient and effective electronically mediated relaxation training method was accompanied at the time by great excitement, partly because of the rapidly expanding biofeedback phenomenon and partly because relaxation methods (typically some abbreviated form of the progressive relaxation training technique developed in 1938 by Jacobson) had begun to establish a firm position within the framework of behavior therapy. The viability of EMG biofeedback as a potentially powerful therapeutic tool was suggested by another early report of these authors concerning the successful treatment of tension headache with frontalis EMG feedback (Budzynski, Stoyva, & Adler, 1970). Basking in the excitement created by the new biofeedback technology, clinicians and many applied researchers tended to ignore both the lack of empirical support for and the naivete of such claims. While more sober assessments cautioned that EMG biofeedback assisted relaxation training had yet to be experimentally verified (Blanchard & Young, 1974), it nevertheless became the most widely employed biofeedback technique in the clinic, and a consensus rapidly developed that in the EMG biofeedback method was to be found the scientifically soundest example of clinical application of biofeedback technology. In fact, although it was not generally acknowledged, much of this reputation was due to the rationality and success of muscle feedback techniques as applied to neuromuscular rehabilitation problems rather than relaxation methods. Regardless, the stage had been set. Wide publicity in the popular media, enthusiastic word-of-mouth promulgation among practitioners uninclined toward cautious clinical appraisal, and a quick proliferation of commercially available EMG biofeedback devices established the method and its industry before researchers had had time to get busy in their laboratories. Single-site muscle biofeedback relaxation training was generally considered to be properly established as a therapeutic tool for stress reduction, and the frontalis muscle (more properly, the two frontalis *muscles* or the *frontales*) was uncritically accepted as the recording site of choice for biofeedback-assisted relaxation training.

The Evaluation Problem

In the near decade which has passed since the appearance of EMG biofeedback-assisted general relaxation training, it has been and is still held by most clinicians who employ biofeedback treatment methods to be a technique with well-established clinical effectiveness. Why this should be, despite increasingly discouraging evidence from carefully controlled experimental studies, can be understood by a perusal of the problems inherent in the interpretation of the great bulk of published reports on EMG biofeedback relaxation. Unfortunately, the question of the viability and efficacy of EMG biofeedback relaxation methods has not been approached in any sort of systematic manner, and this lack has clouded the picture considerably. Another not insignificant factor is that EMG biofeedback has remained the method on which many biofeedback advocates place their faith, largely because of its early security, as the salvation for biofeedback technologies as a whole. This is a poor reason for a favorable appraisal of EMG biofeedback methods. A clear evaluation of the scientific status and worth of EMG biofeedback as a clinical technique has been hampered by the following:

1. Most of the single-case clinical applications, whether published, reported at meetings, or informally shared between practitioners, have imbedded frontalis EMG biofeedback within a treatment package which has included many other therapeutic variables. The enthusiasm of the consumers of these reports combined with the commitment of the authors have all too often resulted in forgetting that the success of a treatment package cannot be blindly attributed to that portion of it which is distinctive, novel, or of current interest to the clinician.

2. The majority of controlled-group comparisons have likewise combined EMG biofeedback with other treatments, especially progressive or autogenic relaxation training and/or nonfeedback home practice, precluding an experimental isolation of the singular contribution of feedback.

3. Many studies include either inadequate or no control for motivation, expectation, or other nonspecific placebo effects. This is true even (or perhaps especially) in studies where investigators think that such control has been achieved (as by the use of yoked, noncontingent or no-feedback conditions) but where inadequate attention has been given to the intrinsic and instructional properties of such conditions in biofeedback experiments. Obvious mistakes include instances in which control subjects can discover that they are in a condition not expected to change (for instance, by the way they are solicited for a biofeedback experiment, by the reputation of the laboratory or the investigator, or by being told that they are just expected to sit quietly or relax as much as possible). Another insidious difficulty is that subjects in control conditions are often in a situation not conducive to a level of performance representative of that which they are otherwise capable. For example, despite instructional cover stories designed to maintain interest, the control situation is very often considerably more boring or even more aggravating than active conditions. These kinds of circumstances, when present alone or in combination, can degrade control performance to such an extent that comparisons between controls and actively trained subjects are hopelessly biased in favor of the experimental condition.

4. Until relatively recently, few investigations have been explicitly and adequately designed to test the assumptions underlying the use of EMG biofeedback techniques.

5. Many investigations have been reported by experimenters woefully unknowledgeable regarding the relevant physiology and/or the bioelectrical recording techniques. This destroys confidence in the reported results and hence the comparability of the results to other studies. Often the instrumentation is employed with no further knowledge than that available in poorly prepared manufacturer's instruction manuals.

6. Frequently, experimenters fail to inform control subjects of the response

of interest (such as forehead tension reduction) and then proceed to compare control performance on that response with the performance of trained subjects, who are either explicitly told of, or can easily ascertain, the response of interest to the experimenter. Such a situation precludes the drawing of any valid conclusions regarding important questions like, "Does contingent feedback training provide a unique advantage over untrained effort?"

7. Very often, EMG reduction at a single site (such as the forehead) is taken as a measure of relaxation when conclusions regarding general relaxation in a psychological sense represent the true interests of the investigator. This amounts to an extreme example of begging the question because the relationship between skeletal muscle tension in general, let alone at a single site, and relaxation in the *psycho*physiological sense has yet to be explicated. It will not do to simply make the assumption that muscle biofeedback experiments, in which all that is recorded is EMG from a single site, are studying relaxation in any form other than in the limited sense of the *physiological relaxation of a circumscribed muscle group*.

Errors of the kinds delineated above, and other types of errors, permeate the area and have conspired to put into the literature many results which, when viewed uncritically, have led to a possibly unfounded optimism regarding the validity and clinical value of EMG biofeedback-assisted relaxation training. In the succeeding sections we will first consider basic laboratory studies which have been aimed at the investigation of the assumptions underlying the use of EMG biofeedback technology. Then, we will review the clinical applications of EMG biofeedback for relaxation to date. Our objective will be to arrive at an appraisal of the scientific status of EMG biofeedback and its uses which will hopefully be dispassionate and based squarely upon what the literature has to say.

BASIC RESEARCH

Tests of Assumptions

In the early uncritical atmosphere of excitement which surrounded biofeedback technology generally, and EMG methods specifically, it was not immediately apparent that many untested assumptions were involved in recommending the use of EMG biofeedback as a general relaxation training method. These assumptions will first be delineated, followed by a consideration of the literature relevant to each.

The Training Effect Itself. Does the availability of the contingent feedback stimulus produce a level of performance unattainable by equivalently goal-directed effort without feedback?

A Particular Muscle as a "Key" Muscle. While several muscles were informally suggested as candidates, (for example, the masseter or the muscles located in the thigh), the frontalis muscles quickly established their prominence in this regard. What was usually meant by this claim was that if a "key" muscle was or could be relaxed, all others would tend to, or could, be relaxed also (generalization), or that a single muscle was a good overall indicator of general muscle tension.

Generalization of Tension Reduction. This assumption may be reduced to the above claim: that trained reduction of tension in a key muscle (for example, the frontales) would produce reduced tension in skeletal muscles throughout the body.

Transfer of Training. Early procedural descriptions (Budzynski & Stoyva, 1972) recommended training on an "easy" muscle prior to initiating training on the "key" muscle. This implied that training on one muscle would facilitate training on another.

Subjective Experience of Being Relaxed Following Learned Reduction of Muscle Tension in a "Key" Muscle. In some sense, this is a particularly important assumption as it represents the sole manner in which the results of EMG biofeedback relaxation training can be related to the psychological experience of the subject.

Correlation of Muscle Tension Reduction with Presumed Autonomic Nervous System Indicators of Relaxation or Low Arousal. Stoyva and Budzynski (1974) had claimed that the so-called advanced stages of frontales EMG training were associated with generalized sympathetic tone reduction. This relationship was held to be further evidence of the generalized relaxing nature of EMG biofeedback training.

Frontalis Muscles as General Indicator of Arousal, Relaxation, or Anxiety. This claim, implicit in many of the above assumptions, was enthusiastically embraced by clinicians who yearned for a way of charting with their machines a patient's level of arousal or anxiety during the course of treatment. In many respects it echoed a similar hope, subsequently frustrated, which had been invested in electrodermal activity.

The available experimental evidence in relation to each of these assumptions will now be considered in turn.

The training effect itself. The question of whether the availability of the contingent feedback stimulus provides the circumstances for a level of specific muscle-tension reduction performance unattainable by unassisted efforts has received attention, but in a less than systematic manner. Six experimental studies have addressed the issue in one form or another. Budzynski and Stoyva (1969) found that after 3 sessions of training, contingent feedback subjects had reduced frontales EMG to lower levels than either a constant tone or no-feedback group. There are several noteworthy features of this study. First, all subjects were told to concentrate on relaxing the forehead. Second, at the end of training, all were paid nominal, performance-contingent sums of money. Third, the no-feedback group also reduced muscle tension, albeit not as much as the contingent group, but no statistical analysis was performed to determine if the decrease for the no-feedback group was statistically significant, nor whether the feedback group was reliably lower than the no-feedback group. On the basis of this seemingly well-controlled experiment, there appeared to develop a consensus that EMG training worked. It was not until 1975 that the next study appeared. Coursey (1975) compared a group given contingent feedback with control groups given a constant tone, with or without specific instructions on how to relax. Unlike the Budzynski and Stoyva experiment, no special attention was given to motivating performance, nor were the subjects told which muscle to relax. This put the controls at a distinct disadvantage, since the contingent feedback stimulus itself provided sufficient information to enable the trained subjects to discover the response of interest. Planned comparisons revealed that after 6 training sessions, the feedback subjects had significantly lower frontales EMG than either of the control groups, who did not differ from each other.

Of particular interest in Coursey's study is that the instructions given to the constant-tone-plus-relaxation-instruction subjects specifically emphasized gently closing the eyes, not blinking or swallowing, letting the jaw sag, and breathing evenly. Because it is known that EMG electrodes placed on the forehead are quite sensitive to muscle activity in the face, especially of the eyes and jaw and to some extent the trunk as well (Basmajian, 1975), there exists the distinct possibility that forehead-trained subjects may largely have been learning to reduce muscle activity in areas other than the forehead. In fact, the two frontales are actually rather quiet when at rest, while the muscles of the eyelids, globes, and jaw are generally active unless they are allowed to find the anatomical position of physiologic rest. Roughly, the latter amounts to the lids being at ''half mast,'' the globes rolled back slightly, and the jaw sagging down with the mouth open a bit. By the end of the second session, Coursey's specially instructed subjects were doing better than the feedback subjects, but failed to continue to decrease. There are two possible explanations of Coursey's results. First, both groups may have initially reduced frontally recorded tension by decreasing muscle activity in the face, eyes, and jaw — the controls by way of the special instructions and the trained subjects by discovering that certain positions of the lids, eyes, and jaw produced decreased feedback. By the end of the second session, both groups may have decreased recorded tension in this way as far as possible. The further decreases in the contingent-feedback group may then have represented additional frontally recorded EMG decreases which were primarily due to true frontales tension reduction unattainable by the no-feedback subjects. A second possibility is that following the substantial drop over the first two sessions, the controls may have lost both the interest and motivation to continue performing as instructed, while interest was maintained in the feedback group by the continued presence of the feedback stimulus.

While problems cloud the interpretation of Coursey's study, in our laboratory we conducted a study (Alexander, White, & Wallace, 1977) which was designed to explicitly investigate the role of the contingent feedback stimulus while paying special attention to the motivation and interest of the no-feedback subjects. All subjects were solicited for a biofeedback experiment and expressed special interest in learning about biofeedback-assisted relaxation. The control subjects received 3 sessions of unaided relaxation followed by 3 contingent feedback sessions. They were specifically instructed that it was absolutely necessary that they try as much as possible to relax a particular area (either the forearm or the forehead) before they were given feedback training, so that both the experimenters and they themselves could scientifically evaluate if subsequent feedback training would enhance their existing abilities. Experimental subjects began with feedback training immediately, receiving similar encouragement to do just as well as possible. After 3 sessions, forehead EMG had dropped significantly in both groups, with the controls manifesting a nonsignificant advantage over the feedback subjects. Similar but less striking results were found with forearm training. These data argue in favor of the motivational interpretation of Coursey's results, but still leave open the possibility that if training had proceeded for more than 3 sessions (recall that Coursey used 6 sessions and that his control subjects failed to show further decreases after the second), the superiority of contingent feedback training may have asserted itself as it apparently did in Coursey's experiment. Still further evidence in favor of the motivational interpretation was provided in our laboratory by White and Alexander (1976), who replicated the Alexander, White, and Wallace (1977) results with headache patients and included 5, rather than 3, training sessions. Again, at the end of training, the motivated controls displayed a slight, but nonsignificant, advantage over the feedback subjects following significant reductions in forehead EMG over the sessions for both groups.

Two other investigations (Haynes, Mosely, & McGowan, 1975; Reinking & Kohl, 1975) failed to provide useful data on this question because controls were not told which muscle to relax and were not provided with any performance motivation. A possible criticism of all of these sorts of studies (the use of normal subjects with nonpathologically elevated muscle tension levels) would appear to be answered by the White and Alexander (1976) investigation with headache patients. Taken together, the results suggest that there has yet to appear any controlled demonstration that the presence of the contingent feedback stimulus provides any unique advantage over what adequately motivated subjects can do without feedback assistance. They further suggest that the main function of the feedback procedure may be to establish and maintain interest and goal-directed performance during tension-reduction sessions, but that the actual tension reduction may be eminently attainable without feedback. That the feedback stimulus is providing crucial information to a subject about muscle tension levels of which it would be difficult for the subject to be otherwise aware, thereby creating a true feedback-assisted *training* experience, must surely be questioned. Additional research is needed to resolve this issue.

A particular muscle as a "key" muscle. The issue of a key muscle has received no experimental attention. Thus far no controlled studies have appeared which have explicitly compared suggested key muscle candidates on generalization effects or subjective and autonomic correlates of training. Nevertheless, given the lack of such findings with the frontales (reviewed below), there is little reason to believe that some other muscle would be found to satisfy the key muscle criteria.

Generalization of tension reduction. The question of generalization has been investigated in two experiments. In the initial study in our laboratory (Alexander, 1975), we failed to find corresponding reductions in forearm and lower leg muscles despite frontales EMG reductions resulting from biofeedback training. Actually, the muscles in the lower leg (but not the forearm) were found to be so inactive from the start that further reductions were unlikely. Also, precise simultaneous recording was not employed. These shortcomings were amended by Shedivy and Kleinman (1977) who likewise failed to find generalization from the frontales during feedback training to either of two neck muscles (sternomastoid and semispinalis/sipenius). The monitoring of the neck muscles in the Shedivy and Kleinman experiment is significant because these muscles are often implicated in complaints of muscle-contraction head and neck pain. These two studies suggest rather convincingly that biofeedback-induced reductions in forehead muscle tension are not accompanied by corresponding tension reduction in other muscles. Earlier, Balshan (1962) had reported that the frontales were the only muscles of the sixteen sites studied that failed to correlate with a general muscle-tension factor. This raises the possibility that trained relaxation of some other muscle might indeed be found to generalize. However, such a circumstance is unlikely given (1) the specific (discriminative) nature of feedback training, and (2) that the skeletal musculature system is designed to provide for profound *differentiation* of muscular activity despite hardwired synergistic and antagonistic relationships for postural and ambulatory purposes. In short, the hypothesis was naive to begin with.

Transfer of training. One investigation has addressed the question of transfer of training. This is a considerably less naive hypothesis and could be predicted from the standpoint of motor skills learning. If indeed biofeedback-assisted muscle-tension reduction is an example of a learnable skill, then training on one muscle *should* be found to facilitate subsequent training on another muscle. In our laboratory (Alexander, White, & Wallace, 1977), this possibility was investigated using a standard skill learning experimental paradigm. No evidence of a transfer of training effect was found from either the forehead to the forearm, or vice versa. Besides arguing against the viability of the strategy of training an "easy" muscle before a "hard" one, these results suggest by implication that it may not be correct to view EMG biofeedback training as a motor-skill learning experience.

Subjective experience of being relaxed following learned reduction of muscle tension in a "key" muscle. Several studies have investigated the issue of the subjective correlates of the biofeedback-induced muscle-tension-reduction experiment (Alexander, 1975; Coursey, 1975; Reinking & Kohl, 1975; Shedivy & Kleinman, 1977; Sime & DeGood, 1977). The results of these studies are in remarkable agreement. Despite differing amounts of forehead EMG reduction between various experimental and control groups, all subjects, trained and untrained alike, were found to report significant increases in subjective feelings of relaxation during sessions, but such groups were never found to differ from each other. Apparently, biofeedback training produces no further subjective experience of relaxation beyond what is afforded by simple unassisted efforts to relax or just sitting quietly. To the extent that relaxation is a psychological experience, such as anxiety, these results are rather crucial. EMG biofeedback training, at least of the frontales, appears to have nothing unique to contribute.

Correlation of muscle tension reduction with presumed autonomic nervous system indications of relaxation or low arousal. Only one study has directly investigated the question of the autonomic correlates of EMG biofeedback training. In the Alexander, White, and Wallace (1977) experiment, measures of heart rate, respiration rate, skin conductance, and skin temperature were obtained during training. Results revealed strong, nonsignificant trends toward increased skin temperature and decreased heart rate and skin conductance over sessions, regardless of whether subjects were relaxing muscles in the forearm or the forehead and with or without feedback aid. Apparently, here again, feedback-induced EMG reductions are not uniquely correlated with generally reduced sympathetic tone. These data cast considerable doubt on the use of EMG biofeedback alone to provide the basis for a "cultivated low arousal" training program.

Frontalis muscles as general indicator of arousal, relaxation, or anxiety. No actual experiment or experimental program has been undertaken to investigate the ability of a single EMG recording site (such as the forehead) to provide a valid, measurable, somatic indicator of general tension, relaxation, or anxiety. It is clear from the studies reviewed thus far that EMG measurements from the forehead region (the "frontalis muscle") certainly do not constitute such a valid indicator. Further, of course, there is little reason to believe that any other site or even an aggregate of sites would do so. The failure to find overall arousal indicators in the behavior of the autonomic nervous system suggests that such a hope, while welcome, is very unlikely to materialize in the skeletal muscular system.

Additional questions. Two other questions relating to basic issues regarding the significance and use of EMG biofeedback training have been investigated. First, is proprioceptive awareness of muscle tension enhanced by feedback information and training? It has long been assumed that the fine-grained training provided by biofeedback procedures should, in fact, result in an increased awareness and may even be the basis for successful feedback assisted EMG reduction. A roughly similar rationale was suggested by Jacobson (1938) as a partial basis for progressive relaxation procedures. Second, how does biofeedback training compare with more traditional, alternative relaxation methods, such as progressive relaxation training and its variants, in the ability to produce EMG reductions at a single site?

Three experiments have been aimed at the awareness question. In the first two (Kinsman, O'Banion, Robins, & Staudenmayer, 1975; Staudenmayer & Kinsman, 1976), worthwhile conclusions regarding the possible enhancement of awareness by biofeedback procedures were precluded because muscle-tension change judgments were obtained immediately following brief trials in which the feedback stimulus was present for experimental, but not of course, for no-feedback (control) subjects. Subjects were required to guess after each trial whether their muscle tension had increased or decreased in relation to the immediately preceding trial. While the authors concluded that the presence of the feedback stimulus seemed to enhance awareness for trained as opposed to untrained subjects, the most plausible interpretation of these results is that feedback subjects were simply, and not surprisingly, reporting a correct discrimination of the differential feedback "click" rates for one trial in comparison to the next. Sime and DeGood (1977) corrected this fatal short-coming in an experiment comparing the effect of forehead EMG feedback, taped progressive relaxation instructions, and a control group which simply heard music on *post-training* tension awareness using the Kinsman guessing procedure. Results indicated that feedback subjects increased guessing accuracy from pre- to posttraining at low, intermediate, and high levels of muscle-tension differences, while the progressive relaxation subjects increased accuracy at the intermediate and high levels, and the controls increased accuracy only at the intermediate level. A problem in interpreting these results, noted by the authors, is created by use of the forehead recording site. As indicated earlier, because the majority of the signal present at frontally located electrodes is probably due to occular and jaw-related muscle activity, the advantage for feedback subjects may be explained by the fact that feedback subjects could have been primarily paying attention to anatomical cues (such as information on the positions of eyes, lids, and jaw which was not available to subjects not receiving feedback) rather than to muscle tension *per se*. It is probably neither possible nor really worthwhile to try to sort out this difficulty in regard to "frontalis" training.

Data on the comparison of the relative effectiveness of feedback-assisted and non-feedback relaxation training methods in producing EMG reductions at a single site (in all cases, the forehead) is available from three studies. Haynes, Mosely, and McGowan (1975) compared five conditions: (1) forehead biofeedback, (2) passive relaxation instruction, (3) progressive relaxation instructions, (4) false feedback, and (5) no treatment. At the end of 1 session, the feedback and passive relaxation groups were found to have significantly lower EMGs than the other three groups. Reinking and Kohl (1975) also compared five conditions: (1) progressive relaxation; (2) forehead feedback, (3) feedback plus progressive relaxation, (4) feedback plus monetary reward, and (5) no treatment. After 12 training sessions all groups except the no-treatment group had reduced frontal EMG significantly. However, the three EMG groups, who did not differ from each other, were superior to the progressive relaxation group. Sime and DeGood (1977) compared forehead feedback with progressive relaxation, and with a control group which heard music. Following 4 days of training, the feedback and progressive relaxation subjects had decreased frontal EMG significantly, but did not differ from each other, while the controls failed to change. In all three of these experiments, feedback training was found to be superior to unaided relaxation (no treatment), but progressive relaxation training was variously found to be completely ineffective (Haynes et al.), somewhat effective — more than no treatment and less than feedback training — by Reinking and Kohl, or as effective as feedback training (Sime & DeGood). This raises the question of what can account for this discrepancy? Only in Sime and DeGood's experiment were *any* subjects told what muscle to relax, and these investigators found progressive relaxation training every bit as effective as the contingent feedback method in reducing EMG at the recording site. It was previously noted that failure to inform subjects of the response of interest strongly biases results in favor of the feedback subjects because the nature of the feedback experience itself serves to confine attention to the recording site. Most likely, all that these experiments tell us is that if subjects are told what to do (for instance, to relax the forehead) and if they want to do it, they can, irrespective of what additional treatment is applied.

Comments. What general conclusions can be drawn from these experiments? First, there seems to be no evidence that feedback-induced muscle tension reductions at a single site have any generalized effect, either on other muscles, on the autonomic nervous system, or on the subjective experience of relaxation. Correspondingly, there appears to be no reason to believe that any single muscle group can be considered to be a key muscle in any sense, especially as a valid barometer of the general state of the organism. Second, there is reason to suspect that EMG biofeedback may be no more effective than unaided, purposeful efforts in the relaxation of *specific* muscles. Quite possibly, people need only be told what to do and motivated to do it in order to perform equivalently to "trained" subjects.

EMG biofeedback training may not represent feedback contingent *learning* at all, even for the physiologic relaxation of a specific muscle group. Third, the virtually exclusive focus on the forehead, presumably the frontales muscles, as a recording site has been both instructive and unfortunate. It can now rather confidently be stated that feedback of EMG activity recorded from electrodes located on the forehead seems to have no unique properties nor probably even any nonunique properties of interest. The unfortunate part is that it is becoming almost embarrassingly evident that we may not have been studying the frontales muscles at all. Because they are known to be generally quiet muscles, unless one is frowning or experiencing surprise, it is likely that what we have been investigating is largely a composite EMG signal arising from an assortment of primarily facial and neck muscles, and that "training" with this imprecise placement may in most cases have represented nothing more than teaching people anatomical tricks.

CLINICAL APPLICATIONS

In the previous section, the consideration of more basic laboratory studies led to rather discouraging conclusions regarding the viability of EMG biofeedback techniques, either as a method of *reducing* specific muscle tension or as a method of *training* general psychophysiological relaxation. The investigations cited were all performed in experimental laboratories on nonpatients. During the same period, many case reports of the application of EMG biofeedback methods to clinical problems in patients and a lesser number of controlled-outcome investigations intended to test the clinical efficacy of EMG biofeedback methods have appeared. Despite the fact that the justification for using these methods in the clinic generally relied on what we have come to see as scientifically unsupported premises, clinical applications proceeded vigorously. As is the case with almost all new and spectacular, essentially psychological, therapies, early reports were positive but became increasingly less so with time as experimental rigor began to catch up with clinical enthusiasm. We will now turn to a review of clinical applications in order to arrive at some general conclusions regarding the scientific status of EMG biofeedback methods as a therapeutic tool.

In general, the clinical applications of EMG biofeedback techniques fall into two broad categories. In the first, EMG biofeedback is used as a means of training profound relaxation. In these instances the rationale is usually that the disorder is thought to be caused or strongly influenced by psychophysiological stress or tension, and thus general relaxation training is considered to be a reasonable treatment strategy. Typically, the target symptom is not attacked directly. Examples of disorders to be covered in this category include chronic anxiety, essential hypertension, and asthma.

In the second category, EMG feedback is more closely related to a target symptom which involves specific inappropriate muscle activity. Often the goal is not the physiological relaxation of muscles but rather the suppression of interfering activity, so that normal muscular work or other desired behavior can occur unhindered. In most of these applications, it is hoped that feedback technology will provide a kind of very specific information about the inappropriate activity of which the patient would otherwise find it difficult to be aware. An example is subvocal speech. Also included are instances of *specific* muscular relaxation treatment, as in writer's cramp.

Not yet mentioned is the reigning monarch of EMG biofeedback clinical applications: the so-called muscle-contraction, or tension, headache, We say ''so-called'' because, as Bakel (1975) points out, there is almost no support in the literature for the widely held belief that tension headaches result from the sustained contraction of one or more muscles in the head region. There is a strong possibility that tension headaches, like migraines, are vascular in nature, but unlike the latter, are characterized by profound vasoconstriction. The pain may result from ischemia rather than muscle contraction directly. Because the rationale for the EMG feedback treatment of tension headache has involved both general relaxation as well as specific muscle-tension reduction, it fits into both of the above categories. Further, its historical importance in the EMG biofeedback clinical literature and the extent of experimental attention paid to it support its consideration apart from other clinical applications.

Tension Headache

The possibility of using EMG biofeedback in the treatment of tension headache was first advanced by Budzynski, Stoyva, and Adler (1970). In their report, they demonstrated the feasibility of this approach by noting the successful reduction of headache activity in 5 patients following 8 to 20 forehead feedback sessions. In several other uncontrolled case studies, similar results have been reported (Wickramasekera, 1972a; McKenzie, Ehrisman, Montgomery, & Barnes, 1974; Epstein, Hersen, & Hemphill, 1976; Reeves, 1976; and Epstein & Abel, 1977). The first controlled-group experiment was performed by Budzynski, Stoyva, Adler, and Mullaney in 1973. They compared EMG biofeedback plus verbal relaxation instruction with a pseudofeedback and a no-treatment control. Results indicated significant superiority for the feedback group. Nevertheless, in assessing the available results in 1974, Blanchard and Young were forced to conclude that while the data looked promising, the unique contribution of EMG feedback had been consistently confounded with both the inclusion of other relaxation methods during training and regular home practice of nonfeedback relaxation.

Subsequent attempts to separate out the individual contributions of EMG biofeedback and other relaxation influences have generally involved comparisons of EMG biofeedback alone and in combination with verbal relaxation instructions to more traditional relaxation training methods, such as progressive relaxation. All manner of outcomes have resulted. Cox, Freundlich, and Meyer (1975) and Haynes, Griffin, Mooney, and Parise (1975) both compared EMG biofeedback to progressive relaxation training, finding the two methods equivalently successful in reducing headache activity when compared to controls. In contrast, Chesney and Shelton (1976) found both relaxation instructions alone, or in combination with EMG feedback, to be superior to feedback alone, while Hutchings and Reinking (1976) found the combination of feedback alone to be superior to verbal relaxation instructions alone. Although details of the exact methods used in these two experiments do differ, it is quite difficult to conjecture with any confidence as to why the findings are in conflict. In this regard, it can be noted that in a follow-up report (Reinking & Hutchings, 1976), the relaxation-only group was found to be equivalent to the feedback conditions 6 and 12 months after treatment. To complicate the matter still further, Masur (1976) and White and Alexander (1976) have both reported that feedback-treated patients do no better than placebo or highly motivated controls, both of which conditions show headache activity reductions of the same magnitude found in the treated patients in other studies. Finally, one current study (Kondo & Canter, 1977) found that feedback is better than false feedback (a generally decreasing feedback tone) in reducing headache measure. However, the latter investigators told the false feedback subjects that the feedback was veridical. The authors indicated their awareness that this represents a poor control condition at best. As noted previously, it is easy for such subjects to conclude that something is amiss and the condition becomes essentially useless as an effective control procedure.

Comment. What can be concluded regarding the efficacy of EMG biofeedback treatment for tension headache? First, it seems to do no harm. In only 1 of the 8 controlled studies reviewed was EMG biofeedback alone found to be inferior to other treatments. Second, it appears to provide no additional treatment benefits when combined or contrasted with more traditional verbal relaxation methods. Again, in only 1 of the 5 relevant studies (Masur, 1976, which also included a progressive relaxation group) was the availability of feedback found to enhance treatment benefit beyond what could be obtained with verbal relaxation alone, and even that advantage disappeared at follow-up. Third, in the many attempts to correlate frontales EMG with headache intensity, a persistently zero-order relationship has resulted.

Fourth, the results taken as a whole point to the distinct possibility that formal relaxation instruction of whatever kind may not be necessary for experimentally inducing self-reported headache activity reductions to the degree typically manifested in biofeedback headache studies. Potentially potent variables which are currently being lumped with nonspecific placebo factors may be active here. One cannot help being struck by the fact that, despite widely varying treatments ranging from none at all, through various active placebos, to elaborate instrumented and noninstrumented relaxation methods, there is an overwhelming tendency for experimental headache patients to obtain benefit no matter what is done. This is especially true in regard to the treatments presumed to be active. Procedural details (the presence of feedback, tensing and releasing muscles, or imagining one's limbs to be heavy and warm, etc.) seem to make little or no difference. It can now be suggested that there are variables, yet to be defined, which are present not only in the active relaxation treatments but are operating, sometimes at considerable strength, in presumably nonactive "control" conditions as well. More systematic attention needs to be paid to these variables. Fifth, the issue of home practice has not yet been sorted out. No one has explicitly compared treatments with and without instructions to practice regularly at home. Most investigators appear to believe that it is not a particularly pressing issue, and they are probably right. There is only one study (White & Alexander, 1976) in which the authors actually state that home practice was not requested, and two others (Haynes et al., 1975; and Kondo & Canter, 1977) where it is not clear whether or not home practice was employed. All three studies found treatment effects in at least some groups. Hence, it would appear that home practice is not necessary; it is probably just helpful.

Sixth, there are no longer any sound, scientific grounds for claiming that "frontalis" EMG biofeedback is the treatment of choice for tension headache. *At best,* it appears to be an equally effective alternative. The crucial question is "an alternative to what?" Put in another way, why do any of the treatments applied thus far work? An answer to this question might reveal a great deal about what we now rather loosely refer to as relaxation training.

Disorders Presumed to be Stress Related

There is a widespread consensus that psychological stress is a potent contributing factor in the production and manifestation of symptoms in many disorders, especially, of course, those which are called psychosomatic. While we will not in this chapter undertake a critical evaluation of this hypothesis, it can be accepted that the notion has considerable merit and some scientific support (as well as massive clinical backing) as long as the hypothesis is not carelessly extended to include emotional *causation* of disease. The most widely recommended ancillary treatment for these disorders is some sort of antistress therapeutic program which includes relaxation training as its core. Because EMG (usually "frontalis") biofeedback training has been thought to be a viable relaxation method, the rationale for the majority of EMG feedback clinical applications has been muscle feedback as a general relaxation or antistress therapy. Despite the fact that to date, there is virtually no totally convincing scientific support for the notion that EMG feedback training produces generalized relaxation of any sort, reports of successful treatments abound.

Anxiety. Chronic anxiety has been the subject of two studies. Raskin, Johnson, and Rondestvedt (1973) found that temporary reductions in anxiety followed forehead EMG biofeedback training in 3 patients. As an uncontrolled case report, however, even this limited treatment effect cannot be attributed to feedback. Similarly, Townsend, House, and Addario (1975) reported that anxiety measures were decreased further by a combination of EMG biofeedback and progressive relaxation training than by conventional group psychotherapy. This is an unspectacular finding in a poorly controlled study from which the individual effects of feedback cannot be isolated.

Essential hypertension. In an unpublished study, Weston (1974) found no difference between forehead EMG feedback and direct systolic blood pressure biofeedback (nor whether additional verbal relaxation was present) in the reduction of both systolic and diastolic blood pressure. Similarly, Blanchard, Miller, Abel, Haynes, and Wicker (1977) compared direct feedback of systolic blood pressure and forehead EMG biofeedback to self-relaxation controls. All groups decreased systolic (but not diastolic) blood pressure significantly each session, and there was a trend in the direction of superiority for both blood-pressure feedback and self-relaxation over EMG biofeedback across sessions. Finally, Surwit, Shapiro, and Good (1978) also found that blood pressure feedback, muscle feedback, and meditation relaxation (Benson, 1975) all produced significant reductions each session but not across sessions and that there were no differences between groups. It would appear that just sitting still will, as expected, produce decreases in systolic blood pressure, but that neither EMG biofeedback nor any other feedback or relaxation methods developed to date can make a clinically significant impact on chronically elevated blood pressure. It is entirely possible that psychological stress variables may play a less prominent role in essential hypertension than has been traditionally believed.

Asthma. Early work in our laboratory suggested the progressive relaxation training resulted in an increase in the peak expiratory flow rates of severely asthmatic children immediately following the period of relaxation (Alexander, Miklich, & Hershkoff, 1972; Alexander, 1972). Subsequently, three studies have investigated the effects of EMG biofeedback-assisted relaxation training on asthma in children. Davis, Saunders, Creer, and Chai (1973) compared progressive relaxation alone or combined with forehead feedback to a self-relaxation control. No long-term benefits emerged at all, and immediate (pre/postsession) changes in flow rates were not different for the two treatment groups; however, a small and statistically untested trend in favor of the combined treatment was noted for children considered to.have "less severe" asthma. Scherr, Crawford, Sergent, and Scherr (1975), also with children, compared a combined progressive relaxation-EMG biofeedback treatment group to a no-attention group measuring only daily peak flow rates obtained at times other than at treatment sessions. Though all subjects improved (the study was conducted at a summer treatment camp), confidence in the superiority noted for the treatment groups is precluded by the lack of an attention-placebo control and by the fact that the control group was independently rated significantly more severely ill than the treated group. Kotses, Glaus, Crawford, Edwards, and Scherr (1976) attempted to study the effectiveness of forehead EMG biofeedback alone on daily flow rates. They assigned asthmatic children to one of three groups: contingent feedback training, noncontingent training (yoked control), and no treatment. At the end of 3 weeks of training, average peak flow was significantly greater in the contingent as compared to the noncontingent and no-treatment groups. There are two major problems with this study. First, as with Scherr et al. (1975), the no-treatment condition fails to control for attention and general relaxation effects. Second, while the noncontingent condition would seem to do so, it does not. The yoked noncontingent subjects were *told to try* to lower the feedback signal, a signal which they in fact could not influence. That this was undoubtedly a counterproductive and frustrating condition is indicated by the fact that recorded EMG *increased* in these subjects.

As should now be expected, there appears to be no unique benefit associated with forehead feedback training in asthmatics. Similar to other applications, EMG feedback is no more effective than alternative relaxation methods. Further, recent evidence suggests that relaxation probably has little if any actual influence on lung function at all. The measure employed in all of the studies cited above (peak expiratory flow rate) has many problems, the most important of which is that it is highly dependent upon subject cooperation, motivation and physical effort during the measurement procedure. Recently in our laboratory, we undertook the replication of our earlier progressive relaxation studies using extensive and definitive assessment of pulmonary function (Alexander, 1979). In children very similar to those studied previously, no clinically significant change in lung function was produced by relaxation training either immediately or on a long-term basis. Apparently, the experimental interventions had been primarily influencing motivation and cooperation with measurement. Relaxation would appear to have no appreciable impact on the asthma itself. It is worth noting that to date no conclusive scientific evidence has surfaced, despite considerable experimental attention, that psychological stress plays any substantial role in the production of symptoms in asthma (Alexander, 1977).

Systematic Desensitization

The obvious possibility of using EMG biofeedback to train relaxation during desensitization treatment has not gone unnoticed. Wickramasekera (1972b) employed forehead biofeedback with verbal relaxation in the successful treatment of test anxiety. Reeves and Mealiea (1975) reported the beneficial treatment of three patients with flight phobias using EMG feedback. In order to promote generalization, they paired low-forehead EMG levels with a convert cue—the word "relax." However, the ultimate significance of these demonstrations is considerably dimmed by the well-established fact that the effectiveness of systematic desensitization is robust to any and all alterations of its components. It seems to work no matter how it is conducted.

Insomnia. Studies by Borkovec and Fowles (1973) and Steinmark and Borkovec (1975) have indicated that progressive relaxation training is effective in treating sleep-onset insomnia. Freedman and Papsdorf (1976) compared forehead EMG feedback and progressive relaxation with a placebo relaxation control in 18 sleep-onset insomniacs. They found that both relaxation techniques were superior to the control condition in reducing self-reported sleep latency; however, neither relaxation method was better than the control condition in reducing sleep-onset time defined by EEG criteria. Additionally, neither forehead, masseter, nor forearm EMG levels were found to be related to sleep-onset latency. This finding is in accord with the results of Good (1975) and Hauri, Phelps and Jordan (1976), who also found forehead EMG levels to be unpredictive of sleep-onset delay. These results confirm that insomnia is not strictly a muscle-tension problem.

Other applications. Fowler, Budzynski, and VandenBergh (1976) have reported the curious treatment of 1 diabetic with forehead EMG feedback. Daily insulin intake decreased following training. Apparently, it was presumed that psychologic stress was somehow involved in the problem.

As an ancillary treatment for alcoholism, Steffen (1975) gave two chronic alcoholics 14 forehead feedback sessions while two other patients received 14 "contemplation" (sic) sessions, followed by a free-drinking phase and then a crossover of conditions and a second test phase. He reported that the treatment phases were associated with decreased subjective disturbance and lowered blood-alcohol levels during test periods.

Finally, Braud, Lupin, and Braud (1975) treated a 6½-year-old hyperactive boy with 11 sessions of forehead biofeedback. They reported that both muscle tension and activity level decreased after treatment, and that the gains were maintained at a 7-month follow-up. Needless to say, the uncontrolled nature and small sample sizes in all of these cases preclude the drawing of conclusions regarding the specific contribution of the feedback treatments.

Comment. A single overriding conclusion seems clear. In studies conducted to date, the clinical use of single-muscle site (usually the forehead) EMG biofeedback techniques as an antistress or general relaxation intervention is largely without scientific justification. In no well-controlled investigation has EMG feedback proven to be superior to even the most simple alternative treatments. Further, except in the case of insomnia, neither feedback nor nonfeedback relaxation methods have proven experimentally superior to unaided self-relaxation conditions. These results appear to be unsupportive of even the considerably more conservative position that EMG biofeedback is a technique which is at least equally effective as other more traditional and simpler "relaxation" methods. It could be maintained that multiple-site EMG feedback training might yet prove to be a viable approach. While such an alternative has indeed received much less systematic attention than it may deserve, in the one study which employed multiple-muscle feedback (Surwit, Shapiro, & Good, 1978) results superior to nonfeedback relaxation (meditation) failed to emerge. Additionally, given the fact that EMG feedback has yet to be convincingly shown to be more effective than unaided efforts in reducing tension in one muscle, there is little reason to hypothesize that its overall effectiveness as a clinical relaxation treatment would be enhanced by trying to "train" many muscles. In the absence of distinctly encouraging results, we can find very little reason to currently recommend EMG biofeedback training in any form as an antistress or relaxation therapy, either in isolation or combined with other treatments. Of course, additional controlled research is still needed in this area.

Specific Rehabilitative Applications

In these applications, EMG feedback is used either to signal the occurrence of interfering muscle activity (as with subvocal speech), or to promote relaxation of specific muscles (as in stuttering, writer's cramp, and spasmodic torticollis). These clinical applications are supported by a more sound scientific rationale. Rather than postulating a usually vague and often questionable relationship between stress and symptoms and relying upon feedback-induced general relaxation as a treatment intervention, the treatments in this category relate the EMG recording and feedback much more directly to the affected organ both conceptually and methodologically.

Subvocal speech. Subvocalization during reading is a fairly widespread phenomenon which detrimentally affects reading speed and is difficult to treat. In one of the earliest applications of EMG biofeedback techniques, Hardyck, Petrinovich, and Ellsworth (1966) obtained immediate and long-lasting cessation of subvocalization during reading in 17 subjects using auditory feedback from the laryngeal muscles. This uncontrolled group study was followed up by two experiments reported by Hardyck and Petrinovich (1969). In the first experiment, one group of college students received 1 hour of laryngeal feedback training, showing complete cessation of subvocalization, while the control group simply read silently with no change in laryngeal EMG activity. Subsequently, the control subjects obtained similar success when they, too, were given training. In a second, uncontrolled study, subvocal speech during reading was eliminated in 1 to 3 sessions in 13 high-school students. One month later, only those students with IQs of 100 or better had maintained the absence of subvocalization. Lastly, Aarons (1971) reported similar dramatic results with the laryngeal feedback method. As concluded by Blanchard and Young (1975), this work is convincing, but as yet it has not been shown that the elimination of subvocalization actually increases reading speed. It does, however, seem to result in less reading fatigue.

Stuttering. Four investigations have reported the successful treatment of stuttering using EMG biofeedback techniques. Guitar (1975) first gave 3 subjects forehead feedback training, and although EMG decreased, no reduction in stuttering was noted on test sentences. Subjects were then sequentially given feedback training on the muscles of the lips, chin, and larynx. Each of the 3 subjects found relaxation of one of the three muscles to be the most helpful in reducing stuttering. The results of this report were supported by Hanna, Wilfling, and McNeill (1975) who found that auditory feedback of laryngeal EMG reduced stuttering in 1 patient. Further data on this treatment strategy have come from Lanyon and his colleagues. Lanyon, Barrington, and Newman (1976) gave 8 stutterers 10 to 18, 1-hour masseter relaxation feedback sessions. Six subjects were reported to have virtually eliminated stuttering. Similarly, Lanyon (1977) claimed to have eliminated stuttering in 7 more subjects given masseter training.

These case studies are completely uncontrolled. While the treatment makes some sense, it is quite impossible to establish the specific contributing role of the feedback method.

Other Applications. In a case study of 1 female patient, Haynes (1976) reported the successful treatment of chronic dysphagia spastica — difficulty in swallowing because of constricted throat muscles. Treatment consisted of 20 forehead EMG biofeedback sessions combined with home practice of verbal relaxation. Decreased swallowing problems were reported by the patient after treatment and at a 6-month follow-up. In addition to the confounding of the two treatments, this study is noteworthy for the lack of recordings from, and EMG feedback of, activity in the throat muscles. In missing this opportunity to provide direct target-muscle feedback, the author opted instead for a general stress/tension rationale.

Direct target-organ feedback has been reported in uncontrolled case studies with two other syndromes, however, neck injuries and writer's cramp. Brudny, Grynbaum and Korein (1974) reported some success with 9 spasmodic torticollis patients given sternocleidomastoid or trapezius feedback training, while Jacobs and Felton (1969) noted similar benefits of trapezius feedback training provided to 10 upper-trapezius, neck-injured patients. Finally, Reavley (1975) successfully treated a single case of writer's cramp with

EMG feedback training from several arm muscles, GSR feedback, and hand-writing retraining. Again, the uncontrolled nature of these studies precludes conclusions regarding the specific value of EMG biofeedback in these cases, or even the role of the feedback stimulus in producing EMG decreases in specific muscles. Nevertheless, these attempts deserve some recognition in that they represent instances in which target-muscle activity is used as the biofeedback recording site.

Comment. While applications in this area make more sense due to the target organ specificity of the feedback treatment, only one controlled study could be found—laryngeal feedback for subvocalization during reading. Even here, the control was for time and maybe, to some extent, attention only. The feedback method has yet to be compared with other treatments. The dramatic case results obtained, however, incline one to be distinctly positive toward this use of muscle-feedback technology. A firm conclusion regarding the effectiveness of EMG feedback in stuttering and neck anomalies must await the availability of controlled experimental investigations. It can be suggested, however, that results from studies using forehead EMG training give one little reason to be particularly optimistic regarding the ability of feedback methods in reducing tension in specifically affected muscles more effectively than unaided, goal-directed efforts.

SUMMARY AND CONCLUSIONS

With the exception of neuromuscular rehabilitation, which was not covered in this review, the overwhelming majority of EMG biofeedback clinical applications have been based upon the presumption that muscular feedback training constitutes a viable general relaxation training method. A comprehensive review of the extensive basic research on this question failed to reveal any convincing scientific support for this notion. It should therefore come as no surprise that a similar review of the clinical interventions which have been based upon the presumed general relaxation or stress reducing properties of EMG feedback training also resulted in finding a more or less complete lack of clinical effectiveness which could be firmly associated with the use of EMG biofeedback in this manner. While all of these applications employed the forehead as the sole recording site for feedback purposes, there would now appear to be sufficient evidence to say with some confidence that feedback from other muscles, or even combinations of muscles, should not be expected to alter the above conclusions.

While these conclusions are admittedly dismal, some optimism surfaced in our review of the more rehabilitative applications of EMG feedback technology. Especially in the case of the reduction of subvocalization during silent reading, the feedback of laryngeal EMG signals was found to be a promising therapeutic approach for this problem. Particularly noteworthy was the failure, in the light of recent evidence, of forehead feedback to maintain its prominence in the treatment of tension headache. As recently as 1974, Blanchard and Young were able to dispassionately conclude that the available data supported the use of forehead EMG biofeedback plus home practice in the treatment of this common and recalcitrant syndrome, it occupies a special position in the defense of biofeedback technology as a whole. That the "home practice" and all that it entails was found to be immeasurably more important than the biofeedback is an outcome which simply must be embraced, no matter how reluctantly, until and unless persuasive evidence to the contrary can be produced.

A tangential finding from the many controlled clinical-outcome studies that have compared EMG biofeedback relaxation with traditional verbal relaxation methods is that more often than not *none* of the active treatments were found to be more clinically effective than the completely unaided efforts of control subjects. While at first blush this may appear to be a potentially damaging result for the future of relaxation methods in general, a more careful appraisal suggests a possible alternative conclusion. Clinical experience still overwhelmingly tells us that psychologic stress remains a potent detrimental influence in physical as well as mental health and that, as a consequence, people still need to "relax." What is necessary is a more physiologically *and* psychologically sophisticated approach to the understanding of the nature of both stress and relaxation. In the area of intervention, it is possible that buried in the unassisted efforts of our patients to relax may be found potent therapeutic factors which have been traditionally labeled placebo, motivation, or expectation variables. As yet, little is known about how these variables, whatever their ultimate nature turns out to be, impact physical and psychological well-being as they interact with the way people go about living. An increased understanding of these factors would put them more under the control of therapists, with the result that they could be better manipulated and become part of the core of behavioral intervention techniques.

Chapter 8
Biofeedback and Migraine
Kenneth P. Price

DESCRIPTION OF MIGRAINE

It has been estimated that 90 percent of chronic headaches are either muscle-contraction headaches or vascular headaches of the migraine type (Dalessio, 1972). Migraine headaches have been classified into two principal categories: classic and common. Classic migraine is a periodic disorder, occuring at regular or irregular intervals. The headache phase is preceded by prodromal symptoms of sharply defined, transient visual disturbances (such as "fortification illusions"), sometimes other sensory or motor disturbances, changes in affect, hunger, water retention, and constipation. During the headache phase itself, the pain is one-sided and throbbing, often developing into a steady ache spreading over the entire head. Anorexia, nausea, and vomiting often accompany the attack. *Common migraine* also occurs periodically. It differs from the classic migraine primarily because of the absence of prodromal symptoms and the fact that the pain is less often unilateral. They both are found predominantly in women.

It is clear that migraine comprises more than just head pain. It is a systematic disorder marked primarily by head pain but also accompanied by general bodily malaise. (There is a phenomenon known as "migraine equivalent" which refers to a disorder characterized by the symptoms associated with migraine but without the headache.) Disturbances in fluid balance are believed to be concomitant with migraine headache and not causally related to it. Such nonspecific alterations of fluid balance — including alterations in the retention and excretion of sodium, potassium, water, and corticosteroids — may be another response of migraine headache-susceptible individuals to stress.

The headache itself is thought to result from dilatation of the extracranial arteries, principally the superficial temporal artery, while the preheadache visual phenomena are believed due to intracranial vasoconstriction. Dalessio

(1972) has hypothesized that the stage of vasodilatation may be an attempt by the organism ''to restore cranial circulatory homeostasis.'' It may be that the painful dilatation of the superficial temporal artery is only an epiphenomenon of the concurrent, nonpainful rebound vasodilatation of intracranial arteries. However, dilatation of the extracranial arteries alone is reported to be generally not painful. It is the release of vasoactive substances such as neurokinin or bradykinin at the site of the artery and in adjacent tissues, producing a sterile inflammation, which, in combination with vascular distention, results in pain (Dalessio, 1972, 1978).

It has been known for some time that the migraine attack is accompanied by depletion of serotonin levels in the brain. The absence of this inhibitory neurotransmitter is hypothesized to allow an uninhibited discharge of central autonomic neurons (Appenzeller, 1976) leading to cerebral vasoconstriction. Recently, the role of the hyperaggregability of platelets in migraineurs has been implicated in the release of serotonin (Dalessio, 1978a; Deshmukh & Meyer, 1977). Platelet aggregation, in turn, has been suggested to be due in some instances to increases in circulating epinephrine resulting from anxiety and stress (Ardlie, Glew & Schwartz, 1966; Deshmukh & Meyer, 1977). Other authors have also noted the importance of increased sympathetic nervous system activity in the precipitation of migraine (Appenzeller, 1976; Symon, Bull, duBoulay, Marshall & Russell, 1973). There thus appears to be a solid scientific rationale for the long-held belief that migraine is a stress-related disorder.

DRUG TREATMENT

Symptomatic relief of migraine has been achieved through various drugs such as the vasoconstrictors (ergotamine tartrate) or prophylactic drugs (methysergide maleate.) Unfortunately, these are not always effective with all patients, and their prolonged use may result in severe side effects (*Headache*, 1965; Friedman, 1972). Recently, interest has been aroused in the use of chemical compounds, such as the beta-adrenergic blocker, propranolol, designed to interfere with sympathetic nervous system arousal. Research is currently in progress to explore the usefulness of platelet antagonists in preventing migraine attacks (Dalessio, 1978a, 1978b; Deshmukh & Meyer, 1977). In this regard, daily ingestion of aspirin has been suggested.

VASOMOTOR CHANGES WITH SUGGESTION

Before discussing the application of biofeedback to the treatment of migraine, I would like to review the attempts that have been made to alter regional blood flow by various ''psychological'' methods. Increased blood flow, blood volume, and temperature in the limbs, brought about through autogenic training with both normal and clinical populations has been reported by a number of investigators (Dobeta, Sugano & Ohno, 1966; Ikemi, Nakagawa, Kimura, Dobeta, Ohno & Sugita, 1965; Luthe, 1970). Experienced subjects have been found to do better than novices, apparently because they are able to perform the exercises passively rather than actively (Tokyo, Tokyo & Naruse, 1965).

Hypnosis has been reported effective in raising and lowering limb temperature in patients suffering from chronic urticaria (Kaneko & Takaishi, 1963). Specially selected normal subjects, highly hypnotically susceptible or extensively trained, have been reported to react with vasomotor changes to hypnosis (Maslach, Marshall & Zimbardo, 1972). Interestingly, Maslach et al. report that during the initial pretest given to subjects, they gave verbal feedback to the subjects when they produced the desired response and this had a *negative* effect, resulting in the loss of the desired response. Because of this, the idea of using feedback in subsequent experimental sessions was dropped. Paul (1963) reviews studies showing the production of blisters or wheals through hypnosis. Chapman, Goodell & Wolff (1959) hypnotized 10 healthy adults and 3 patients suffering from urticaria and suggested that one arm was hypersensitive to pain and the other was normal or anaesthetized. When a standard noxious stimulus was applied to both arms (rapidly alternating from one arm to the other), it was found that the inflammatory reaction and tissue damage was greater on the arm of suggested hypersensitivity or vulnerability.

Graham, Stern, and Winokur (1958) hypnotized normal subjects and suggested to them attitudes that had been found characteristic of patients suffering from hives and Raynaud's disease. Results showed increased temperature associated with the hives suggestion and decreased temperature associated with the Raynaud's suggestion (confirming their hypothesis). Graham and Kunish (1965) failed to replicate these results with unhypnotized subjects. Peters and Stern (1971) repeated the essence of Graham et al.'s (1958) experiment using both hypnosis and method acting instructions only, with subjects of high suggestibility. They found no effect for attitude suggestion, but general vasoconstriction under the hypnotized condition and vasodilatation under the unhypnotized condition. In a related experiment, Beahrs, Harris, and Hilgard (1970) failed to alter skin reactivity to mumps antigen by direct hypnotic suggestion to well-trained hypnotic subjects. They suggest that the reason for this may have been their use of subjects with normal, as opposed to labile, skin reactivity. Suggestion alone has been found to alter blood volume in the hand or arm of normals and patients (Hadfield, 1920; Li Chao-i, Len Yuan-lien & Wang, 1964).

CLASSICAL CONDITIONING OF VASOMOTOR ACTIVITY

Several early studies demonstrated the classical conditioning of digital vasoconstriction in normal subjects (Gottschalk, 1946; Menzies, 1937, 1941; Roessler & Brogden, 1943). Shmavonian (1959) confirmed these findings in a better controlled experiment. Teichner and Levine (1968) also successfully conditioned both vasoconstriction and vasodilatation. Interestingly, in a review of Menzies' and Roessler and Brogden's experiments, Crafts, Schneirla, Robinson, and Gilbert (1950, p. 279) suggested that classical conditioning could be used to treat migraine headache by inducing a "general relaxation of the musculature and a vasomotor condition different from that which underlies the headache." In fact, influenced by Menzies' (1937) paper, Korn (1949) undertook a conditioning study with the goal of applying the results to therapy for migraine. He used a normal college student as his sole subject, ice as the unconditioned stimulus and a bell as the conditioned stimulus. He reported the successful conditioning of constriction in the *superficial temporal artery*. Korn's initial experiment appears not to have been followed up in the literature.

OPERANT CONDITIONING OF VASOMOTOR ACTIVITY

A number of studies have shown the modification of pulse volume (or skin temperature) by means of operant techniques. These have been reviewed in depth by Taub (1977). Two studies are worth emphasizing. The first is one undertaken by Christie and Kotses (1973). Unlike previous research focusing on digital vasomotor activity, these researchers studied the conditioning of *cephalic* vasoconstriction and vasodilatation. Two groups of 4 male subjects were negatively reinforced (with white noise) for either constriction or dilatation. It appears that instructions to the subjects to avoid the noise were not given until the fourth of 6 half-hour sessions. The dependent variable was the number of beats occurring above some criterion during periods when reinforcement was available during the sixth session. Although the amount of data presented is meager, the authors conclude that conditioning of both vasoconstriction and vasodilatation was achieved.

The only study that used migraine patients as subjects was that of Koppman, McDonald, and Kunzel (1974). They presented a tone to subjects showing dilatation of superficial temporal artery pulse volume and requested subjects to alternately keep the tone on or off. They found significant differences between the amount of time the tone was on or off during training trials, indicating learning of the desired response. The authors remarked that using tone-on time as the dependent measure, rather than a direct measure of amplitude, may have indicated only small consistent changes in pulse volume, and therefore, their clinical significance was unknown.

ORIGIN OF BIOFEEDBACK FOR THE TREATMENT OF MIGRAINE

The use of biofeedback in the treatment of migraine was first reported by Sargent, Green, and Walters (1972, 1973) and Sargent, Walters, and Green (1973). Their idea for employing biofeedback for migraine was the result of a serendipitous finding. In the course of training one female subject "to learn to control brain waves, to reduce electromyographic potential in the forearm musculature and to increase blood flow in the hands," the subject spontaneously recovered from a migraine headache. This was detected by the experimenters, who noted a 10° F rise in differential hand and forehead temperature within the space of two minutes.

Clinical trials of the procedure were then undertaken. The procedure used consisted of two techniques. First, patients were given training in autogenic relaxation. This involves reciting to oneself such phrases as "my hands are warm" and visualizing the physiological changes that are supposed to ensue. Patients were then provided with analog feedback of temperature changes occurring while they were relaxing. Originally, feedback was provided for the difference in temperature between the forehead and the right index finger. Since this made it impossible to know whether temperature was increasing or decreasing at one or the other of the two sites or changing in the same direction but at different rates, the procedure was changed so that feedback was provided only for absolute digital temperature change.

Results reported (Sargent et al., 1972) were as follows: of 33 patients for whom pretreatment data were available, 90 percent, 80 percent, and 68 percent were rated as improved by a physician and each of two psychologists, respectively. Of 62 patients treated, regardless of the availablility of pretreatment baseline data, 74 percent were rated as improved. These positive results were explained by Sargent et al. as most likely due to the mechanism of inhibition of sympathetic nervous system outflow (thus preventing the sequence of events leading to migraine as discussed earlier) rather than to a hydraulic system of shunting blood flow from the head to the hands.

The research reported by Sargent and his colleagues at the Menninger Clinic opened up a promising new area for biofeedback researchers. In fact, primarily as a result of the Menninger studies, headaches appear to have become the most heavily applied area for biofeedback. There are a number of drawbacks to the work of Sargent et al. which have been pointed out previously (Blanchard & Young, 1974; Price, 1974). No control groups or procedures were run to isolate and identify the effective components of the treatment package and to rule out nonspecific or placebo factors. Secondly, lack of objective criteria for improvement, beyond clinical judgments, and the absence of statistical treatment of the data that were presented detract from the value of the studies. To their credit, the Menninger group conducted a long-term follow-up of patients completing their program (Solbach & Sargent, 1977). This is a practice sorely lacking in most reports of biofeedback therapy. Unfortunately, the results of this follow-up vitiate even the modest positive results that were reported earlier. Of 110 headache sufferers who entered the Menninger program, 74 completed 270 days of training and follow-up. Thirty-six patients dropped out of the program before completing the 270 days. At some point after completion of the follow-up, questionnaires were sent to all participants. The report by Solbach and Sargent (1977) is based on the responses of 56 of the "graduates" and 12 of the dropouts. At their termination from the project, patients had been judged on the criteria of percentage reduction of "headache activity" as experiencing improvement in one of the following categories: none, slight, moderate, good, very good. Slightly more than a third of the patients fell in the no-improvement or slight-improvement categories, about a fifth in the moderate, and over two-fifths in the good-to very-good improvement categories. Results of the questionnaire follow-up were that all graduate groups decreased the frequency of headaches with *no differences* between them according to accepted levels of statistical significance. There were also no differences in the measures of headache intensity or duration. The only significant difference was between the slight and no-improvement groups on the one hand, and the moderate, good and very-good groups on the other, with the latter groups showing a greater reduction in the use of medication. Graduates differed from dropouts primarily in that the former had a greater decrease in headache duration and amount of medication used.

Looked at in a positive way, these data could indicate that autogenic feedback enabled the very good, good, and moderate groups to maintain the same degree of improvement that the slight and no improvement groups derived from medication (but without the side effects of the medication). However, specific data on medication consumption is not presented. So, it is impossible to know whether the statistically significant difference between the groups in the use of drugs is a clinically significant one as well. On the subjective level, Solbach and Sargent note that respondents reported that they found that the relaxation exercises and staff interest and support were the most helpful parts of training.

In summary, the studies by Sargent and his colleagues, which have been used as the foundation for biofeedback with migraine, provide weak justification for the use of biofeedback (or autogenic feedback) for migraine. They were, nevertheless, highly influential on the work of others. I will present, below, what I believe is a comprehensive, although not exhaustive, review of the literature on biofeedback and migraine. With three exceptions, I will include only published studies, because their methodology and results have been subjected to peer review and their data are readily available for the reader's inspection. Studies have been organized according to the criteria suggested by Blanchard in Chapter 3 of this volume.

BIOFEEDBACK AND THE TREATMENT OF MIGRAINE

Case Reports, Single- and Multiple-Systematic Case Studies

Success in treating migraine with biofeedback has been reported anecdotally (Adler & Adler, 1976; Fried, Lamberti & Sneed, 1977; Graham, 1975; Legalos, 1973). Single or multiple case studies with information on methodology and presentation of data have been reported by Johnson and Turin (1975), Kentsmith, Strider, Copenhaver, and Jacques (1976), Reading and Mohr (1976), Stambaugh and House (1977), and Wickramasekera (1973). The case study of Kentsmith et al. is noteworthy because of the finding that the meditation-biofeedback treatment was accompanied by a reduction of plasma dopamine-beta-hydroxylase (DBH) in the migraine patient treated. DBH is involved in the synthesis of norepinephrine, and is believed to be an indicant of sympathetic nervous system activity. Higher levels of DBH have been found in migraine patients during headache-free intervals than in a control group of nonmigraineurs (Gotoh, Kanda, Sakai, Yamamoto, & Takeoka, 1976). Thus, Kentsmith et al. speculate that their relaxation-biofeedback treatment is related to the patient's learning to suppress sympathetic nervous system activity during periods of stress.

Single-Group Outcome Studies

Temperature biofeedback combined with autogenic relaxation treatment has been applied to larger groups of patients by Fahrion (1977), Medina, Diamond, and Franklin (1976), and Mitch, McGrady, and Iannone (1976). Fahrion treated 11 patients suffering from migraine and 10 patients suffering from combined migraine and tension headaches. Patients were followed up for 6 to 13 months. About 72 percent of them were reported improved. Nearly 50 percent almost completely eliminated medication. Medina et al. treated 13 patients with migraine and 14 patients with combined migraine and muscle-contraction headache. Sixty-four percent of the migraineurs and 30 percent of the mixed headache group were reported improved. A praiseworthy aspect of this study is the relatively long baseline (2 to 60 months) and follow-up periods (7 to 34 months). Mitch et al. treated 12 migraineurs and 8 mixed headache patients. Sixty-five percent of them were reported improved.

While these studies report the improvement of chronic headache sufferers, many of whom had not responded to other therapies, they suffer from at least two lacunae. First, data are not presented regarding the relationship of success in digital temperature training to headache activity. Second, the absence of control groups does not allow one to identify the active components of the treatments.

Single-Subject and Replicated Single-Subject Experiments

Turin and Johnson (1976) treated seven patients using only feedback for finger warming, without training in relaxation. The exception to this statement is that the patients were asked to practice at home without a feedback device. Since the patients did not have a feedback device at home, the only thing they could practice must have been relaxation. In any case, all patients improved. Three of the patients were trained in finger cooling prior to finger warming. None showed improvement under this condition, one got worse, and all subsequently improved with finger warming.

Feuerstein and Adams (1977) and Feuerstein, Adams and Beiman (1976) used a novel feedback approach. They provided feedback for constrictions of the superficial temporal artery. All of the five patients treated were reported improved. One of the migraine patients showed improvement in headache activity while receiving "control" EMG feedback, and one tension headache sufferer improved while receiving "control" cephalic vasomotor feedback. While not definitive, these two studies suggest that direct conditioning of vasoconstriction in the superficial temporal artery is an alternative to the popular finger-warming approach.

Controlled-Group Outcome Studies

It is rather surprising that the wide interest in biofeedback and migraine did not generate more controlled-outcome research. Table 8.1 presents some parameters of four such recent studies. Andreychuk and Skriver (1975) compared three treatments: (1) autohypnosis, consisting of relaxation instructions, visual imagery, verbal reinforcers, and direct suggestion for dealing with pain, (2) feedback for hand temperature, combined with autogenic relaxation instructions, and (3) feedback for EEG alpha production, combined with relaxation instructions. All subjects were asked to practice at least twice each day at home between sessions (the instructions they were given are not presented). All patients improved, and no differences were found between treatments. Additionally, when subjects were divided into high- and low-hypnotic susceptible groups within each treatment, the high-hypnotic susceptibles improved more than the low-hypnotic susceptibles. Two criticisms that could be leveled at this study are that relaxation training is confounded with all of the treatments, and insufficient information is provided regarding the criteria for headache improvement.

Friar and Beatty (1976) compared biofeedback for temporal artery constric-

TABLE 8:1 Controlled-Group Outcome Studies of Biofeedback and Migraine

	NUMBER OF SUBJECTS (SEX)	DURATION OF BASELINE	TYPES OF TREATMENT	DURATION OF TREATMENT (SESSIONS/WEEK)	DURATION OF FOLLOW-UP
Andreychuk & Skriver (1975)	24 (F) 4 (M)	6 weeks	Temperature biofeedback; alpha biofeedback; autohypnosis	10 weeks (1/week)	none
Blanchard et al. (1978)	25 (F) 5 (M)	4 weeks	Temperature biofeedback; relaxation training; waiting list	6 weeks (2/week)	3 months
Friar & Beatty (1976)	16 (F) 3 (M)	30 days	Pulse-volume biofeedback in temporal artery or digital vessels	(3/week)	30 days
Mullinex et al. (1978)	7 (F) 4 (M)	8.8 weeks avg. (?)	Veridical temperature biofeedback; false temperature biofeedback	2 to 3 weeks (2 to 3 sessions per week) plus booster sessions 1, 2, and 6 weeks posttraining	3 months

tion to training in digital vasoconstriction. Results showed that patients given the temporal artery training improved on a number of headache measures while the other group did not. Unlike other studies (Turin & Johnson, 1976) Friar and Beatty did not report increased headache symptomatology in the group trained in digital vasoconstriction.

Veridical feedback for increases in hand temperature was compared to false feedback by Mullinex, Norton, Hack, and Fishman (1978). The majority of patients treated in each group improved; there were no differences between the experimental and control treatments. In addition, there was no relationship between success in learning to raise skin temperature and a decrease in headache symptomatology. One weakness in the study as reported is that data are not presented regarding the relationship between the false feedback (controlled by the experimenter) and actual skin temperature in the control group. It is possible that the false feedback group was actually receiving true feedback, and thus would not be a control group. One finding reported does speak to this issue. It is that the veridical-feedback group produced greater temperature increases than the false-feedback group, suggesting that the false-feedback treatment was an appropriate control.

Blanchard, Theobold, Williamson, Silver, and Brown (1978) compared three treatments: (1) biofeedback for fingertip temperature combined with autogenic training, (2) relaxation training, and (3) no-treatment control. At the end of treatment, it was found that both active treatments brought about greater improvement than no-treatment. Additionally, patients receiving relaxation training improved more than those receiving autogenic feedback. At the end of a 3-month follow-up, there were no longer any significant differences between the two active treatments. The majority of patients were improved.

The results of this study are interesting, in part, because they reveal that in the short term, biofeedback training was inferior to Jacobsonian relaxation training, even though the former was combined with autogenic relaxation training. This suggests that the active (tension activation and reduction) relaxation procedure was more efficient than the passive relaxation. With sufficient practice, however, differences between the two disappear.

A comparison of relaxation treatment to training in temporal artery vasoconstriction was reported by Zamani (1974) in an unpublished doctoral dissertation. In this study, 8 patients were given at least 8 sessions of feedback to reduce extracranial temporal pulse amplitude; 6 patients in a control group were exposed to the same number of sessions, where either a Jacobsonian relaxation tape or narrated instructions from the Stanford Hypnotic Susceptibility Scale was played. The group exposed to the relaxation procedure demonstrated no statistically significant improvement in headache activity, while the feedback group showed significant decreases in the number of headaches per week, and in their duration and intensity. Both groups were asked to practice at home, and it is not known to what extent the feedback group practiced temporal artery constriction or relaxation at home.

Finally, as reported in another doctoral dissertation, Kewman (1978) compared three groups of migraine patients: 11 trained to increase finger temperature, 12 trained to decrease finger temperature, and 11 not treated. All patients, including the untreated controls, improved on a number of measures of migraine activity. When subjects were regrouped on the basis of success in learning to control finger temperature, there were still no differences between patients who learned to raise finger temperature, patients who did not learn to raise finger temperature and untreated controls. However, subjects who learned to decrease finger temperature tended to show *increased* symptomatology.

Summary of Biofeedback Studies and Discussion

The biofeedback treatment of migraine has been carried out under two paradigms. In the first, dilatation of digital arteriovenous beds (as measured by increased skin temperature) has been encouraged by contingent feedback, usually visual, often accompanied by various imagery stratagems aimed at priming or facilitating vascular dilatation. The rationale for this has not always been clear. Most often, it is hypothesized that increased digital skin temperature is accompanied by or indicative of inhibition of sympathetic nervous system tone. Through a process that is probably more complex than we currently understand, this autonomic inhibition is assumed to forestall the biochemical prodromal events that result in migraine.

Only three studies have been found which essayed an assessment of the physiological mechanisms underlying biofeedback. Sovak, Fronek, Helland, and Doyle (1976) studied a small number of normal subjects (4 male, 2 female). The subjects were first trained to increase digital vasodilation by means of feedback and autogenic training and then in a second series of sessions (for 5 of the previous subjects) were exposed to currents of hot air directed at the hands. Results for the autogenic feedback series were that digital vasodilatation took place accompanied by extracranial vasodilatation as well. The authors suggest that the mechanism for the presumed therapeutic efficacy in migraine of training in digital vasodilatation is "a reflectoric vasoconstriction of . . . affected carotid arteries together with an overall reduction of the sympathetic nervous outflow." To properly judge their data, it would be useful to have more information on the duration of the changes (data is reported on maximum rather than average change and the time period is not reported), and other details or methodology. It would also be useful to replicate this study, especially with a sample of migraineurs.

Mathew, Largen, Claghorn, Dobbins, and Meyer (1977) used a noninvasive [133] xenon inhalation technique to measure regional cerebral bloodflow during volitional hand vasodilatation and vasoconstriction in a sample of 12 normal females. They found no effect (and no differences between the vasodilation and vasoconstriction groups) of digital temperature manipulation on regional cerebral blood flow. They tentatively suggest that the therapeutic effects of biofeedback may not be due to any specific feedback effect but instead may be due to generalized relaxation or other demand characteristics of the training situation.

Price and Tursky (1976) exposed 40 female migraineurs and 40 matched normal controls to one of four treatments: (1) veridical feedback for digital blood volume changes; (2) false feedback for digital blood volume changes (yoked to the feedback viewed by subjects in the first treatment); (3) relaxation training provided by a tape recording; and (4) exposure to a neutral tape recording. Results were that subjects in the veridical feedback, yoked feedback, and relaxation training groups all tended to dilate digital vessels with no differences among them (subjects in the neutral tape group tended to constrict over time). In addition, a moderate to high correlation was found between blood-volume changes in the hand and blood-volume changes in the superficial temporal artery. It was suggested that inhibition of sympathetic nervous system activity through relaxation may be the mechanism enabling migraineurs to abort headaches.

We noted that longer-term studies needed to be done to replicate the results of this one-session study. The reports by Andreychuk and Skriver (1975), Blanchard et al. (1978), and Mullinex et al. (1978) seem to confirm these results of no advantage for biofeedback over relaxation. One interesting finding in Price and Tursky (1976) was that migraineurs responded differently to the treatments than normal controls. This may have been due to differential responding to the experimental situation or to differences in learning in the autonomic nervous system. Recent experiments in our laboratory have confirmed differences between migraineurs and normals in response to classical conditioning. In a similar finding the case study by Kentsmith et al. (1976) reported that the migraineur studied did *not* learn to increase digital temperature as well as her normal control. In sum, the physiological mechanisms underlying biofeedback training have not been clearly described. Furthermore, there is some evidence that these mechanisms may be different in migraine sufferers and nonsufferers.

The second biofeedback paradigm has involved feedback for temporal artery pulse volume activity, with training for vasoconstriction. This technique presumably works in a fashion parallel to that of the vasoconstrictor drugs. Both the relaxation procedure and the temporal artery vasoconstriction training are said to work through their routine use by migraineurs at the first sign of a headache. It would be useful to have data on just what physiological events actually accompany self-control behaviors employed at the onset of a headache. Does the temporal artery dilate, indicating intracranial and extracranial vasodilation, which is known to abort classic migraine? Is it possible to volitionally constrict temporal arteries at the beginning of a headache, and is this sufficient to abort it? More research on the specificity and effectiveness of volitional control of cephalic vasoconstriction is needed.

RELAXATION AS A TREATMENT FOR MIGRAINE

Although some studies have reported no effect for relaxation training in migraine (Zamani, 1974), the vast majority have reported great benefit from relaxation training (Benson, Klemchuk & Graham, 1974; Paulley & Haskell, 1975; Warner & Lance, 1975). Furthermore, almost every biofeedback study that has been conducted (including the controlled-group outcome studies reviewed earlier) has combined biofeedback with some kind of relaxation treatment, thus confounding the two treatments. It is, thus, largely impossible to separate out the effects of biofeedback *per se* from those of relaxation training. Now, it could be argued that if a self-control procedure such as "autogenic feedback" is truly effective in reducing the frequency or intensity of migraine, it is as irrelevant to ask why as it used to be to question why aspirin worked for common headaches. This argument can be answered as follows: in the first place, all the data is not yet in on the long-term effectiveness of autogenic feedback. Secondly, considering the intemperate claims that have been made for biofeedback, it is incumbent upon us to show that it is biofeedback *per se,* rather than biofeedback as an epiphenomenon of some other treatment that is responsible for therapeutic improvement in migraine. This is important because of our obligation to justify what we do on a scientific basis (rather than on superstitious learning) as well as on the pragmatic grounds of labor- and cost-effectiveness. The literature on systematic desensitization (Yates, 1975) could serve as a model of how a technique may be investigated parametrically to yield data on the effectiveness and theoretical "correctness" of its component parts. It is important to know whether autogenic phrases, imagery, or relaxation instructions are useful in priming a response that is shaped and conditioned through feedback or whether they constitute the treatment itself.

CONCLUSION

The current status of biofeedback in the treatment of migraine is still equivocal. On the one hand, there are numerous studies, reviewed above, which report therapeutic benefit for migraine from biofeedback. On the other hand, most of these studies suffer from one or more methodological weaknesses. One primary defect is that biofeedback has generally not been found to be superior to training in relaxation only. A second defect found even among the best studies is the inadequate duration of baseline and follow-up. A 3-month follow-up is simply inadequate for proving the adequacy of treatment. This is especially so in light of the fact that many patients improve for a short time in response to practically any treatment. Miller (1978) has pointed out two issues often overlooked in a consideration of the therapeutic effects of biofeedback. First, many conditions get better spontaneously without treatment. Second, patients often seek help when they are feeling worst, and since their disorder is naturally cyclical, they are likely to improve. Because they are discharged when feeling better, the therapist is likely to take an exaggerated view of their improved state. Moreover, the act of being seen by a professional creates strong placebo conditions for at least short-term improvement. It has long been known that a significant percentage of migraine sufferers respond positively to drug placebos (46 to 58 percent as reported by Friedman, 1957). Perusal of the recent literature reveals that this is still the case (Diamond & Medina, 1976; Ryan, 1977).

While a rather bleak picture has been painted of the state of the art in biofeedback and migraine, I think it would be wrong to dismiss self-control procedures as a treatment for migraine. While not convincing in themselves, the studies reviewed in this chapter are suggestive enough to warrant further research in the area. Such research *must* be long-term and properly controlled. Even then, procedures for developing self-control over autonomic activity may by themselves be inadequate to produce sustained, major reduction in headache activity. They may serve best as adjuncts to therapy aimed at influencing patients' responses to life situations (Adler & Adler, 1976; Mitchell & Mitchell, 1971; Price, 1974; Schwartz, 1973).

Chapter 9
Biofeedback and the Treatment of Fear and Anxiety*

Robert J. Gatchel

One of the important potential applications which attracted many clinical researchers to the field of biofeedback was the possible use of learned control of physiological responses as a means of treating anxiety. Over the years, a number of treatment techniques were developed with the main goal of reducing the physiological component of anxiety. For example, in therapies such as progressive relaxation therapy (Jacobson, 1938), autogenic training (Schultze & Luthe, 1959), and systematic desensitization (Wolpe, 1958), which were developed to eliminate anxiety and tension states, the primary aim is the production of a low state of sympathetic arousal that competes against the stress response and accompanying elevated arousal level. Many of these biobehavioral approaches were developed on the basis of theoretical accounts of anxiety which suggested the importance of physiological responsivity in fear behavior. Biofeedback technology was viewed as possibly providing a more direct means of modifying the physiological underpinning of this aversive emotional state. In this chapter, I will review studies which have assessed the treatment efficacy of biofeedback techniques in alleviating anxiety. Before reviewing this research, however, a brief summary of issues involved in the definition and measurement of anxiety and a discussion of theoretical learning accounts of anxiety will be presented.

*The writing of this paper was supported in part by a grant to the author from the National Heart, Lung, and Blood Institute (Grant No. NIH HL 21426-01).

DEFINITION AND MEASUREMENT OF ANXIETY

Although most individuals have a subjective feeling as to what anxiety is, there is no universally accepted definition of this emotional state. Indeed, as Lang (1977a) indicates: "It is curious that a phenomenon so widely remarked and considered fundamental to psychopathology should be so resistant to precise definition." This lack of a precise definition is highlighted by the fact that there are no less than 120 procedures available that are purported to measure anxiety (Cattell & Scheier, 1961).

The major problem associated with defining and measuring anxiety is that, rather than being an actual entity or "thing," anxiety is a construct which is inferred in order to account for some form of behavior. Anxiety is usually viewed as a mediator, that is, an unobservable inferred construct which is hypothesized to account for a certain observable behavior such as task performance differences between individuals. Of course, if one uses a construct to explain some form of behavior, it is essential that one develops a precise operational definition and employs objective and quantifiable behavioral referents as measures of the construct.

Presently, more and more clinical researchers interested in the study of anxiety operationally define it as a complex of responses consisting of three broad components of behavior: (1) subjective or self-report measures, (2) physiological arousal involving primarily the sympathetic branch of the autonomic nervous system, and (3) overt somatic-motor behaviors such as trembling or stuttering. What makes the study and measurement of anxiety so difficult is that one cannot always assume that these three broad behavior component measures will be highly correlated (Lang, 1977a). A patient may verbally report that he is not anxious, but yet be observed trembling and stuttering and displaying a greatly accelerated heart rate. Therefore, it is important to assess all three components in specific situations whenever possible, with the expectation that there may be complex interactions between components that may differ from one type of anxiety situation to the next. In addition, within the physiological component, there may be low correlations among various measures (Lacey, 1967). In the context of a biofeedback study, this was recently demonstrated by Gatchel, Korman, Weis, Smith, and Clarke (1978). In that study, an EMG biofeedback group was able to maintain a low level of frontalis EMG activity during a stress-induction procedure. However, this low level of EMG activity did not generalize to other physiological responses. Heart rate and skin conductance levels both increased, which coincided with the subjects' self-report of anxiety.

It is also important to realize that many measures of anxiety are also indicants of other arousal states. For example, a greatly elevated heart rate is not only associated with anxiety but also with a state of sexual arousal.

However, if a patient reports that he is anxious and tense, is observed to be trembling and sweating, and displays a greatly accelerated heart rate, then one would be on relatively solid ground to infer the presence of anxiety in that individual.

Proponents of social learning/behavioral approaches have been most vocal in emphasizing the importance of clearly specifying stimulus conditions and then assessing how they modulate response symptom interactions when dealing with a maladaptive behavior such as anxiety (Lang, 1977a). This approach has increasingly been demonstrated to be both practical and heuristic in its emphasis upon an individual's behavior in specific situations (Mischel, 1976). An anxiety treatment procedure can then be developed to modify an individual's maladaptive response pattern to a specific stress situation. Treatment success is able to be subsequently assessed in terms of the amount of desirable changes in the specific target behaviors which occur before and after therapy. Such an approach emphasizes the integration of assessment and treatment. Assessment is a vital procedure used in order to clearly define the focal problem behavior and, also, to allow quantifiable interpretation of therapy results. As will be apparent, the biofeedback studies I review vary greatly in the precision of this assessment-treatment procedure.

THEORETICAL ACCOUNTS OF ANXIETY

One of the earliest behavioristic accounts of anxiety was essentially a physiological model based on simple Pavlovian conditioning. Briefly summarized, this model states that the repeated pairing of a conditioned stimulus (CS) and the unconditioned stimulus (UCS) eventually results in the elicitation of a conditioned response (CR) by the CS alone. In the case of an aversive conditioning situation, the CR is viewed as being composed of both autonomic and skeletal responses. Both the frequency and intensity of CS/UCS presentations are important in the maintenance of the conditioned CS/UCR relationship. Extinction was viewed as a result of repeated CS presentations in the absence of the UCS. Watson and Rayner's (1920) early demonstration of the course of conditioned fear acquisition in the child Little Albert, and the program developed by Jones (1924) for the elimination of acquired fear, were both based on this model. It should be noted, however, that there have been only a few isolated studies such as these which have unequivocally demonstrated that fear can be classically conditioned in human subjects (Davison & Neale, 1978).

The above Pavlovian model was not wholeheartedly embraced by all psychologists because it was viewed as incomplete. Mowrer (1947) attacked the monistic theories of Pavlov and Watson and proposed a two-factor theory of learning to account for conditioned anxiety. His is credited as being the first widely accepted theoretical model to account for anxiety. This two-factor theory suggests that neither the principle of association nor the law of effect alone can adequately provide a comprehensive and unified theory of learning. Rather, it was argued that two basic learning processes need to be taken into account: "The process whereby the solutions to problems, i.e., ordinary 'habits' are acquired; and the process whereby emotional learning, or 'conditioning,' takes place," (Mowrer, 1947, p. 114).

With respect to conditioned fear behavior, this model dictates the occurrence of a two-process sequence: (1) The acquisition of the emotional or fear response (CR) to the CS by means of classical conditioning involving the smooth musculature and mediated by the autonomic nervous system. (2) This fear then serves as an acquired drive and acts to motivate subsequent escape and avoidance behavior. It also serves as a reinforcer of such behavior via its drive-reduction consequences. These instrumental responses involve the skeletal musculature mediated by the central nervous system. Thus, for example, the temporal contiguity of a CS such as a bell with painful electric shocks was sufficient to produce a conditioned fear response to the bell. An active instrumental avoidance or escape response to the CS was subsequently reinforced because it reduced the fear drive.

Mowrer's (1947) two-factor theory has generated a great deal of experimental research. His model has served as a theoretical framework for a great many behavior therapy researchers interested in the modification of anxiety-related disorders. However, although this learning model of anxiety is embraced by many psychologists, it cannot be uncritically accepted because there are certain limitations associated with it. A major limitation is that, even though conditioned anxiety has been produced time and time again in laboratory animals, there have been few controlled experimental demonstrations of the effect with human subjects. One reason is that, because of ethical considerations, the high-intensity aversive UCSs which need to be employed in order to produce such conditioning cannot be employed in experimentation with human subjects. A related point is that there are no clear-cut and objective clinical data definitively demonstrating a causal relationship between the development of anxiety and avoidance and a specific aversive conditioning experience.

It is generally accepted that there is presently no one model or classical theory of learning which comprehensively explains the development and maintenance of anxiety behavior. This is partially due to the fact that there is still a great deal of disagreement among theorists about the basic principles governing learning. However, even though Mowrer's learning model is associated with certain limitations, many experimental and clinical researchers use it because it provides an effective theoretical framework to use in the further investigation and integration of research and clinical data on anxiety. In passing, it should also be noted that this theory is undergoing change. For example, the concepts of "response preparedness" (Seligman & Hager, 1972) and "stimulus prepotency" (Marks, 1977) appear to be important factors to take into account. The concept of "stimulus prepotency" refers to the observation that the fear of certain things such as heights and snakes are common in human subjects because of an innate avoidance of them but that other stimuli such as trees do not produce such innate avoidance. Indeed, it appears that it is much easier to condition fear to the former stimuli than to the latter type (Marks, 1977). Thus, different stimuli may possess different capacities for eliciting conditioned emotional responses. Similarly, the concept of "response preparedness" refers to the observation that there are certain responses which are biologically highly prepared or "prewired," such as certain types of fear and avoidance responses to specific objects. Such differential capacities for evoking anxiety and the ways in which that anxiety is expressed, will need to be taken into account in any future comprehensive model of anxiety.

Although the autonomic component of behavior has been viewed as central in the course of development of anxiety in the above reviewed learning model of Mowrer, and has long been used in the behavioral definition of anxiety, direct investigation of this component has been, surprisingly, almost totally ignored. Biofeedback technology provides an ideal means by which one can directly examine the functional role of autonomic responding in theories of anxiety. Indeed, some of the biofeedback studies to be reviewed next bear directly upon this issue.

CLINICAL APPLICATIONS OF BIOFEEDBACK

There is currently a paucity of well-controlled research which has adequately assessed the effectiveness of biofeedback techniques in the treatment of fear and anxiety. In this section, I will review clinical case studies and controlled-group studies which have been conducted to date. I will then discuss a number of biofeedback-treatment evaluation studies conducted in my laboratory during the past few years which demonstrate the significant role that placebo factors play in biofeedback therapy directed at the elimination of fear and anxiety. Of course, it should be kept in mind that a necessary condition in all these studies is a demonstration that subjects learn to control the desired physiological response with biofeedback training. Failure to find evidence for a learning effect would invalidate any conclusions about the efficacy of biofeedback training for the particular problems being examined.

Clinical Case Studies

Individual case studies involving uncontrolled observations without attempts at measurement have basically no formal scientific value in assessing therapeutic outcome. Indeed, without some form of measurement, the evaluation of change is at a purely subjective, inferential level. By introducing at least some form of assessment at pretreatment and posttreatment stages, there will be some basis for evaluation of change in even the individual case study.

Of course, this still does not allow the precise establishment of treatment outcome cause-effect relationships because of the absence of control over alternative factors, such as therapist contact, placebo/expectancy effects, etc., that may be equally important in affecting changes in the patient's maladaptive behavior. Barlow, Blanchard, Hayes, and Epstein (1977) have recently reviewed basic procedures in the use of single-case experimental designs in clinical biofeedback evaluation and research.

When there is a combination of case studies into a single-group design, there is an increase in confidence in the reliability of a clinical finding because of the presence of a number of replications. However, all the problems associated with the single-case study approach apply equally to the single-group design.

Currently in the literature, there are a number of single-case studies and single-group studies examining the clinical effectiveness of biofeedback in the treatment of anxiety. These studies should only be viewed as suggestive of potential clinical effectiveness and not as scientifically valid and conclusive demonstrations.

EMG Biofeedback. In the only single-group study assessing the clinical effectiveness of EMG biofeedback training in reducing anxiety, Raskin, Johnson, and Rondestvedt (1973) assessed the effects of daily deep- muscle relaxation, achieved through frontalis EMG biofeedback training, on the symptoms of 10 chronically anxious patients. All 10 patients reported that their anxiety symptoms markedly disrupted their lives. The training consisted of administering biofeedback sessions until the patient could remain deeply relaxed for 25 minutes. Once this was achieved, sessions without biofeedback were interspersed every 2 or 3 days. This training period varied from 2 weeks to 3 months, with the average training period being 6 weeks. Eight weeks of daily relaxation practice was initiated once the patient could sustain deep muscle relaxation for 25 minutes with and without feedback. During this period, the patients were also requested to practice at home for 2 half-hour sessions each day.

Therapist ratings of anxiety, insomnia, and tension headaches were made weekly for 8 weeks prior to the relaxation training, during the period of feedback training, and during the 8 weeks of daily relaxation practice. On the basis of an assessment of these ratings, it was determined that the biofeedback intervention had beneficial effects on the anxiety of 4 of the 10 patients. One of these patients experienced a dramatic decrease of all his anxiety symptoms, while the other 3 learned to utilize the relaxation technique to lessen previously intolerable situational anxiety. These results demonstrate promise for the use of muscle-biofeedback training in alleviating certain symptoms associated with chronic anxiety in some patients.

Wickramasekera (1972) reported a single case study in which EMG biofeedback-assisted muscle relaxation training was used as an adjunct to the treatment of test anxiety with systematic desensitization. Two initial relaxation training sessions were administered using EMG biofeedback of frontalis muscle activity. The female patient was then taught to present the hierarchical scenes to herself and was instructed to terminate the scene whenever the EMG biofeedback signal reached a certain predetermined high level. This treatment was successful in eliminating the anxiety and in allowing the patient to pass an examination that she had avoided taking many times in the past because of her high anxiety. Budzynski and Stoyva (1973) have also reported the successful use of EMG biofeedback as an adjunctive procedure in behavior-therapy techniques for eliminating anxiety.

Of course, these anecdotal case studies do not provide any solid evidence for the clinical effectiveness of EMG biofeedback training, since the basic systematic desensitization treatment procedure is well established and has been shown to produce significant and reliable therapeutic improvement. An evaluation of whether EMG assisted relaxation adds anything significant to the basic systematic desensitization procedure will need to be conducted.

Electrodermal Biofeedback. In the only electrodermal biofeedback study in the literature, Shapiro, Schwartz, Schnidman, Nelson, and Silverman (1972), in a single-group study, assessed the possibility of directly controlling electrodermal responses to fear stimuli through feedback and reward. The investigators based their study on research showing increased electrodermal activity to phobic stimuli (Geer, 1966). Using an operant paradigm, the study employed 20 snake-phobic women who were rewarded for either reducing or increasing their electrodermal responses to pictures of snakes arranged to provide increasing levels of fear. The results suggested that subjects could gain some control over their electrodermal responses to fearful stimuli in a single brief session. Also, this control was accompanied by a relative decrease in fear to the snake stimuli as gauged by a postexperimental questionnaire.

Of course, the above study did not contain an appropriate experimental control group and, as a result, the findings of reduced fear may have been due to a host of uncontrolled factors. Better controlled clinical trials have yet to be conducted.

Heart-Rate Biofeedback. There have been a number of promising results reported in case studies which have used heart rate as the target behavior in biofeedback training. In one such study, Wickramasekera (1974) reported the treatment of a chronic case of cardiac neurosis. The 55-year-old male patient treated had developed an extreme fear of developing a "heart attack" and became extremely sensitive to slight increases in heart rate, shortness of breath, and feelings of "passing out." This chronic fear seriously disrupted his daily course of living. Wickramasekera administered a treatment program which consisted of heart-rate deceleration biofeedback training, self-administered systematic desensitization, and a therapist-administered verbal flooding procedure. At the end of 16 sessions of this treatment, the patient was free of anxiety episodes for 2 months. There were also no episodes at 6- and 12-month follow-up evaluations.

Of course, the separate contribution of biofeedback training to therapeutic improvement cannot be assessed in the above clinical case study. However, the results indicate that biofeedback training directed at a target problem behavior — heart rate — in combination with adjunctive behavioral treatment approaches produced rapid and clinically significant therapeutic improvement.

In a case study which involved the use of only a heart-rate biofeedback treatment procedure, Blanchard and Abel (1976) treated a 30-year-old female patient who suffered ''spells'' of passing out. Because of an early traumatic rape experience, certain thoughts of rape and sex precipitated in this patient episodes of tachycardia followed by bradycardia and then passing out. During an initial baseline evaluation period, the therapists had the client listen to a tape which included descriptions of thoughts and events which distressed her. This produced heart-rate increases of greater than 140 beats per minute.

At the start of therapy, the patient was trained to voluntarily lower heart rate. After 8 such training sessions, the patient was then required to listen to the distressing tape while lowering heart rate with the assistance of feedback. After 25 such sessions, she was required to listen to the tape without feedback present; it was found that her ability to maintain a low heart rate transferred to this no-feedback condition. This treatment program was found to produce significant clinical improvement. The patient's ''spells'' also remained absent at a 4-month follow-up. These findings suggest that heart-rate biofeedback training might be a clinically effective therapeutic technique with patients demonstrating a significant cardiac response to anxiety-producing situations.

Blanchard and colleagues reported a number of other case studies which similarly found heart-rate biofeedback to be therapeutically effective. Scott, Peters, Gillespie, Blanchard, Edmunson, and Young (1973) treated a 61-year-old psychiatric inpatient who was suffering from chronic anxiety and moderate tachycardia. Biofeedback training produced a heart rate which averaged 16 beats per minute lower than the patient's average baseline rate. The patient also reported feeling less tense and made fewer requests for medication. Scott, Blanchard, Edmunson, and Young (1973) treated 2 other patients suffering from chronic anxiety and tachycardia. In both studies, biofeedback training produced a slowing of heart rate to a normal range, as well as a decrease in verbal reports of being ''anxious, tense, or nervous.'' It should be noted, however, that in none of these 3 cases was a systematic collection of self-report improvement data conducted.

In another case study which similarly suggests the therapeutic efficacy of heart-rate biofeedback, Gatchel (1977) administered heart-rate deceleration biofeedback for the treatment of a claustrophobic type problem behavior which was highlighted by significant tachycardia. The patient was a 23-year-old male college student who had developed an intense fear of enclosed places. This fear was significantly interfering with his daily functioning. Fourteen sessions of heart-rate biofeedback training were administered over the course of 2 months. It should be pointed out that, since biofeedback training required the client to remain in a small enclosed subject cubicle for the duration of each training session, a "built-in" feature of the therapy procedure was extensive exposure to aversive claustrophobic cues while performing the heart-rate deceleration task. The client was also requested to practice heart-rate control between sessions whenever possible.

For 2 weeks prior to therapy, during therapy, and for 2 weeks after therapy, the client was requested to keep a daily record of the number and severity of anxiety attacks he experienced during the course of the day. A time-series analysis of pretreatment and posttreatment assessment of anxiety attacks indicated a statistically significant amount of fear reduction due to the biofeedback treatment intervention.

The above findings again suggest the treatment efficacy of biofeedback in reducing anxiety. It should also be noted that the time-series analysis employed in this case study by Gatchel allows one to systematically evaluate a single subject over time, using the subject as his own control and thus permitting the statistical assessment of the effect of the therapeutic intervention over time. It is a useful tool in the evaluation of therapy-outcome studies, and has several significant advantages over simple pre- and posttreatment change. This method is to be recommended in the analysis of future biofeedback case study results (see Gottman, 1973, for a discussion of this type of analysis).

Conclusions. The heart-rate biofeedback case study results by Blanchard and colleagues, Gatchel (1977), and Wickramasekera (1974) suggest that cardiac-rhythm biofeedback training may be an effective therapeutic technique for alleviating anxiety when heart rate is a major component of the anxiety response. Of course, as indicated earlier, these results should only be viewed as suggestive of possible clinical effectiveness because of the absence of control over factors such as placebo effects, which may have been primarily responsible for the observed changes.

The single-group EMG biofeedback study reported by Raskin et al. (1973) demonstrated some therapeutic improvement for some of the chronically anxious patients assessed (4 out of 10). These results obviously do not testify to the overwhelming effectiveness of this biofeedback procedure.

Finally, the electrodermal biofeedback technique examined by Shapiro et al. (1972) suggests the possible therapeutic benefit of such a procedure. However, their study was only a preliminary, one-session analogue investigation. Additional studies focusing on an actual clinically anxious population that is administered more than a single biofeedback training session are needed in order to more adequately assess the possible fear-reducing effects of this procedure.

Control-Group Studies

A "true experiment" of treatment outcome consists of one group of patients receiving treatment while an equivalent group either does not or receives some form of pseudotherapy, with both groups being assessed before and after the treatment procedure. Using such an experimental design, there is a possibility that certain cause-effect relationships can be statistically isolated. Such experiments, however, can vary greatly in the precision associated with isolating such relationships, depending upon the adequacy of the experimental paradigm utilized. For example, without the inclusion of appropriate types of control groups, controlling for such factors as expectancy/placebo or the amount of therapist contact which could possibly have an important impact on the form of behavior disorder being examined, it may be impossible to establish a clear, unconfounded cause-effect relationship. There are a wide variety of experimental designs varying in precision which can be used in evaluation research. Campbell and Stanley (1970) provide a good review of many such designs. As will become evident, the studies to be reviewed next vary greatly in the adequacy of their experimental designs and thus the resultant ability to clearly isolate treatment-outcome effects.

EMG Biofeedback. Townsend, House, and Addario (1975) assessed the therapeutic effectiveness of frontalis EMG biofeedback-mediated relaxation in the treatment of chronic anxiety. Chronically anxious patients were matched in pairs on a combination of resting frontalis EMG, state-trait anxiety, and total mood disturbance scores, and assigned to one of two treatment groups. The first group, an EMG biofeedback group, received 9, 20-minute biofeedback sessions over the course of 2 weeks. They also practiced deep muscle relaxation with taped instructions for one-half hour each day. They continued self-practice without taped instructions during the third and fourth weeks of therapy. A comparison group received group psychotherapy. This was a short-term structured group therapy experience dealing specifically with anxiety. Sixty-minute sessions were held for groups of 4 or 5 patients. A total of 16 sessions was administered.

At the start of the study, there were 15 patients assigned to each of the above two groups. Due to a variety of attrition factors, however, only 10 subjects in the biofeedback group and 8 in the group therapy condition completed the full 4 weeks of therapy. Evaluation of change from pretreatment assessment to change during and after treatment indicated significant decreases in EMG levels, mood disturbance as measured by the Profile of Mood States, trait anxiety, and to a lesser extent, state anxiety (as measured by the State-Trait Anxiety Inventory) evidenced by the biofeedback group. No such decreases occurred in the comparison group-therapy condition. These findings point to the potential effectiveness of EMG biofeedback, although the individual contribution of deep muscle relaxation via taped instructions cannot be separately assessed.

In another EMG biofeedback study which did make such a separate assessment, Canter, Kondo, and Knott (1975) compared the therapeutic effectiveness of frontalis EMG biofeedback to that of traditional Jacobson progressive-relaxation muscle training. Twenty-eight psychiatric patients diagnosed as anxiety neurotics were treated in this study. One-half of these patients reported having acute panic episodes associated with their condition and the remaining one-half were typically more chronically anxious without acute panic episodes. The number of training sessions administered to patients ranged from 10 to 25. Results of this investigation indicated that both EMG biofeedback and progressive muscle relaxation training produced significant reductions in frontalis tension levels. The EMG biofeedback training, however, was found to be generally more effective in producing greater reductions in muscle activity with a coincident greater relief in anxiety symptoms for a larger number of patients. Thus it appears that the EMG biofeedback training produces therapeutic improvement above and beyond that which is effected by traditional progressive muscle relaxation training.

In neither of the above two EMG biofeedback studies was the effect of placebo factors on therapeutic improvement assessed. As will be discussed later in this chapter, such factors have been shown to play a significant role in the therapeutic improvement produced by heart-rate biofeedback techniques. Future EMG biofeedback studies will need to control for these factors.

In another treatment-comparison study, Jessup and Neufeld (1977) reported some preliminary results which evaluated the ability of four techniques — frontalis muscle biofeedback, noncontingent biofeedback, unaided self-relaxation, and autogenic phrases — to help hospitalized psychiatric patients to relax. The noncontingent biofeedback training consisted of tape-recorded tones characteristic of those produced by biofeedback subjects who were able to successfully relax. The subjects were instructed simply to listen to the tape and ''let the tone relax you.'' The patient sample consisted of 7 males and 13 females, for whom some form of depression was the primary clinical diagnosis (15 patients). These patients were not suffering from any marked psychotic episodes at the time of testing.

A host of physiological measures, as well as the Nowlis Mood Adjective Check List (MACL), were assessed before and during 4 daily 20-minute training sessions. Results indicated that heart rate and MACL anxiety scores decreased significantly in subjects receiving the noncontingent biofeedback. However, except for a decrease in MACL anxiety scores for autogenic-phrase group subjects, the other three treatments did not significantly affect any of the dependent measures.

The lack of therapeutic impact of the other three treatments, all of which are usually found to produce some degree of relaxation, may have been due to the limited amount of training administered. Also, for the type of patient group employed (predominantly depressed), a relaxation response may not have been an appropriate problematic behavior upon which to focus treatment.

The fact that the noncontingent biofeedgack group produced the greatest amount of relaxation-related behavior indicates the significant impact that such a nonspecific treatment procedure can have. It suggests the important role that placebo-type effects can play in techniques directed at the alleviation of anxiety.

Alpha Biofeedback. Chisholm, DeGood, and Hartz (1977) examined whether brief alpha biofeedback training would significantly alter the degree of physiological and self-reported stress evidenced in an aversive laboratory situation, the anticipation and administration of electric shock. Subjects were assigned to one of three groups: (1) A contingent alpha feedback group which received 24 minutes of training; (2) a noncontingent alpha feedback group which received 24 minutes of training; and (3) a no-feedback control group. Results of this study indicated that subjects in the contingent-feedback group could produce enhanced alpha density which was maintained during the post-treatment aversive shock situation. However, this was not accompanied by a corresponding heart-rate and self-report reduction in this situational anxiety. The investigators conclude that alpha feedback training was not effective in producing a generalized relaxation response to the aversive situation. However, one must temper this statement somewhat because one brief alpha biofeedback training session may not provide an adequate test of clinical effectiveness.

The authors also note that the average group differences in self-reported anxiety and tension paralleled heart-rate changes more closely than the alpha changes, further suggesting that a decrease in alpha suppression did not serve to produce a generalized relaxation response. These data also suggest that heart rate is more closely tied to the self-reported experience of anxiety. Indeed, Klorman, Weissberg, and Wisenfeld (1977) have recently demonstrated a close relationship between cardiac reactions and individual differences in fear. This suggestion that heart rate is an appropriate target behavior to modify when treating anxiety with biofeedback techniques will be discussed at further length later in this chapter.

The above results questioning the potential clinical utility of alpha biofeedback training in reducing anxiety are compatible with some earlier findings reported by Orne and Paskewitz (1974). These investigators assessed whether anticipation of electric shock would depress alpha activity in a biofeedback situation. Subjects in this study learned to enhance alpha activity through biofeedback training, after which they were exposed to a stressful threat-of-shock anticipation situation. Results indicated that, although heart rate and electrodermal activity increased in response to the threat of shock, as well as the subjects' postexperimental reports of anxiety, there was not any sharp decrease in alpha density as the result of exposure to this stress. Even though this study lacked appropriate control groups, the results do suggest that individuals can demonstrate experiential and autonomic concomitants of fear and apprehension without any associated changes in cortical alpha density. Such results seriously question the assumption that alpha biofeedback training will directly lead to a reduction in overall anxiety level.

Finally, a study by Valle and DeGood (1977) assessed the relationship between self-reported anxiety as measured by the State-Trait Anxiety Inventory and the presence of alpha control produced by biofeedback training. Results of this study indicated that momentary state-anxiety scores were unrelated to both the direction (suppression or enhancement) and success of alpha control. These data further indicate that alpha level per se is not directly related to self-reported anxiety.

Heart-Rate Biofeedback. Sirota and colleagues (Sirota, Schwartz, & Shapiro, 1974; 1976) conducted two studies which assessed the effects of heart rate deceleration biofeedback training on self-rated aversiveness of painful electric shocks. In the first study, it was found that subjects who were lowering their heart rates rated the electric shocks as less aversive than those who were instructed to raise their heart rates. It should be pointed out that these latter subjects did not actually raise their heart rates, but could merely hold their rates steady. In their second study, two groups of subjects were run in a counterbalanced order through heart-rate deceleration and heart-rate acceleration biofeedback training. Results demonstrated a near-significant trend (.07 level) for subjects lowering heart rhythm to rate the electric shocks as less aversive than these same subjects during heart rhythm increase trials. In both of these studies, it was also found that subjects scoring high in cardiac awareness demonstrated the greatest reduction in perceived aversiveness of shock while voluntarily showing their heart rates and the greatest increase in perceived aversiveness while raising their heart rates, relative to subjects scoring low in perception of cardiac activity. These results suggest the potential significance of the interaction between physiological control and at least one individual-difference variable, cardiac awareness.

The above results suggest that the voluntary lowering of heart rate by subjects while they are being exposed to painful electric shocks leads to a relative reduction in the perceived aversiveness of these noxious stimuli. However, one must be cautious in wholeheartedly embracing such an interpretation, since the effect may have been indirectly due to changes in pain thresholds. Of course, such an alteration of pain threshold produced by biofeedback training would be an important finding in its own right. Heart-rate slowing may lead to an increase in pain threshold and a consequent lower rating of aversiveness; heart-rate elevation may increase the subjects' rating of shocks as more aversive due to a decreased pain threshold. Indeed, pain threshold is decreased under conditions of fear and anxiety, both of which are typically accompanied by slight increases in cardiac rate. Future research will need to assess whether anxiety is being directly affected by the biofeedback, or whether pain threshold is being affected.

In another similar type of study, Victor, Mainardi, and Shapiro (1978) assessed the effects of heart-rate biofeedback training on subjective reactivity to a cold-pressor test (immersion of the hand in ice water for 30 seconds). This test is often used to evaluate cardiovascular response to stress. Five experimental conditions were employed in this study. Two groups were provided biofeedback training (one group increased heart rate and the other decreased heart rate), and were requested to continue controlling their heart rates during the cold-pressor test. Two other groups were not provided with biofeedback training but were simply asked to voluntarily control their heart rates (either increasing or decreasing rate) during the cold-pressor test. A fifth condition was a simple no-treatment habituation control group. Subjects in the two biofeedback groups received 25, 30-minute training trials, followed by 5 no-feedback transfer trials in which they were asked to continue controlling heart rate without feedback. Subjects in the two no-feedback groups read magazines during a comparable period of 25 feedback trails and were then requested to control their heart rates during 5 no-feedback trials. The habituation group read magazines for the entire training period. Cold-pressor tests were administered before and after this training period.

Results of this study indicated a relationship between heart-rate change and subjective reports of pain to the cold pressor test. Significant differences in heart rate during the cold-pressor test were found among the five groups. The greatest effects were found between the two biofeedback groups. Similar, but smaller, effects were obtained in the groups simply asked to control their heart rates. Reports of pain also varied significantly, with higher heart rates associated with higher ratings of pain. Thus, again, these results indicate that the voluntary lowering of heart rate may lead to a relative reduction in the perceived aversiveness of a noxious stimulus. However, as indicated earlier, additional research is needed to determine whether this anxiety is being affected directly by biofeedback or indirectly by changes in pain thresholds.

In yet another study, DeGood and Adams (1976) evaluated the comparative effectiveness of brief heart-rate deceleration biofeedback training (25 minutes), deep muscle relaxation training, and a no-feedback/music-listening procedure on heart-rate reactivity to an aversive situation (10 trials in which a 1-second tone preceded the delivery of an electric shock by 30 seconds). Using a pre- to posttreatment assessment design, it was shown that the biofeedback group subjects evidenced the greatest amount of heart-rate reduction, followed by the muscle-relaxation group, and then the no-feedback/music group when exposed to the tone-shock trials. Moveover, although the transfer of this heart-rate control was incomplete for biofeedback-group subjects on trials in which the feedback signal was not present, it still remained lower than the level of the other two experimental groups. Thus, again, it appears that heart-rate control training effectively transfers to a classic aversive situation.

Using actual clinical populations, Nunes and Marks (1975; 1976) conducted two separate group outcome studies assessing the effectiveness of heart-rate biofeedback. The patients were all females with phobias of small animals. The main treatment administered was graduated *in vivo* exposure to the feared object. This particular form of desensitization treatment had been shown to be effective with these kinds of disorders (Watson, Gaind, & Marks, 1971). A major purpose of these two outcome studies was to assess whether heart-rate deceleration biofeedback training would serve as an effective adjunctive treatment to the basic *in vivo* therapy. In both studies, a group receiving graduated *in vivo* desensitization and biofeedback was compared to a group receiving only graduated *in vivo* exposure. Results of these investigations indicated that there was no added therapeutic benefit of biofeedback training above and beyond the improvement produced by *in vivo* exposure alone.

The failure of the biofeedback training to produce additional clinical improvement does not necessarily argue against its use as an effective therapeutic agent. Since the small-animal phobias treated in these studies respond so successfully to graduated *in vivo* exposure (Marks, 1972), biofeedback, or for that matter, any other type of treatment might not be expected to add significantly to the clinical improvement produced.

In an analog-treatment study conducted by Prigatano and Johnson (1972), spider-fearful subjects, after a behavioral pretest of their level of fear of spiders, were administered 2 heart-rate biofeedback sessions during which they were training to control heart-rate variability. They were then exposed to slides of spiders while continuing to receive heart-rate feedback. These subjects were compared to a group of subjects who received false heart-rate biofeedback during the training sessions. Results demonstrated that both groups evidenced improved approach behavior after treatment. However, there was no difference between groups. The fact that the false-biofeedback group learned to reduce heart-rate variability, and could show this control in the absence of feedback as effectively as the biofeedback-treatment group may have been the reason for this lack of difference in therapeutic improvement. Moreover, the fact that the false-biofeedback condition produced some significant fear reduction suggests that it may be a significant placebo procedure. Research to be discussed later in the chapter appears to support this suggestion.

Multiple-Response Biofeedback Training. To date, Garrett and Silver (1976; 1978) have been the only investigators to examine the effects of multiple-response biofeedback training in reducing anxiety. In two such experiments, Garrett and Silver (1976) assessed whether such biofeedback training could be used to effectively reduce test anxiety. In the first experiment, 36 college students who expressed an interest in participating in research which might alleviate test anxiety were employed. These subjects were administered three tests assumed to be sensitive to test anxiety — a reading test, a block-design test, and a digit-span test — before and after training sessions. The pretraining test scores were used to form 18 matched pairs of subjects, with the members of each pair being randomly assigned to an experimental group which received EMG and alpha biofeedback training and a no-contact control group which received no treatment. In the biofeedback treatment group, one-half of the subjects started with alpha training and the other half began with EMG training. Each subject received 2 training sessions on consecutive days for one response, and then 2 sessions on consecutive days for the other response. Results indicated that the biofeedback group evidenced a significant decrease in test anxiety, as measured by a test-anxiety questionnaire, and increased significantly in class academic rank while control subjects did not. There was no effect on the performance levels on the three tests administered in the laboratory.

In a second experiment, these investigators assessed the comparative effectiveness of alpha biofeedback training, EMG biofeedback training, a combination of alpha and EMG biofeedback training, relaxation training designed to control for placebo effects, and a no-contact control group in reducing test anxiety. Ten subjects were assigned to each group. The four training groups received 2 training sessions per week on alternate weeks for a total of 10 sessions. Subjects in the combination biofeedback group alternated between alpha and EMG training on different weeks, with half beginning with alpha training and half with EMG training. Results demonstrated that the three biofeedback groups showed a decrease in test anxiety, while the relaxation and no-contact control groups did not. The three biofeedback groups were found to be equally effective in reducing this anxiety. There was no effect found on semester grade-point averages.

The above two studies demonstrate that a specific type of anxiety — a fear of test situations — can be effectively reduced with the use of biofeedback. In a subsequent investigation, Garrett and Silver (1978) examined whether combined alpha and EMG biofeedback training was as effective as systematic desensitization in reducing test anxiety. Eleven test-anxious subjects were assigned to the biofeedback group, and 9 to the desensitization group. Ten treatment sessions were administered to each subject. Test anxiety was measured by a test-anxiety questionnaire. Results demonstrated that biofeedback training was as effective as desensitization in reducing test anxiety.

These studies by Garrett and Silver indicate that EMG biofeedback, alpha biofeedback, combined EMG and alpha biofeedback, and desensitization are equally effective in reducing test anxiety. In these studies, test anxiety was measured by a self-report questionnaire. In future research, the assessment of anxiety in real test situations and whether any such reduction will lead to an increase in test performance is needed to more directly determine the impact of these procedures on test anxiety.

Conclusions. Results reported by Townsend et al. (1975), employing chronically anxious patients and Canter et al. (1975), using anxiety neurotics, suggest that EMG biofeedback training may be effective in reducing anxiety. The study by Canter et al., moreover, indicated that the therapeutic change produced is above and beyond that produced by muscle relaxation training alone. These findings are encouraging for the clinical utilization of EMG biofeedback. Positive results were also reported by Garrett and Silver (1976). However, there has been a study reported by Jessup and Neufeld (1977) which did not find positive therapeutic results. As was pointed out, though, this may have been due to the limited amount of training administered (only 4, 20-minute training sessions) for the type of patient studied (predominantly depressed). Moreover, the goal of alleviating tension and anxiety by this biofeedback technique may not have been an appropriate target behavior to focus on in depressed patients. Thus, in spite of these negative results, it still appears that EMG biofeedback may be clinically effective with patients suffering primarily from anxiety. These preliminary findings warrant additional research.

An alpha biofeedback study reported by Chisholm et al. (1977) found no evidence for the effectiveness of brief (1-session) alpha biofeedback training in reducing physiological and self-report components of anxiety in a laboratory-induced stress situation. They found that self-reported anxiety paralleled heart-rate changes more closely than alpha changes. Results reported by Valle and DeGood (1977) and Orne and Paskewitz (1974) have also questioned the clinical utility of alpha biofeedback training for reducing anxiety. Garrett and Silver (1976), however, found that more extended alpha biofeedback training (10 sessions) had a significant impact on reducing test anxiety. Obviously, additional controlled research is needed.

Results of experiments which assessed the therapeutic effectiveness of heart-rate biofeedback are somewhat mixed on the utility of this procedure. Sirota et al. (1974; 1976) and Victor et al. (1978) conducted studies which indicate that brief training in heart-rate slowing altered pain threshold to some extent. A study by DeGood and Adams (1976) also demonstrated that brief heart-rate control training effectively transfers to an aversive situation. Results of clinical studies conducted by Nunes and Marks (1975; 1976) did not find that heart-rate biofeedback produced additional clinical improvement above and beyond the improvement produced by graduated *in vivo* exposure alone. However, since the type of anxiety treated in these studies responds so significantly to *in vivo* exposure, biofeedback might not be expected to add significantly to clinical improvement. Finally, a study by Prigatano and Johnson (1972) failed to find treatment improvement differences between a heart-rate biofeedback group and a false-biofeedback group. This may have been due to the fact that both groups showed a reduction in the target physiological response, heart-rate variability. Again, additional research is needed to more adequately assess the heart-rate biofeedback procedure, especially in light of the positive case study results reported earlier. Individual differences in the ability to control heart rate will need to be carefully taken into account in this future research.

A series of studies by Garrett and Silver (1976; 1978) assessed the effects of multiple-response biofeedback training in reducing test anxiety. There was no difference found between combined alpha and EMG biofeedback training and each individually administered technique. These procedures were found to be as effective as desensitization. It would be of great interest in future research to assess the combination biofeedback training of a somatic response system such as EMG and an autonomic measure such as heart rate. Since autonomic responding appears to be an important component of the anxiety response, the direct modification of it along with a skeletal muscular response may provide a more comprehensive treatment of the physiological underpinning of anxiety.

HEART-RATE BIOFEEDBACK AND PLACEBO EFFECTS

A number of years ago, I embarked on a research program designed to assess whether biofeedback could be employed as an effective therapeutic strategy to alleviate anxiety. Specifically, I was interested in determining whether anxiety could be directly restrained through inhibition of the heart-rate component of sympathetic arousal. It was reasoned that this would provide one test of the possible importance of autonomic activity in the development/maintenance of anxiety which is suggested in the earlier reviewed model proposed by Mowrer (1947). There were a number of factors that prompted me to focus on heart rate as the target physiological behavior in this biofeedback research. First of all, one of the common concomitants of self-reported anxiety is an increase in sympathetic nervous-system activity (Lader & Mathers, 1968), with heart rate appearing to be an especially sensitive measure associated with fear (Lang, Rice, & Sternbach, 1972). Secondly, Lang, Melamed, and Hart (1970) have shown that those subjects demonstrating the steepest heart-rate habituation gradient across therapy sessions gained the greatest profit from systematic desensitization. It was therefore thought that training individuals to voluntarily decrease heart rate might be a more direct and powerful method for bringing about fear reduction. Also related to these findings with human subjects are data reported by DiCara and Weiss (1969) which indicated that the operant conditioning of heart rate altered emotional reactivity in rats. In this study, curarized rats were trained to decrease heart rate in order to avoid electric shock. They subsequently showed good learning under noncurarized conditions. In contrast, when these rats were trained to increase heart rate, they demonstrated poor subsequent avoidance learning.

A third factor taken into consideration was the casual observation that subjects undergoing heart-rate biofeedback training frequently report feeling calm and relaxed at the end of heart-rate slowing sessions, but they often report feeling anxious and tense at the end of speeding sessions (Headrick, Feather, & Wells, 1971). In a more systematic assessment of this subjective phenomenon, Hatch (1977) recently conducted an investigation in my laboratory in which he measured the transitory anxiety state of subjects immediately before and again immediately after each of 4 separate heart rate biofeedback sessions. He used the State-Trait Anxiety Inventory (STAI) (Spielberger, Gorsuch, & Lushene, 1970) to measure this anxiety. An assessment of STAI scores before and after the 4 heart-rate slowing sessions indicated a small decrease in perceived state anxiety which, however, was not statistically significant. For the speeding session, though, there was a very large and statistically significant increase in the mean state-anxiety scores following heart-rate speeding performance. Therefore, although a significant reduction in state anxiety was not found to accompany heart rate slowing performance, the findings obtained for heart rate speeding performance indicate that the direct manipulation of a physiological component of anxiety (heart rate) generalizes to a self-report component of anxiety as well (STAI). These data suggest that the restraint of heart-rate acceleration through the use of biofeedback training might be useful in inhibiting situational anxiety states.

Finally, a fourth major factor was the growing amount of research which indicated that human subjects could significantly learn to voluntarily control their heart rates when provided with exteroceptive feedback. A standard automated heart-rate feedback training program was developed and shown to produce very reliable and significant learning of heart rate control (Gatchel, 1974; Lang, 1974).

In the first of a series of studies, Gatchel and Proctor (1976) examined whether heart rate biofeedback could be employed as a therapeutic strategy to alleviate speech anxiety. After a pretest assessment of the level of anxiety in speech-anxious subjects, which consisted of an evaluation of self-report, overt motor, and physiological components of behavior while subjects were preparing and actually giving a brief speech, 2 separate biofeedback training sessions were given during which subjects learned to significantly control heart-rate deceleration. Subjects were then retested for anxiety while preparing and giving another speech and during which they were requested to try to maintain a low heart rate. Results demonstrated that those subjects who received biofeedback training showed significantly less self-report, physiological (heart rate and skin conductance) and overt signs of anxiety relative to control group subjects.

As a follow-up to the Gatchel and Proctor study, an experiment by Gatchel, Hatch, Watson, Smith, and Gaas (1977) investigated whether a muscle relaxation self-control technique found by Goldfried and Trier (1974) to produce a significant reduction in anxiety was as effective as the heart-rate biofeedback technique in bringing about fear reduction. Since, as indicated earlier, heart rate is strongly associated with fear (Lang, Rice, & Sternbach, 1972), it was felt that the use of learned control over this visceral response might be a more direct and powerful tool for reducing anxiety than the traditional muscle-relaxation technique. This study directly compared the therapeutic effectiveness of these two procedures in reducing speech anxiety. In addition, a combined muscle-relaxation/biofeedback treatment group was included in order to examine whether a combination of the two procedures produces greater therapeutic improvement than each separately administered technique. All three treatment groups were compared to a false-biofeedback control group. This placebo group was led to believe that it was successfully learning to voluntarily decrease heart rate, a skill which would later serve as an effective means of alleviating anxiety. Similar to the Gatchel and Proctor (1976) study, pretreatment assessment of anxiety consisted of self-report, overt motor, and physiological components of behavior while preparing and giving a speech. Four treatment training sessions were then administered, after which a posttreatment assessment of anxiety was conducted.

Results of this study indicated that all four experimental groups demonstrated a significant reduction in the self-report component of anxiety as a result of the treatment they received. There were no significant differences among the four groups. The fact that the false-biofeedback placebo group evidenced as much of a reduction in anxiety as the active-treatment groups indicates that this placebo condition has a powerful therapeutic impact. Indeed, therapeutic expectancy/demand characteristics have been shown to be significant factors in analogue therapy research (Borkovec, 1973). The significant amount of publicity and exaggerated accounts of "cure-all" biofeedback techniques, which regularly appear in the news media, may make a false-biofeedback group an extremely powerful placebo condition because of the accompanying significant amount of therapeutic expectancy. As I have suggested elsewhere (Gatchel, 1978), the perception, even if nonveridical, that an individual can control a physiological response which is a major component of anxiety may play an important role in eliminating that anxiety. The earlier reviewed study by Prigatano and Johnson (1973) also demonstrated that a false-biofeedback condition produces some significant fear reduction.

Even though there were no significant differences among groups for the self-report measure of anxiety, assessment of the physiological measures produced some interestingly different results. Findings demonstrated that the three treatment conditions produced significantly less heart-rate and skin-conductance level increases during the posttest assessment phase than the false-biofeedback group. In addition, among the three treatment groups, the combined relaxation/biofeedback group evidenced the greatest decrease in physiological responding. The interesting question which these data raise is what component(s) is the most valid and clinically reliable measure of anxiety reduction? This is not a novel or recent concern. As was pointed out earlier in this chapter, it has been empirically demonstrated that the three major component measures of behavior are not always highly correlated (Lang, 1977a).

There are some recent data reviewed by Hodgson and Rachman (1974) that shed light on these findings of a low relationship between response systems. These investigators have proposed that *level of demand* is an important variable which affects the degree of discordance among the different behavioral response systems. They review an experiment conducted by Miller and Bernstein (1972) which demonstrated that avoidance behavior is partially a function of this demand factor. In that investigation, claustrophobics were required to remain in a darkened chamber while heart rate and respiration were recorded. Under a low-demand condition, in which subjects were under no external pressure to remain in the chamber longer than "a point at which you would usually want to leave the situation if it happened to you in your daily life," correlations were relatively high between time in chamber and self-reported anxiety ($-.42$), heart rate ($-.56$), and respiration rate ($-.51$). However, under high-demand conditions in which subjects were instructed to remain in the chamber for 10 minutes and were told, "If you should become fearful, please control it as best you can so that you can remain for this full period," the relationships between systems dropped to .00, .00, and .07, respectively. These results therefore demonstrate that concordance between response systems is greater under low-demand level conditions. When there are high levels of demand, discordance between systems is produced. In explaining these findings of discordance under high-demand conditions, Hodgson and Rachman (1974) point out that it appears ". . . a highly motivated subject is able to control a tendency towards flight in spite of autonomic and experiential signs of fear" (p. 321).

The false-biofeedback group condition employed in the earlier reviewed study by Gatchel and colleagues can be viewed as a high-demand level condition. Because subjects were informed that the biofeedback training technique was effective in reducing anxiety, it was likely that they may have become highly motivated to force themselves to control their fear even though physiological cues were still present. This may have helped trigger the resultant discordance among response systems. These results again highlight the fact that the use of only one masure alone to assess a construct such as anxiety is not to be recommended since it can lead to erroneous conclusions. In assessing results, the response topography of the interaction of these various behaviors needs to be evaluated in the context of a specific situation.

One method for assessing the reative importance of the three major components of behavior is the determination of both the short-term *and* long-term effects on these components produced by a particular treatment procedure. In the Gatchel et al. (1977) study, only short-term improvement, measured immediately after therapy administration, was evaluated. An important question is whether the improvement demonstrated by the various treatment groups is maintained when speech anxiety is assessed at a later point in time, and whether it generalizes to other speech situations dissimilar to the one in which the anxiety assessment procedure was first conducted. One might expect that an effective and active therapeutic procedure would produce long-lasting clinical improvement which would maintain its strength and effectiveness over time. A recently completed study by Gatchel, Hatch, Maynard, Turns, and

Taunton-Blackwood (1979) investigated these questions in a study comparing three treatment groups: (1) the combined muscle, relaxation/biofeedback group, which was found to produce the greatest reduction of physiological responding in the earlier study by Gatchel et al. (1977); (2) the false-biofeedback control group, which produced a significant reduction in speech anxiety in this earlier study; and (3) a systematic desensitization group. This group was included in the study because, even though the active muscle relaxation group was demonstrated to produce therapeutic improvement greater than an attention-placebo group by Goldfried and Trier (1974), no study has assessed whether that technique is as effective as the standard systematic desensitization procedure in reducing anxiety.

Results of this investigation indicated that, again, the false-biofeedback placebo group demonstrated as much reduction in self-reported speech anxiety as the two treatment groups. Physiologically, however, it did not demonstrate as much reduction. One month later, when subjects were again tested for speech anxiety but in a different speaking situation (a larger room with an audience of 6 individuals, rather than the smaller room with an audience of 2 observers used in the earlier speech evaluation), the self-report improvement was maintained in all groups including the false-biofeedback group. Thus, the improvement effects produced by this placebo condition do not appear to be illusory or short-lived. Indeed, in an earlier study by Paul (1967), maintenance of gains over 2 years for treatment groups in his therapy evaluation study including an "attention-placebo" group were found. In the Paul study, however, the "attention-placebo" group did not improve as much as the desensitization group. In our study, though, the false-biofeedback group did improve as much as the active treatment groups. The perception by subjects in this group that they had active control over an anxiety-competing response, heart rate, appears to have significantly influenced their self-report of anxiety. Future research will hopefully provide further insight into the mechanisms involved in biofeedback treatment processes, especially those involved in the perceived control-placebo phenomenon.

CONCLUSIONS AND SUMMARY

In reviewing a number of case studies, it was noted that there was some evidence for the clinical effectiveness of heart-rate biofeedback training when heart rate is a major component of the anxiety response. Results of control-group studies are somewhat mixed as to the clinical utility of this training technique. Additional research is sorely needed. Studies such as those by Gatchel and colleagues, moreover, have demonstrated the important role that placebo factors play in heart-rate biofeedback therapy. This placebo factor in biofeedback treatment was found to exert its major effect on the self-report component of behavior. It was found that, although subjects in a false-biofeedback/placebo treatment group did not display as much of a reduction in physiological responding as did the other treatment groups, their self-report component of anxiety did show a clinically significant reduction. Moreover, this clinical improvement was not illusory or short-lived. Subjects in this false-biofeedback/placebo condition maintained their improvement when evaluated at a later time and in a different speech situation. These findings clearly demonstrate the important role that placebo factors play in producing and maintaining fear reduction in a biofeedback-treatment program.

The great amount of publicity and exaggerated accounts of "cure-all" biofeedback techniques that appear with relative regularity in the news media may help to make a false-biofeedback control group an extremely powerful placebo condition due to the large amount of therapeutic expectancy/demand characteristics produced by this publicity. Because of the demonstrated power of this placebo condition, the inclusion of it in future therapy-evaluation research, especially biofeedback studies, will insure an adequate test of the therapeutic effectiveness of presumed active clinical techniques.

One of the major shortcomings of the EMG-biofeedback control-group studies which suggested the therapeutic effectiveness of EMG-control training was the lack of an adequate placebo control group. Additional research is required which effectively controls for placebo factors before any conclusive statement can be made concerning therapeutic effectiveness of EMG-biofeedback procedures for the treatment of fear and anxiety.

An important question that requires investigation is whether biofeedback techniques and/or biofeedback-placebo techniques are more effective than less expensive and easily administered procedures, such as muscle-relaxation training and meditation exercises, in reducing anxiety. A study by Garrett and Silver (1978) recently demonstrated that desensitization was as effective as combined alpha and EMG biofeedback training in reducing test anxiety. Also, Gatchel et al. (1979) found that desensitization was equivalent to muscle relaxation/heart rate biofeedback in reducing speech anxiety. Indeed, Lang (1977b) has recently suggested that these easily administered methods are preferred because they appear to be equally effective. He based this suggestion on some of his recent research, which assessed the comparative effectiveness of heart rate biofeedback, EMG biofeedback, and simple meditation exercises similar to those developed and employed by Benson and colleagues (Benson, Rosner, Marzetta, & Klemchuck, 1974) in producing heart-rate slowing. He found no major differences among groups. Lang's suggestion, however, may be somewhat premature. His research compared techniques without exposing subjects to an anxiety-producing situation. The fact that there were no differences found under these training conditions does not necessarily mean that they would have equal impact on reducing anxiety. For example, in the study by Gatchel et al. (1977), there were no differences found among the heart-rate biofeedback, muscle relaxation, and combined muscle-relaxation and heart-rate biofeedback groups in the amount of heart-rate deceleration during the actual training sessions. However, when subjects were exposed to a stress situation, the combined muscle relaxation/heart-rate biofeedback group demonstrated less of an increase in heart rate and skin conductance level than the other two groups. A combination of techniques may therefore prove to be more effective across all behavioral component systems than separately administered techniques. Birbaumer (1978) has recently pointed out the potential effectiveness of pattern biofeedback training in the treatment of anxiety disorders. Indeed, Schwartz (1975) has reported that feedback for an "integration" pattern (simultaneous decrease of both heart rate *and* blood pressure) produced greater subjective experiences of relaxation and calmness. It should be noted, though, that these results were from only a single-session experiment. Additional research in such combination training techniques is obviously needed.

One important line of research which has yet to be initiated is the examination of individual differences in response to biofeedback treatment. The majority of studies reviewed in this chapter were between-group designs which employed biofeedback modification of one specific target behavior across all subjects without independently determining whether the target behavior was a major component of anxiety for a specific individual and whether an individual could learn to exert a significant amount of control over the specific physiological response. Individual differences in physiological responding have been well documented (Lacey, 1967). It would appear necessary to take into account these individual differences in deciding upon the target physiological response to tailor the biofeedback training around. Heart-rate biofeedback therapy may not be effective for all clients, but only for those who can learn to voluntarily control heart rate, and for whom heart rate is a dominant component of the anxiety response, as was the case in the successful individual treatment results reported by Blanchard and colleagues and Gatchel (1977). For other individuals, some other physiological response, or combination of responses, may be dominant. For still other individuals, the physiological component of anxiety may not be dominant but, rather, the cognitive component may be more important. In such cases, some form of cognitive behavior therapy would need to be employed. The concept of tailoring therapy to each individual client is not new in the field of behavior therapy (Goldfried & Davison, 1976). Such "tailoring" will be required for biofeedback therapy techniques with the expectation that biofeedback will not be clinically useful for all patients. This is an important area for future research exploring the clinical application of biofeedback in the treatment of fear and anxiety.

One last point needs to be highlighted concerning the clinical utilization of biofeedback techniques. It may be unrealistic to expect that learning to control a physiological response or responses will lead to an overall decrease in general anxiety. Rather, its usefulness may be primarily in the realm of allowing an individual to more adequately cope with some specific situational stress. Providing only a small number of training sessions would not be expected to lead to an overall reduction in the general anxiety level of an individual. This would probably require many months, and even years of training. However, such limited training might be capable of having some momentary impact on an aversive situation, since the subject will now have a self-control skill that he can actively employ to compete against the momentary experienced anxiety. Researchers must be careful not to become too grandiose in expecting global reductions in the anxiety state of an individual in studies providing only limited biofeedback training.

Chapter 10
The Placebo Effect and Biofeedback

Edward S. Katkin and Steve Goldband

INTRODUCTION

The purpose of this chapter will be to critically review the empirical evidence that has accrued in support of the specific therapeutic efficacy of biofeedback techniques. That biofeedback is a therapeutic tool firmly entrenched in the clinician's armamentarium is well documented by both the phenomenal growth of the Biofeedback Society of America and by the emerging concern of clinicians about how they might best use the technique and protect themselves from legal and ethical liabilities (see Fuller, 1978). Biofeedback research, having its origins in both learning theory and psychophysiology, has been adopted and applied clinically by psychiatrists, clinical psychologists, and therapists of diverse backgrounds and levels of training. Hence, what to some looks like a new and challenging area of basic research, to others looks like the latest form of effective therapy.

To be more specific, it seems clear that from the vantage point of the clinician, biofeedback therapy is, in fact, a variation of psychotherapy. Like any other form of psychotherapy, its effects may be either treatment-specific or nonspecific. Psychotherapy (as well as pharmacomedical therapy) is notorious for having nonspecific, or placebo, effects, and biofeedback indeed has been viewed by some researchers in the field as "the ultimate placebo" (Stroebel & Glueck, 1973). Whether biofeedback treatment has specific therapeutic qualities that can be shown to be independent of demand characteristics, therapist bias, subject expectancy, base rates of spontaneous remission, and other nonspecific factors must be demonstrated through properly controlled studies. In this chapter, we will briefly review some of the issues that must be addressed in evaluating the specific effectiveness of treatment in general and biofeedback in particular; then we will review the empirical evidence on the effectiveness of a variety of clinical applications of biofeedback therapy; and finally, we will suggest some possible strategies for future research in the area.

CONCEPTUAL ISSUES CONCERNING PLACEBOS

Strictly speaking, the concept of "placebo" refers to the use of a pharmacologically inactive agent which is administered to a patient for a variety of reasons including the failure to identify a diagnosable disorder. Often, but not always, the placebo administration results in symptom reduction. It must be understood that the positive therapeutic results of placebo administration should be relatively random. That is, it is expected that a placebo will show neither disease specificity nor interpatient reliability. In either of these events, the agent would lose its definition of placebo and be reclassified as an active treatment even if its mechanism were not well understood. It is not the case that a treatment is classified as a placebo because its mechanism is not understood; rather, it is classified as a placebo precisely when its mechanism is well understood and there is no pharmacologically valid reason for it to succeed.

In the area of psychotherapy, the term placebo has been borrowed from medicine and employed frequently. In the psychotherapeutic sense, therefore, a placebo should refer to a type of treatment that is known to have no valid specific treatment effect, but which superficially appears to the patient to be an active form of psychotherapy. In other words, placebo psychotherapy should look like therapy, should sound like therapy, and *should cause the patient to expect that he is receiving therapy*. Nevertheless, the treatment should be understood to have no valid theoretical mechanism by which it could actually *be* therapy.

Types of Therapy

Traditional psychotherapy. When one takes the definition of placebo seriously, it becomes apparent that an attempt to evaluate the effectiveness of traditional psychotherapy against placebo effects is an extremely difficult task. There is not sufficient specificity of knowledge about the process of effective therapy to warrant assumptions about credible interpersonal interactions that would be placebos. How does one create a continuing interpersonal relationship that is presented to the client as therapy and which can be demonstrated to be incapable of actually being therapy? By definition, it appears there can be no genuine and credible placebo forms of psychodynamic psychotherapy. For this reason, much of the outcome research in psychotherapy has focused on the role of patient expectancy, therapist warmth or empathy, and other supposedly nonspecific aspects of therapeutic relationships as approximations to placebo effects. To the extent that many theorists

(Frank, 1973; Shapiro, 1971; Truax & Mitchell, 1971) suggest that these factors are central to the successful utilization of therapeutic procedures, they become active treatment effects and not placebos.

Behavior modification. Among the many reasons for the rapid development of the field of behavior modification in the past two decades has been the greater precision with which outcome studies of its effectiveness could be designed. Many forms of behavior modification, especially systematic desensitization, specified precise theoretical mechanisms supposedly independent of therapist characteristics which were expected to produce operationally defined symptom reduction. Within the context of this greater definitional precision, a variety of placebo possibilities presented themselves.

Controlled research on placebo effects in behavior-modification techniques has usually focused on the issue of patient expectancy for success. The general strategy has been to define a placebo therapy that is presented to the patient with instructions that lead the patient to expect success as much as he would with the actual treatment. Careful steps are usually taken to equate time and effort of the therapist and to create conditions that are similar to the actual therapy. Finally, care is usually taken to ensure that there are no experimenter bias or demand characteristics associated with the outcome evaluation.

As careful as these procedures have been, it is not clear that they have been entirely effective. Kazdin and Wilcoxon (1976) have suggested that the procedures of the treatments themselves, rather than any characteristics of the therapist or demands of the evaluation, may generate different expectancies for success because of differential credibility. Kazdin and Wilcoxon have criticized the employment of the traditional ''attention-placebo'' control strategy in which the experimenter simply designates his placebo as any treatment that is roughly equivalent to the actual treatment in terms of its attentional demands on the patient. They have argued that there is no empirical evidence to support the assumption that differential expectancy is actually induced in the control groups. As alternatives, Kazdin and Wilcoxon have suggested that use of the ''treatment element control strategy'' or the ''empirically derived control strategy.''

The *treatment element control strategy* involves using the identical elements of treatment in the control group as are used in the treatment group, but presenting them in such a manner as to render them theoretically inert. Thus relaxation exercises may be conducted and a relevant hierarchy of fear-inducing scenes presented, but the time sequence of the presentation is such as to render the procedure theoretically ineffective. Alternatively, the treatment element control strategy may be used to isolate specific components of treatment (such as when comparing a desensitization therapy group with a group that gets identical therapy without the relaxation component). According to Kazdin and Wilcoxon, this strategy also suffers from insufficient attention to empirical evidence concerning the degree to which it engenders equal degrees of expectancy for success in the control group.

The *empirically derived control strategy* is an attempt to assess the extent to which the control strategy successfully creates equal expectancies of success. This can be done either through pilot studies prior to treatment or through postexperimental interviewing of the subjects.

All of these approaches to the development of placebo control in behavior therapy have focused on the concept of expectancy for success as the crucial medium by which a placebo may operate. In a recent paper, Lick and Bootzin (1975) have focused on the mechanisms by which such placebo effects may work in research on systematic desensitization. Assuming that there is no magical or mystical manner by which "expectancy" leads to therapeutic success, Lick and Bootzin state that to "the extent to which placebo manipulations work, they must operate by mechanisms different from those traditionally proffered to explain the efficacy of (systematic desensitization)" (1975, p. 926). They then suggested the following possible mechanisms. First, expecting to be cured of fear, the patient may test the expectancy by exposing himself to the feared object, thus leading to some increment in extinction of the fear. Second, expectancy changes may encourage greater attention to cues that represent improvement, leading to greater report of gain. Third, since the expectancy of improvement would be cognitively dissonant with knowledge that one still had symptoms, the dissonance may create heightened drive to continue testing reality as described above, further facilitating the actual desensitization process. Lick and Bootzin have speculated that any or all of these mechanisms might lead to changes in a patient's self-report of therapeutic gain as well as to changes in overt behavior indicative of such gain.

Biofeedback therapy. Biofeedback therapy, as a specific subtype of behavior modification, seems unusually resistant to the shortcomings of placebo control described above. Even if a placebo therapy for biofeedback should lead to differential expectancy, it is unlikely that the mechanisms postulated by Lick and Bootzin would be applicable. First, self-reports of symptom reduction are rarely the primary criteria for success in biofeedback; quantitative changes in psychophysiological response activity are. Second, if the effect of the placebo is to cause the subject to voluntarily test the therapeutic hypothesis, it is less likely to be carried out in the visceral arena. A patient can approach a feared object in a runway more readily than he can reduce his blood pressure just to test a hypothesis. Biofeedback for tension headaches, migraine headaches, or other forms of subjective distress is theoretically presumed to work via specific measurable alterations of muscle tension, vasoconstriction, skin temperature, etc. While a placebo treatment may significantly alter the patient's subjective report of symptom reduction, it is not likely that it would similarly result in altered physiological patterns. To be sure, it is still possible that proper placebo-control research on biofeedback may be contaminated. As we will discuss in detail below, the subject's employment of physical or cognitive mediators may be crucial to the success of biofeedback. To the extent that use of such mediators can be construed as "work," the subject's expectancy for success may influence his motivation to work and as a result, his success with the technique. Nevertheless, our thesis is that biofeedback therapy by its very nature is a better candidate for careful evaluation with placebo control than other forms of behavior modification; and it is certainly better suited for such research than general psychotherapies. With that in mind, the following section will briefly review the current research literature on the clinical effectiveness of biofeedback therapy along a number of dimensions, specifically analyzing the degree to which treatment effectiveness has been demonstrated to be greater than that attributable to a placebo.

REVIEW OF EMPIRICAL LITERATURE

Because a great deal of this literature is extensively reviewed in the other chapters of this volume, we will here only briefly summarize the current status of the various areas of clinical applications of biofeedback.

Striate Musculature

Clinically, there have been three main foci of interest in skeletal muscular biofeedback: (1) rehabilitation of patients who have lost normal musculature control; (2) headache treatment; and (3) anxiety reduction and relaxation enhancement.

Rehabilitation. Successful use of muscle potential feedback in rehabilitation medicine has been reported by several investigators, who have used three general treatment strategies. These include
1. Detecting and feeding back neuromuscular potentials in currently nonfunctional muscles in conditions such as hemiplegia, nerve injury, and reversible physiological block.
2. Inhibiting undesired motor activity and increasing voluntary control of desired movement in conditions such as spasmodic torticollis and various kinds of spasticity.
3. Coordinating and controlling a series of muscle actions in conditions such as chronic fecal incontinence.
As reviewed by Basmajian and Hatch in Chapter 6, there have been a number of case studies reporting the effective use of EMG biofeedback in the above three areas. The use of electromyogram feedback for muscular rehabilitation is impressive in that many of the patients treated were from a chronically disabled population in which traditional rehabilitation efforts had been par-

tially or completely unsuccessful. Yet the successful reports all take the form of case studies, and there are no placebo-controlled experimental evaluations of the specific efficacy of biofeedback.

Treatment of tension headache. Although muscular feedback has met with little success in the treatment of migraine (Sargent, Green, & Walters, 1973; Wickramasekera, 1973b), electromyographic feedback from the frontal muscles of the forehead has been reported to be effective in relieving tension headache. For example, some positive results have been reported for the treatment of tension headaches both in case reports (Budzynski, Stoyva, & Adler, 1970) and in one controlled study (Budzynski, Stoyva, Adler, & Mullaney, 1973). However, the particular role of biofeedback has not been clarified by the case studies, as the successful technique usually included both laboratory feedback training and home relaxation practice. Even in Budzynski et al.'s (1973) controlled outcome study, the authors emphasized that they considered daily practice outside of the laboratory setting "critical." In addition, it is highly likely that the attention-placebo control used in this study was quite ineffective, for two-thirds of the subjects in Budzynski et al.'s control group dropped out of the study complaining that "the training was having no effect on their headaches" (p. 290). Only half as many subjects in their no-treatment control group dropped out. Further research is clearly needed to investigate the specific versus the interactive effects of muscle-tension biofeedback and relaxation in the treatment of headache.

Anxiety reduction and relaxation enhancement. Muscle-tension feedback has been used, with mixed results, in a number of uncontrolled attempts to reduce anxiety and/or enhance relaxation. Alexander and Smith have exhaustively reviewed this research in Chapter 7 of this text. The general conclusion that can be made concerning this literature is that, although there is considerable face validity for the effective treatment of skeletal muscular disorders with electromyographic feedback, as well as a considerable number of clinical case reports to support its use, there are no adequately controlled experiments to document the specific effectiveness of such treatment. Similarly, there appears to be no conclusive evidence that muscle-tension biofeedback treatment is effective in reducing anxiety. As with studies of tension headache treatment, those studies reporting positive results used other procedures, such as EEG theta feedback, relaxation, or systematic desensitization, combined with muscle-tension feedback to achieve positive results. Thus, the specific role of muscle-tension feedback in the alleviation of anxiety remains unclear.

Heart Rate

There has been a great deal of experimental work aimed at controlling the human heart rate, much of it done with normal subjects. These studies have typically shown that normal subjects can raise and lower their heart rates to some extent and can decrease heart rate variability, but there are some limitations on how the results of these studies may be interpreted. It is difficult to assess whether the small decreases in rate obtained were the results of the feedback process itself or could be accounted for by general relaxation or could be more efficiently obtained by other methods. Studies of physiological changes associated with transcendental meditation (Wallace, 1970; Wallace & Benson, 1972) and progressive relaxation (Paul, 1969), for instance, have found heart-rate decreases that equal and sometimes exceed changes obtained in biofeedback experimentation.

Typically the clinician has not adopted cardiac-rate biofeedback techniques for the purpose of raising or lowering heart rate in and of itself. Rather, the strategies more commonly employed have been to use cardiac rate feedback to treat a specific type of cardiac dysfunction, such as cardiac arrhythmias.

Cardiac Arrhythmias. In his chapter (Chapter 3), Blanchard has concluded that the treatment of cardiac arrhythmias with biofeedback continues to look promising. However, definitive data on the issue are still lacking. A great deal of additional controlled outcome research is needed.

Blood-Pressure Control

Again, Blanchard has reviewed this research in his chapter. To summarize, although there have been a series of successful attempts to train normotensives to control their blood pressure, mixed results have been found with hypertensives. None of the reported clinical studies has presented evidence that the magnitude of blood-pressure decrease obtained by biofeedback is greater than could be obtained by simple methods of suggestion, relaxation, or merely adapting to the training situation. Grenfell, Briggs, and Holland (1963) have detailed the enormous power of placebo and expectancy effects in the pharmacological treatment of hypertension; there is little reason to believe that biofeedback treatment is less vulnerable. Controlled experimental studies are needed to tease out the specific components that lead to successful outcome.

Electrical Activity of the Brain

One of the most widely investigated and widely publicized applications of biofeedback involves control of the electrical rhythms of the brain. Much public attention has been focused on the specific application of biofeedback to the control of alpha rhythm. Outside of the research laboratory, this research was often seen as ushering in a new era of mind-body unity, and many centers sprang up around the country (usually near campuses) promising that the feats of Eastern Zen and Yoga masters, who had practiced for decades, might soon be possible for anyone with a feedback machine and a few days of training.

Several years and many research articles later, reports of alpha biofeedback sound much more cautious. Kuhlman and Kaplan (Chapter 5) have provided an excellent review of this research. They conclude that, "whatever therapeutic value the 'alpha state' may have, it does not necessarily include the alpha rhythm." Placebo and nonspecific factors can account for a large component of therapeutic effectiveness.

Epilepsy. While many lay centers have been "experimenting" with alpha feedback for "growth experiences," a number of investigators in research laboratories have been attempting to evaluate the potential effectiveness of brain-wave feedback for the alleviation of disorders such as epilepsy. Again, Kuhlman and Kaplan have provided a thorough review of this research in Chapter 5. Their basic conclusion is that "clinical improvement in epileptics can occur as a result of EEG feedback training." However, the exact mechanisms involved in its success are not known. A great deal of additional research is needed before EEG feedback can make a significant contribution to the treatment of epilepsy.

Summary

Shapiro and Surwit (1976) reviewed the biofeedback literature a few years ago and arrived at the gloomy conclusion that "there is *not one* well-controlled scientific study of the effectiveness of biofeedback and operant conditioning in treating a particular physiological disorder" (p. 113). Unfortunately, our update provides little reason to revise that conclusion. On the other hand, Katkin, Fitzgerald, and Shapiro (in press) have pointed out that although there have not been well-controlled experimental demonstrations of the efficacy of biofeedback therapy, the dramatic results reported with neuromuscular reeducation and with amelioration of seizure disorders were "suggestive" of active treatment effects. Rogers and Kimball* however, have adhered to stricter criteria. Discussing neuromuscular biofeedback research, they have concluded that while "most of these studies showed fantastic results, several sources of internal invalidity . . . may well account for these effects. These studies are . . . inadequate in their control for the operation of even the most weak confounding variable . . ." (p. 43).

Whether one wishes to focus on the "fantastic" outcomes of the clinical case studies or on the inadequacy of the experimental controls employed to evaluate them, the inescapable facts are not only that no well-controlled

---

*Rogers, T., & Kimball, W. H. Nonspecific factors in biofeedback therapy. Paper presented at the meetings of the Society for Psychophysiological Research, Philadelphia, Pa., October, 1977.

scientific studies of the effectiveness of biofeedback therapy exist, but that there are remarkably few attempts to demonstrate such effectiveness. Researchers too frequently have omitted appropriate controls from their experiments. Even single-patient case reports rarely include appropriate baseline controls or other single-case control observations which might enhance the credibility of their conclusions (Hersen & Barlow, 1976). In the next section, we will discuss some of the placebo-control conditions that we believe may be of value in biofeedback therapy research.

SUGGESTED PLACEBO CONTROLS

Milieu and Instructions

Although the mechanisms by which differential "expectancy" may lead to therapeutic change is not well understood, it remains incumbent upon the serious biofeedback researcher to try to control differential expectancies of success between experimental and control subjects. To this end, it is recommended that any instructions leading to an expectancy of positive (or negative) treatment outcome be administered equally to experimental and control subjects. Furthermore, it should be obvious that all subjects should be run in similar if not identical environments. No-treatment control groups or waiting-list control groups are insufficient in the face of the implicit promise of treatment communicated by the impressive electronic equipment used to provide biofeedback. Following equivalent treatment of experimental and control subjects, it is necessary to *assess* empirically their expectancy for successful treatment (Lick & Bootzin, 1975). Only when such an assessment reveals equivalent expectancy can any subsequent treatments be viewed as adequately similar to justify comparison.

After guaranteeing that control subjects are exposed to the same procedures as treatment subjects with respect to treatment milieu and instructional set, how can the biofeedback researcher provide the control subjects with credible placebo treatment? Our position on this issue is quite simple: the researcher must first possess some articulated sense of the mechanism by which the active treatment effect of biofeedback works, and then choose a form of placebo treatment which resembles it in all or most respects, but which cannot be expected to operate according to the principles of effective treatment of the biofeedback.

It has been argued (Black, Cott, & Pavloski, 1977) that the effective principles by which biofeedback operates are the principles of operant reinforcement. As Katkin et al. (in press) have noted "biofeedback . . . may be seen to derive from the scientific fields of psychophysiology, learning theory, and the experimental analysis of behavior. Specifically . . . it emerged from the exciting milieu of basic research on the instrumental conditioning of autonomically mediated behavior'' (p. 2). Although there has been continuing controversy over the role of so-called mediators in the operant control of autonomic responses (Crider, Schwartz, & Shnidman, 1969; Katkin, 1971; Katkin & Murray, 1968; Katkin, Murray, & Lachman, 1969), there has been little controversy about the basic assumption that reinforcement procedures can be used to modify autonomic behavior. Some investigators have interpreted these phenomena in traditional operant terms while others have preferred to couch their interpretations in the language of ''skills acquisition'' or motor-skills learning models (Lang, 1974). Still others have focused on the role of reinforcement in modifying cognitive mediators of autonomic responses (Katkin, 1971). Regardless of the theoretical system preferred, it is widely recognized that effective control of autonomic functions requires the establishment of response-reinforcement contingencies, for it is apparent that noncontingent reinforcement of a response should have no therapeutic effect. The implications of the use of noncontingent versus contingent reinforcement as a strategy for placebo control are discussed below.

Noncontingent Reinforcement

The simplest and most straightforward type of placebo control is false-physiological feedback. It should be understood that false physiological feedback is essential to a noncontingent reinforcement paradigm, for it is likely that, given veridical feedback, the subject will generate implicit reinforcements based upon knowledge of results gleaned from the feedback. Using false feedback and providing reinforcements (such as monetary rewards) that are randomly or noncontingently applied appears to be a proper control strategy. Further, one can choose to yoke control subjects with experimental ones, so that each control receives a number of noncontingent reinforcements equivalent to the number of contingent reinforcements received by an experimental subject.

As appealing and simple as this strategy appears, nevertheless it presents formidable problems. As Rogers and Kimball (see footnote) have pointed out, if the subject can discriminate his physiological response, he will soon discover the noncontingency of feedback and inquire one way or another about the discrepancy. This is a particularly acute problem in the area of skeletal-muscular feedback. Hanna, Wilfling, and McNeill (1975) used false feedback of laryngeal muscle potentials in a case study of biofeedback treatment for stuttering. When they presented their patient with an interspersed control period of false feedback, he complained that the feedback instrument had gone out of adjustment. Obviously, this patient was able to discriminate veridically his laryngeal muscle tension and could perceive a discrepancy between his own internal feedback and the external feedback.

Hanna et al.'s (1975) report highlights the nature of a serious problem engendered by the use of false physiological feedback — if a response is discriminable, false feedback will not be credible; therefore, false feedback may only be a useful control strategy for nondiscriminable responses. However, Brener (1977) has argued, and we agree, that response-reinforcement contingencies require that reinforceable responses be discriminable. He has demonstrated that subjects are able to learn to make sensory discriminations of their visceral responses and that such discrimination enables them to gain voluntary control over those responses. Brener, Kleinman, and Goesling (1969) also have demonstrated that subjects who received successful discrimination training of their heart rates showed better heart-rate control. This line of research and theory suggests that if a response is not discriminable, then a response-reinforcement contingency most likely cannot be established. Herein lies a paradox. If false feedback of a discriminable response is employed as a placebo control, it is likely to be detected by the subjects and thereby lose its credibility; if a nondiscriminable response is employed, according to Brener (1977), it is unlikely that the contingent treatment condition will be successful. Hence, despite its inherent appeal, the use of false physiological feedback as a placebo control for biofeedback is probably inappropriate and ineffective.

Alternate Control Strategies

Black et al. (1977) have argued that Brener (and others) has postulated unnecessary "awareness" concepts to explain what are simply instrumental conditioning phenomena. In their view, a major failure of research on biofeedback has been the failure to borrow from the methodological literature on instrumental learning. "It is astonishing that so little of the theoretical and experimental armamentarium of operant conditioning has been mobilized in research on the development of control over (autonomic system) and (central nervous system) responses" (Black et al., 1977, p. 96). Black et al. have argued that research on biofeedback should take as a starting point the wealth of knowledge concerning the parameters of instrumental learning and should systematically study the extent to which these parameters are characteristic of treatment effects in biofeedback.

It is our contention that this advice is not only good research strategy, but that it represents a sound conceptual base for the analysis of placebo effects. Within this paradigm, schedules of reinforcement, timing of reinforcement, magnitude of reinforcement, and other parameters of the operant experiment, can be evaluated for systematic effects on biofeedback treatment. If response to biofeedback follows the empirical laws of operant conditioning, then we can be confident that biofeedback indeed is a form of "active treatment" and not a nonspecific effect. Although Brener's (1977) discussion of the importance of sensory discrimination of visceral events as an essential element of visceral self-control has devastating implications for the use of false feedback as a placebo control, it does not invalidate other strategies which may be logically derived from the operant literature. For instance, if it could be shown that the treatment effect of biofeedback varied systematically with the schedule of reinforcement used, one could conclude that there was an active treatment effect due to operant conditioning. A variety of experimental manipulations are possible in order to gain greater insight into the nature of the active treatment effect of biofeedback. These will be described below.

Delay of reinforcement. It is generally recognized that if reinforcement is delayed, response acquisition is interferred with, and that with very long delays there is no acquisition at all. For those treatment paradigms in which the feedback of physiological function is construed as a reinforcement in itself, the feedback of a physiological response can be delayed in varying degrees. Note that such a procedure, however, is isomorphic with false feedback to the extent that the subject can discriminate his physiological response. Thus it is suggested that in this situation, the subject be given specific instructions indicating that the feedback is truly of his own responses but that the apparatus will delay it in time. If contingent reinforcement is the crucial variable for treatment effect (and not some nonspecific placebo effect), the results should indicate progressively weaker treatment effect as the feedback is progressively delayed.

In a treatment paradigm in which some discrete reinforcer such as a light flash representing money is utilized, the delay-of-reinforcement procedure is more straightforward. Here presentation of the discrete reinforcer can simply be delayed. Once again, if the treatment effect is dependent on a response-reinforcement contingency, slower and less complete acquisition of visceral control should be associated with longer delays of reinforcement.

Partial versus continuous reinforcement. If the effects of biofeedback treatment are attributable to placebo effects, then it is likely that partial reinforcement will lead to outcomes quite similar to those achievable by continuous reinforcement. However, if the effects follow the well-established principles of reinforcement learning, then partial reinforcement schedules should result in slowed acquisition and greater resistance to extinction. With respect to biofeedback treatment, this would suggest that training with partial reinforcement should result in longer periods of symptom relief without remission or reinforcement than would be obtained with continuous reinforcement. This could be tested *in vivo,* or in a laboratory period of extinction training in which all reinforcement is discontinued. Partial reinforcement in a biofeedback paradigm can be carried out on either interval or ratio schedules.

Schedules of reinforcement. It is well established that ratio schedules of reinforcement result in higher rates of responding than interval schedules for simple operant conditioning. It does not follow that autonomic-response conditioning will follow similiar patterns, but it does seem plausible that if the effects of biofeedback are specific to the active effect of response-reinforcement contingencies and not attributable to nonspecific effect, then some clear differentiation of response acquisition should be discernible for ratio schedules of reinforcement as opposed to interval schedules.

One possible technique for providing, say, fixed-ratio reinforcement for heart-rate decrease would be to present the subjects with a visual display that is capable of feeding back each heart beat interval which is longer than a predetermined criterion for reinforcement. On a fixed-ratio schedule, then, the subject would receive the information that he had successfully passed the criterion level only on some fixed proportion of actual successes. For a fixed-interval schedule, the subject would get feedback only if the success occurred after some fixed time period had elapsed. The demonstration that ratio schedules and interval schedules resulted in different acquisition functions would clearly substantiate the notion that the treatment effect was active and not nonspecific.

Black et al. (1977) have demonstrated that in rats reinforced with lateral hypothalamic stimulation, the use of a percentile-reinforcement schedule led to significant differences (57 bpm) between rats reinforced for increases and decreases of heart rate, but that using a reinforcement-density schedule, the rats "displayed neither significantly elevated heart rates nor significantly lowered heart rates" (p. 102). It is not necessary here to go into the detailed reasons for the differing results produced by two techniques of reinforcement. It is important to note, however, that the discrepancies are understandable and, more important, predictable, based on a clear analysis of the effects of these differing reinforcement schedules on the pattern of response acquisition.

Contingency reversal. In order to rule out the possibility that apparent reinforcement effects are attributable to sensitization, the technique of contingency reversal, or bidirectional conditioning, has been employed. It is generally believed that if a subject can show instrumental increases and decreases in the operant level of a response as a function of differential reinforcement, then the response is not likely attributable to a placebo effect. Such considerations have guided much of Miller's early work on the instrumental modification of heart-rate response in curarized rats (Miller & DiCara, 1967). As Black et al. have pointed out, this bidirectional control was originally introduced in operant conditioning as a test for artifactual effects of sensitization or classical conditioning. It is essential to the proper use of this control procedure that a baseline period be employed which is characterized by random presentations of the discriminative stimuli and the reinforcers. This is necessary in order to subsequently demonstrate that both increases and decreases from baseline were actually conditioned.

CONCLUSIONS

We have noted that the short history of biofeedback research is characterized by a dreary record of poorly controlled research. The techniques of clinical biofeedback are clearly defined and the results to date are sometimes dramatic, but the confidence which can be placed in these results is low because there is little evidence bearing on the possible contribution of nonspecific or placebo effects to therapeutic outcome.

False or random feedback, which appears superficially to be an appropriate placebo-control condition, is probably inappropriate and is not likely to resolve the issue of specific versus nonspecific treatment effects. We have suggested that the crucial distinction between an active treatment effect and a placebo effect lies in the degree to which the mechanisms underlying their effectiveness are understood. It is not legitimate to define placebo effects as those which are not understood; rather, a placebo effect is one which leads to positive outcome when knowledge of its mechanism suggests that it should not.

We have argued that the active treatment effect of biofeedback requires the establishment of response-reinforcement contingencies and that the proper elucidation of active versus placebo effects resides in careful analysis of the relationship between visceral learning and systematic manipulations of reinforcement parameters. Among the strategies suggested were delaying reinforcement, varying reinforcement schedules, and demonstrating bidirectional control of responses.

At the beginning of this chapter, we noted that biofeedback is a therapeutic tool that is well entrenched in the clinician's armamentarium. Perhaps more than any other of the clinician's tools, it is susceptible to meaningful evaluation for its specific treatment effect. The tools for this evaluation are available, and hopefully, future research will focus on the demonstration of the specific treatment effects of biofeedback therapy.

Chapter 11
Instrumentation in Biofeedback

John D. Rugh

Clinical and research applications of biofeedback rely heavily upon relatively sophisticated electronic instrumentation. Currently the three most popular clinical biofeedback devices are electromyographic (EMG), temperature, and galvanic skin response (GSR) devices. With these instruments, the clinician may monitor or feedback minute changes in muscle electrical activity, peripheral temperature, and skin resistance, or impedance. A variety of less popular devices are also available which may be used to monitor other functions such as heart rate, stomach acidity, penile erection, mastication, nasality in speech, salivary flow, respiration, brain waves, blood pressure, and anal-sphincter pressure. These instruments extend the clinician's sensory capabilities and may prove therapeutically useful with some stress-related disorders.

Most of the basic principles and technologies employed in biofeedback instrumentation are not new or unique. Basic physiological monitoring devices which display specific body functions have been available and used in research for several decades. What is unique is the widespread clinical usage and belief that physiological functions and disease states may be altered if sufficient information is provided to the organism. The theoretical and practical problems related to this belief are viewed from an instrumentation perspective in this chapter. This chapter will describe and critically evaluate clinical biofeedback instrumentation.

HISTORICAL PERSPECTIVE

Most biofeedback companies began by developing small portable EEG devices during the "alpha obsession" in the late 60s and early 70s. Although the clinical efficacy of alpha training had not been demonstrated, the publicity given a few early investigations created a large market for inexpensive brain wave feedback devices. Claims were made relating the "alpha experience" to self-enlightenment, extrasensory perception, natural "highs," and various therapeutic effects. Many clinicians, hungry for new therapeutic modalities, incorporated alpha training into their practices. Sales were not limited to health professionals. The American public with its fascination for gadgets, mysticism, and psychic powers provided a large market for portable biofeedback devices, which was met by approximately 30 small manufacturing firms.

Inexpensive alpha-training devices were commonly sold through mail-order houses or magazine ads. Many of these devices were of poor technical quality, were subject to artifact, and were grossly misrepresented. Schwitzgebel and Rugh (1975) examined a series of these early EEG feedback devices. Wide variability was found in functional characteristics. Input impedance was found to be as low as 500 ohms on 1 unit. Alpha filter bandwidths ranged from 0.9 to 16.5 Hz, and 5 of 13 devices studied did not employ differential-input amplifiers and were subject to 60-Hz interference. As a method to reduce 60-Hz interference, one manufacturer recommended using the device in large open fields away from power lines.

These early biofeedback devices were plagued with problems. Several units had current drains which limited battery life to less than 15 hours. Unsecured batteries presented a common problem. During shipping, the electronic components were frequently damaged and wires were broken by loose batteries. Inadequate labeling of controls and dials was common. Instruction books, when supplied, were usually inadequate. Specifications, safety considerations, and maintenance instructions were seldom provided. A number of these early biofeedback devices had the circuitry encased in plastic, which prevented trouble shooting and component replacement. Finally, many of these devices were very poor aesthetically.

Although there was a large body of research published regarding electrodes, amplication, and filtering of bioelectric signals, many early biofeedback devices were apparently designed without reference to this literature. It is generally agreed, for example, that the input-impedance of a bioelectric amplifier should be at least 10 times greater than the electrode or source impedance (Geddes, 1972). Electrode impedances are frequently as high as 20 K ohms, yet Schwitzgebel and Rugh (1975) reported 6 or 13 devices tested to have input impedances of less than 200 K ohms. These low-input impedance devices are subject to amplitude errors due to changes in the scalp-electrode impedance. During a training session, the amplitude of the alpha signal appears to increase as the scalp-electrode impedance decreases. With these devices, what is interpreted as learning to control or increase the alpha rhythm may thus be simply a result of changes in the scalp-electrode impedance. This problem points to the need for continuous interaction between the biomedical industry and basic research efforts.

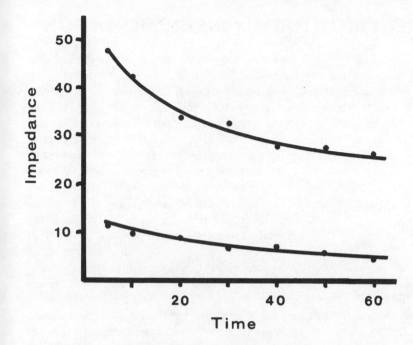

Fig. 11.1. Skin-electrode impedance slowly decreases over time (top curve), which may result in changes in output levels, noise levels and performance. As the bottom curve indicates, this source of error may be reduced if the electrode-skin impedance is made low at the beginning of the session. This may be done by careful cleaning of the skin and "rubbing in" of electrode cream.

Although few, if any, of the behavioral or therapeutic claims regarding alpha training were ever substantiated (Johnson, 1977), alpha training became very popular. A large number of elaborate, well-designed clinical quality brain-wave feedback devices were and still are marketed. These devices are used in a variety of clinical capacities ranging from pain control to weight reduction. Unlike the inexpensive mail-order units, these devices are of good technical quality and are aesthetically appealing. The popularity and sales of these devices are dropping as an increasing number of negative reports are published regarding the therapeutic effectiveness of EEG feedback. With a few exceptions, it is expected that this trend will continue.

As investigators shifted their interest from alpha feedback to EMG, tempera-ture, and GSR, manufacturers broadened their product lines to include these and other feedback modalities. It is interesting to note that this occurred after the public market was saturated with alpha devices. Because of this, one does not find a large number of inexpensive EMG, temperature, and GSR devices designed for public consumption. With a few exceptions, recent devices are designed for and sold only to the clinical market. The characteristics and problems of these later clinical devices are the subjects of the next section.

CURRENT BIOFEEDBACK INSTRUMENTATION

There are currently over 50 small companies marketing more than 150 different biofeedback devices intended for clinical applications. Most of the clinical devices currently on the market do not suffer from the technical and manufacturing problems of the early alpha-feedback devices. Most have differential-input amplifiers (3 electrodes), high input impedance, and good 60-Hz rejection characteristics. They may be used in relatively noisy electrical environments and are very professional in appearance. Battery life is as high as 500 hours on some devices, and others employ recharageable batteries. Putting circuitry in plastic is no longer common, and the quality of instruction books has greatly improved. The devices do, however, have some serious problems which will be discussed later in this chapter. Before discussing instrumentation problems, we will discuss the more serious problem of operator error.

Much of the confusion and many of the misconceptions surrounding biofeedback result from a lack of understanding of the physiological signals being measured. Users of biofeedback devices must have an understanding of the characteristics, natural variations, and limits of the physiological signals they are dealing with. It should be understood, for example, that the surface EMG signal is a small electrical signal which has been found to correlate with muscular contraction. It is believed to be the result of action potentials from muscle and nerve fibers. The signal on the skin surface is the summation of electrical activity originating frequently from more than one muscle. It is most often recorded with surface electrodes and is *not* a measure of "aura" or "psychic energy." For mild to strong muscular contraction, the power spectrum of the muscle signal peaks at about 40 to 60 Hz (Hayes, 1960). A small amount of signal may be observed at frequencies as high as 1000 Hz. Different muscles show slightly different power spectra. There is some evidence that the power spectrum of the EMG signal shifts upward following sustained contraction (Johansson, Larsson, & Ortengren, 1970). Furthermore, the spectrum may shift slightly with different contractile levels (Duxbury et al., 1976). The EMG signal recorded from electrodes placed on the forehead is not necessarily an ideal measure of anxiety, mental anguish, or tranquillity. Rather, it is an indication of the contractile level of the facial, scalp, and neck muscles. Periodic fluctuations of this signal are frequently due to talking, eye movement, chewing, swallowing, and wrinkling of the brow. Each of these activities must be carefully controlled before claims regarding resting EMG levels can be made.

The most common error in using EMG devices is made when interpreting resting muscle activity levels from frontal electrode placements using an integrator. As noted above, this electrode placement picks up a variety of facial muscle activities. The integrator does not discriminate between basal

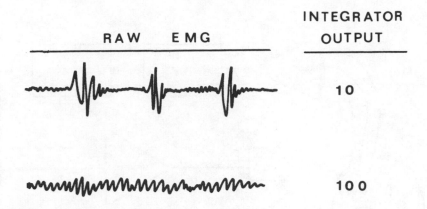

Fig. 11.2. EMG integrators provide an indication of the area under the curve of the rectified raw EMG signal. The same reading may be obtained with quite different signals as indicated in the figure. In the upper trace, a series of eye blinks raised the integrator output level to 100, even though the resting EMG was lower than that of the lower trace.

EMG levels and the large periodic EMG activity associated with swallowing and eye movement. When integrated over several minutes, the resulting readout is more related to the number of swallows than the resting EMG level of the forehead muscles. Many of the dramatic reductions in EMG levels shown in the first few sessions of many published studies are possibly due to the subjects learning not to swallow during trial periods. An examination of the raw EMG signal may provide a more accurate indication of the resting EMG level. Artifacts such as swallows may be easily detected when viewed in this manner.

Hardt and Kamiya (1976) have demonstrated very clearly the importance of attending to instrument characteristics. These investigators compared two popular methods of scoring alpha activity. "Percent time" measures of alpha activity are made by computing the time spent in alpha (above a specific amplitude) and displayed as a ratio of the total trial time period. This measure is very sensitive to changes in the duration of the alpha signal but is not well suited for measurement of amplitude changes. A second method integrates the area under the curve of the alpha signal and thus takes into account both amplitude and duration of the signal. Hardt and Kamiya recorded both measures simultaneously from 16 subjects. They report that the two measures were not equivalent, nor was there a linear relationship between the two measures. The investigators note that these differences may be sufficient to account for the conflicting outcomes of many published reports dealing with alpha training. The authors further recommend the use of the integrated measure to accurately reflect alpha activity and to provide more complete feedback to the

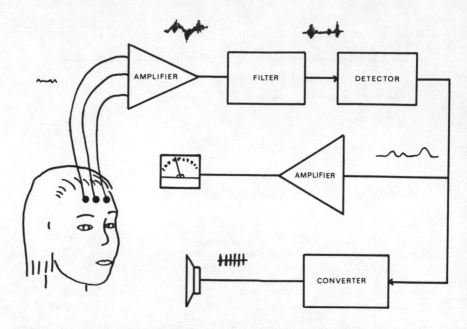

BIOFEEDBACK INSTRUMENTATION

Fig. 11.3. Block diagram of a simplified EMG feedback device. The center electrode is a common, or reference, electrode. Audio and visual feedback modes are shown.

subject. An earlier report by Travis, Kondo, & Knott (1974) is consistent with this conclusion. Unfortunately, most commercial EEG devices employ the time-period measure of alpha activity.

A number of errors in clinical judgments can be made as a result of a lack of understanding of the responses being measured. A clear understanding of the natural variation and the stimuli-response characteristics of skin impedance is necessary to interpret GSR recordings. A case in point is Barnett's (1940) observation that the forearm skin impedance changes with the seasons. The impedance was found to more than double. It was felt this was due to changes in the epidermal thickness but could also be due to simple drying of the skin. If this same change is found on the hand where the GSR is normally recorded, the gradual increase in impedance as summer approaches may be mistaken for an improved ability to relax.

Instruments currently available for clinical work have major weaknesses. It has been the author's experience, however, that the most nagging problems related to biofeedback instrumentation are human. They result from an inadequate study of the physiological system and a lack of understanding of basic bioinstrumentation principles. The user of biofeedback devices should have an understanding of the basic principles of operation of these devices. Detailed knowledge of circuit design is not necessary; however, a knowledge of the input-output characteristics of each circuit is essential.

EMG Operational Characteristics

The small electrical differences between the two active electrodes are amplified about 1 million times by various amplifying stages which are shown here as one stage. Signals which are common to the two active electrodes with respect to the ground electrode are greatly reduced. The amount of reduction of these noise signals is indicated by the common mode rejection figure. The higher the figure, the better the noise rejection. Several "front-end" problems such as electrode polarization, electrode-skin impedance, input impedance, and amplifier noise will be discussed later.

After amplification, the signal is filtered to further suppress unwanted noise and to select the signal desired. Two filters are generally employed. A notch filter selectively rejects 60-Hz noise. A bandpass filter is usually tuned from 90 to 500 Hz and is used to select the EMG signal. Signals outside this range of frequencies are suppressed. It should be understood that the device's noise level is closely related to the filter bandwidth. Narrow-band devices (100 to 150 Hz) will usually have very low noise levels ($< 1.0 \mu$V RMS). These devices, however, will be sampling only a portion of the EMG signal and may not provide an accurate indication of EMG amplitude. Wide-band devices (20 to 1000 Hz) will have higher noise levels but will provide a more representative measure of muscle activity. As will be discussed later, variability in filter characteristics between devices poses a serious problem when attempts are made to compare the work of different investigators.

After amplification and filtering, the EMG signal is rectified and averaged or smoothed. This process is performed by the detector and its associated circuitry. Several methods of signal rectification and signal averaging are possible, which adds to the variability between instruments. Many devices provide the user with a front-panel control, which can be used to vary the time constant or signal averaging. This control sets the degree to which the feedback tone will follow rapid changes in the input signal. With a long time constant, small fluctuations in the muscle activity will not be represented in the feedback signal. Only gross trends will be observed. When the time constant is very short, the feedback signal will follow even the slightest change in input signal. Very short time constants may not be ideal for clinical biofeedback as the subject is flooded with information, confused, and possibly annoyed by the feedback tone. Unfortunately, parametric studies have not been done to determine the optimum time constant. If biofeedback training is based upon operant conditioning (for instance, a shaping process) the nature of the information provided by the feedback signal is a critical factor in the learning process and should be carefully studied.

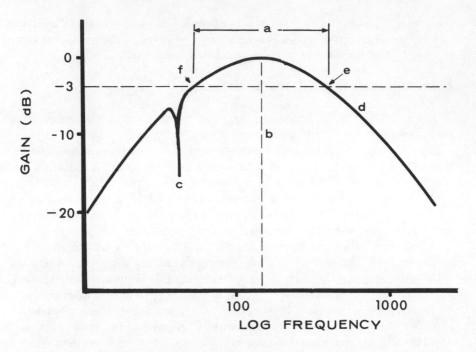

Fig. 11.4. Filter characteristics are usually displayed on a graph of frequency versus instrument gain. Filter bandwidth (a) is normally specified by the upper and lower frequencies (e and f) at which the signal amplitude is reduced by one-half (3 dB). Center frequency (b) is the point of maximum signal gain. The rejection characteristics of 60-Hz filters (c) can easily be determined by this plot. The selectivity, steepness, or "roll-off" of the filter (d) may be specified in dB per octave.

The feedback signal itself may be very critical. Lang (1977) has discussed evidence which suggests that the information-processing demands of the feedback task may not allow the individual to achieve low states of arousal. The feedback signal must be attended to and may produce an orienting reflex continuously working to maintain cognitive arousal. In support of this position, Lang presented data which showed that subjects practicing meditation showed significantly greater heart-rate reductions than subjects receiving feedback. The meditation subjects also showed more stable respiratory patterns and more reduction in frontalis-muscle tension. This position is also supported by the subjective comments of biofeedback users, who often express a preference for slow auditory clicks and long time constants, which carry relatively little information, rather than the high-frequency, short time constants, which provide much more detailed information.

The signal out of the detector is typically a slowly varying DC signal which rises and falls as the muscle contracts and relaxes. The signal at this point may be amplified and displayed on a meter. To be usable in an auditory modality, the slowly varying DC signal must be converted to a signal which is within the auditory range. This is usually done using a voltage-to-frequency converter. This circuit provides an AC output signal whose frequency is dependent upon the level of the DC input signal. Rather than using a pure tone, a series of auditory clicks are frequently used. The frequency of the clicks is dependent upon the DC input signal. The circuit is usually designed such that increases in muscle activity result in an increase in the click rate. Although the relationship between input and output of the converter is usually linear, some manufacturers use nonlinear functions which may be useful in learning. A logarithmic function or transformation of the signal makes changes at the low end of the scale more salient and may thus facilitate learning (Leaf & Gaarder, 1971). Again, this question has not been rigorously tested.

The EMG system described above is very simplified; however, it does contain the essential components of most commercial biofeedback devices. A large variety of "add-on" features are available in most commercial units. Features range from electrode-test functions to digital integrations and derivative feedback modes. Many devices offer threshold controls which can be used to set the upper or lower level of EMG amplitude at which feedback will be initiated. Adjustable bandpass, digital readouts, multiple inputs, light-bar readouts, optically coupled output signals, and RMS signal processing are added features of many current biofeedback devices. Some of the features such as battery- and electrode-test functions reduce misuse of the devices and are highly recommended. Although advertising claims suggest otherwise, it is important to remember that there is no evidence that any of these extra features make the feedback process more therapeutic or clinically relevant.

Temperature and GSR Operational Characteristics

Except for differences in the input stages, the basic operating principles of temperature and GSR feedback devices are similar. Both amplify a slowly varying DC signal and display it on a meter. Many clinical units also convert the DC signal to a tone whose frequency is dependent upon temperature or skin resistance. Temperature feedback devices usually employ a thermistor sensor in one leg of an input bridge or voltage divider. The thermistor changes resistance as its temperature changes. This results in a change in the voltage across the bridge. The voltage is amplified by a low-drift DC amplifier and used to drive a variety of displays.

Traditional concerns of temperature measurement include the problem of response time, that is, how quickly the thermistor follows a change in temperature. Several seconds are usually necessary for thermistors to accurately indicate a temperature change. Generally the smaller-sized thermistors are quicker to respond but are more fragile. The problem of stability and drift is critical to accurate measurement. Temperature devices may give inaccurate

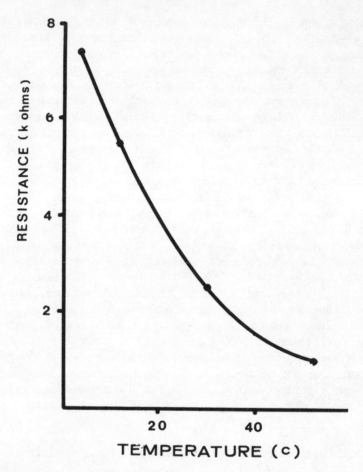

Fig. 11.5. Thermistor probes normally have a nonlinear relationship between temperature change and resistance change. This problem must be compensated for by nonlinear labeling of the meter dial or through electronic means.

temperature readings due to several sources of drift, including battery-voltage drop, ambient temperature changes, component aging, and/or moisture leaking into the thermistor. The thermistor itself is very stable and not usually influenced by aging. Another common concern is the resolution of the temperature device, the smallest change in temperature which can be registered. Temperature changes of as little as 0.0005°C can be indicated with modern thermistors, which provide about 75 ohms change-per-degree-C-change in temperature. A 1°C full-scale meter output is possible; however, it has not been shown that this degree of resolution is necessary for temperature training.

Rather than sensing the resistance of a thermistor, the GSR device senses the resistance or impedance of the body. A small current is passed through the tissue via electrodes placed across the palm or fingers. The flow of current or change in voltage dropped across the tissue is amplified and may be displayed on a meter calibrated in ohms (resistance) or mhos (conductance). There is a very large body of literature on GSR instrumentation which should be reviewed by individuals interested in using this modality (e.g., Edelberg, 1972).

Accurate GSR measurements depend upon a number of factors. Of considerable importance is the nature of the electrodes and the test current through the body. Edelberg, Greiner, & Burch (1960) noted that to prevent tissue damage, the test current passed through the body should not exceed about 11 micro-amps per cm² of electrode surface area. It was also noted that currents of less than 5 micro-amps are too low and the signal is lost in noise. The noise, drift, and battery effect of a variety of electrode materials have been studied by Lykken (1959). Also of interest for users of GSR devices is a paper by Lykken, Rose, Luther, & Maley (1966), which describes procedures to correct for individual differences in the GSR range.

The origin of the GSR response is still unclear. It is generally believed that the GSR is a measure of sweat gland activity. This belief is primarily due to the early work of Darrow (1934), who demonstrated a linear relationship between the rate of secretion of the sweat glands and electrical skin conductance. The response is normally measured on the hands; however, it is also found on the insole of the foot. Human basal skin resistance may range from 5 K ohm to over 1 meg ohm cm². Transient responses following stimulation typically have a latency of about 2 seconds. The response usually reaches a peak after 5 seconds, followed by a slow return to baseline. It must be recognized that the baseline level and transient responses of the GSR are influenced by a wide range of factors including temperature, humidity, sudden noise, sexual arousal, fear, exercise, sex, and race. The GSR is influenced by such a large number of variables that some have argued against using it as an emotional index. An excellent review of GSR research and application is provided by Edelberg (1972). A careful study of this material would seem a necessary prerequisite to the clinical application of GSR feedback.

A broad range of features is available on commercial temperature and GSR feedback devices. Light-bar displays which indicate relative and absolute temperature or skin resistance are increasingly common. Digital displays reading in Fahrenheit or Celsius, a variety of auditory feedback modes and devices with 0.01° resolution are available. There is no evidence, however, that any of these special features make the devices more clinically useful.

Problems in Instrumentation

By what criteria does the clinician select a biofeedback device? What are ideal instrument characteristics? What should the feedback latency be for optimum learning? What feedback modality is most effective? These questions point to the major problem currently facing clinical biofeedback instrumentation. At this time, we do not know how to design instruments for optimum clinical results. Instrument characteristics are usually determined in one of two ways. First, parametric studies may be run in which each instrument characteristic is systemically varied while observing clinical effectiveness. Alternatively, if the mediating mechanisms responsible for the instrument's effectiveness are understood, then ideal instrument characteristics can be deduced from their properties. Unfortunately, there is no body of literature which has explored most biofeedback instrument characteristics, nor is there an accepted theory upon which to determine important functional characteristics.

The lack of agreement upon desirable characteristics is reflected in the variability currently found in clinical instruments. Rugh and Schwitzgebel (1977a) recently ran comparative tests on 11 commercial EMG feedback devices. Wide variability was found in several important instrument characteristics. Filter bandwidth, for example, varied from 55 to 2600 Hz. Center frequency ranged from 60 Hz to a high of 800 Hz. No consistency was found in methods of signal averaging or in calibration procedures. The nature of the feedback signals ranged from pulsed auditory tones to very elaborate frequency-modulated visual and auditory systems. Some instruments provide the user with logarithmic transfer functions; others provide only linear input/output functions. Clearly there is little agreement upon how best to design an instrument.

Most biofeedback devices are currently designed with the simplistic assumption that clinical biofeedback is essentially operant conditioning. The client, for example, learns to reduce muscular tension in a specific muscle which is causing a pathological condition. Devices are thus designed with variable thresholds and adjustable-gain settings to allow standard operant-shaping procedures. Based upon learning theory, feedback latency is kept short to increase the temporal relationship between the level of the EMG (response) and the feedback (reinforcement). Unfortunately, there is little evidence to support the claim that the clinical effectiveness of biofeedback is due to simple operant conditioning of specific physiological responses. To the contrary, the author has noted that frequently those patients who show the most clinical improvement are not the ones who are best able to control the specific response.

The effectiveness of biofeedback may be due to a variety of mediating mechanisms that current biofeedback devices are not designed to augment or enhance. Clinical biofeedback may be effective because it improves motivation, distracts the patient from his problems, produces general relaxation, or helps the subject to identify phobic stimuli. Biofeedback may also be effective by helping the subject to realize the relationship between physiological arousal and different emotional states. Any one aspect or combination of these aspects may account for clinical improvement. Clearly, the design of the biofeedback instrument will be much different if its effectiveness is based upon distraction

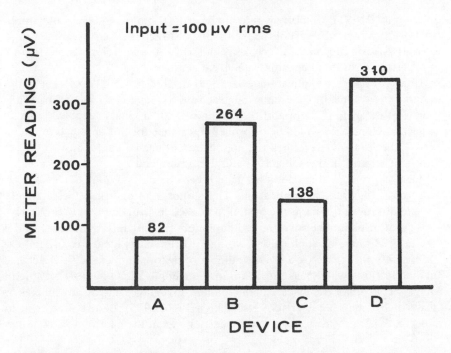

Fig. 11.6. Variability between instrument filters, calibration, and signal-processing techniques result in different devices providing very different results. Meter readings of different instruments are thus not comparable as indicated by this test of 4 different EMG devices.

rather than operant conditioning. If distraction is a salient feature of the therapy, then one would want to design a device along the lines of a pinball machine with lots of bells, lights, and whistles. On the other hand, if changes in motivation and recognition of emotional arousal are key factors, the device would be designed with features which facilitate record-keeping for progress charts and with multimodality capabilities such that more than one physiological parameter could be measured. At this time, the basis of the reputed effectiveness of biofeedback training is not known; thus there is little to guide instrument design.

Some applications of biofeedback instruments are relatively straightforward and preferred instrument characteristics can be indicated. For example, Aarons (1971) described the study of digastric muscle activity related to subvocalization during reading. Certain instrument characteristics would be desirable for this application. The device would ideally have silver-silver chloride electrodes, high input-impedance (> 1 meg ohm), a broad band filter (20 to 1000 Hz) with a 60-Hz notch, a raw EMG output for the chart recorder, and perhaps an integrator to cumulatively store muscle activity during specific trial periods. Also of value might be a logarithmic meter readout calibrated in microvolts RMS. Portability would not be critical, nor would special features such as a calibrated threshold, seven modes of feedback, or a variable time constant. Aesthetic features such as walnut cabinets and chrome knobs may or may not be desirable depending upon the setting.

Consider another application where it is desired to signal a subject in the natural environment of muscular contractions associated with daytime bruxism (teeth clenching). Portability, simplicity, and a binary feedback with an adjustable threshold would be of prime importance for this application. Rugh and Solberg (1974) described the application of such a device in identifying stressful stimuli in the subject's natural environment.

Ideal instrument characteristics cannot be specified without a clear knowledge of the instrument application. The author is often asked the relatively simple question, "What is the best biofeedback instrument to buy?" Clearly, this question cannot be answered without more specific information regarding the desired range of application. No one instrument is ideal for all applications. Currently there are a sizable number of instruments available. Each has unique features which make it useful in some applications but unworkable in others. The author has discussed the relative advantages and disadvantages of many instrument characteristics elsewhere (Rugh, 1975). Before attempting to select an instrument, the user must specify in detail the nature of his application.

Even after specifying instrument requirements, the potential consumer will likely have difficulty selecting a device. Manufacturers' specification sheets frequently lack pertinent information on instrument functional characteristics. For example, a recent survey indicated that 21 of 44 items of advertising literature did not provide specifications on input impedance (Rugh & Schwitzgebel, 1977b). Other important characteristics such as filter characteristics are frequently not given or are inadequate. When specifications are provided, they frequently cannot be used to compare between instruments, as different manufacturers use a variety of test procedures to measure the same instrument characteristic. A variety of test procedures are available to test instrument characteristics. Manufacturers often select the test procedure which makes their device look the best. Clearly, there is a need for standardized test procedures and agreement upon which specifications should be provided.

There is no clear relationship between the technical quality of biofeedback devices and the price. The input impedance of one $695 EMG device, for example, was found to be only 13 K ohm, while 7 less expensive devices were found to have input impedances greater than 1 meg ohm. The noise level and 60-Hz suppression of a $49 EMG kit were comparable to 4 units which ranged in price from $450 to $695 (Rugh & Schwitzgebel, 1977a). The buyer simply cannot pay a high price and assume that he is purchasing a technically sound instrument. The question remains, however, whether there is a relationship between the technical quality of a device and the clinical effectiveness of the device.

Use and Maintenance

When accurate measurements of various physiological responses are required, the user must:

1. Understand the characteristics and natural variation of the physiological
   parameters being recorded.
2. Be familiar with the instrument being used, the device's limitations, and
   how the signal is processed.
3. Have knowledge of possible artifacts which can influence the signal or
   affect the instrument.

There is little evidence that most users of biofeedback devices currently
have the foregoing knowledge. Apparatus sections of published articles are
frequently inadequate or incomplete. EMG microvolt readings are frequently
used as if they were absolute rather than relative values. Reductions in hand
temperature due to evaporative cooling of perspiration have been ignored.
Electrode polarization has been responsible for some very impressive learning
curves caused by the amplifier slowly providing less and less output signal due
to DC offset driving the amplifier into cutoff. Some of the early alpha training
has been suspect because muscle activity was not controlled. Eye movements
and eyelid quivers are believed responsible for some of the reported "alpha
bursts." Many analog filters used in EEG devices have a tendency to "ring"
at their tuned frequency. These and other sources of artifact can lead to
misinterpretation of data and overly optimistic clinical results. The instrument
user must study all aspects of instrument usage and be extremely careful in
interpreting results.

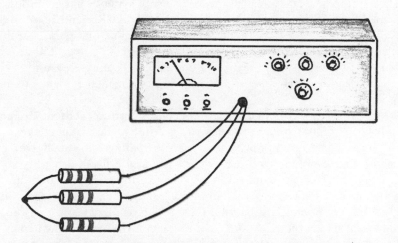

Fig. 11.7. Instrument noise level should be tested so that realistic goals may be set for the
instrument user. Three 10-K ohm resistors connected to the device's input as indicated above will
provide an indication of instrument noise level.

Tips on Instrument Usage

1. Many electrode creams and gels are transparent and difficult to see. Adding food coloring will reduce chances of inadvertently "shorting out" two electrodes with electrode paste.
2. The technical characteristics vary between instruments; thus, users must develop normative data for each device. It is often useful to use the device on a series of "normals" to develop standards.
3. Electrodes and batteries are the most common maintenance problems. Ensure that spares are available. Check electrodes weekly for intermittent opens using an ohmeter. The degradation in performance due to weak batteries may be observed by temporarily placing known weak batteries in the device.
4. Electrical noise from nearby apparatus should be evaluated by energizing the apparatus and observing correlated changes in the feedback device.
5. Electrostatic discharges can be a source of artifact and can be very damaging to solid-state electronic devices. Nylon clothing, carpets, and upholstery should be avoided. Aerosol sprays are available which can be used to reduce static buildup.
6. Electrodes should be routinely checked for wire breakage, particularly at points of stress.

SUMMARY AND DISCUSSION

The development of clinical biofeedback instrumentation has not followed a systematic, orderly pattern as is common in traditional scientific or clinical pursuit. Before research has even begun to determine optimum instrument design characteristics, over 50 companies are marketing over 150 different devices. Thousands of clinicians are currently accepting fees for services using devices for which there is virtually no experimental evidence to guide their design.

Wide variability exists in clinical biofeedback instrumentation. Comparisons between clinics or laboratories using different instruments cannot be made. Instruments vary in filter characteristics, calibration, signal-averaging methods, time constant, and the type of feedback. This variability is not accurately reflected in manufacturers' specification sheets, which are frequently incomplete. Even when instrument specification sheets are provided, they are frequently unusable because there are no standard tests or procedures used to measure the specifications. The problem is further complicated by the refusal of some manufacturers to supply schematic diagrams of their products. Without such material, the user cannot adequately understand the functional characteristics of his instrument.

The problems in instrumentation appear to stem from a strong interest in clinical application at the expense of attending to instrumentation and basic studies of the mechanisms responsible for clinical effectiveness. Of the 48 papers which have been published in the first issues of *Biofeedback and Self-Regulation*, only two have remotely dealt with instrument design characteristics. A lack of technical sophistication is further indicated in a review Ancoli and Kamiya (1977). These investigators found that 38 of 46 studies reviewed did not provide adequate information in instrument-filter characteristics.

Pressures from several sources are expected to prompt a change in this rather bleak instrumentation picture. Mild pressures from the Federal Food and Drug Administration have already resulted in a reduced number of false advertising claims and improper labeling. The Biofeedback Society of America will likely impose severe restrictions upon manufacturers who display at annual meetings.

Finally, the ultimate pressures to improve instrumentation will come from clinical failures. Biofeedback devices are not now designed for optimum clinical performance, and less than optimum clinical results are being obtained. Much of the clinical effectiveness of biofeedback devices is undoubtedly due to expectancy and patient tolerance. Both of these effects, however, will soon be exhausted. To be a viable clinical tool, biofeedback training and instrumentation design must be based upon careful systematic research.

Chapter 12
Biofeedback Research Methodology: Need for an Effective Change

Bernard Tursky

One has only to examine the back issues of *Psychophysiology*, *Psychosomatic Medicine*, and various psychological and medical journals for the past few years to realize the degree of proliferation of experimental and clinical biofeedback research studies. Hundreds of laboratory studies have been published to demonstrate that a consistent learning effect can be achieved in various autonomically controlled physiological response systems as a result of reinforcing a unidirectional response in these systems. These reported results are usually small in magnitude but statistically significant (Katkin & Murray, 1968; Kimmel, 1967, 1974). Attempts have also been made to utilize biofeedback training techniques to shape the physiological response functions that relate to a number of psychological, psychosomatic, and physiological disorders ranging from simple nervous tension to migraine headache and essential hypertension. Several recent review articles and book chapters (Blanchard & Young, 1974; Miller & Dworkin, 1977; Shapiro, Mainardi, & Surwit, 1977) indicate that the demonstrated effectiveness of the use of biofeedback as a therapeutic technique is unclear. These references illustrate a lack of confidence in the therapeutic value of biofeedback as presently used. In the conclusion of their review of the clinical literature, Blanchard and Young make these statements: "Based on this summary, it would seem premature to hail biofeedback training as a panacea for psychosomatic and other disorders." "Wholesale therapeutic application of biofeedback techniques cannot be supported by available data." "Without a doubt, biofeedback techniques must be regarded as experimental."

Miller and Dworkin (1977) in their chapter on critical issues in therapeutic applications of biofeedback, state that "to date the therapeutic applications of biofeedback have had an exorbitantly high ratio of enthusiastic claims to evaluated fact.'' These statements of concern for the clinical effectiveness of biofeedback suggest that the present concept of biofeedback and its methodology should be carefully evaluated.

The purpose of this paper is first, to overview the general methodology and some of the strategies utilized in biofeedback research and clinical studies, second, to argue that the limited success of this technique in laboratory studies and the reported failure of biofeedback to produce long-term results in many clinical applications may be related to the methodology and strategy most commonly utilized, and third, to suggest some possible alternative to this methodology based on proven engineering and psychological concepts.

BIOFEEDBACK METHODOLOGY

The discussion of biofeedback methodology can be divided into two distinct areas, one dealing with the technical development of instrumentation and the other, perhaps even more significant, dealing with the strategies developed and utilized by biofeedback researchers and therapists to try to achieve the ultimate goal of therapeutic success. Because Chapter 11 (of this volume) by Rugh deals with issues of instrumentation, only the latter area will be discussed here.

It is obvious that over the past ten years the expanded research and clinical interest in biofeedback has resulted in rapid and dramatic progress in the area of biofeedback instrumentation and methodology. Companies specializing in the production of quality biofeedback equipment have been organized and are flourishing. The development of integrated circuits has made it possible to reduce the physical size of biofeedback equipment so that portable devices are now available for home use. The utilization of special-purpose transducers and signal processors has resulted in significant noise reduction and an increased reliability in signal production. The only facet of biofeedback methodology that remains relatively unaltered through the years is the feedback display.

Audio and visual displays are almost universally used as response consequence signals in biofeedback research and clinical applications. Occasionally these reinforcers have been linked to monetary or esthetic rewards (Shapiro, Crider, & Tursky, 1964; Shapiro, Tursky, & Schwartz, 1970; Benson, Shapiro, Tursky, & Schwartz, 1971). The basic assumption is that a light flash or tone burst presented as a consequence of a specific alteration in an organ system function will provide the individual with information about alteration in that physiological measure. It also assumes that this response-contingent information can be utilized by an organism to voluntarily control or, at the very least, therapeutically modify the contingent physiological function. Concretely put, it means that a light flash contingent upon the production of predetermined fluctuation in blood pressure is providing the individual with information that is meaningfully associated with that change in blood pressure, and that repeated delivery of this response-consequent information will eventually alter the individual's blood pressure level in the reinforced direction. It is even deemed possible that this procedure could reduce the individual's blood pressure from a hypertensive to a normal level.

The literature to date does not clearly support this notion of permanent or voluntary alteration or control. The experimental studies have indeed demonstrated that operant conditioning of the physiological functions controlled by the atuonomic nervous system is possible. However, this learning effect in many instances has been relatively small in magnitude, and the evidence for therapeutic usefulness has been ambiguous and sporadic.

To explain this lack of success, an examination of the literature must be conducted to separate the successful from the unsuccessful areas of biofeedback research and treatment. A comprehensive review for this paper is impractical. Fortunately, the review articles by Blanchard and Young (1974), Miller and Dworkin (1977), Shapiro, Mainardi, and Surwit (1977), and the chapter by Blanchard in this text provide enough information to make reasonable distinctions between clinical successes and failures. The success reported in the treatment of certain clinical and psychological disorders are clouded by the use of self-report and observational measures to evaluate success and failure. Miller and Dworkin (1977) suggest that a number of factors must be considered in evaluating the therapeutic effectiveness of biofeedback. They argue that patients cyclically feel better or worse, and initially seek treatment when they are feeling poorly. Thus, any new treatment may be grossly overestimated in the self-report of a patient since it fits in with the natural fluctuations of the severity of the disease symptoms.

This consideration makes it difficult to evaluate self-report data about the incidence and severity of some of the psychosomatic and psychological problems that have been treated with biofeedback. The evaluation of tension and migraine headache studies as well as reduction of anxiety may be particularly affected by this treatment-seeking behavior. The positive self-reports of reduction of incidence and intensity of these chronic pain syndromes may be explained by this and other placebo effects. As A. K. Shapiro (1960) points out, these placebo effects can be clinically useful; however, one can imagine less expensive and less time-consuming methods of producing such placebo effects.

For disorders that can be evaluated by more objective criteria, such as the relearning of muscle function or the control of essential hypertension, some very interesting progress is reported. One needs only read the other chapters in this volume in order to gain an appreciation of some of these advances. There have been numerous illustrations of the successful therapeutic use of biofeedback training, indicating that this procedure can be effectively used to alter some disease states. Why were these studies successful while others failed? Does the answer lie in the disease state being treated, in the physiological response system being trained, in some particular aspect of the methodology being used, or does it lie in some fortuitous combination of all these factors? One possible answer to this question may lie in the experimental and therapeutic strategies utilized in biofeedback training.

BIOFEEDBACK STRATEGIES

Let us examine some of the strategies that have been devised and employed to strengthen the reinforcing effect of the response consequence. The simplest of these is the manipulation of instructions. In the early biofeedback research, investigators intentionally masked their instructions (Shapiro, Crider, & Tursky, 1964) to demonstrate that learning was due to the response-reinforcer interaction. Both the introduction of regulations governing the use of deception in laboratory studies and the hope that more specific instructions would increase the biofeedback learning effect produced a movement toward greater specificity of instruction. These specific instructions were designed to help the subject choose advantageous strategies to produce the desired effects. Brener and colleagues clearly demonstrated the added experimental effectiveness of instructional manipulations (Brener, Kleinman, & Goesling, 1969).

A second biofeedback strategy relates to the type of feedback and reinforcer utilized in each study. They range from a simple binary presentation of a light flash or tone burst for each successful production of a criterion response to a complex presentation of proportional audio or visual feedback related to the ability of the subject to alter the tonic levels of the physiological measure under investigation. Simple and complex combinations of binary and proportional feedback have been employed in various biofeedback studies. Young and Blanchard (1974) found that auditory binary and proportional feedback did not produce differential results in helping subjects to learn to control heart rate. However, in the most recent study, Colgan (1977) tested the effect of binary and proportional feedback on bidirectional control of heart rate. Using a meter for proportional feedback and a light flash as a binary indicator of success, he found that proportional feedback was superior to binary and that the addition of binary signal does not enhance control. Lang and Twentyman (1974) found that by utilizing a complex analog computer display, the best results were produced for teaching subjects heart-rate control.

One innovative strategy that is presently being investigated is the use of classical conditioning to enhance the effectiveness and specificity of the auditory or visual responses consequence. Furedy and Poulos (1976) have been utilizing this procedure in the training of heart-rate deceleration. Subjects are first conditioned to produce a large deceleration in heart rate by pairing a tilt table UCS to a simple visual CS. The subject is then instructed to visualize the tilt every time he sees the CS in the biofeedback training period. Thus, this new CS of light plus visualization of tilt becomes a meaningful heart-rate deceleration response consequence. Experimental results from the utilization of this strategy have been promising.

Another strategy concerns the controlled use of somatomotor activity. The early concerns about the validity of operant conditioning of physiological behavior because of somatic involvement (Obrist, Webb, Sutterer, & Howard, 1970; Katkin & Murray, 1968) has been replaced by the rationalization that any mediating influence that can assist a patient in gaining useful control over a malfunctioning physiological system is beneficial. Brener (1974) advances the argument that correlative physiological behaviors should be considered to be components of a general behavioral adjustment of which the measure to be manipulated is one component. In other words, alteration of breathing or the tensing or relaxation of the musculature may be part of patterns of response that accompany a desired change in heart rate or blood pressure. If this is correct, these coincidental responses should not be eliminated by instructions. Schwartz (1972) discusses this phenomenon in terms of a patterning of physiological behavior. He argues that certain patterns of physiological relationships exist as related measures and, therefore, operate under certain interactive constraints. Reinforcement of one must necessarily have an effect on the others in proportion to their phasic or tonic correlation with the measure of interest. Schwartz (1974) also treats the notion of biological constraints in terms of limitations imposed on the subject, such as the physiological and psychological states of the patient, the instructions provided by the experimenter, the neural integration of functionally related physiological system, and the range of possible responses with a given organ system. Schwartz (1974) and Miller and Dworkin (1977) both touch briefly on the idea that a major constraint on physiological learning may be the imcompatability of the response to the response consequence. Elmore and Tursky (1976) have recently suggested that a possible reason for the variable and limited therapeutic success of biofeedback may be a direct result of a lack of selective associability between the response and the reinforcing signal.

For a particular organism, it has clearly been demonstrated that certain stimuli are highly associable with certain consequences while others are not. Garcia and Koelling (1966) demonstrated this principle of selective associability beyond any doubt. They placed thirsty rats in an operant situation in which they drank water flavored with saccharine in the presence of light and white noise. For half the rats, the response consequence that followed was a strong electric shock to the feet; for the other half, the response consequence was exposure to x-rays or ingestion of lithium chloride, which induces sickness and vomiting. When later tested to ascertain which elements of the stimulus (lights, noise, or sweet taste) were responsible for the obtained suppression of drinking, Garcia and Koelling (1966) found that those rats which had been shocked would not drink freely of sweet-tasting water in the presence of noise and light. Those rats which had been made ill drank plain water in the presence of noise and light, but avoided sweet-tasting water.

Clearly, the notion of meaningful consequence (in terms of the selective associability of responses and their reinforcers) in biofeedback experiments has not been considered systematically. In nearly all the studies conducted, the response consequences have been some visual and auditory stimuli. Here, a desired response such as an incremental reduction in systolic blood pressure is produced by the subject and a tone sounds or a light flashes. What, by way of natural association, do flashes of light and bursts of noise have to do with changes in the internal systems implicated in the regulation of heart rate, blood pressure, skin temperature, and muscle tension? It is hard to believe that a visual or auditory stimulus initiated by a small change in systolic or diastolic blood pressure can influence the complex physiological control system that regulates blood pressure. In Fig. 12.1, the complex network of interacting neural and physiological systems that are involved in the regulation of human blood pressure is shown. The sensory biofeedback response consequence (visual or auditory) is not shown in this diagram. It must find its way into the system through the auditory or visual cortex before it can exert any influence

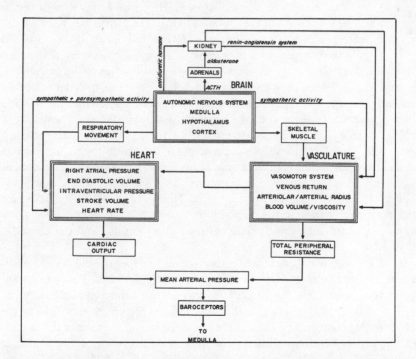

Fig. 12.1. Schematic diagram summarizing the physiological mechanisms which are involved in the regulation of arterial blood pressure. (Reprinted from David Shapiro, Richard S. Surwit, "Learned Control of Physiological Function and Disease," in *Handbook of Behavior Modification and Behavior Therapy*, edited by Harold Leitenberg, 1976, p. 109. Reprinted by permission of Prentice-Hall, Inc., Englewood Cliffs, N.J.)

on the autonomic nervous system and through that avenue on the blood-pressure control system. Similar diagrams can be developed for most of the physiological measures that we have systematically tried to influence with sensory biofeedback. This illustration demonstrates the lack of selective associability between the sensory-response consequence and most of the physiological responses controlled by the autonomic nervous system.

ALTERNATIVE METHODOLOGY

What can be done to restructure the prevailing biofeedback experimental methodology to take into greater account the idea of the selective association principle? In other words, how can we select response-consequent signals that will be directly associable with the particular autonomically mediated physiological process that we want to alter? The answer may lie in approaching the problem from an engineering viewpoint. Noback (1967) has argued that an understanding of servomechanisms can be useful for gaining insight into certain control activities in the nervous system. He points out that most neural control is accomplished by closed-loop systems that utilize negative or degenerative feedback to maintain homeostasis or constancy in the internal physiological systems (examples are temperature, blood pressure, heart rate).

Mulholland (1976) in a number of recent articles has pointed out the importance of understanding engineering feedback systems in order to design better and more meaningful biofeedback studies. The importance of the time and phase relationships between the physiological response and the feedback signal is discussed. His remarks are primarily directed toward the relationship between the visual response consequence and the conditioning of various components of the central nervous system-mediated EEG signal. These arguments may have even greater application to the physiological functions controlled by the autonomic nervous system. The linkage between audio and visual input and change in heart rate, blood pressure, and temperature seem more out of phase than the linkage between these stimuli and the centrally mediated EEG response.

Feedback in electrical engineering terms describes specific electronic modifications of amplifiers widely used in servocontrol systems. Feedback amplifiers differ from simple amplifiers in that a portion of the output signal of the amplifier is returned (feedback) to the input stage of the instrument. The phase and amplitude relationship between the feedback output signal and the incoming input signal determines the operational characteristics of the amplifier system. Out-of-phase (degenerative) feedback causes a reduction of output gain and greater stability; in-phase (regenerative) feedback causes an increase in gain and a reduction in stability.

If it can be argued that the "biofeedback" process is analogous to the use of signal feedback in electrical engineering, some thought has to be given to which of the above-described relationships could best accomplish the clinical goals of the biofeedback process. Since the goal of biofeedback is to enhance the occurrence of a particular physiological response to the point where this alteration becomes permanent and voluntary, it would seem to indicate that the in-phase (regenerative) feedback model is more appropriate if proper precautions to avoid oscillation are taken.

The present use of sensory feedback in the form of tones and lights as reinforcers of appropriate responses results in the return or feeding back of information to the subject that is different in character or out of phase with the subject's physiological output signal. To carry the analogy further, it might be argued that the cerebral processing of the sensory response information may act as a phaseshift network that alters the phase relationship between the output and input signals. This out-of-phase (degenerative) feedback results in small but consistent changes in physiological functioning that cannot be altered beyond a certain level. This stabilization effect has been demonstrated by the small but consistent results achieved in many of the laboratory and clinical studies that utilize sensory feedback, and it has been demonstrated that increased amounts of training do not necessarily produce greater alterations in the physiological function that is being manipulated. Thus, out-of-phase (degenerative) feedback seems to reduce the possibility of achieving voluntary control of autonomic functions.

In Fig. 12.2, an equivalent circuit diagram of the biofeedback system is shown. The complex feedback transfer function (FTF) made up of the subject's sensory perceptions, the neural connections between the audiovisual input, the brain, and the autonomic nervous system, must produce a time and phase alteration in the information delivered to the organ system under manipulation.

It should, therefore, follow that the feedback amplifier model that biofeedback should emulate is the in-phase (regenerative) model. The response-consequent signal should be as similar as possible to the input signal, both in waveform and phase relationships, so as to make the feedback path as direct as possible. This manipulation would alter the phase-shift circuitry to produce an in-phase, input/output relationship.

How can the phase relationship between the physiological response and its consequent stimulus be altered? One clear solution to this problem is to eliminate some of the sources of time lag and phase shift. Theoretically, this goal would be achieved if the feedback stimulus could have a direct input into the afferent pathways that connect the function controlling the physiological behavior being manipulated. There are three available modalities of afferent input: exteroceptive, which respond to external agents; proprioceptive, which are primarily associated with body position and movements; and introceptive, which are associated with visceral activities.

It is critical to note that one implication of this classification is that the feedback stimuli (visual and auditory signals) used in the major proportion of

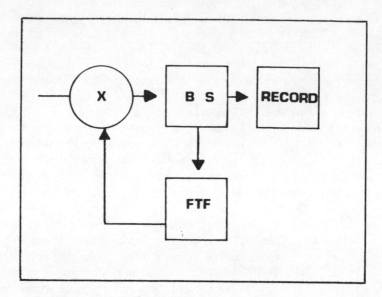

Fig. 12.2. Equivalent Circuit Diagram of a Biofeedback System. In this example, a particular physiological system (X) of the subject's (O) is evaluated. The Biofeedback System (BS) consists of a preamplifier, a signal processor, and a feedback display. The Feedback Transfer Function (FTF) is comprised of the subject's sensory perceptions of auditory or visual reinforcers, neural connections between audio-visual input, the brain, the autonomic nervous system, and the organ system under manipulation.

biofeedback studies do not produce direct input into the afferent systems controlling the behaviors being manipulated.

How can we explain these examples of successful application of biofeedback therapy? The success of the provision of visual and auditory feedback in the "retraining" of lost skeletal muscle-group function may be characterized in terms of reestablishing perception of the patient's neurologically powerful source of information. The hemiplegic subject must relearn to attend to such sensory information as he or she has utilized formerly. The sensory-feedback stimuli provided in this instance may need to serve only as discriminatory stimuli to cue the perception of *kinesthetic sensation* provided by the training movement of the affected limb.

Much of the biofeedback research is concerned with responses which are innervated by the autonomic nervous system. The question of why a study such as that by Engel, Nikoomanesh, and Schuster (1974) was so effective with the autonomic nervous system-mediated rectal sphincter muscles is extremely crucial. In that study, the use of visual feedback (polygraph record) and the additional feedback of actual rectal muscle distentions caused by an inflatable balloon inserted into the rectum resulted in therapeutically significant improvement in all six patients studied. It is my belief (though this view is not shared by Dr. Engel) that the signals from the balloon inflation actually served to produce an interoceptive response signaling a change in the sphincter musculature. The visual polygraph displays only served to direct the patient's attention. Thus, the feedback stimulus operated directly upon the response system via the natural neural afferent pathways.

The highly successful Kristt and Engel (1975) hypertension study provides an indication of the viability of the hypothesis that a physiological function (in this instance, blood pressure) can be successfully altered when an effective response-consequent signal is chosen. A long-term effect was demonstrated in a three-phase study designed to train patients to use biofeedback to lower their blood pressure in the hospital and then to utilize a home version of the hospital procedure to maintain their lowered pressure. It was found that all patients in this study reduced their blood pressure to normotensive levels and maintained this reduction during a 3-month follow-up. The authors speculate that the patients involved in this study learned to directly regulate their peripheral vascular resistance. The effective feedback at home in this instance cannot be the visual response-consequent signals provided in the laboratory, since these were not used during the 7-week follow-up period at home. Instead, there is a strong possibility that the continuing use of the blood-pressure cuff and the previously learned biofeedback training procedure provided proprioceptive and interoceptive input in the form of the reduction of pressure and the phasic reduction of koratkoff sound or pressure pulses in the cuff to enable the system to "learn" to control blood pressure level.

A third example of effective in-phase afferent feedback is related to the use of biofeedback to modify sexual functioning. Genital responsivity provides naturally effective afferent feedback. Penile tumescence and vaginal sensations can be conceptualized as natural in-phase feedback devices. Sensory feedback in this instance serves the purpose of a discriminative stimulus.

The suggestion that is being made on the basis of the observed success of biofeedback applications and our brief look at the afferent feedback systems is that the external consequent stimuli should be chosen with an eye for those which are most likely to result in actual afferent input to the response system being manipulated.

It seems reasonable to suggest that each physiological response function can be examined and analyzed to enable the researcher or clinician to choose the most appropriate external response consequent signal for that function. It can now be argued that response consequences which are more in concert with naturally occurring afferent information will be more effective in producing sustained control of the response system. The rectal balloon, the blood pressure cuff, and the movement of paralyzed limbs are all examples of such meaningful response consequences already in use. Carrying this argument even further, one can see the possibility of utilizing heating or cooling of the skin as reinforcers to alter circulatory dysfunctions and even the possibility of manipulating internal control systems such as the baroreceptors in the carotid sinus for training a reduction of blood pressure. The important point is to realize that possibly there is a way to expand the domain of successful application of biofeedback through modification of the type of response consequences arranged by the investigator.

CONCLUSIONS

Biofeedback as a clinical tool has gained popularity without clearly demonstrating its effectiveness in most areas of investigation. A review of the most often utilized methodology and strategies indicate that a major improvement in the technical elements of the biofeedback process has been achieved. The weak link in the system seems to be the connection between the physiological response system and the reinforcer. Audio and visual response consequences are remote from and out of phase with the physiological response system. Several strategies for improving this relationship have been discussed in this paper. Among the most innovative are the use of classical conditioning to enhance the stimulus-response relationship and the use of response consequences that are more selectively associable with the physiological measure being treated. In my opinion, if the effective clinical use of biofeedback is to be realized, an effort must be made to solve the problem of providing an effective response consequence.

Chapter 13
General Discussion and a Review of Recent Results with Paralyzed Patients*

Neal E. Miller

One of the difficulties in discussing the chapters in this book is the wealth of material that has been presented. I have selected for discussion the following topics that appear in one or more of the chapters.†

NEED FOR EXPERT KNOWLEDGE ABOUT CLINICAL CONDITIONS

One of the excellent points that came out of Basmajian's stimulating chapter is the need to know the essential details about the specific field to which one is applying the technique of biofeedback. The knowledge of the technical details of biofeedback and of the principles of learning is not enough. One must know about the clinical condition with which one is working and/or in many cases have close collaboration with a medical specialist in that field. For example, Basmajian pointed out one has to have correct knowledge about the muscles

* The work on paralyzed patients described here was supported by U.S. Public Health Service Grant HL 21532 and by the Department of Rehabilitation Medicine at Goldwater Memorial Hospital.

† The papers discussed correspond to Chapters 2, 3, 4, 6, and 12 of this text. As indicated in the Preface, these chapters are partially based on papers delivered at a biofeedback symposium held in the Spring of 1977 at the University of Texas at Arlington, at which I served as a discussant (Gatchel & Price, 1977).

involved in holding the shoulder in place — something that he had to discover — before one knows what response to record and reward. To carry the argument beyond his example, in other cases one has to know whether or not the symptom one is trying to reverse is a physiologically necessary compensation for some underlying pathology. Similarly, certain symptoms of muscular tension, physical pain, or visceral disturbance may serve some rewarding function (in psychiatric terms, a primary or secondary gain) for the patient. To treat these cases effectively, a knowledge of psychotherapy is needed. As the new area of *behavioral medicine* develops, new types of training will be needed to teach medical specialists more about behavioral science and to teach psychologists and other behavioral scientists more about physical medicine. These points have been discussed in more detail elsewhere (Miller, 1978; Miller & Dworkin, 1977).

BIDIRECTIONAL TRAINING

In training patients to relax, I am pleased to note that Basmajian pointed out that it is often useful to train them to tense a muscle as well as to relax it in order to get the contrast between these two responses. Similarly, when he wanted to train patients to tense a muscle, he often found it necessary also to train them to relax it, not only to get the contrast but also to prevent them from remaining tense all the time when actually what they needed was a phasic response of tension followed by relaxation. Weiss and Engel (1971) have used bidirectional training in the treatment of premature ventricular contractions.

In his chapter, Blanchard pointed out that one of the features of Engel's procedure in dealing with hypertension was to train his patients to increase blood pressure as well as to reduce it and hence emphasize the contrast between these two opposite responses (Kristt & Engel, 1975).

A bidirectional training procedure was also used in an early systematic case study of learned reduction in blood pressure reported from my laboratory (Miller, 1972).

In addition to the value of the contrast between the two directions, which helps to clarify for the patient what he is doing and what the sensory consequences of it are, bidirectional training gives the patient more practice in producing changes and keeps up his motivation because he is repeatedly succeeding in producing appreciable changes instead of constantly straining to produce a small change after he has already gone about as far as he can in a given direction. Finally, bidirectional performance clearly demonstrates learned control, both to the patient and the therapist. The ability to produce a change in either of two specific directions could scarcely be a nonspecific placebo effect. We need more research specifically aimed at comparing the effectiveness of bidirectional with that of unidirectional training.

EVALUATION OF THERAPEUTIC EFFECTS

Basmajian has reported the encouraging experience of having patients discard their short leg braces. But, as he knows, there are large piles of discarded crutches around various shrines throughout the world. Fortunately, Basmajian has also reported an excellently designed study in which the effects of physical therapy alone are compared with an equal amount of time divided between physical therapy and EMG feedback. The need for such a study is shown by the fact that the patients given physical therapy alone showed improvement, indicating that although they had apparently reached a plateau under the previous conditions, they still had untapped potential for improvement. While the patients with EMG feedback did still better, Basmajian did not report any indices of the statistical reliability of the difference. We need more controlled studies of this kind on larger numbers of cases. Certainly, the preliminary results to date on the use of feedback in rehabilitation, as well as in the therapy of a number of other conditions, are promising enough to merit, indeed to demand, the effort required to conduct the rigorous tests necessary to determine therapeutic effectiveness. As ever increasing percentages of medical expenses are being paid by third parties (insurance companies or the government), one can anticipate increasing demands for proof of therapeutic effectiveness. Thus, rigorous studies will have cash value for the clinician.

Blanchard's excellent review of applications to cardiovascular dysfunctions clearly points out what needs to be done to evaluate therapeutic effectiveness. I am glad to note that he does find some better evidence than was available at the time of his earlier review (Blanchard & Young, 1974).

Blanchard has emphasized the value of a series of truly systematic case studies. To this I would add that such studies can be particularly valuable when enough thorough evidence is available on a prior history of failure to respond to alternative types of treatment. This prior history must be detailed enough, however, to be sure that there was not an initial period of favorable response to the prior treatment which, because of its transience, was later discounted. Furthermore, the follow-up must be extensive enough to be sure that any improvement observed during treatment by biofeedback was not merely another such transient effect. The rigorous prior history of longstanding difficulty is necessary to control for a number of factors that can make an ineffective treatment appear to be effective. One of these is the remarkable ability of the body to heal itself. Another is the powerful placebo effect. Finally, there is the fact that patients with fluctuating chronic conditions usually come for treatment when they are feeling worse than usual and are discharged from treatment when they are feeling better than usual. Thus, there is likely to be a double selective factor making the treatment appear to be more beneficial than it actually was. Factors that can inflate the estimate of the effectiveness of treatment have been discussed elsewhere (Miller, 1978: Miller & Dworkin, 1977).

NEED FOR GOOD EQUIPMENT

Tursky has emphasized the need for good equipment and the potentialities of recent advances in electronics to supply such equipment. To this I would add that the demands on biofeedback equipment are much greater than those on equipment for other types of psychophysiological applications. In ordinary psychophysiological applications, the subject has no knowledge of the responses he is producing and usually no motivation to change them. The biofeedback situation is strikingly different; the subject is trying to cause a signal to change in a given direction, and he knows when it does change. If it is easier to produce the change by an artifact than by the response that the experimenter thinks he is recording, the patient will learn to produce the artifact; he may be completely unaware of the fact that he is producing the change in some therapeutically irrelevant way. This puts unusually high demands on the design of the equipment and the way the experimenter uses it.

TRANSFER FROM THE LABORATORY TO LIFE

When biofeedback is used to train the patient to produce one type of change, for example, warming the hands, in order to have an effect on a different type of phenomenon, for example, a headache, Blanchard has pointed out the desirability of collecting data to determine the relationship between the two. Without such a relationship, it is highly questionable to attribute the improvement to the training in the temperature. I heartily agree with this point. It is a pity that the kind of data that he calls for has not been collected more systematically and frequently.

The foregoing problem does not come up where the training is aimed directly at a function that is the symptom: for example, high blood pressure. In that case, there is another problem: does the training transfer from the laboratory to a measure of blood pressure in the physician's office? If it does not do this, it obviously is not useful. But even if the training does transfer to the physician's office, the question remains of whether the patient has merely learned to reduce his blood pressure whenever it is being measured so that he may be fooling the physician into taking him off anti-hypertensive drugs that he really needs when he is out under stressful conditions of life and not concentrating on controlling his blood pressure. In the case of blood pressure, this question is not yet easy to answer short of using a portable device that involves a chronic catheter into an artery. That is why special efforts should be made to check for improvements in clinical signs such as the condition of the grounds of the retina.

In the case of cardiac arrhythmias, it is now technically feasible to have patients carry around a portable recording ECG and to have a computer score the records in order to determine baseline levels in the life situation both before and after training. Engel and Bleecker (1974) have used such devices to secure follow-up data on some of their patients. Unfortunately, no one has used them yet in extensive before-and-after studies.

During the latter stages of training, Engel and Bleecker (1974) have used the procedure of gradually introducing periods without feedback in order to help the patients to perform without the need for special equipment. To the extent that patients can learn to discriminate the response they are making, they can substitute their improved perception for the biofeedback devices. Such substitution greatly facilitates transfer from the laboratory to life.

CORRECTING MISPERCEPTIONS

Engel and Bleecker (1974) have reported that some of the patients with premature ventricular contractions (PVCs) mistake the skipped beats, which they can feel, for the normal state of affairs. These patients become anxious when their heart is beating normally; because they cannot feel it, they are afraid that it has stopped. It is easy to see how such a misperception might reinforce the irregular beats. Engel reports that correcting this misperception is an important part of therapy. Similarly, Dr. Gordon Ball (personal communication) has reported that some patients with bruxism (abnormal grinding of the teeth) feel a tension in their jaws which can be relieved by clenching them. Using the EMG to demonstrate to these patients that clenching their teeth increases muscular tension instead of relieving it seems to play a significant role in their therapy.

ROLE OF IMAGERY

The chapters by Geer, by Lang, and by Tursky all deal with attempts to discover how to produce larger changes in visceral responses. Geer indicates that when different scripts are used in behavior therapy, feedback on the responses that they produce can be used to guide the therapist in how to produce a script that will be most effective in eliciting the desired response from a particular patient. Lang presents intriguing evidence that in eliciting anxiety as measured by an increase in heart rate, scripts involving imagery of the patient's responses are more effective than those involving imagery of the environmental situation. While I do not question the importance of his results, I wonder whether or not at this point we can be sure that it always is the action that produces the effects rather than the results of the action, results which might be considered to be part of the total stimulus situation. In one of his examples, a man was told to imagine that he was completely out of control, trembling and vomiting, while there was a crowd of people around. I wonder whether it was the imagery of the responses *per se* of vomiting that caused his heart rate to increase or the imagery of the vomit and of the people watching him being completely out of control. I daresay that this script might have produced less of an emotional effect if the setting had been one in which there was no one present to observe the patient. Conceivably, including the outcome of such responses allows the author to compose scripts containing more stimulus elements that are more disturbing to the patient than are those not including imagery of action. These and other points certainly merit further research on the fascinating problem that Lang has so trenchantly raised.

That imagery of a stimulus situation can, under certain circumstances, induce large changes in visceral responses is indicated by Luria's (1968) example of a mnemonist who had an unusually vivid memory of imagery. He could produce a 3.5°C difference between the two hands by imagining that one was on a hot stove while the other was squeezing a piece of ice, or raise his heart rate 30 beats per minute by imagining he was running to try to catch a train. That imagery is not always effective, however, is demonstrated by my experience with two hypnotized subjects who were amazed that they had failed to produce a difference between the temperatures of their two hands but had only vividly hallucinated one.

FEEDBACK THAT IS MORE RELEVANT

Tursky has suggested that one of the ways of training patients to produce larger visceral responses is to use a type of feedback that is more relevant. That I completely agree with him is demonstrated by the following quotation:

> Many learning theorists make the implicit assumption that, provided no strong, conflicting, unconditioned response is involved and the magnitudes are comparable, one drive and reinforcement may be substituted for another. Miller (1959, p. 241) has made this assumption explicit but has pointed out that it has not been subjected to any systematic tests. Recent work by investigators such as Garcia and Koelling (1966) and Garcia, Ervin, and Koelling (1966) is questioning this assumption by showing that the reinforcement of nausea is more effective in training animals to avoid food with a particular flavor than to avoid a particular place, whereas reinforcement by electric shock is more effective in training the animal to avoid the place than the food.
>
> Most of the reinforcements used in human work on biofeedback have been signals that tell the subject that he is succeeding or failing. Such signals derive their reinforcing value from the cognitive process that determines their meaning. Will a more primitive type of reinforcement, such as the avoidance of or escape from mild pain be more effective than

a cognitively derived one in the therapeutic applications of biofeedback, especially those involving visceral responses?

It is also possible that a more relevant type of drive and reward would be more effective. For example, in trying to produce a learned change in a cardiovascular function, it might be useful to use mild peripheral ischemia produced by a pressure cuff as the drive, and relief from it as the reward. We believe that, in many cases, instrumental learning plays an important role in refining the homeostatic regulation of a specific function and in adjusting the priorities among the different functions being regulated (Miller, 1969). If this hypothesis is correct, it may be advantageous to discover and use the reinforcements that are involved in normal regulation in order to correct instances of maladaptive regulation (Miller and Dworkin, 1977, p. 150.)

While I agree with the possibility that Tursky has raised, I have to disagree completely with the evidence that he uses to support this possibility. In the study by Kristt and Engel (1975), during home study patients got knowledge about blood pressure by using a cuff that had a microphone so that they received feedback from the Korotkoff sound in the same way as they had in the laboratory. Tursky assumes that the patient stopped responding to the Korotkoff sounds and started responding to feedback from the feeling of the pressure of the cuff. Conceivably, this could have happened, but I see no evidence whatsoever to suggest that it did happen. With respect to his example of anal incontinence, there are two points. In the first place, the external sphincter is not under the control of the autonomic nervous system but is under the control of the somatic nervous system, so that the response is a skeletal one of the same kind that Basmajian has dealt with. This could be one of the reasons for the success. Secondly, inflation of the balloon in the rectum was not used as a feedback signal but was used as a means of eliciting sphincter contractions; it produced a distension of the rectum analogous to the distention produced by the feces — a kind of signal that the patient had received many times but to which he had not responded correctly. Then the patient was given visual information on what his internal and external sphincters were doing. According to Engel, it was this feedback that enabled the patient to learn the correct response.

While I believe that a type of feedback that is more relevant and/or more directly motivational may be more effective, it certainly is not true that all perfectly arbitrary, irrelevant types of feedback are ineffective; and I don't believe that Tursky has claimed this, although some learning theorists might do so. To cite just a few arbitrary types of feedback, in training patients to control their PVCs, Weiss and Engel (1971) have used flashing red, green, and yellow lights, and Pickering and Miller (1977) have sometimes used the

ECG on an oscilloscope screen. Harris et al. (1973) have trained baboons to produce a 40-mm. mercury increase in blood pressure and to maintain it for 12 hours a day in order to avoid electric shock and to get food. As you will see soon, we have used a tone as a feedback signal to train patients with spinal lesions to produce large increases in blood pressure.

THE PROBLEM OF THE RESPONSE

Tursky had emphasized the possible utility of imagery, classical conditioning and the use of mediating responses to get large visceral responses to occur. I heartily agree with the need to try these and other maneuvers to get large responses to occur so that they can be reinforced (Miller & Dworkin, 1974). It is also true that we do not know what parameters of the response to reinforce (Miller & Dworkin, 1977). Should we reinforce more frequently occurring small changes, or are most of these merely noise so that it would be much better to reinforce only the much rarer large changes? Is it more efficient to set the criterion to reward an absolute level or rate, or should one primarily reward changes in the correct direction?

There are still other problems. For example, blood pressure varies with each heart beat. In order to train a reduction, should one reward only the depth of the trough of the diastolic pulse wave? Rhythmic changes in blood pressure, the sinus arrhythmia, occur with breathing. Should one reward each downward fluctuation of the sinus arrhythmia? Then there is a longer Traube-Hering rhythm. Should one reward the downward fluctuations in this rhythm? Are the changes involved in these rhythms learnable responses, or from the point of view of learning, are they only noise? In the latter case, the ideal procedure might be to use a computer to try to predict what the pressure would be on the basis of the foregoing rhythms and to reward any deviation in the correct direction from that prediction.

From the discussion under the last three headings, it should be obvious that there are many things that need to be tried in the attempt to produce larger learned changes. The ability to produce such larger changes would be useful for further basic research as well as for therapeutic applications.

RESEARCH ON PARALYZED PATIENTS

Following a long tradition established by discussants in countless other symposia, I would like to include a little new data of my own in this discussion. With these data, I shall conclude.

In one of our attempts to produce larger learned changes in blood pressure, my colleagues and I turned to patients paralyzed by polio or muscular dystrophy, since these diseases paralyze the skeletal muscles without appreciably affecting visceral responses (Pickering, Brucker, Frankel, Mathias, Dworkin, & Miller 1977). We thought that the paralysis of the skeletal muscles would reduce the noise that responses mediated by them induce and also might make the visceral changes more perceptually perspicuous. We were disappointed in this expectation. The changes in blood pressure learned by these patients were relatively small, averaging about 5 mm. mercury in each direction. However, these changes were highly reliable statistically; and, by a number of controls, we were able to make it seem unlikely that they could have been produced by changes in respiration, by contractions of the nonparalyzed muscles, or even by commands to the paralyzed ones. We found that contraction of normal muscles or even commands to the paralyzed muscles produced increases in blood pressure and also in heart rate. By contrast, the learned changes in blood pressure were not accompanied by changes in heart rate, a marked difference which made it seem unlikely that they could have been induced by the contractions of normal muscles or by commands to paralyzed ones.

After this study was completed, a purely chance occurrence led to the discovery of what we had been looking for but not found — considerably larger learned changes in blood pressure. A patient who had had his spinal cord severed at T4 (about the middle of his chest) by a gunshot wound three years before had been trying with great persistence to learn to use his powerful arms and shoulders to walk with crutches and braces. But he failed because every time he was helped into an upright position, his blood pressure fell so low that he fainted. After practice on the tilt-table and other procedures, physical therapists had given up.

When he heard we had been working on blood pressure, he begged one of my collaborators, Mr. Bernard Brucker, to try to train him to increase his blood pressure. In view of the small changes we had produced on the other patients and the fact that this one had so much of his body disconnected from the brain, prospects of success seemed dim indeed. Finally, the patient persuaded Mr. Brucker to try and, to everyone's surprise, showed unusual ability in learning to produce large increases (Brucker & Ince, 1977). Perhaps because he could produce large, prompt increases, this patient became able to perceive them, which enabled him to practice by himself. In a typical test after training, if this patient was helped into an upright position and told not to try to do anything to his blood pressure, it fell from a systolic level of 110 mm. mercury down to one of 50 mm. mercury within 2 minutes, at which point he was about to faint so that he had to be helped to sit down again. But if he was asked voluntarily to raise his blood pressure and keep it up, he could increase it within a minute from 110 mm. mercury to 145 mm. mercury. Then when he was helped to stand, it fell down to a bit under 110 mm. mercury, but it was still at the safe level of 90 mm. mercury at the end of 5 minutes. The prompt specific increases which he could produce on request conclusively demonstrated specific voluntary control and could scarcely have been a placebo effect. This voluntary control generalized from the laboratory to the life situation, so that he was able to learn to walk with crutches and braces. At first, he occasionally would feel his blood pressure falling and have to stand still to concentrate on raising it. He is still doing this, now in his own apartment, 4 years after the end of training.

In his doctoral dissertation, Brucker (1977) showed that 9 out of 10 patients with spinal lesions at different levels, none of whom could produce appreciable increases in blood pressure on pretraining trials, were able to increase their systolic pressure on the fifth training session by an average of 8 mm. mercury and by the twenty-fifth session, by an average of slightly more than 15 mm. mercury. The tenth patient was suffering from depression and negativism.

Two of these patients suffered from extreme postural hypotension so that they had to be kept in a semi-reclining position with their feet about the same level as their heads in order to avoid fainting. One of these lesions, between C3 and C4, had occurred approximately 2 years before starting and the other, between C4 and C5, approximately 3 years before the start of training. Both of these patients learned well enough to achieve the desirable therapeutic effect of being able to sit in a normal position with their legs down without fainting.

In contrast with the polio and muscular dystrophy patients, tests with the 9 spinal patients showed that commands to contract the paralyzed muscles as strongly as possible produced little if any effect on blood pressure. Commands to produce maximal contraction of intact muscles did increase blood pressure and heart rate. However, increases in blood pressure from attempts maximally to contract all normal and paralyzed muscles were somewhat less than the learned changes produced without any apparent involvement of skeletal muscles. Similarly, virtually no changes in breathing or the percent CO_2 of expired air were recorded during large voluntary increases in blood pressure; considerably larger changes in breathing produced much smaller changes in blood pressure.

Additional tests were run on the patient with the highest lesion, between C3 and C4 (Miller & Brucker, 1978). Widely placed electrodes on the neck and frontalis very probably recorded any appreciable response from any of the nonparalyzed muscles of this patient. When he made a voluntary increase of 24 mm. mercury, there were only minimal signs of muscular activity from either of these pairs of electrodes. When he attempted maximally to contract all of his muscles, paralyzed or not, the EMG activity was increased to levels many times higher but the blood pressure was increased only 10 mm. mercury. These and other tests make it seem quite likely that he was producing his learned increases in blood pressure directly without involving any mediation by any responses of the skeletal muscles.

Interviews with the thoroughly studied patients, those who suffered from orthostatic hypotension and hence achieved therapeutic effects, indicated that during the early stages of learning they used various images, such as those of sexual activities or a horse race, but that as they gained skill, these images completely dropped out.

Since these patients have unusually large spontaneous fluctuations in blood pressure, it seems plausible that the lesion may have interfered with the mechanism for maintaining blood pressure under tight homeostatic control and that this antihomeostatic effect may have been the reason why some of them could learn such large changes. The largest one that I have personally observed in one of the patients who gave himself considerable additional practice after the end of formal training is an increase of 70 mm. mercury in systolic pressure. It would be interesting if a drug could be found that produced a similar release from tight homeostatic controls. It would be very valuable for research with animals and might even be of therapeutic use in training patients. However, since such a drug would produce fluctuations in vital signs, it probably would be promptly discarded in any pharmaceutical test as having an undesirable side effect.

The high motivation and extra practice also may have contributed to this patient's unusual performance. Many experiments on visceral learning probably use too few trials.

Another intriguing question is, how do the patients with so much of their bodies disconnected from the brain by high cervical lesions produce these large changes in blood pressure? Is it entirely via the vagus, and, if so, how could some of them change their blood pressure without changing their heart rate? Do they use humoral factors controlled by the brain? We hope to be able to investigate some of these problems.

Chapter 14
A Perspective
on Clinical Biofeedback

Kenneth P. Price and Robert T. Gatchel

As we suggested in the first chapter of this volume, the technology of biofeedback has come to occupy the attention and imagination of researchers, clinicians, and consumers primarily because of its promise of an effective therapy for psychophysiologic and other "somatic" and "psychological" disorders. Biofeedback has been considered a possible alternative to some traditional somatic or psychotherapeutic interventions, which have been seen as either ineffective or fraught with unpleasant or dangerous side effects. Furthermore, the idea of self-regulation of bodily processes struck a responsive chord among a generation of psychologists that believed it had freed itself from the bonds of the "medical model" in psychopathology and saw an opportunity to escape the confines of the medical model in medicine as well. In fact, the rise of biofeedback accompanied and, in part, encouraged the development of a renewed interest in a holistic approach to physical illness as exemplified by Engel (1977), Lipowski (1977), and Schwartz and Weiss (1977). These authors have written about the need for a new "biobehavioral" model of health and disease. This model views health and illness as aspects of an individual's total behavioral (conceived broadly) repertoire and response to daily living (Price, Gaas-Abrams, & Browder, 1977). As such, the model requires input from the full range of basic science researchers and health-care professionals. The approach of behaviorally and cognitively oriented psychologists is believed to be of special importance in implementing the holistic model and translating it from theory to practice. Biofeedback technology has been seen as one of the chief contributions of psychology to behavioral medicine.

Like many new therapeutic developments, biofeedback was invested prematurely with far-reaching therapeutic implications on the basis of innovative, yet meager, clinical data. Unlike other modalities, biofeedback also had to bear the burden of being thought of as heralding a conceptual revolution, marking the beginning of a "new mind," "a new body" (Brown, 1974). Biofeedback was endowed in some quarters, professional as well as lay, with an almost mystical aura. Biofeedback was not merely a psychophysiological or psychotherapeutic tool but became a discipline in itself. As a discipline, it established its own professional society, its own journal, and its own licensing rules as to who can employ biofeedback (the latter is still at the embryonic and debated stage as of this writing).

Clinicians' exaggerated confidence in the therapeutic efficacy of biofeedback procedures is illustrated by the following quotation taken from a letter criticizing traditional medical interventions as often more dangerous but no more effective than placebos: "Why should migraine patients be given Sansert®, tranquilizers and other drugs when good biofeedback training can more effectively and more safely help 80 percent of them? Biofeedback deserves first choice. Can we continue to ignore the overwhelming evidence that self-regulation safely can control symptoms in 80 percent of patients with stress diseases?" (Shealy, 1977, p. 133). On the other hand, disillusionment, too, has set in. In 1976, Shapiro and Surwit concluded a review of biofeedback with a disappointing summation: "There is *not one* well-controlled scientific study of the effectiveness of biofeedback and operant conditioning in treating a particular physiological disorder" (Shapiro & Surwit, 1976, p. 113). Katkin and Goldband (Chapter 10) claim that this verdict is still accurate. In another review, Miller (1978) describes three levels of research strategies in order of increasing precision and scientific validity: (1) pilot studies to suggest promising effects worthy of investigation, (2) controlled comparisons with the best available techniques or placebo, and (3) broad clinical trials. He laments that "therapeutic applications of biofeedback already have too high a ratio of uncontrolled pilot studies in Phase 1 to controlled studies in Phase 2. It is time to leave Phase 1 behind and move on to Phase 2" (p. 396).

It is almost always the case, however, that no matter how negative a review, it does not recommend the abandonment of biofeedback research. To the contrary, data are always sufficiently suggestive, though not conclusive, that further research in the area is proposed.

Let us summarize and discuss some of the conclusions of the contributors to this volume.

CARDIOVASCULAR DYSFUNCTIONS

The evidence for the utility of direct biofeedback for blood pressure responses in the treatment of hypertension is inconclusive. Regular practice of relaxation or meditation does appear to be helpful in reducing blood pressure in hypertensives. In a more recent review of the literature on the role of relaxation in biofeedback training, which postdates Blanchard's chapter, Tarler-Benlolo (1978) concluded that both biofeedback and relaxation training, either alone or in combination, appear to have some effect in lowering blood pressure of essential hypertensives. Tarler-Benlolo also points out that due to a lack of standardization of biofeedback and relaxation techniques, it is currently impossible to determine the relative effectiveness of the two procedures. Although there were some equivocal findings, the majority of the studies did indicate that either method was equally effective in producing positive results. Future studies are needed to more systematically evaluate the relative effectiveness of these procedures alone and in combination, in the treatment of essential hypertension as well as other forms of psychophysiological disorders. In a recent systematic study with normotensive subjects, Fey and Lindholm (1978) reported that a combination of progressive relaxation and blood-pressure biofeedback produced the greatest degree of blood-pressure reduction. Studies such as these are needed employing hypertensives.

It should also be noted that, if relaxation training alone is found to be an effective alternative to biofeedback, an important question which requires investigation is why does it work? Is it an efficient method for producing generalized sympathetic deactivation or a "wakeful hypometabolic state" (Wallace, Benson, & Wilson, 1971)? In her review, Tarler-Benlolo noted that relaxation techniques such as modified Jacobsonian progressive relaxation, autogenic training, and adaptions of meditation methods involving passive mental concentration are beginning to appear more effective than "active" techniques requiring a great deal of concentrated attention. Biofeedback may be found to be too "active" a technique to produce the maximum degree of psychological deactivation (Cuthbert & Lang, 1976).

For the treatment of two other forms of cardiovascular dysfunction, premature ventricular contractions and Raynaud's disease, biofeedback continues to look promising. However, definitive data on the issue are still lacking, and a great deal of additional controlled outcome research is needed.

SEXUAL DYSFUNCTIONS

While genital responses have been shown to be responsive to both instructions and feedback, there is currently no evidence that the direct conditioning of genital responses has therapeutic value. It is suggested that biofeedback may have a role to play in guiding the development of erotic and nonerotic fantasies, which can, in turn, have significant therapeutic value. This is a relatively new area of biofeedback research which currently has a paucity of well-controlled investigations. Again, a great deal of additional research is needed.

EEG PATTERNS

There is little support for the notion that "alpha conditioning" (which may very well be artifactual to factors such as oculomotor adjustments) is accompanied by any unusual state of consciousness or has any other therapeutic value for tension or anxiety. A great deal of the excitement about alpha biofeedback was produced by the reports of "pleasantness" of subjects in the earliest studies on alpha conditioning. These early reports are currently viewed with some skepticism. Indeed, it has been argued by many investigators (Mulholland, 1971) that the "pleasantness" state probably has as much to do with the subject's feelings and expectations of success in the biofeedback situation as with any inherent effects. There is no such thing as a unitary alpha state. As Hassett (1978) notes, ". . . the brain is not a single undifferentiated mass of tissue that remains in one state or another" (p. 143).

Biofeedback has shown itself useful in the treatment of epilepsy. However, it appears to be effective, not through the enhancement of specific brain wave frequencies, but through training in EEG normalization by shifting EEG frequencies upward, enhancing alpha production, and reducing slow-wave activity. It shows promise as a therapeutic tool in this area.

SKELETAL MUSCULAR DYSFUNCTIONS

Biofeedback is very helpful when used to reeducate weak muscles and to relax hyperactive muscles. However, this conclusion is based primarily upon single and multiple case studies and poorly controlled group studies employing questionable outcome measures. The great bulk of this research had been conducted with patients in clinical settings. As a result, the clinical needs of the patients were considered first, with experimental design given a subordinate role. Currently, controlled group-outcome studies are sorely needed, as well as the refinement of existing therapeutic techniques.

MUSCLE TENSION

As Alexander and Smith state in Chapter 7: "First there is no evidence that feedback induced muscle tension reductions at a single site have any generalized effect whatsoever, either on other muscles, in the autonomic nervous system, or on the subjective experience of relaxation. . . . Second, there is reason to suspect that EMG biofeedback may be no more effective than unaided, purposeful efforts in the relaxation of specific muscles." These authors also review the use of EMG biofeedback in the treatment of tension headache, anxiety, hypertension, asthma, and insomnia. They report that it has not been found to be any more effective than instructions alone, relaxation, or placebo in treating these disorders. Again, however, additional research appears to be needed. In particular, controlled investigations of EMG biofeedback in combination with other techniques in the treatment of such disorders are greatly needed.

MIGRAINE HEADACHE

To date, research suggests that biofeedback for finger temperature increases may be useful for treating migraine but has no advantage over relaxation training. In addition, biofeedback training for constriction of the superficial temporal artery may be effective, but there are insufficient data for stronger conclusions. Many more long-term, controlled-outcome studies are needed. It should also be noted that a great deal of additional research is needed to assess why biofeedback and relaxation may be effective in treating migraine. What underlying physiological mechanisms are being affected by these procedures?

ANXIETY

Gatchel and colleagues have found that biofeedback for reductions in heart rate may be useful for inhibiting cardiac acceleration during periods of acute stress. This research has also demonstrated the important role that placebo factors play in producing and maintaining fear reduction in a biofeedback treatment program. Shapiro (1971) has carefully traced the history of the potent effect of suggestion in psychiatry and medicine. Present medical practice has continued to rely upon the placebo effect. In the area of biofeedback, the great degree of enthusiasm for the new biofeedback technology may have as much to do with its therapeutic success as the treatment itself. Indeed, biofeedback has been referred to as "the ultimate placebo" (Stroebel & Glueck, 1973). Only recently have studies such as those by Gatchel and colleagues been conducted to carefully tease out placebo effects from the presumed active treatment agent in biofeedback programs directed at the reduction of fear and anxiety. A great deal of additional such controlled research is sorely needed in the area. Even if placebo factors are eventually found to be the major active ingredient in biofeedback treatment, such a finding would not detract from its therapeutic effectiveness *as long as clinicians realize this* so that they can best choose the appropriate treatment for their various patients. Indeed, there is a long-accepted maxim in medicine which states: "Treat many patients with new remedies while they still have the power to heal" (Shapiro, 1971).

CURRENT STATUS OF THE FIELD

What, then, is the verdict on clinical biofeedback? Quite frankly, it is difficult to answer this without appearing to beg the question. On the other hand, it is quite clear that the claims for the therapeutic efficacy for biofeedback have been grossly exaggerated and sometimes even wrong. On the other hand, large numbers of people with a variety of different disorders seem to have been helped (although possibly for only a short time) by treatments including or exclusively using biofeedback procedures. Under these circumstances, we think it justified to conclude that "biofeedback" still has therapeutic potential, but the hard work of realizing that potential and elucidating the type of biofeedback, methodology, and circumstances of its use is still to be done. The pessimistic overreaction leading to a negative evaluation of anything connected with biofeedback (which is evident among many serious investigators) is an understandable response to the unrestrained initial overenthusiasm to biofeedback, which has not yet been moderated by some writers. We think it would be unfortunate if the pendulum of fashion swung biofeedback into oblivion, as has happened to so many other treatment modalities in the past (Shapiro, 1971). A balanced, unemotional approach to the field, accompanied by careful research, is most likely to yield data that are rigorous, acceptable, and therapeutically useful.

We would like to enumerate below some of the issues that ought to be considered in future biofeedback research.

Use of Appropriate Methodology

Shapiro has recently qualified his earlier statement (Shapiro & Surwit, 1976) about the lack of controlled studies of biofeedback with the admission that he is not sure what the prerequisities of a well-controlled study should be (Shapiro, Mainardi, & Surwit, 1977). This undoubtedly reflects the belief that many different kinds of variables need to be controlled in biofeedback research.

Let us list, in paraphrased form, Blanchard's criteria for appropriate methodological concerns:

1. Change should be clinically meaningful.
2. An appropriate experimental design should be used in gathering the data. Appropriate statistical techniques should be employed to evaluate the results.
3. All clinical biofeedback studies (as well as any therapy outcome study, for that matter) must have follow-up data. The duration of follow-up should be lengthy.
4. The proportion of treated patients that improved should be reported, to

avoid misinterpretation when only a few subjects respond with much change.

5. It is desirable to show that the changes that occur in the laboratory also obtain in the patient's natural environment.
6. Results should be replicable. Thus, single case studies have little or no value at this point.
7. Change should be shown in the physiological response that is trained in order to relate the feedback to therapeutic improvement. In the present volume, Rugh has written, for example, that ''frequently those patients who show the most clinical improvement are not the ones who are best able to control the specific response.''

Both Katkin and Goldband and Tursky have suggested new approaches to biofeedback methodology. Katkin and Goldband have proposed using schedules of reinforcement to test biofeedback paradigms. This has been explored in the past (Gatchel, 1974), but surely merits future work. Indeed, Hatch and Gatchel (1978) have argued that the operant paradigm remains the most viable theoretical formulation from which to view voluntary control of physiological responses such as heart rate because it draws attention to important response controlling variables, such as feedback characteristics, in a way that encourages precision and systematic control. Finally, Tursky has recalled for us that all stimuli are not equally associable and has proposed using different feedback modalities (proprioceptive or interoceptive) to aid in learning a response and in maintaining transfer of training.

Knowledge of Equipment Characteristics

Rugh has made an important contribution by alerting us to the dangers of using a ''black box'' biofeedback device. He has listed some possibilities for erroneously concluding that a physiological change has occurred, when, in fact, the signal change is due to artifact from the equipment or the preparation. We once witnessed a dramatic demonstration of the reduction in forehead temperature by one patient, over 5°F in the space of a few minutes. It turned out that the tape holding the thermistor in place had gradually worked itself loose, making the thermistor's connection with the skin increasingly tenuous.

Understanding of Physiology

Almost every contributor to this volume has emphasized the importance of understanding the physiology of the response system that the experimenter tries to modify. Alexander and Smith have pointed out, for example, the dangers of relying on forehead EMG as a measure of frontalis activity or general anxiety. By the same token, to intervene intelligently with migraine, one must understand the physiology of a migraine attack (Price, Gaas-Abrams, & Browder, 1977; Taub, 1977).

The Need for Appropriate Biofeedback Therapist Training

It is readily apparent that a clinician or researcher who wishes to use the technology of biofeedback is required to have some broad expertise in at least three areas: in psychology, in order to develop and utilize the most effective methodology and psychological principles for his or her biofeedback program; in electronics, in order to be totally aware of the "inner workings" and safety characteristics of the biofeedback devices being used; and in physiology and physical medicine, in order to understand the biological nature of the response system that is being modified. As Miller noted in his chapter, as the field of behavioral medicine develops, of which biofeedback will be just one small portion, "new types of training will be needed to teach psychologists and other behavioral scientists more about physical medicine." A close collaboration between the biofeedback therapist and the medical specialist will be required. For example, a thorough physical examination is routinely essential in order to be certain that a condition is not successfully amenable to conventional medical techniques (such as headaches caused by a brain tumor that is operable if found early).

Presently, many who prescribe the use of biofeedback do not have the broad training and expertise required in all of the above three areas. This raises some very important ethical, legal, and medical issues. The modification of physiological responses may produce undesirable and medically dangerous side-effects in certain individuals. Some liken the use of biofeedback to the use of drugs that alter physiological responding. The federal Food and Drug Administration carefully monitors and controls the introduction of any new drug to the market. No such monitoring occurs for new innovations in biofeedback technology. At the least, some "watchdog" agency in the field of behavioral medicine is needed to develop licensing rules in order to insure the use of biofeedback by only competent and adequately trained clinicians or researchers. A clinical psychology-psychophysiology training program is an example of a program in which an individual could acquire the necessary technical, scientific, and professional training to be able to utilize biofeedback and to investigate it in a competent fashion.

Biofeedback as a Psychophysiological Tool

Lang has reminded us that biofeedback may be used not just as a therapy but also a means for understanding psychophysiological disorders. This is illustrated by the finding that patient groups cannot control autonomic activity as well as normals (Lang, Troyer, Twentyman & Gatchel, 1975; Price & Tursky, 1976). This has implications for learning theorists' hypotheses about the etiology of psychophysiological disorders (Lachman, 1972). An understanding of precisely how self-control develops and what are the underlying psychobiological mechanisms and constraints may provide valuable insights into such disorders.

Biofeedback and Therapy

Lazarus (1977) has placed biofeedback within the context of psychotherapy in general (as have Katkin and Goldband). He writes: "First, we cannot in our thinking isolate the somatic disturbances and their self-regulation in biofeedback from the larger context of the person's adaptive commerce with his environment. Second, this adaptive commerce is constantly being mediated by social and psychological processes" (p. 73). A similar view has been expressed by Schwartz (1973) and Price (1974). Biofeedback does not offer a simplistic solution to life's ills, whether they be a dysfunctioning colon or a disquieting anxiety. While in some instances, biofeedback alone for a disordered organ system may be adequate (as for Miller's hypotensive spinal patients), it may be more often the case that skilled clinical intervention is required to discover what role a symptom plays in a patient's life and how best to help that patient cope with his or her environment. Indeed, in his chapter, Miller reminds us that in order to treat some cases effectively with biofeedback, a knowledge of psychotherapy is required. This is true in cases in which certain symptoms of physiological dysfunction are providing some primary or secondary gains for the patients.

Individual Difference Variables in Biofeedback

An important area of research which has yet to produce any fruitful results is the evaluation of individual differences and how they relate to the effectiveness of biofeedback training. One of the reasons for some of the disarray in the biofeedback therapy literature may be the differential responses of individuals to treatment. Attempts to relate a number of individual differences and personality characteristics, such as autonomic perception, locus of control, and hypnotic susceptibility, to biofeedback have not been too successful. Miller (1978) has recently reviewed much of this research and, therefore, we will not again review it here. In passing, it should be pointed out that McCanne and Sandman (1975) have demonstrated that the use of initial baseline, rather than immediately preceding rest periods, to determine heart-rate changes yields results that are contaminated by habituation. The two methods might therefore be expected to produce different results. The great majority of studies assessing the relationship between individual difference/personality variables and biofeedback employed heart rate as the target physiological response. It may well be that one of the reasons for many of the equivocal results reported in this literature is the differing methods of computing rate change from one study to the next. Indeed, Miller (1978) has demonstrated that this might be the case for the equivocal relationships found between locus of control and voluntary heart-rate change. Future investigations will need to take into account such potentially contaminated measures.

Research into the relationship between individual differences in physiological responding and biofeedback is well worthwhile. In response to the same stressor, different individuals will demonstrate different response topographies. As Gatchel noted in his chapter, to apply biofeedback training to the same target response across all individuals, for example, in order to allow them to relax more effectively and cope with the physiological component of anxiety might not be maximally effective. An approach which tailors the biofeedback training to the target response(s) most involved in, say, an individual's anxiety reaction, might have a more significant therapeutic impact. Such "tailoring" will be required for biofeedback therapy techniques, with the expectation that biofeedback will not be clinically useful for all patients. Similarly, various nomothetic variables may suggest which patients will respond best to biofeedback and which to relaxation procedures.

CONCLUSIONS

Ironically, biofeedback caught the imagination of clinicians because of its presumed success in training autonomic activity, while a review of the literature discloses that biofeedback's greatest therapeutic successes have come in the area of training voluntary (striated muscle) activity. Nevertheless, biofeedback continues to have great potential for application to areas where disordered autonomic activity plays a role. The task remaining for biofeedback researchers is to elucidate which aspects of biofeedback, under what circumstances, work best for individuals with specific disorders.

Finally, as was noted time and time again throughout this text, the clinician or researcher employing biofeedback needs knowledge in a number of different areas: the pathophysiology of the disorder being treated and the physiology of the response systems to be voluntarily regulated, the relation of such response systems to the etiology and symptoms of the particular disorder, the electrical functioning of the feedback device itself, the nature of the self-regulation process involved in biofeedback "learning," and the knowledge and use of appropriate methodology. Without such expertise, it cannot be expected that useful and reliable biofeedback treatment procedures can be developed.

REFERENCES

Chapter 1

Annent, J. *Feedback and Human Behavior*. Baltimore: Penguin Books, 1969.

Bagchi, B.K. Mysticism and mist in India. *Journal of the American Society of Psychosomatic Dentistry and Medicine*, 1969, **16**, 1–32.

Bagchi, B.K. & Wenger, M.A. Electro-physiological correlates of some yogi exercises. *Electroencephalography and Clinical Neurophysiology*, 1957, supplement **7**, 132–149.

Basmajian, J.V. Control and training of individual motor units. *Science*, 1963, **141**, 440–441.

Basmajian, J.V., Baeza, M. & Fabrigar, C. Conscious control and training of individual spinal neurons in normal human subjects. *Journal of New Drugs*, 1965, **5**, 78–85.

Brener, J. & Kleinman, R.A. Learned control of decreases in systolic blood pressure. *Nature*, 1970, **226**, 1063–1064.

Crider, A., Shapiro, D. & Tursky, B. Reinforcement of spontaneous electrodermal activity. *Journal of Comparative and Physiological Psychology*, 1966, **61**, 20–27.

Deckner, C.S., Hill, J.T. & Bourne, J.R. Shaping of human gastric motility. Paper presented at the meeting of the American Psychological Association, Honolulu, 1972.

Engel, B.T. Operant conditioning of cardiac function: A status report. *Psychophysiology*, 1972, **9**, 161–177.

Fowler, R.L. & Kimmel, H.D. Operant conditioning of the GSR. *Journal of Experimental Psychology*, 1962, **63**, 563–567.

Freeza, D.A. & Holland, J.G. Operant conditioning of the human salivary response. *Psychophysiology*, 1971, **8**, 581–587.

Goesling, W.J. & Brener, J. Effect of activity and immobility upon subsequent heart rate conditioning in curarized rats. *Journal of Comparative and Physiological Psychology*, 1972, **81**, 311–317.

Hefferline, R.F., Keenan, B. & Harford, R.A. Escape and avoidance conditioning in human subjects without observation of their responses. *Science*, 1959, **130**, 1338–1339.

Hnatiow, M. & Lang, P.J. Learned stabilization of cardiac rate. *Psychophysiology*, 1965, **1**, 330–336.

Hothersall, D. & Brener, J. Operant conditioning of changes in heart rate in curarized rats. *Journal of Comparative and Physiological Psychology*, 1969, **68**, 338–342.

Kamiya, J. Operant control of the EEG alpha rhythm and some of its reported effects on consciousness. In C. Tart (Ed.), *Altered States of Consciousness*. New York: Wiley, 1969.

Kamiya, J., Barber, T.X., Miller, N.E., Shapiro, D. & Stoyva, J. *Biofeedback and Self-control: An Aldine Annual on the Regulation of Bodily Processes and Consciousness*. Chicago: Aldine, 1977.

Katkin, E.S. & Murray, E.N. Instrumental conditioning of autonomically mediated bahavior: Theoretical and methodological issues. *Psychological Bulletin*, 1968, **70**, 52–68.

Kimmel, H.D. & Hill, F.A. Operant conditioning of the GSR. *Psychological Reports*, 1960, **7**, 555–562.

Kimmel, E. & Kimmel, H.D. Replication of operant conditioning of the GSR. *Journal of Experimental Psychology*, 1963, **65**, 212–213.

Kimble, G.A. & Perlmuter, L.C. The problem of volition. *Psychological Review*, 1970, **77**, 361–384.

Klinge, V. Effects of exteroceptive feedback and instructions on control of spontaneous galvanic skin response. *Psychophysiology*, 1972, **9**, 305–317.

Lang, P.J. Autonomic control or learning to play the internal organs. *Psychology Today*, October, 1970.

Lang, P.J., Sroufe, L.A. & Hastings, J.E. Effects of feedback and instructional set on the control of cardiac rate variability. *Journal of Experimental Psychology*, 1967, **75**, 425–431.

Lapides, J., Sweet, R.B. & Lewis, L.W. Role of striated muscle in urination. *Journal of Urology*, 1957, **77**, 247–250.

Lindsley, D.B. & Sassaman, W.H. Autonomic activity and brain potentials associated with "voluntary" control of pilomotors. *Journal of Neurophysiology*, 1938, **1**, 342–349.

Lisina, M.I. The role of orientation in the transformation of involuntary reactions to voluntary ones. In L.G. Voronin; A.N. Leontiev; A.R. Luria; E.N. Sokolov; & O.B. Vinobradova (Eds.), *Orienting Reflex and Exploratory Behavior*. Washington: American Institute of Biological Sciences, 1965.

Luria, A.R. *The Mind of a Mnemonist*, trans. by L. Solotaroff. New York: Basic Books, 1958.

McClure, C.M. Cardiac arrest through volition. *California Medicine*, 1959, **90**, 440–448.

Miller, N.E. Learning of visceral and glandular responses. *Science*, 1969, **163**, 434–445.

Miller, N.E. Biofeedback and visceral learning. In M.R. Rosenzweig & L.W. Porter (Eds.), *Annual Review of Psychology*. Palo Alto, Cal.: Annual Reviews, 1978.

Miller, N.E. & Dworkin, B. Visceral learning: Recent difficulties with curarized rats and significant problems for human research. In P.A. Obrist; A.H. Black, J. Brener, & L.V. DiCara (Eds.), *Cardiovascular Psychophysiology*. Chicago: Aldine, 1974.

Ogden, E. & Shock, N.W. Voluntary hypercirculation. *American Journal of the Medical Sciences*, 1939, **198**, 329–342.

Roberts, A.H., Kewman, D.G. & MacDonald, H. Voluntary control of skin temperature: Unilateral changes using hypnosis and feedback. *Journal of Abnormal Psychology*, 1973, **82**, 63–168.

Rosen, R.C. Suppression of penile tumescence by instrumental conditioning. *Psychosomatic Medicine*, 1973, **35**, 509–514.

Sargent, J.D., Green, E.E. & Walters, E.D. The use of autogenic feedback training in a pilot study of migraine and tension headaches. *Headache*, 1972, **12**, 120–124.

Schwartz, G.E. Voluntary control of human cardiovascular integration and differentiations through feedback and reward. *Science*, 1972, **175**, 90–93.

Schwartz, G.E. Biofeedback as therapy: Some theoretical and practical issues. *American Psychologist*, 1973, **28**, 666–673.

Shapiro, D., Schwartz, G.E. & Tursky, B. Control of diastolic blood pressure in man by feedback and reinforcement. *Psychophysiology*, 1972, **9**, 296–304.

Shapiro, D., Tursky, B., Gershon, E., & Stern, M. Effects of feedback and reinforcement on the control of human systolic blood pressure. *Science*, 1969, **163**, 588–590.

Shearn, D.W. Operant conditioning of heart rate. *Science*, 1962, **137**, 530–531.

Skinner, B.F. *The Behavior of Organisms*. New York: Appleton-Century-Crofts, 1938, p. 112.

Slaughter, J., Hahn, W. & Rinaldi, P. Instrumental conditioning of heart rate in the curarized rat with varied amounts of pretraining. *Journal of Comparative and Physiological Psychology*, 1970, **72**, 356–360.

Snyder, C. & Noble, M. Operant conditioning of vasoconstriction. *Journal of Experimental Psychology*, 1968, **77**, 263–268.

Sroufe, L.A. Learned stabilization of cardiac rate with respiration experimentally control. *Journal of Experimental Psychology*, 1969, **81**, 391–393.

Sroufe, L.A. Effects of depth and rate of breathing on heart rate and heart rate variability. *Psychophysiology*, 1971, **8**, 648–655.

Wenger, M. & Bagchi, B. Studies of autonomic functions in practitioners of Yoga in India. *Behavioral Science*, 1961, **6**, 312–323.

Wenger, M., Bagchi, B. & Anand, B. Experiments in India on "voluntary" control of the heart and pulse. *Circulation*, 1961, **24**, 1319–1325.

Chapter 2

Elder, S. T. & Eustis, N. K. Instrumental blood pressure conditioning in out-patient hypertensives. *Behavior Research and Therapy*, 1975, **13**, 185–188.

Katkin, E. S. & Murray, E. N. Instrumental conditioning of automatically mediated behavior: Theoretical and methodological issues. *Psychological Bulletin*, 1968, **70**, 52–68.

Lang, P. J. Acquisition of heart rate control: Method, theory, and clinical implications. In D. C. Fowles (Ed.), *Clinical Applications of Psychophysiology*. New York: Columbia University Press, 1975. ·

Lang, P. J. The psychophysiology of anxiety. In H. Akiskal (Ed.), *Psychiatric Diagnosis: Exploration of Biological Criteria*. New York: Spectrum, 1977.

Lang, P. J. & Lazovik, A. D. Experimental desensitization of a phobia. *Journal of Abnormal and Social Psychology*, 1963, **66**, 519–525.

Lang, P. J., Melamed, B. G. & Hart, J. H. A psychophysiological analysis of fear modification using an automated desensitization procedure. *Journal of Abnormal Psychology*, 1970, **76**, 220–234.

Lang, P. J., Troyer, W. G., Twentyman, C. T. & Gatchel, R. J. Differential effects of heart rate modification training on college students, older males, and patients with ischemic heart disease. *Psychosomatic Medicine*, 1975, **37**, 429–446.

Schwartz, G. E. Biofeedback, self-regulation and the patterning of physiological processing. *American Scientist*, 1975, **63**, 314–324.

Weerts, T. C. & Lang, P. J. The psychophysiology of fear imagery: Differences between focal phobia and social performance anxiety. Manuscript submitted for publication, 1977.

Wolberg, L. R. *Medical Hypnosis.* New York: Grune & Stratton, 1948.

Wolpe, J. *Psychotherapy by Reciprocal Inhibition.* Stanford: Stanford University Press, 1958.

Chapter 3

Alexander, F. *Psychosomatic Medicine.* New York: Norton, 1950.

Baddeley, R. M. The place of upper dorsal sympathectomy and the treatment of primary Raynaud's disease. *British Journal of Surgery,* 1965, **52**, 426–430.

Benson, H. *The Relaxation Response.* New York: William Morrow, 1975.

Benson, H., Rosner, B. A. & Marzetta, B. R. Decreased systolic blood pressure in hypertensive subjects who practiced meditation. *Journal of Clinical Investigation,* 1973, **52**, 8a.

Benson, H., Rosner, B. A., Marzetta, B. R. & Klemchuk, H. P. Decreased blood pressure in borderline hypertensive subjects who practiced meditation. *Journal of Chronic Diseases,* 1974, **27**, 163–169.

Benson, H., Rosner, B. A., Marzetta, B. R. & Klemchuk, H. M. Decreased blood pressure in pharmacologically treated hypertensive patients who regularly elicited the relaxation response. *Lancet,* 1974, **1**, 289–291.

Benson, H., Shapiro, D., Tursky, B. & Schwartz, G. E. Decreased systolic blood pressure through operant conditioning techniques in patients with essential hypertension. *Science,* 1971, **173**, 740–742.

Blanchard, E. B. & Abel, G. G. An experimental case study of the biofeedback treatment of a rape-induced psychophysiological cardiovascular disorder. *Behavior Therapy,* 1976, **7**, 113–119.

Blanchard, E. B. & Epstein, L. H. Clinical applications of biofeedback. In M. Hersen; R. M. Eisler; & P. M. Miller (Eds.), *Progress in Behavior Modification,* Vol. 4. New York: Academic Press, 1977.

Blanchard, E. B. & Haynes, M. R. Biofeedback treatment of a case of Raynaud's Disease. *Journal of Behavior Therapy and Experimental Psychiatry,* 1975, **6**, 230–234.

Blanchard, E. B., Haynes, M. R., Kallman, M. D. & Harkey, L. A comparison of direct blood pressure feedback and electromyographic feedback on the blood pressure of normotensives. *Biofeedback and Self-Regulation,* 1976, **1**, 445–451.

Blanchard, E. B., Miller, S. T., Abel, G. G., Haynes, M. R. & Wicker, R. The failure of blood pressure feedback in treating hypertension. Unpublished manuscript, 1977.

Blanchard, E. B. & Young, L. D. Clinical applications of biofeedback training: *Archives of General Psychiatry,* 1974, **30**, 530–589.

Blanchard, E. B. & Young, L. D. Of promises and evidence: A reply to Engel. *Psychological Bulletin,* 1974, **81**, 44–46.

Blanchard, E. B. & Young, L. D. Self-control of cardiac functioning: A promise as yet unfulfilled. *Psychological Bulletin*, 1973, **79**, 145–163.

Blanchard, E. B., Young, L. D. & Haynes, M. R. A simple feedback system for the treatment of elevated blood pressure. *Behavior Therapy*, 1975, **6**, 241–245.

DeQuattro, V. & Miura, Y. Neurogenic factors in human hypertension: Mechanism or myth? In J. H. Laragh, (Ed.), *Hypertension Manual*. New York: Dun-Donnelley, 1974.

Elder, S. T. & Eustis, N. K. Instrumental blood pressure conditioning in out-patient hypertensives. *Behaviour Research & Therapy*, 1975, **13**, 185–188.

Elder, S. T., Ruiz, Z. B., Deabler, H. L. & Dillenkoffer, R. L. Instrumental conditioning of diastolic blood pressure in essential hypertensive patients. *Journal of Applied Behavior Analysis*, 1973, **6**, 377–382.

Engel, B. T. Comment on self-control of cardiac functioning: A promise as yet unfulfilled. *Psychological Bulletin*, 1974, **84**, 43.

Engel, B. T. & Bleecker, E. R. Applications of operant conditioning techniques to the control of cardiac arrhythmias. In P. A. Obrist; A. H. Black; J. Brener; & L. V. DiCara (Eds.), *Cardiovascular Psychophysiology*. Chicago: Aldine, 1974.

Epstein, L. H. & Blanchard, E. B. Biofeedback, self-control and self-management: An integration and reappraisal. *Biofeedback and Self-Regulation*, (in press).

Goldman, H., Kleinman, K. M., Snow, M. Y., Bidus, D. R. & Korol, B. Relationship between essential hypertension and cognitive functioning: Effects of biofeedback. *Psychophysiology*, 1975, **12**, 569–573.

Kristt, D. A. & Engel, B. T. Learned control of blood pressure in patients with high blood pressure. *Circulation*, 1975, **51**, 370–378.

Love, W. A., Montgomery, D. D. & Moeller, T. A. Working paper no. 1. Unpublished manuscript. Nova University: Ft. Lauderdale, Fla., 1974.

MacKenzie, J. The hypersensitive nervous system in heart disease. In *Principles of Diagnosis and Treatment Heart Affections*. London: Oxford University Press, 1916, pp. 81–84.

Miller, N. E. Clinical applications of biofeedback: Voluntary control of heart rate, rhythm, and blood pressure. In H. I. Russek (Ed.), *New Horizons in Cardiovascular Practice*. Baltimore: University Park Press, 1975, pp. 245–246.

Miller, N. E. Postscript. In D. Singh & C. T. Morgan (Eds.), *Current Status of Physiological Psychology: Readings*. Monterey, Cal.: Brooks-Cole, 1972.

Moeller, T. A. & Love, W. A. A method to reduce aterial hypertension through muscular relaxation. Unpublished manuscript. Nova University: Ft. Lauderdale, Fla., 1974.

Patel, C. H. Twelve-month follow-up of yoga and biofeedback in the management of hypertension. *Lancet*, 1975, **1**, 62–67.

Patel, C. H. Yoga and biofeedback in the management of hypertension. *Lancet*, 1973, **2**, 1053–1055.

Patel, C. H. & North, W. R. S. Randomized controlled trial of yoga and biofeedback in management of hypertension. *Lancet*, 1975, **2**, 93–99.

Pickering, G. W. *High Blood Pressure*, 2nd ed. New York: Grune & Stratton, 1968.

Pickering, T. & Gorham, G. Learned heart-rate controlled by a patient with a ventricular parasystolic rhythm. *Lancet*, 1975, **2**, 252–253.

Podell, R. N., Kent, D & Keller, K. Patient ,psychological defenses and physician response in the long-term treatment of hypertension. *Journal of Family Practice*, 1976, **3** 145–149.

Porter, J. N., Snider, R. L., Bardana, E. J., Rosch, J. & Eidemiller, L. R. The diagnosis and treatment of Raynaud's phenomenon. *Surgery*, 1975, **77**, 11–23.

Schwartz, G. E. Clinical applications of biofeedback: Some theoretical issues. In D. Upper & D. S. Goodenough (Eds.), *Behavior Modification with the Individual Patient: Proceedings of Third Annual Brockton Symposium on Behavior Therapy*. Nutley, N.J.: Roche, 1972.

Schwartz, G. E. & Shapiro, D. Biofeedback and essential hypertension: Current findings and theoretical concerns. In L. Birk (Ed.), *Biofeedback: Behavioral Medicine*. New York: Grune & Stratton, 1973.

Scott, R. W., Blanchard, E. B., Edmundson, E. D. & Young, L. D. A shaping procedure for heart rate control in chronic tachycardia. *Perceptual and Motor Skills*, 1973, **37**, 327–338.

Shapiro, D. Operant-feedback control of human blood pressure: Some clinical issues. In P. A. Obrist; A. H. Black; J. Brener; & L. V. DiCara (Eds.), *Cardiovascular Psychophysiology*. Chicago: Aldine, 1974.

Shapiro, D., Schwartz, G. E. & Tursky, B. Control of diastolic blood pressure in man by feedback and reinforcement. *Psychophysiology*, 1972, **9**, 296–304.

Shapiro, D., Tursky, B., Gershon, E. & Stern, M. Effects of feedback and reinforcement on control of human systolic blood pressure. *Science*, 1969, **163**, 588–590.

Shapiro, D., Tursky, B. & Schwartz, G. E. Control of blood pressure in man by operant conditioning. *Circulation Research*, 1970, **26**, Suppl. 1: 27–32.

Shoemaker, J. E. & Tasto, D. L. The effects of muscle relaxation on blood pressure of essential hypertensives. *Behaviour Research and Therapy*, 1975, **13**, 29–43.

Stambler, J., Stambler, R., Riedlinger, W. F., Algera, G. & Roberts, R. H. Hypertension screening of 1 million Americans. *JAMA*, 1976, **235**, 2299–2306.

Stephenson, N. L. Two cases of successful treatment of Raynaud's disease with relaxation in biofeedback training in supportive psychotherapy. Paper presented to Seventh Annual Meeting of Biofeedback Research Society, Colorado Springs, Colorado, February 1976.

Stone, R. A. & DeLeo, J. Psychotherapeutic control of hypertension. *New England Journal of Medicine*, 1976, **294**. 80–84.

Tursky, B., Shapiro, D. & Schwartz, G. E. Automated constant cuff-pressure system to measure average systolic and diastolic blood pressure in man. *IEEE Transactions in Bio-Medical Engineering*, 1972, **19**, 271–276.

Weiss, T. & Engel, B. T. Operant conditioning of heart rate in patients with premature ventricular contractions. *Psychosomatic Medicine*, 1971, **33**, 301–321.

Chapter 4

Abel, G. C., Blanchard, E. B., Barlow, D. H. & Mavissahalian, H. Indentifying specific erotic cues in sexual deviations by audiotaped description. *Journal of Applied Behavior Analyses*, 1975, **8**, 247–260.

Bancroft, J. Aversion therapy of homosexuality. *British Journal of Psychiatry*, 1969, **15**, 1417–31.

Bancroft, J. *Deviant sexual behavior: Modification and assessment.* Oxford: Clarendon Press, 1974.

Bancroft, J., & Marks, I. Elective aversion therapy of sexual deviations. *Proceedings, Royal Society of Medicine*, 1968, **61**, 796–799.

Barlow, D. H. An overview of behavioral assessment in clinical settings. In John D. Cone and Robert P. Hawkins (Eds.), *Behavioral Assessment: New Directions in Clinical Psychology.* New York: Brunner-Mazel, 1977.

Barlow, D. H., Agras, W. S., Abel, G. G., Blanchard, E. B. & Young, L. D. Biofeedback and reinforcement to increase heterosexual arousal in homosexuals. *Behavior Research and Therapy*, 1975, **13**, 45–50.

Blanchard, E. G. & Young, L. D. Self-control of cardiac functioning: A promise as yet unfulfilled. *Psychological Bulletin*, 1973, **79**, 145–163.

Callahan, E. J. & Leintenberg, H. Aversion therapy for sexual deviation: Contingent shock and covert sensitization. *Journal of Abnormal Psychology*, 1973, **81**, 60–73.

Crider, A. B., Schwartz, G. E. & Shnidman, S. On the criteria for instrumental conditioning: A reply to Katkin and Murray. *Psychological Bulletin*, 1969, **71**, 455–461.

Csillag, E. R. Modification of penile erectile response. *Journal of Behavior Therapy and Experimental Psychiatry*, 1976, **7**, 27–29.

Davison, G. C. Elimination of a sadistic fantasy by a client-controlled counterconditioning technique: A case study. *Journal of Abnormal Psychology*, 1968, **73**, 84–90.

Davison, G. C. Homosexuality: The ethical challenge. *Journal of Consulting and Clinical Psychology*, 1976, **33**, 157–162.

Dodson, B. *Liberating Masturbation.* New York: Bodysex Designs, 1974.

Ellmore, A. M. & Tursky, B. A model and improved methodology to enhance biofeedback's therapeutic success. Paper presented at Society for Psychophysiological Research Meeting, October 1976, San Diego.

Fuhr, R. A. Facilitation of sexual arousal through imagery. Doctoral dissertation, SUNY at Stony Brook, 1976.

Gagnon, J. & Simon, W. *Sexual Conduct: The Social Sources of Human Sexuality.* Chicago: Aldine, 1973.

Geer, J. H. Direct measurement of genital responding. *American Psychologist*, 1975, **30**, 415–418.

Geer, J. H. Sexual functions — some data and speculations on psychophysiological assessment. In J. D. Cone and R. P. Hawkins (Eds.), *Behavioral Assessment: New Directions in Clinical Psychology.* New York: Brunner/Mazel, 1977.

Geer, J. H. & Fuhr, R. Cognitive factors in sexual arousal: The role of distraction. *Journal of Consulting Clinical Psychology*, 1976, **44**, 238–243.

Gold, S. & Newfeld, I. A learning theory approach to the treatment of homosexuality. *Behaviour Research and Therapy*, 1965, **2**, 201–204.

Heiman, J. A psychophysiological explanation of sexual arousal patterns in males and females. *Psychophysiology*, 1977, **14**, 266–274.

Heiman, J. Issues in the use of psychophysiology to assess female sexual dysfunction. *Journal of Sex and Marital Therapy, 1976*, **3**, 197–274.

Herman, S. H. & Prewett, M. An experimental analysis of feedback to increase sexual arousal in a case of homosexual and heterosexual impotence. A preliminary report. *Journal of Behavior Therapy and Experimental Psychiatry*, 1974, **5**, 271–274.

Hensen, D. E. & Rubin, H. B. Voluntary control of eroticism. *Journal of Applied Behavioral Analyses*, 1971, **4**, 37–44.

Hoon, P. W., Wincze, J. P. & Hoon, E. K. The effects of biofeedback and cognitive mediation upon vaginal blood volume. *Behavior Therapy*, 1977, **8**, 694–702.

Kaplan, H. S. *The New Sex Therapy*. New York: Brunner/Mazel, 1974.

Katkin, E. S. & Murray, E. N. Instrumental conditioning of autonomically mediated behavior: Theoretical and methodological issus. *Psychological Bulletin*, 1968, **70**, 52–68.

Kinsey, A. C., Pomeroy, W. B., Marin, C. E. & Gebhard, P. H. *Sexual Behavior in the Human Female*. Philadelphia: Saunders, 1953.

Lang, P. J. Imagery in therapy: An information processing analysis of fear. *Behavior Therapy*, 1977, **8**, 862–886.

Lang, P. J. Learned control of human heart rate in a computer directed environment. In P. A. Obrist; A. H. Black; J. Brener; & L. V. DiCara (Eds.), *Cardiovascular Psychophysiology*. Chicago: Aldine, 1974.

Laws, D. R. & Rubin, H. B. Instrumental control of an autonomic sexual response. *Journal of Applied Behavioral Analysis*, 1969, **2**, 93–99.

Laws, D. R. & Pawlowski, A. V. A multipurpose biofeedback device for penile plethysmography. *Journal of Behavior Therapy and Experimental Psychiatry*, 1976, **7**, 27–29.

Lobitz, C. W. & LoPiccolo, J. New methods in the behavioral treatment of sexual dysfunction. *Journal of Behavior Therapy and Experimental Psychiatry*, 1972, **2**, 265–271.

Marks, I. & Gelder, M. G. Transvestism and fetishism: Clinical and psychological changes during favadic aversion. *British Journal of Psychiatry*, 1969, **113**, 711–730.

McGuire, R. J. & Vallance, M. Aversion therapy by electric shock: A simple technique. *British Medical Journal*, 1964, **1**, 151–153.

Price, K. P. & Geer, J. H. Feedback effects on penile tumescence. Paper read at 1973 Eastern Psychological Association Meeting, Washington, D.C.

Quinn, J. T., Harbison, J. J. M. & McAllister, H. An attempt to shape human penile responses. *Behaviour Research and Therapy*, 1970, **8**, 213–216.

Quinsey, V. L. & Bergersen, S. G. Instructional control of penile circumference in assessment of sexual preference. *Behavior Therapy*, 1976, **7**, 489–493.

Reynolds, B. S. Psychological treatment models and outcome results for erectile dysfunction: A critical review. *Psychological Bulletin*, 1977, **84**, 1218–1238.

Rosen, R. C. Suppression of penile tumescence by instrumental conditioning. *Psychosomatic Medicine*, 1973, **35**, 509–514.

Rosen, R. C. Genital blood flow measurement: Feedback applications in sexual therapy. *Journal of Sex and Marital Therapy*, 1976, **2**, 184–196.

Rosen, R. C. & Kopel, S. Penile plethysmography and biofeedback in the treatment of a transvestite-exhibitionist. *Journal of Consulting Clinical Psychology*, 1977, **45**, 908–916.

Rosen, R. C., Shapiro, D. & Schwartz, G. E. Suppression of penile tumescence. *Psychosomatic Medicine*, 1975, **37**, 479–483.

Schachter, S. The interaction of cognitive and physiological determinants of emotional states. In L. Berkowitz (Ed.), *Advances in Experimental Social Psychology*, Vol. 1. New York: Academic Press, 1964.

Schaefer, H. H., Tregarthan, G. T. & Colgan, A. H. Measured and self-estimated penile erection. *Behavior Therapy*, 1976, **7**, 1–7.

Spiess, W. F. J. The psychophysiology of premature ejaculation: Some factors related to ejaculatory latency. Doctoral dissertation, Stony Brook, 1977.

Wincze, J. P., Hoon, E. F. & Hoon, P. W. Physiological responsivity of normal and sexually dysfunctional women during erotic stimulus exposure. *Journal of Psychosomatic Research*, 1976.

Chapter 5

Anand, B. K., China, G. A. & Singh, B. Some aspects of electroencephalographic studies in yogis. *Electroencephalography and Clinical Neurophysiology*, 1961, **13**, 452–456.

Ancoli, S. & Kamiya, J. Methodological issues in alpha biofeedback training. *Biofeedback and Self-Regulation*, 1978, **3**, 159–183.

Andreychuk, T. & Skriver, C. Hypnosis and biofeedback in the treatment of migraine headache. *International Journal of Clinical and Experimental Hypnosis*, 1975, **23**, 172–183.

Benjamins, J. Alpha feedback relaxation procedures with high and low mental image clarity; an analogue desensitization study. *Proceedings of the Biofeedback Society of America*, Albuquerque, March 1978.

Benjamins, J. The effectiveness of alpha feedback training and muscle relaxation procedures in systematic desensitization. *Biofeedback and Self-Regulation*, 1976, **1**, 352.

Besner, H. Biofeedback: Possible placebo in treating chronic onset insomnia. *Proceedings of the Biofeedback Society of America*, Albuquerque, March 1978.

Black, A. H. The operant conditioning of central nervous system electrical activity. In G. H. Bower (Ed.), *The Psychology of Learning and Motivation: Advances in Research and Theory*, New York: Academic Press, 1972, pp. 47–95.

Black, A. H., Cott, A. & Pavloski, R. The operant learning theory approach to biofeedback training. In G. Schwartz and J. Beatty (Eds.), *Biofeedback: Theory and Research*, New York: Academic Press, 1977, pp. 89–127.

Blanchard, E. B. & Young, L. D. Clinical applications of biofeedback training. *Archives of General Psychiatry*, 1974, **30**, 573–589.

Brazier, M. A. B. The problem of periodicity in the electroencephalogram: Studies in the cat. *Electroencephalography and Clinical Neurophysiology*, 1963, **15**, 287–298.

Brown, B. B. Recognition of aspects of consciousness through association with EEG alpha activity represented by a light signal. *Psychophysiology*, 1970, **6**, 442–452.

Budzynski, T. Biofeedback procedures in the clinic. In L. Birk (Ed.), *Biofeedback: Behavioral Medicine*, New York: Grune & Stratton, 1973.

Cabral, R. J. & Scott, D. F. Effects of two desensitization techniques, biofeedback and relaxation, on intractable epilepsy: Follow-up study. *Journal of Neurology, Neurosurgery and Psychiatry*, 1976, **39**, 504–507.

Chase, M. H. & Harper, R. M. Somatomotor and visceromotor correlates of operantly conditioned 12–14 c/sec sensorimotor cortical activity. *Electroencephalography and Clinical Neurophysiology*, 1971, **31**, 85–92.

Chatrian, G. E., Petersen, M. C. & Lazarte, J. A. The blocking of the rolandic wicket rhythm and some central changes related to movement. *Electroencephalography and Clinical Neurophysiology*, 1959, **11**, 497–510.

Cohen, H. D., Graham, C., Fotopoulos, S. S. & Cook, M. R. A double-blind methodology for biofeedback research. *Psychophysiology*, 1977, **14**, 603–608.

Eberlin, P. & Mulholland, T. B. Bilateral differences in parieto-occipital EEG induced by contingent visual feedback. *Psychophysiology*, 1976, **13**, 212–218.

Epstein, L. H. & Blanchard, E. G. Biofeedback, self-control, and self-management. *Biofeedback and Self-Regulation*, 1977, **2**, 201–211.

Feinstein, B. & Sterman, M. B. Effects of sensorimotor rhythm biofeedback training on insomnia. *Proceedings of the Biofeedback Research Society*, Colorado Springs, February 1974.

Fetz, E. E. Operant conditioning of cortical unit activity. *Science*, 1969, **163**, 955–957.

Finley, W. W. Effects of sham feedback following successful SMR training in an epileptic: Follow-up study. *Biofeedback and Self-Regulation*, 1976, **1**, 227–236.

Finley, W. W. Operant conditioning of the EEG in two patients with epilepsy: Methodologic and clinical considerations. *Pavlovian Journal of Biological Science*, 1977, **12**, 93–111.

Finley, W. W., Smith, H. A. & Etherton, M. D. Reduction of seizures and normalization of the EEG in a severe epileptic following sensorimotor biofeedback training: Preliminary study. *Biological Psychology*, 1975, **2**, 189–203.

Gannon, L. & Sternbach, R. A. Alpha enhancement as a treatment for pain: A case study. *Behavior Therapy and Experimental Psychiatry*, 1971, **2**, 209–213.

Gastaut, H. Etude électrocorticographique de la réactivité des rythmes rolandiques. *Revue Neurologique*, 1952, **87**, 176–182.

Gastaut, H. & Broughton, R. *Epileptic Seizures*. Springfield, Ill.: Charles C. Thomas, 1972.

Glueck, B. C. & Stroebel, C.F. Biofeedback and meditation in the treatment of psychiatric illnesses. *Comprehensive Psychiatry*, 1975, **16**, 303–321.

Green, J. Brainwave feedback training for seizure reduction in epilepsy. Unpublished doctoral dissertation, Union Graduate School, 1976.

Hardt, J. V. & Kamiya, J. Anxiety change through electroencephalographic alpha feedback seen only in high anxiety subjects. *Science*, 1978, **201**, 79–81.

Hauri, P. Biofeedback techniques in the treatment of chronic insomnia. In R. L. Williams and I. Karacan (Eds.), *Sleep Disorders: Diagnosis and Treatment*, in press.

Howe, R. C. & Sterman, M. B. Cortical-subcortical EEG correlates of suppressed motor behavior during sleep and waking in the cat. *Electroencephalography and Clinical Neurophysiology*, 1972, **32**, 681–695.

Jacobson, E. *Progressive Relaxation*. Chicago: University of Chicago Press, 1938.

Johnson, L. Learned control of brain wave activity. In J. Beatty and H. Legewie (Eds.), *Biofeedback and Behavior*, New York: Plenum, 1977, pp. 73–94.

Johnson, R. K. & Meyer, R. G. Phased biofeedback approach for epileptic seizure control. *Journal of Bahavior Therapy and Experimental Psychiatry*, 1974, **5**, 185–187.

Kamiya, J. Conditioned discrimination of the EEG alpha rhythm in humans. Presented at the Western Psychological Association meeting, 1962.

Kamiya, J. Operant control of the EEG alpha rhythm and some of its reported effects on consciousness. In C. Tart (Ed.), *Altered States of Consciousness*. New York: Wiley, 1969, pp. 489–501.

Kaplan, B. J. Biofeedback in epileptics: Equivocal relationship of reinforced EEG frequency to seizure reduction. *Epilepsia*, 1975, **16**, 477–485.

Kasamatsu, A. & Hirai, T. An electroencephalographic study of the Zen meditation (Zazen). *Folia Psychiatrica et Neurologica Japonica*, 1966, **20**, 315–336.

Katkin, E. S. & Murray, E. N. Instrumental conditioning of autonomically mediated behavior: Theoretical and methodological issues. *Psychological Bulletin*, 1968, **70**, 52–68.

Kuhlman, W. N. EEG feedback training of epileptic patients: Clinical and electroencephalographic analysis. Unpublished doctoral dissertation, Yale University, 1976.

Kuhlman, W. N. and Allison, T. EEG feedback training in the treatment of epilepsy: Some questions and some answers. *Pavlovian Journal of Biological Science*, 1977, **12**, 112–122.

Kuhlman, W. N. Functional topography of the human mu rhythm. *Electroencephalography and Clinical Neurophysiology*, 1978*a*, **44**, 83–93.

Kuhlman, W. N. EEG feedback training: Enhancement of somatosensory cortical activity. *Electroencephalography and Clinical Neurophysiology*, 1978*b*, **45**, 290–294.

Kuhlman, W. N. EEG feedback training of epileptic patients: clinical and electroencephalographic analysis. *Electroencephalography and Clinical Neurophysiology*, 1978*c*, **45**, in press.

Lubar, J. F. & Bahler, W. W. Behavioral management of epileptic seizures following EEG biofeedback training of the sensorimotor rhythm. *Biofeedback and Self-Regulation*, 1976, **1**, 77–104.

Lubar, J. F. & Shouse, M. N. EEG and behavioral changes in a hyperkinetic child concurrent with training of the sensorimotor rhythm (SMR): A preliminary report. *Biofeedback and Self-Regulation*, 1976, **1**, 293–306.

Luthe, W. Autogenic training: Method, research, and application in medicine. *American Journal of Psychotherapy*, 1963, **17**, 174–195.

Mattson, R. H., Heninger, G. R., Gallagher, B. B. & Glaser, G. H. Psychophysiologic precipitants of seizures in epileptics. *Neurology*, 1970, **20**, 407.

McLaughlin, T. J. & Lewis, C. N. Feedback EEG reactivity and the social responsivity of psychiatric patients. *Journal of Nervous and Mental Disease*, 1975, **161**, 336–342.

Melzack, R. & Perry, C. Self-regulation of pain: The use of alpha-feedback and hypnotic training for the control of chronic pain. *Experimental Neurology*, 1975, **46**, 452–469.

Mills, G. K. & Solyom, L. Biofeedback of EEG alpha in the treatment of obsessive ruminations: An exploration. *Journal of Behavior Therapy and Experimental Psychiatry*, 1974, **5**, 37–41.

Mostofsky, D. I. & Balaschak, B. A. Psychobiological control of seizures. *Psychological Bulletin*, 1977, **84**, 723–750.

Mulholland, T. B. Biofeedback as a scientific method. In G. Schwartz and J. Beatty (Eds.), *Biofeedback: Theory and Research*, New York: Academic Press, 1977, pp. 9–28.

Mulholland, T. B. & Benson, F. Detection of EEG abnormalities with feedback stimulation. *Biofeedback and Self-Regulation*, 1976, **1**, 47–61.

Mulholland, T. B., McLaughlin, T. J. & Benson, F. Feedback control and quantification of the response of EEG alpha to visual stimulation. *Biofeedback and Self-Regulation*, 1976, **1**, 411–422.

Murphy, P. J., Darwin, J. & Murphy, D. A. EEG feedback training for cerebral dysfunction: A research program with learning disabled adolescents. *Biofeedback and Self-Regulation*, 1977, **2**, 288.

Nowlis, D. & Kamiya, J. The control of electroencephalographic alpha rhythms through auditory feedback and the associated mental activity. *Psychophysiology*, 1970, **6**, 476–484.

Olds, J. Operant conditioning of single unit responses. *Twenty-third International Congress of Physiological Science*, Tokyo, 1965, pp. 372-380.

Paskewitz, D. A., Lynch, J. J., Orne, M. T. & Costello, J. The feedback control of alpha activity: Conditioning or disinhibition. *Psychophysiology*, 1970, **6**, 637–638.

Paskewitz, D. A. & Orne, M. T. Visual effects on alpha feedback training. *Science*, 1973, **181**, 360–363.

Patmon, R. & Murphy, P. J. Differential treatment efficacy of EEG and EMG feedback for hyperactive adolescents. *Proceedings of the Biofeedback Society of America*, Albuquerque, March 1978.

Peek, C. J. A critical look at the theory of placebo. *Biofeedback and Self-Regulation*, 1977, **2**, 327–335.

Plotkin, W. B. On the social psychology of experiential states associated with EEG alpha biofeedback training. In J. Beatty and H. Legewie (Eds.), *Biofeedback and Behavior*, New York: Plenum, 1977, pp. 121–134.

Plotkin, W. B. & Cohen, R. Occipital alpha and the attributes of the "alpha experience." *Psychophysiology*, 1976, **13**, 16–21.

Quy, R. J. Biofeedback training in the treatment of epilepsy. Paper presented at the Psychophysiology Group, London, December 1976.

Rémond, A. (Ed.). *Handbook of Electroencephalography and Clinical Neurophysiology, vol. 6, part A: The EEG of the waking adult.* Amsterdam: Elsevier, 1976.

Rosenfeld, J. P. & Rudell, A. P. Mediation of operant controlled neural activity. In D. A. Mostofsky (Ed.), *Behavior Control and Modification of Physiological Activity*, Englewood Cliffs, N.J.: Prentice Hall, 1976, pp. 115–137.

Roth, S. R., Sterman, M. B. & Clemente, C. D. Comparison of EEG correlates of reinforcement, internal inhibition, and sleep. *Electroencephalography and Clinical Neurophysiology*, 1967, **23**, 509–520.

Rouse, L., Peterson, J. & Shapiro, G. EEG alpha entrainment reaction within the biofeedback setting and some possible effects on epilepsy. *Physiological Psychology*, 1975, **3**, 113–122.

Schacter, D. L. EEG theta waves and psychological phenomena: A review and analysis. *Biological Psychology*, 1977, **5**, 47–82.

Schmidt, E. M., Bak, M. J., MacIntosh, J. S. & Thomas, J. S. Operant conditioning of firing patterns in monkey cortical neurons. *Experimental Neurology*, 1977, **54**, 467–477.

Shapiro, A. K. Contribution to a history of the placebo effect. *Behavior Science*, 1960, **5**, 109–135.

Shinkman, P. G., Bruce, C. J. & Pfingst, B. E. Operant conditioning of single-unit response patterns in visual cortex. *Science*, 1974, **184**, 1194–1196.

Shouse, M. N. & Lubar, J. F. Management of the hyperkinetic syndrome with methylphenidate and SMR biofeedback training. *Biofeedback and Self-Regulation*, 1977, **2**, 290.

Sittenfeld, P. Die Konditionierung der Theta-Aktivität des Elektroencephalogramms durch akustische Rückmeldung in Abhängigkeit von der Muskelspannung der Stirnmuskulatur. Unpublished doctoral dissertation, University of Dusseldorf, West Germany, 1973.

Sterman, M. B. Neurophysiologic and clinical studies of sensorimotor EEG biofeedback training: Some effects on epilepsy. In L. Birk (Ed.), *Seminars in Psychiatry*, 1973, **5**, 507–526.

Sterman, M. B. & Friar, L. Suppression of seizures in an eplieptic following sensorimotor EEG feedback training. *Electroencephalography and Clinical Neurophysiology*, 1972, **33**, 89–95.

Sterman, M. B., Howe, R. C. & Macdonald, L. R. Facilitation of spindle-burst sleep by conditioning of electroencephalographic activity while awake. *Science*, 1970, **167**, 1146–1148.

Sterman, M. B., LoPresti, R. W. & Fairchild, M. D. Electroencephalographic and behavioral studies of monomethylhydrazine toxicity in the cat. Technical Report AMRL-TR-69-3, Wright-Patterson Air Force Base, Ohio, 1969.

Sterman, M. B. & Macdonald, L. R. Effects of central cortical EEG feedback training on seizure incidence in poorly controlled epileptics. *Epilepsia*, 1978, **19**, 207–222.

Sterman, M. B., Macdonald, L. R. & Stone, R. K. Biofeedback training of the sensorimotor EEG rhythm in man: Effects on epilepsy. *Epilepsia*, 1974, **15**, 395–416.

Stevens, J. R. Endogenous conditioning to abnormal cerebral transients in man. *Science*, 1962, **137**, 974–976.

Stoyva, J., Budzynski T., Sittenfeld, P. & Yaroush, R. A two-step EMG-theta feedback training in sleep onset insomnia: preliminary results. *Proceedings of the Biofeedback Research Society*, Colorado Springs, February 1974.

Travis, T. A., Kondo, C. Y. & Knott, J. R. Alpha enhancement research: A review. *Biological Psychiatry*, 1975, **10**, 69–89.

Upton, A. R. M. & Longmire, D. The effects of feedback on focal epileptic discharges in man: A preliminary report. *Canadian Journal of Neurological Sciences*, 1975, **3**, 153–167.

Wargin, M. & Fahrion, S. L. A case study: Synchronized alpha training for the obsessive-compulsive headache patient. *Biofeedback and Self-Regulation*, 1977, **2**, 299.

Weber, E. S. P. & Fehmi, L. G. The therapeutic use of EEG biofeedback. *Proceedings of the Biofeedback Research Society*, Colorado Springs, February 1974.

Wolpe, J. *The Practice of Behavior Therapy*. New York: Pergamon Press, 1969.

Wyler, A. R. & Fetz, E. E. Behavioral control of firing patterns of normal and abnormal neurons in chronic epileptic cortex. *Experimental Neurology*, 1974, **42**, 448–464.

Wyler, A. R., Fetz, E. E. & Ward, A. A. Effects of operantly conditioned epileptic unit activity on seizure frequencies and electrophysiology of neocortical experimental foci. *Experimental Neurology*, 1974, **44**, 113–125.

Wyler, A. R., Lockard, J. S., Ward, A. A. & Finch, C. A. Conditioned EEG desynchronization and seizure occurrence in patients. *Electroencephalography and Clinical Neurophysiology*, 1976, **41**, 501–512.

Wyrwicka, W. & Sterman, M. B. Instrumental conditioning of sensorimotor cortex EEG spindles in the waking cat. *Physiology and Behavior*, 1968, **3**, 703–707.

Chapter 6

Amato, A., Hermsmeyer, C. A. & Kleinman, K. M. Use of electromyographic feedback to increase inhibitory control of spastic muscles. *Physical Therapy*, 1973, **53**, 1063–1066.

Andrews, J. M. Neuromuscular reeducation of the hemiplegic with the aid of the electromyograph. *Archives of Physical Medicine and Rehabilitation*, 1964, **45**, 530–532.

Baker, M. P., Regenos, E. M., Wolf, S. L. & Basmajian, J. V. Developing strategies for biofeedback: Applications in neurologically handicapped patients. *Physical Therapy*, 1978, in press.

Basmajian, J. V. *Muscles Alive: Their Functions Revealed by Electromyography*, 3rd ed. Baltimore: Williams & Wilkins, 1974.

Basmajian, J. V. Motor learning and control: A working hypothesis. *Archives of Physical Medicine and Rehabilitation*, 1977, **58**, 38–41.

Basmajian, J. V., Kukulka, C. G., Narayan, M. C. & Takebe, K. Biofeedback treatment of foot-drop after stroke compared with standard rehabilitation techniques, Part 1. Effects on voluntary control and strength. *Archives of Physical Medicine and Rehabilitation*, 1975, **56**, 231–236.

Basmajian, J. V., Regenos, E. M. & Baker, M. P. *Rehabilitation biofeedback for stroke patients*. Second Joint Conference on Stroke, American Heart Association, Miami, Florida, 1977.

Booker, H. E., Rubow, R. T. & Coleman, P. J. Simplified feedback in neuromuscular retraining: An automated approach using electromyographic signals. *Archives of Physical Medicine and Rehabilitation*, 1969, **50**, 621–625.

Brown, D. M. Biofeedback in occupational therapy: New horizons in upper extremity rehabilitation (Cassette tape, cat. no. T–81). In J. V. Basmajian (Ed.), *New Methods in Physical Rehabilitation* series. New York: Biomonitoring Applications, 1976.

Brucker, B. S. & Ince, L. P. Biofeedback as an experimental treatment for postural hypotension in a patient with a spinal cord lesion. *Archives of Physical Medicine and Rehabilitation*, 1977, **58**, 49–53.

Brudny, J., Grynbaum, B. B. & Korein, J. Spasmodic torticollis: Treatment by feedback display of the EMG. *Archives of Physical Medicine and Rehabilitation*, 1974, **55**, 403–408.

Brudny, J., Korein, J., Grynbaum, B. B., Friedman, L. W., Weinstein, S., Sachs-Frankel, G. & Belandres, P. V. EMG feedback therapy: Review of treatment of 114 patients. *Archives of Physical Medicine and Rehabilitation*, 1976, **57**, 55–61.

Brudny, J., Korein, J., Levidow, L., Grynbaum, B. B., Leiberman, A. & Friedman, L. W. Sensory feedback therapy as a modality of treatment in central nervous system disorders of voluntary movement. *Neurology*, 1974, **24,** 925–932.

Budzynski, T. H., Stoyva, J. M., Adler, C. S. & Mullaney, D. J. EMG biofeedback and tension headache: A controlled outcome study. *Psychosomatic Medicine*, 1973, **35,** 484–496.

Carlsson, S. G. & Gale, E. N. Biofeedback in the treatment of long-term temporomandibular joint pain. *Biofeedback and Self-Regulation*, 1977, **2**, 161–171.

Carlsson, S. G., Gale, E. N. & Ohman, A. Treatment of temporomandibular joint syndrome with biofeedback training. *Journal of the American Dental Association*, 1975, **91**, 602–605.

Cleeland, C. S. Behavioral tactics in the modification of spasmodic torticollis. *Neurology*, 1973, **23**, 1241–1247.

Fair, P. L. & Basmajian, J. V. Relaxation therapy in physical rehabilitation (Cassette tape, cat. no. T–82). In J. V. Basmajian (Ed.), *New Methods in Physical Rehabilitation* series. New York: Biomonitoring Applications, 1976.

Finley, W. W., Ninman, C., Standly, J. & Ender, P. Frontal EMG biofeedback training of athetoid cerebral palsy patients: A report of six cases. *Biofeedback and Self-Regulation*, 1976, **1**, 169–182.

Finley, W. W., Ninman, C. A., Standly, J. & Wansley, R. A. Electrophysiologic behavior modification of frontal EMG in cerebral palsied children. *Biofeedback and Self-Regulation*, 1977, **2**, 59–79.

Harris, F. A., Spelman, F. A. & Hymer, J. W. Electronic sensory aids as treatment for cerebral-palsied children. Inappropriception: Part 2. *Physical Therapy*, 1974, **54**, 354–365.

Jacobs, A. & Felton, G. S. Visual feedback of myoelectric output to train muscle relaxation in normal persons and patients with neck injuries. *Archives of Physical Medicine and Rehabilitation*, 1969, **50**, 34–39.

Johnson, H. E. & Garton, W. H. Muscle reeducation in hemiphlegia by use of electromyographic device. *Archives of Physical Medicine and Rehabilitation*, 1973, **54**, 320–325.

Kukulka, C. G., Brown, D. M. & Basmajian, J. V. Biofeedback training for early finger joint mobilization. *The American Journal of Occupational Therapy*, 1975, **29**, 469–470.

Lee, K., Hill, E., Johnston, R. & Smiehorowski, T. Myofeedback for muscle retraining in hemiphlegic patients. *Archives of Physical Medicine and Rehabilitation*, 1976, **57**, 588–591.

MacPherson, E. L. R. Control of involuntary movement. *Behavior Research and Therapy*, 1967, **5**, 143–145.

Marinacci, A. & Horande, M. Electromyogram in neuromuscular reeducation. *Bulletin of the Los Angeles Neurological Society*, 1960, **25**, 57–71.

Netsell, R. & Cleeland, C. S. Modification of lip hypertonia dysarthria using EMG feedback. *Journal of Speech and Hearing Disorders*, 1973, **38**, 131–140.

Peck, D. F. The use of EMG feedback in the treatment of a severe case of blepharospasm. *Biofeedback and Self-Regulation*, 1977, **2**, 273–277.

Pickering, T. G., Brucker, B., Frankel, H. L., Mathias, C. J., Dworkin, B. R. & Miller, N. E. Mechanisms of learned voluntary control of blood pressure in patients with generalized bodily paralysis. In J. Beatty and H. Legewie (Eds.), *Biofeedback and Behavior*. New York: Plenum, 1977.

Smith, H. M., Basmajian, J. V. & Vanderstoep, S. F. Inhibition of neighboring motoneurons in conscious control of single spinal motoneurons. *Science*, 1974, **183**, 975–976.

Spearing, D. L. & Poppen, R. Single case study: The use of feedback in the reduction of foot dragging in a cerebral palsied client. *The Journal of Nervous and Mental Disease*, 1974, **159**, 148–151.

Swaan, D., Van Wieringer, P. C. W. & Fokkema, S. D. Auditory electromyographic feedback therapy to inhibit undesired motor activity. *Archives of Physical Medicine and Rehabilitation*, 1974, **55**, 251–254.

Takebe, K. & Basmajian, J. V. Gait analysis in stroke patients to assess treatments of foot-drop. *Archives of Physical Medicine and Rehabilitation*, 1976, **57**, 305–310.

Takebe, K., Kukulka, C. G., Narayan, M. G. & Basmajian, J. V. Biofeedback treatment of foot drop after stroke compared with standard rehabilitation technique. Part 2: Effects on nerve conduction velocity and spasticity. *Archives of Physical Medicine and Rehabilitation*, 1976, **57**, 9–11.

Teng, E. L., McNeal, D. R., Kralj, A. & Walters, R. L. Electrical stimulation and feedback training: Effects on the voluntary control of paretic muscles. *Archives of Physical Medicine and Rehabilitation*, 1976, **57**, 228–233.

Wooldridge, C. P. & Russel, G. Head position training with the cerebral palsied child: An application of biofeedback techniques. *Archives of Physical Medicine and Rehabilitation*, 1976, **57**, 407–414.

Chapter 7

Aarons, L. Aural and EMG feedback in reading. *Perceptual and Motor Skills*, 1971, **33**, 271–306.

Alexander, A. B., Miklich, D. R. & Hershkoff, H. The immediate effects of systematic relaxation on peak expiratory flow rates in asthmatic children. *Psychosomatic Medicine*, 1972, **34**, 388–394.

Alexander, A.B. Systematic relaxation and flow rates in asthmatic children: Relationship to emotional precipitants and anxiety. *Journal of Psychosomatic Research*, 1972, **16**, 405–410.

Alexander, A. B. An experimental test of assumptions relating to the use of electromyographic biofeedback as a general relaxation training technique. *Psychophysiology*, 1975, **12**, 656–662.

Alexander, A. B. Behavioral methods in the clinical management of chronic asthma. In R. B. Williams & W. D. Gentry (Eds.), *Behavioral Approaches to Medical Practice*, Cambridge: Ballinger, 1977.

Alexander, A. B. Behavioral methods in the clinical management of chronic asthma. In Williams, R. B. & Gentry, W. D. (Eds.), *Behavioral Approaches to Medical Practice*, Cambridge: Ballinger, 1977.

Alexander, A. B. Effects of relaxation training on pulmonary mechanics in children with asthma. *Journal of Applied Behavior Analysis*, 1979, in press.

Bakal, D. A. A biopsychological perspective. *Psychological Bulletin*, 1975, **82**, 369–382.

Balshan, I. D. Muscle tension and personality in women. *Archives of General Psychiatry*, 1962, **7**, 436.

Basmajian, J. V. Facts vs. myths in EMG biofeedback. *Biofeedback and Self-Regulation*, 1976, **1**, 369–372.

Benson, H. *The Relaxation Response.* New York: William Morrow, 1975.

Blanchard, E. B. & Young, L. D. Clinical applications of biofeedback training. *Archives of General Psychiatry*, 1974, **30**, 373–389.

Blanchard, E. B., Miller, S. T., Abel, G. C., Haynes, & Wicker, R. The failure of blood pressure feedback in treating hypertension. *Journal of Applied Behavior Analysis*, 1978, in press.

Borkovec, T. D. & Fowles, D. Controlled investigation of the effects of progressive and hypnotic relaxation on insomnia. *Journal of Abnormal Psychology*, 1973, **82**, 153–158.

Braud, L. W., Lupin, M. N. & Braud, W. G. The use of electromyographic feedback in the control of hyperactivity. *Journal of Learning Disabilities*, 1975, **8**, 21–26.

Brudny, J., Grynbaum, B. B. & Korein, J. Spasmodic torticollis: Treatment by feedback display of the EMG. *Archives of Physical Medicine & Rehabilitation*, 1974, **55**, 403–408.

Budzynski, T. H. & Stoyva, J. M. An instrument for producing deep muscle relaxation by means of analog information feedback. *Journal of Applied Behavior Analysis*, 1969, **2**, 231–237.

Budzynski, T. H., Stoyva, J. M. & Adler, C. Feedback-induced muscle relaxation: Application to tension headache. *Journal of Behavior Therapy & Experimental Psychiatry*, 1970, **1**, 205–211.

Budzynski, T. H. & Stoyva, J. M. Biofeedback techniques in behavior therapy. In N. Birbaumer (Ed.), *Die Bewältigung von Angst. Beiträge der Neuropsychologie zur Angstforschung. (The making of anxiety. Contributions of neuropsychology to anxiety research.)* Reihe Fortschritte der Klinischen Psychologie, Band 4, München Wien: Verlag Urban & Schwarzenberg, 1972.

Budzynski, T. H., Stoyva, J. M., Adler, C. S. & Mullaney, D. J. EMG biofeedback and tension headache: A controlled outcome study. *Psychosomatic Medicine*, 1973, **35**, 484–496.

Chesney, M. A. & Shelton, J. L. A comparison of muscle relaxation and electromyogram biofeedback treatments for muscle contraction headache. *Journal of Behavior Therapy & Experimental Psychiatry*, 1976, **7**, 221–225.

Coursey, R. D. Electromyograph feedback as a relaxation technique. *Journal of Consulting & Clinical Psychology*, 1975, **43**, 825–834.

Cox, D. J., Freundlich, A. & Meyer, R. G. Differential effectiveness of electromyograph feedback, verbal relaxation instructions and medication placebo and tension headache. *Journal of Consulting & Clinical Psychology*, 1975, **43**, 892–898.

Davis, M. H., Saunders, D. R., Creer, T. L. & Chai, H. Relaxation training facilitated by biofeedback apparatus as a supplemental treatment in bronchia asthma. *Journal of Psychosomatic Research*, 1973, **17**, 121–128.

Epstein, L. H., Hersen, M. & Hemphill, D. P. Music feedback in the treatment of tension headache: An experimental case study. *Journal of Behavior Therapy & Experimental Psychiatry*, 1974, **5**, 59–63.

Epstein, L. H. & Abel, G. G. An analysis of biofeedback training effects for tension headache patients. *Behavior Therapy*, 1977, **8**, 37–47.

Fowler, J. E., Budzynski, T. H. & VandenBergh, R. L. Effects of an EMG biofeedback relaxation program on the control of diabetes. *Biofeedback and Self-Regulation*, 1976, **1**,105–112.

Freedman, R. & Papsdorf, J. D. Biofeedback and progressive relaxation treatment of sleep-onset insomnia: A controlled, all-night investigation. *Biofeedback & Self-Regulation*, 1976, **1**, 253–271.

Good, R. Frontalis muscle tension and sleep latency. *Psychophysiology*, 1975, **12**, 465–467.

Guitar, B. Reduction of stuttering frequency using analog electromyographic feedback. *Journal of Speech & Hearing Research*, 1975, **18**, 672–685.

Hanna, R., Wilfling, F. & McNeill, B. A biofeedback treatment for stuttering. *Journal of Speech & Hearing Disorders*, 1975, **40**, 270–273.

Hardyck, C. D., Petrinovich, L. F. & Ellsworth, D. W. Feedback of speech muscle activity during silent reading: Rapid extinction. *Science*, 1966, **154**, 1467–1468.

Hardyck, C. D. & Petrinovich, L. F. Treatment of subvocal speech during reading. *Journal of Reading*, 1969, **1**, 1–11.

Hauri, P., Phelps, P. J. & Jordan, J. B. Biofeedback as a treatment for insomnia. Paper presented at the meeting of the Biofeedback Research Society, Colorado Springs, Colorado, 1976.

Haynes, S. N., Moseley, D. & McGowan, W. T. Relaxation training and biofeedback in the reduction of frontalis muscle tension. *Psychophysiology*, 1975, **12**, 547–552.

Haynes, S. N., Griffin, P., Mooney, D. & Parise, M. Electromyographic biofeedback and relaxation instructions in the treatment of muscle contraction headaches. *Behavior Therapy*, 1975, **6**, 672–678.

Haynes, S. N. Electromyographic biofeedback treatment of a woman with chronic dysphagia. *Biofeedback & Self-Regulation*, 1976, **1**, 121–126.

Hutchings, D. F. & Reinking, R. H. Tension headaches: What form of therapy is most effective? *Biofeedback & Self-Regulation*, 1976, **1**, 183–190.

Jacobs, A. & Felton, G. S. Visual feedback of myoelectric output to facilitate muscle relaxation in normal persons and patients with neck injuries. *Archives of Physical Medicine & Rehabilitation*, 1969, **50**, 34–39.

Jacobson, E. Progressive Relaxation. Chicago: University of Chicago Press, 1938.

Kinsman, R. A., O'Banion, K., Robinson, S. & Staudenmayer, H. Continuous biofeedback and discreet post trial verbal feedback in frontalis muscle relaxation training. *Psychophysiology*, 1975, **12**, 30–35.

Kondo, C. & Canter, A. True and false electromyographic feedback: Effect of tension headache. *Journal of Abnormal Psychology*, 1977, **86**, 93–95.

Kotses, H., Glaus, K. D., Crawford, P. L., Edwards, J. E. & Scherr, M. S. Operant reduction of frontalis EMG activity in the treatment of asthma in children. *Journal of Psychosomatic Research*, 1976, **20**, 453–459.

Lanyon, R. I., Barrington, C. C. & Newman, A. C. Modification of stuttering through EMG biofeedback: A preliminary study. *Behavior Therapy*, 1976, **7**, 96–103.

Lanyon, R. I. Effect of biofeedback on stuttering during reading and spontaneous speech. *Journal of Consulting & Clinical Psychology*, 1977, 45, **5**, 860–866.

Masur, F. T. A comparison of EMG biofeedback, relaxation instructions, and attention-placebo in the treatment of chronic tension headaches. Paper presented to the Duke Conference on Behavioral Approaches to Medical Practice, Durham, North Carolina, 1976.

McKenzie, R. E., Ehrisman, W. J., Montgomery, P. S. & Barnes, R. H. The treatment of headache by means of electroencephalographic biofeedback. *Headache*, 1974, **13**, 164–172.

Raskin, M., Johnson, G. & Rondestvedt, J. W. Chronic anxiety treated by feedback-induced muscle relaxation: A pilot study. *Archives of General Psychiatry*, 1973, **28**, 263–267.

Reavley, W. The use of biofeedback in the treatment of writer's cramp. *Journal of Behavior Therapy & Experimental Psychiatry*, 1975, **6**, 335–338.

Reeves, J. L. & Mealiea, W. L. Biofeedback-assisted cue-controlled relaxation for the treatment of flight phobias. *Journal of Behavior Therapy & Experimental Psychiatry*, 1975, **6**, 1–5.

Reeves, J. L. EMG-biofeedback reduction of tension headache: A cognitive skills-training approach. *Biofeedback & Self-Regulation*, 1976, **1**, 217–225.

Reinking, R. H. & Kohl, M. L. Effects of various forms of relaxation training on physiological and self-report measures of relaxation. *Journal of Consulting & Clinical Psychology*, 1975, **43**, 595–600.

Reinking, R. H. & Hutchings, D. Follow up and extension of "Tension headaches — what method is most effective?" Paper presented at the meeting of the Biofeedback Research Society, Colorado Springs, Colorado, 1976.

Scherr, M. S., Crawford, P. L., Sergent, C. B. & Scherr, C. A. Effect of biofeedback techniques on chronic asthma in a summer camp environment. *Annals of Allergy*, 1975, **35**, 289–295.

Schedivy, D. I. & Kleinman, K. M. Lack of correlation between frontalis EMG and either neck EMG or verbal ratings of tension. *Psychophysiology*, 1977, **14**, 182–186.

Sime, W. E. & DeGood, D. E. Effect of EMG biofeedback and progressive relaxation training on awareness of frontalis muscle tension. *Psychophysiology*, 1977, **14**, 522–530.

Staudenmayer, H. & Kinsman, R. A. Awareness during electromyographic biofeedback: Of signal or process? *Biofeedback & Self-Regulation*, 1976, **1**, 191–199.

Steffen, J. J. Electromyographically induced relaxation in the treatment of chronic alcohol abuse. *Journal of Consulting & Clinical Psychology*, 1975, **43**, 275.

Steinmark, S. & Borkovec, T. Active and placebo treatment effects on moderate insomnia under counterdemand and positive demand instructions. *Journal of Abnormal Psychology*, 1975, **83**, 157–163.

Stoyva, J. & Budzynski, T. H. Cultivated low arousal — an anti-stress response? In L. V. DiCara (Ed.), *Recent Advances in Limbic and Autonomic Nervous System Research*. New York: Plenum, 1974, pp. 265–290.

Surwit, R. S., Shapiro, D. & Good, M. I. A comparison of cardiovascular biofeedback, neuromuscular biofeedback, and meditation in the treatment of borderline essential hypertension. *Journal of Consulting and Clinical Psychology*, 1978, in press.

Townsend, R., House, J. & Addario, D. A comparison of biofeedback-mediated relaxation and group therapy in the treatment of chronic anxiety. *American Journal of Psychiatry*, 1975, **132**, no. **6**, 598–601.

Weston, A. Perception of autonomic processes, social acquiescence and cognitive development of a sense of self-control in essential hypertensives trained to lower blood pressure using biofeedback procedures. Unpublished doctoral dissertation, Nova University, Ft. Lauderdale, Florida, 1974.

White, P. D. & Alexander, A. B. EMG biofeedback as a treatment for tension headache: Viable intervention or placebo? Paper presented at the meeting of the Society for Psychophysiological Research, San Diego, California, 1976.

Wickramasekera, I. Electromyographic feedback training and tension headache: Preliminary observations. *American Journal of Clinical Hypnosis*, 1972, **15**, 83–85.

Wickramasekera, I. Instructions and EMG feedback in systematic desensitization: A case report. *Behavior Therapy*, 1972, **3**, 460–465.

Chapter 8

Adler, C. S. & Adler, S. M. Biofeedback-psychotherapy for the treatment of headaches: A five-year follow-up. *Headache*, 1976, **16**, 189–191.

Andreychuk, T. & Skriver, C. Hypnosis and biofeedback in the treatment of migraine headache. *International Journal of Clinical and Experimental Hypnosis*, 1975, **23**, 172–183.

Appenzeller, O. Monoamines, headache and behavior. In O. Appenzeller (Ed.), *Pathogenesis and Treatment of Headache*. New York: Spectrum, 1976.

Ardlie, N. G., Glew, G. & Schwartz, C. J. Influence of catecholamines on nucleotide-induced platelet aggregation. *Nature*, 1966, **212**, 415–417.

Beahrs, J. O., Harris, D. R. & Hilgard, E. R. Failure to alter skin inflammation by hypnotic suggestion in five subjects with normal skin reactivity. *Psychosomatic Medicine*, 1970, **32**, 627–631.

Benson, H., Klemchuk, H. P. & Graham, J. R. The usefulness of the relaxation response in the therapy of headache. *Headache*, 1974, **14**, 49–52.

Blanchard, E. B., Theobald, D. E., Williamson, D. A., Silver, B. V. & Brown, D. A. A controlled evaluation of temperature biofeedback in the treatment of migraine headaches. *Archives of General Psychiatry*, 1978, in press.

Blanchard, E. B. & Young, L. D. Self-control of cardiac functioning: A promise as yet unfulfilled. *Psychological Bulletin*, 1974, **79**, 145–163.

Chapman, L. F., Goodell, H. & Wolff, H. G. Increased inflammatory reaction induced by central nervous system activity. *Transactions of the Association of American Physicians*, 1959, **72**, 84–109.

Christie, D. J. & Kotses, H. Bidirectional operant conditioning of the cephalic vasomotor response. *Journal of Psychosomatic Research*, 1973, **17**, 167–170.

Crafts, L. W., Schneirla, T. C., Robinson, E. E. & Gilbert, R. W. *Recent Experiments in Psychology*. New York: McGraw-Hill, 1950.

Dalessio, D. J. *Wolff's Headache and Other Head Pain*, 3rd ed. New York: Oxford University Press, 1972.

Dalessio, D. J. Migraine, platelets, and headache prophylaxis. *Journal of the American Medical Association*, 1978a, **239**, 52–53.

Dalessio, D. J. Of platelets, their antagonists, and transient cerebral ischemia. *Journal of the American Medical Association, 1978b*, **239**, 228–229.

Deshmukh, S. V. & Meyer, J. S. Cyclic changes in platelet dynamics and the pathogenesis and prophylaxis of migraine. *Headache*, 1977, **17**, 101–108.

Diamond, S. & Medina, J. L. Double-blind study of propranolol for migraine prophylaxis. *Headache*, 1976, **16**, 24–27.

Dobeta, H., Sugano, H. & Ohno, Y. Circulatory changes during autogenic training. In J. J. Lopez Ibor (Ed.), *Fourth World Congress of Psychiatry, Madrid, 5-11, IX, 1966*. International Congress Series, No. 117, p. 45. Excerpta Medica Foundation. Amsterdam, 1966.

Headache. Editorial, 1965, **5**, 60–61.

Fahrion, S. L. Autogenic biofeedback treatment for migraine. *Mayo Clinic Proceedings*, 1977, **52**, 776–784.

Feuerstein, M. & Adams, H. E. Cephalic vasomotor feedback in the modification of migraine headache. *Biofeedback and Self-Regulation*, 1977, **2**, 241–254.

Feuerstein, M., Adams, H. E. & Beiman, I. Cephalic vasomotor and electromyographic feedback in the treatment of combined muscle contraction and migraine headaches in a geriatric case. *Headache*, 1976, **16**, 232–237.

Friar, L. R. & Beatty, J. Migraine: Management by trained control of vasoconstriction. *Journal of Consulting and Clinical Psychology*, 1976, **44**, 46–53.

Fried, F. E., Lamberti, J. & Sneed, P. Treatment of tension and migraine headaches with biofeedback techniques. *Missouri Medicine*, 1977, **74**, 253–255.

Friedman, A. P. Use of tranquilizers in the treatment of headache. *American Practitioner and Digest of Treatment*, 1957, **8**, 94–97.

Friedman, A. P. Reflections on the treatment of headache. *Headache*, 1972, **11**, 148–155.

Gotoh, F., Kanda, T., Sakai, F. Yamamoto, M. & Takeoka, T. Serum dopamine-β-hydroxylase activity in migraine. *Archives of Neurology*, 1976, **33**, 656–657.

Gottschalk, L. A. A study of conditioned vasomotor responses in ten human subjects. *Psychosomatic Medicine*, 1946, **8**, 16–27.

Graham, D. F., Stern, J. A. & Winokur, G. Experimental investigation of the specificity of attitude hypothesis in psychosomatic disease. *Psychosomatic Medicine*, 1958, **20**, 446–457.

Graham, F. K. & Kunish, N. O. Physiological responses of unhypnotized subjects to attitude suggestions. *Psychosomatic Medicine*, 1965, **27**, 317–329.

Graham, G. W. Hypnotic treatment for migraine headaches. *The International Journal of Clinical and Experimental Hypnosis*, 1975, **23**, 165–171.

Hadfield, J. A. The influence of suggestion on body temperature. *Lancet*, 1920, **2**, 68–69.

Ikemi, Y., Nakagawa, S., Kimura, M., Dobeta, H., Ohno, Y. & Sugita, M. Blood-flow change by autogenic training — including observations in a case of gastric fistula. In W. Luthe (Ed.), *Autogenic Training: Correlationes Psychosomaticae* (International Edition). New York: Grune & Stratton, 1965.

Johnson, W. G. & Turin, A. Biofeedback treatment of migraine headache: A systematic case study. *Behavior Therapy*, 1975, **6**, 394–397.

Kaneko, Z. & Takaishi, N. Psychosomatic studies on chronic urticaria. *Folia Psychiatrica et Neurologica Japonica*, 1963, **17**, 16–24.

Kentsmith, D., Strider, F., Copenhaver, J. & Jacques, D. Effects of biofeedback upon suppression of migraine symptoms and plasma dopamine-β-hydroxylase activity. *Headache*, 1976, **16**, 173–177.

Kewman, D. G. Voluntary control of digital skin temperature for treatment of migraine headaches. *Dissertation Abstracts International*, 1978, **38**, (7), 3400-B.

Koppman, J. W., McDonald, R. D. & Kunzel, M. G. Voluntary regulation of temporal artery diameter by migraine patients. Paper presented at the Fifteenth Annual Meeting of the American Association for the Study of Headache, New York, New York. June 1973.

Korn, R. R. Vasomotor conditioning and the vascular headache: Toward a therapeutic synthesis. (Preliminary Report). *Intercollegiate Psychology Association*, 1949, **1**, 51–67.

Legalos, C. N. Biofeedback and psychotherapy. *Seminars in Psychiatry*, 1973, **5**, 529–533.

Li Chao-i, Lin Yuan-lien & Wang, S. Influence of attention on the state of the dermal vessels. *Acta Psychologica Sinica*, 1964, **3**, 298–302.

Luthe, W. *Autogenic Therapy, vol. 4 Research and Theory*. New York: Grune & Stratton, 1970.

Maslach, C., Marshall, G. & Zimbardo, P. G. Hypnotic control of peripheral skin temperature: A case report. *Psychophysiology*, 1972, **9**, 600–605.

Mathew, R. J., Largen, J. W., Claghorn, J. L., Dobbins, K. & Meyer, J. S. Relationship between volitional alteration in skin temperature and regional cerebral blood flow in normal subjects. Paper presented at annual meeting of the Biofeedback Society of America, Albuquerque, New Mexico, March 1978.

Medina, J. L., Diamond, S. & Franklin, M. A. Biofeedback therapy for migraine. *Headache*, 1976, **16**, 115–118.

Menzies, R. Conditioned vasomotor responses in human subjects. *Journal of Psychology*, 1937, **4**, 75–120.

Menzies, R. Further studies of conditioned vasomotor responses in human subjects. *Journal of Experimental Psychology*, 1941, **29**, 457–482.

Miller, N. E. Biofeedback and visceral learning. In M. R. Rosenzweig and L. W. Porter (Eds.), *Annual Review of Psychology,* vol. 29. Palo Alto: Annual Reviews, 1978.

Mitch, P. S., McGrady, A. & Iannone, A. Autogenic feedback training in migraine: A treatment report. *Headache,* 1976, **15**, 267–270.

Mitchell, K. R. & Mitchell, D. M. Migraine: An exploratory treatment application of programmed behavior therapy techniques. *Journal of Psychosomatic Research,* 1971, **15**, 137–157.

Mullinex, J. M., Norton, B. J., Hack, S. & Fishman, M. A. Skin temperature biofeedback and migraine. *Headache,* 1978, **17**, 242–244.

Paul, G. L. The production of blisters by hypnotic suggestion: Another look. *Psychosomatic Medicine,* 1963, **25**, 233–244.

Paulley, J. W. & Haskell, D. A. L. The treatment of migraine without drugs. *Journal of Psychosomatic Research,* 1975, **19**, 367–374.

Peters, J. E. & Stern, R. M. Specificity of attitude hypothesis in psychosomatic medicine: A reexamination. *Journal of Psychosomatic Research,* 1971, **15**, 129–135.

Price, K. P. The application of behavior therapy to the treatment of psychosomatic disorders: Retrospect and prospect. *Psychotherapy: Theory, Research and Practice,* 1974, **11**, 138–155.

Price, K. P. & Tursky, B. Vascular reactivity of migraineurs and nonmigraineurs: A comparison of responses to self-control procedures. *Headache,* 1976, **16**, 210–217.

Reading, C. & Mohr, P. D. Biofeedback control of migraine: A pilot study. *British Journal of Social and Clinical Psychology,* 1976, **15**, 429–433.

Roessler, R. L. & Brogden, W. J. Conditioned differentiation of vasoconstriction to subvocal stimuli. *American Journal of Psychology,* 1943, **56**, 78–86.

Ryan, R. E., Sr. Motrin — a new agent for the symptomatic treatment of muscle contraction headache. *Headache,* 1977, **16**, 280–283.

Sargent, J. D., Green, E. E. & Walters, E. D. The use of autogenic feedback training in a pilot study of migraine and tension headaches. *Headache,* 1972, **12**, 120–124.

Sargent, J. D., Green, E. E. & Walters, E. D. Preliminary report on the use of autogenic feedback training in the treatment of migraine and tension headaches. *Psychosomatic Medicine,* 1973, **35**, 129–135.

Sargent, J. D., Walters, D. & Green, E. Psychosomatic self-regulation of migraine headaches. *Seminars in Psychiatry,* 1973, **5**, 415–428.

Schwartz, G. E. Biofeedback as therapy, some theoretical and practical issues. *American Psychologist,* 1973, **28**, 666–673.

Shmavonian, B. M. Methodological study of vasomotor conditioning in human subjects. *Journal of Comparative and Physiological Psychology,* 1959, **52**, 315–321.

Solbach, P. & Sargent, J. D. A follow-up evaluation of the Menninger pilot migraine study using thermal training. *Headache,* 1977, **17**, 198–202.

Sovak, M., Fronek, A., Helland, D. R. & Doyle, R. Effects of vasomotor changes in the upper extremities on the hemodynamics of the carotid arterial beds: A possible mechanism of biofeedback therapy of migraine. (A preliminary report). In J. I. Martin (Ed.), *Proceedings of the San Diego Biomedical Symposium,* vol. 15. New York: Academic Press, 1976.

Stambaugh, E. E. & House, A. E. Multimodality treatment of migraine headache: A case study utilizing biofeedback, relaxation, autogenic and hypnotic treatments. *The American Journal of Clinical Hypnosis,* 1977, **19**, 235–240.

Symon, L., Bull, J. W. D., duBoulay, E. P. G. H., Marshall, J. & Russell, R. W. R. Reactivity of cerebral vessels. In J. N. Cummings (Ed.), *Background to Migraine,* New York: Springer-Verlag, 1973.

Taub, E. Self-regulation of human tissue temperature. In G. E. Schwartz and J. Beatty (Eds.), *Biofeedback Theory and Research.* New York: Academic Press, 1977.

Teichner, W. H. & Levine, J. M. Digital vasomotor conditioning and body heat regulation. *Psychophysiology,* 1968, **5**, 67–76.

Tokyo, K. H., Tokyo, K. O. & Naruse, G. A study of plethysmography and skin temperature during active concentration and autogenic exercise. In W. Luthe (Ed.), *Autogenic Training: Correlations Psychosomaticae* (International Edition). New York: Grune & Stratton, 1965.

Turin, A. & Johnson, W. G. Biofeedback therapy for migraine headaches. *Archives of General Psychiatry,* 1976, **33**, 517–519.

Warner, G. & Lance, J. W. Relaxation therapy in migraine and chronic tension headache. *The Medical Journal of Australia,* 1975, **1**, 298–301.

Wickramasekera, I. E. Temperature feedback for the control of migraine. *Journal of Behavior Therapy and Experimental Psychiatry,* 1973, **4**, 343–345.

Yates, A. J. *Theory and Practice in Behavior Therapy.* New York: Wiley, 1975.

Zamani, R. Treatment of migraine headache through operant conditioning of vasoconstriction of the extracranial temporal artery (biofeedback), and through deep muscle relaxation. *Dissertation Abstracts International,* 1974, **35** (6), 3046-B.

Chapter 9

Barlow, D. H., Blanchard, E. B., Hayes, S. C. & Epstein, L. H. Single-case designs and clinical biofeedback experimentation. *Biofeedback and Self-Regulation,* 1977, **2**, 221–239.

Benson, H., Rosner, B. A., Marzetta, B. R. & Klemchuk, H. P. Decreased blood pressure in borderline hypertensive subjects who practice meditation. *Journal of Chronic Disease,* 1974, **27**, 163–169.

Birbaumer, N. Biofeedback training: A critical review of its clinical applications and some possible future directions. *European Journal of Behavioral Analysis and Modification,* 1978, in press.

Blanchard, E. B. & Abel, G. G. An experimental case study of the biofeedback treatment of a rape-induced psychological cardiovascular disorder. *Behavior Therapy,* 1976, **7**, 113–119.

Borkovec, T. D. The role of expectancy and physiological feedback in fear reduction: A review with special reference to subject characteristics. *Behavior Therapy,* 1973, **4**, 491–505.

Budzynski, T. & Stoyva, J. Biofeedback techniques in behavior therapy. Reprinted in D. Shapiro; T. X. Barber; L. V. DiCara; J. Kamiya; N. E. Miller; & J. Stoyva (Eds.), *Biofeedback and Self-control: 1972.* Chicago: Aldine, 1973.

Campbell, D. T. & Stanley, J. C. *Experimental and Quasi-experimental Designs for Research*. Chicago: Rand-McNally, 1970.

Canter, A., Kondo, C. Y. & Knott, J. R. A comparison of EMG feedback and progressive muscle relaxation training in anxiety neurosis. *British Journal of Psychiatry*, 1975, **127**, 470–477.

Cattell, R. B. & Scheier, I. H. *The Meaning and Measurement of Neuroticism and Anxiety*. New York: Ronald, 1961.

Chisholm, R. C., DeGood, D. E. & Hartz, M. A. Effects of alpha feedback training on occipital EEG, heart rate, and experiential reactivity to a laboratory stressor. *Psychophysiology*, 1977, **14**, 157–163.

Davison, G. C. & Neale, J. M. *Abnormal Psychology: An Experimental Clinical Approach*. New York: Wiley, 1978.

DeGood, D. E. & Adams, A. S. Control of cardiac response under aversive stimulation: Superiority of a heart-rate feedback condition. *Biofeedback and Self-Regulation*, 1976, **1**, 373–385.

DiCara, L. V. & Weiss, J. M. Effect of heart-rate learning under curare on subsequent noncurarized avoidance learning. *Journal of Comparative and Physiological Psychology*, 1969, **69**, 368–374.

Garrett, B. L. & Silver, M. P. The use of EMG and alpha biofeedback to relieve test anxiety in college students. In I. Wickramasekera (Ed.), *Biofeedback, Behavior Therapy, and Hypnosis: Potentiating the Verval Control of Behavior for Clinicians*. Chicago: Nelson-Hall, 1976.

Garrett, B. L. & Silver, M. P. A comparison of EMG and alpha biofeedback with desensitization with test-anxious college students. *Biofeedback and Self-Regulation*, 1978, in press.

Gatchel, R. J. Frequency of feedback and learned heart rate control. *Journal of Experimental Psychology*, 1974, **103**, 274–283.

Gatchel, R. J. Perceived control: A review and evaluation of therapeutic implications. In A. Baum; J. Singer; & S. Valins (Eds.), *Advances in Environmental Psychology*. Hillsdale, N.J.: Erlbaum. In press.

Gatchel, R. J. & Proctor, J. D. Effectiveness of voluntary heart rate control in reducing speech anxiety. *Journal of Consulting and Clinical Psychology*, 1976, **44**, 381–398.

Gatchel, R. J., Hatch, J. P., Maynard, A., Turns, R. & Taunton-Blackwood, A. Comparative effectiveness of heart rate biofeedback, false-biofeedback, and systematic desensitization in reducing speech anxiety: Short- and long-term effectiveness. *Journal of Consulting and Clinical Psychology*, 1979, in press.

Gatchel, R. J., Hatch, J. P., Watson, P. J., Smith, D. & Gaas, E. Comparative effectiveness of voluntary heart-rate control and muscular relaxation as active coping skills for reducing speech anxiety. *Journal of Consulting and Clinical Psychology*, 1977, **45**, 1093–1100.

Gatchel, R. J., Korman, M., Weis, C. B., Smith, D. & Clarke, L. A multiple-response evaluation of EMG biofeedback performance during training and stress-induction conditions. *Psychophysiology*, 1978, in press.

Geer, J. H. Fear and autonomic arousal. *Journal of Abnormal and Social Psychology*, 1966, **71**, 253–255.

Goldfried, M. R. & Davison, G. C. *Clinical Behavior Therapy*. New York: Holt, Rinehart, & Winston, 1976.

Goldfried, M. R. & Trier, C. S. Effectiveness of relaxation as an active coping skill. *Journal of Abnormal Psychology*, 1974, **83**, 348–355.

Gottman, J. M. N-of-one and N-of-two research in psychotherapy. *Psychological Bulletin*, 1973, **80**, 93–105.

Hatch, J. P. The effects of biofeedback schedules on the operant modification of human heart rate. Unpublished doctoral dissertation, University of Texas at Arlington, 1977.

Headrick, M. W., Feather, B. W. & Wells, D. T. Unidirectional and large magnitude heart rate changes with augmented sensory feedback. *Psychophysiology*, 1971, **8**, 132–142.

Hodgson, R. & Rachman, S., II. Desynchrony in measure of fear. *Behavior Research and Therapy*, 1974, **12**, 319–320.

Jacobson, E. *Progressive Relaxation*. Chicago: University of Chicago Press, 1938.

Jessup, B. A. & Neufeld, R. W. J. Effects of biofeedback and "autogenic relaxation" techniques on physiological and subjective responses in psychiatric patients: A preliminary analysis. *Behavior Therapy*, 1977, **8**, 160–167.

Jones, M. C. A laboratory study of fear: The case of Peter. *Pedagogical Seminary*, 1924, **31**, 308–315.

Klorman, R., Weissberg, R. P. & Wiesenfeld, A. R. Individual differences in fear and autonomic reactions to affective stimulation. *Psychophysiology*, 1977, **14**, 45–51.

Lacey, J. I. Somatic response patterning and stress: Some revisions of activation theory. In M. H. Appley & R. Trumbull (Eds.), *Psychological Stress*. New York: McGraw-Hill, 1967.

Lader, M. H. & Mathews, A. M. A physiological model of phobic anxiety and desensitization. *Behavior Research and Therapy*, 1968, **6**, 411–421.

Lang, P. J. Learned control of human heart rate in a computer directed environment. In P. Obrist; A. Black; J. Brener, & L. DiCara (Eds.), *Contemporary Trends in Cardiovascular Psychophysiology*. Chicago: Aldine-Atherton, 1974.

Lang, P. J. The psychophysiology of anxiety. In H. Akiskal (Ed.), *Psychiatric Diagnosis: Exploration of Biological Criteria*. New York: Spectrum, 1977a.

Lang, P. J. Research on the specificity of feedback training: Implications for the use of biofeedback in the treatment of anxiety and fear. In J. Beatty and H. Legweie (Eds.), *Biofeedback and Behavior*, Proceedings of the NATO Symposium on Biofeedback and Behavior, Munich. New York: Plenum Press, 1977b.

Lang, P. J., Melamed, B. G. & Hart, J. A psychophysiological analysis of fear modification using an automated desensitization procedure. *Journal of Abnormal Psychology*, 1970, **76**, 220–234.

Lang, P. J., Rice, D. C. & Sternbach, R. A. Psychophysiology of emotion. In N. Greenfield & R. Sternbach (Eds.), *Handbook of Psychophysiology*. New York: Holt, Rinehart, & Winston, 1972.

Marks, I. M. Flooding (implosion) and allied treatments. In W. S. Agras (Ed.), *Behavior Modification: Principles and Clinical Applications*. Boston: Little, Brown, 1972.

Marks, I. M. Phobias and obsessions: Clinical phenomena in search of a laboratory model. In J. D. Maser & M. E. P. Seligman (Eds.), *Psychopathology: Experimental Models*. San Francisco: Freeman, 1977.

Miller, B. V. & Bernstein, D. A. Instructional demand in a behavioral avoidance test for claustrophobic fears. *Journal of Abnormal Psychology*, 1972, **80**, 206–210.

Mischel, W. *Introduction to Personality*. New York: Holt, Rinehart, & Winston, 1976.

Mowrer, O. H. On the dual nature of learning: A reinterpretation of "conditioning" and "problem-solving." *Harvard Educational Review*, 1947, **17**, 102–148.

Nunes, J. S. & Marks, I. M. Feedback of true heart rate during exposure in vivo. *Archives of General Psychiatry*, 1975, **32**, 933–936.

Nunes, J. S. & Marks, I. M. Feedback of true heart rate during exposure in vivo: Partial replication with methodological improvement. *Archives of General Psychiatry*, 1976, **33**, 1346–1350.

Orne, M. T. & Paskewitz, D. A. Aversive situational effects on alpha feedback training. *Science*, 1974, **186**, 458–460.

Paul, G. L. Insight versus desensitization in psychotherapy two years after termination. *Journal of Consulting Psychology*, 1967, **31**, 333–348.

Prigatano, G. P. & Johnson, H. J. Biofeedback control of heart rate variability to phobic stimuli: A new approach to treating spider phobia. In *Proceedings of Annual Convention, APA*. Washington: American Psychological Association, 1972, pp. 403–404.

Raskin, M., Johnson, G. & Rondestvedt, T. Chronic anxiety treated by feedback-induced muscle relaxation. *Archives of General Psychiatry*, 1973, **28**, 263–266.

Schultz, J. H. & Luthe, W. *Autogenic Training: A Psycho-physiologic Approach in Psychotherapy*. New York: Grune & Stratten, 1959.

Schwartz, G. E. Biofeedback, self-regulation, and the patterning of physiological processes. *American Scientist*, 1975, **63**, 314–324.

Scott, R. W., Blanchard, E. B., Edmunson, E. D. & Young, L. D. A shaping procedure for heart rate control in chronic tachycardia. *Perceptual and Motor Skills*, 1973, **37**, 327–338.

Scott, R. W., Peters, R. D., Gillespie, W. J., Blanchard, E. B., Edmunson, E. D. & Young, L. D. The use of shaping and reinforcement in the operant acceleration and deceleration of heart rate. *Behavior Research and Therapy*, 1973, **11**, 179–185.

Seligman, M. E. P. & Hager, J. L. (Eds.), *Biological Boundaries of Learning*. New York: Appleton-Century-Crofts, 1972.

Shapiro, D., Schwartz, G. E., Shnidman, S., Nelson, S. & Silverman, S. Operant control of fear-related electrodermal responses in snake-phobic subjects. *Psychophysiology*, 1972, **9**, 271 (abstract).

Sirota, A. D., Schwartz, G. E. & Shapiro, D. Voluntary control of human heart rate: Effect on reaction to aversive stimulation. *Journal of Abnormal Psychology*, 1974, **83**, 261–267.

Sirota, A. D., Schwartz, G. E. & Shapiro, D. Voluntary control of human heart rate: Effect on reaction to aversive stimulation: A replication and extension. *Journal of Abnormal Psychology*, 1976, **85**, 473–477.

Spielberger, C., Gorsuch, R. & Lushene, R. *State-Trait Anxiety Inventory Manual*. Palo Alto, Ca.: Consulting Psychologists Press, 1970.

Townsend, R. E., House, J. F. & Addario, D. A comparison of EMG feedback and progressive muscle relaxation training in anxiety neuroses. *American Journal of Psychiatry*, 1975, **132**, 598–601.

Valle, R. S. & DeGood, D. E. Effects of state-trait anxiety on the ability to enhance and suppress EEG alpha. *Psychophysiology*, 1977, **14**, 1–7.

Victor, R., Mainardi, J. A. & Shapiro, D. Effects of biofeedback and voluntary control procedures on heart rate and perception of pain during the cold pressor test. *Psychosomatic Medicine*, in press.

Watson, J. P., Gaind, R. & Marks, I. M. Prolonged exposure: A rapid treatment for phobics. *British Medical Journal*, 1971, **1**, 13–15.

Watson, J. B. & Rayner, R. Conditioned emotional reactions. *Journal of Experimental Psychology*, 1920, **3**, 1–14.

Wickramasekera, I. Heart rate feedback and the management of cardiac neurosis. *Journal of Abnormal Psychology*, 1974, **83**, 578–580.

Wickramasekera, I. Instructions and EMG feedback in systematic desensitization: A case report. *Behavior Therapy*, 1972, **3**, 460–465.

Wolpe, J. *Psychotherapy by Reciprocal Inhibition*. Stanford, Calif.: Stanford University Press, 1958.

Chapter 10

Black, A. H., Cott, A. & Pavloski, R. The operant theory approach to biofeedback training. In G. E. Schwartz & J. Beatty (Eds.), *Biofeedback: Theory and Research*. New York: Academic Press, 1977.

Brener, J. Sensory and perceptual determinants of voluntary visceral control. In G. E. Schwartz and J. Beatty (Eds.), *Biofeedback: Theory and Research*. New York: Academic Press, 1977.

Brener, J., Kleinman, R. & Goesling, W. J. The effects of different exposures to augmented sensory feedback on the control of heart rate. *Psychophysiology*, 1969, **5**, 510–516.

Budzynski, T., Stoyva, J. & Adler, C. Feedback-induced muscle relaxation: Application to tension headache. *Journal of Behavior Therapy and Experimental Psychiatry*, 1970, **1**, 205–211.

Budzynski, T. H., Stoyva, J. M., Adler, C. S. & Mullaney, D. J. EMG biofeedback and tension headache: A controlled outcome study. *Psychosomatic Medicine*, 1973, **35**, 484–496.

Crider, A., Schwartz, G. E. & Shnidman, S. On the criteria for instrumental autonomic conditioning: A reply to Katkin and Murray. *Psychological Bulletin*, 1969, **71**, 455–461.

Frank, J. D. *Persuasion and Healing*. Baltimore: Johns Hopkins University Press, 1973.

Fuller, G. D. Current status of biofeedback in clinical practice. *American Psychologist*, 1978, **33**, 39–48.

Grenfell, R. F., Briggs, A. H. & Holland, W. C. Antihypertensive drugs evaluated in a controlled double-blind study. *Southern Medical Journal*, 1963, **56**, 1410–1416.

Hanna, R., Wilfling, F. & McNeill, B. A biofeedback treatment for stuttering. *Journal of Speech and Hearing Disorders*, 1975, **40**, 270–273.

Hersen, M. & Barlow, D.M. *Single Case Experimental Designs*. New York: Pergamon Press, 1976.

Katkin, E. S. *Instrumental Autonomic Conditioning*. New York: General Learning Press, 1971.

Katkin, E. S. & Murray, E. N. Instrumental conditioning of autonomically mediated behavior: Theoretical and methodological issues. *Psychological Bulletin*, 1968, **70**, 52–68.

Katkin, E. S., Fitzgerald, C. R. & Shapiro, D. Clinical applications of biofeedback: Current status and future prospects. In M. L. Pick, M. W. Leibowitz, J. E. Singer, A. Steinschneider, & H. W. Stevenson (Eds.), *Applications of Basic Research in Psychology*. New York: Plenum, in press.

Katkin, E. S., Murray, E. N. & Lachman, R. Concerning instrumental autonomic conditioning: A rejoiner. *Psychological Bulletin*, 1969, **71**, 462–466.

Kazdin, A. E. & Wilcoxon, L. A. Systematic desensitization and nonspecific treatment effects: A methodological evaluation. *Psychological Bulletin*, 1976, **83**, 729–758.

Lang, P. J. Learned control of human heart rate in a computer directed environment. In P. A. Obrist, A. H. Black, J. Brener, & L. V. DiCara (Eds.), *Cardiovascular Psychophysiology*. Chicago: Aldine, 1974.

Lick, J. & Bootzin, R. Expectancy factors in the treatment of fear: Methodological and theoretical issues. *Psychological Bulletin*, 1975, **82**, 917–931.

Miller, N. E. & DiCara, L. Instrumental learning of heart rate changes in curarized rats: Shaping, and specificity to discriminative stimulus.

Paul, G. L. Physiological effects of relaxation training and hypnotic suggestion. *Journal of Abnormal Psychology*, 1969, **74**, 425–437.

Sargent, J. D., Green, E. E. & Walters, E. D. Preliminary report on the use of autogenic feedback training in the treatment of migraine and tension headaches. *Psychosomatic Medicine*, 1973, **35**, 129–135.

Shapiro, A. K. Placebo effects in medicine, psychotherapy, and psychoanalysis. In A. E. Bergin and S. L. Garfield (Eds.), *Handbook of Psychotherapy and Behavior Change*. New York: Wiley, 1971.

Shapiro, D., Mainardi, J. A. & Surwit, R. S. Biofeedback and self-regulation in essential hypertension. In G. E. Schwartz & J. Beatty (Eds.), *Biofeedback: Theory and Research*. New York: Academic Press, 1977.

Shapiro, D. & Surwit, R. S. Learned control of physiological function and disease. In H. Leitenberg (Ed.), *Handbook of Behavior Modification and Behavior Therapy*. Englewood Cliffs, N.J.: Prentice-Hall, 1976.

Stroebel, C. F. & Glueck, B. C. Biofeedback treatment in medicine and psychiatry: An ultimate placebo? *Seminars in Psychiatry*, 1973, **5**, 379–393.

Truax, C. B. & Mitchell, K. M. Research on certain therapist interpersonal skills in relation to process and outcome. In A. E. Bergin & S. L. Garfield (Eds.), *Handbook of Psychotherapy and Behavior Change*. New York: Wiley, 1971.

Wallace, R. K. Physiological effects of transcendental meditation. *Science*, 1970, **167**, 1751–1754.

Wallace, R. K. & Benson, H. The physiology of meditation. *Scientific American*, 1972, **226**, 85–90.

Wickramasekera, I. Temperature feedback for the control of migraine. *Journal of Behavior Therapy and Experimental Psychiatry*, 1973, **4**, 343–345.

Chapter 11

Aarons, L. Subvocalization: Aural and EMG feedback in reading. *Perceptual and Motor Skills*, 1971, **33**: 1, 271–306.

Ancoli, S. & Kamiya, J. Methodological issues in alpha feedback training. *Proceedings of the Biofeedback Society of America, 8th Annual Meeting*, Orlando, Florida, 1977.

Barnett, A. Seasonal variations in the epidermal impedance of human skin. *American Journal of Physiology*, 1940, **129**, 306–307.

Darrow, C. W. The significance of the GSR in the light of its relation to quantitative measures of perspiration. *Psychological Bulletin*, 1934, **31**, 697–698.

Duxbury, A. J., Hughes, D. F. & Clark, D. E. Power spectral distribution of the masseter electromyogram from surface electrodes. *Journal of Oral Rehabilitation*, 1976, **3**, 333–339.

Edelberg, R. Electrical activity of the skin. In N. S. Greenfield & R. A. Sternbach (Eds.), *Handbook of Psychophysiology*. New York: Holt, Rinehart & Winston, 1972, 367–418.

Edelberg, R., Greiner, T. & Burch, N. R. Some membrane properties of the effector in the galvanic skin response. *Journal of Applied Physiology*, 1960, **15**, 691.

Geddes, L. A. *Electrodes and the Measurement of Bioelectric Events*. New York: Wiley, 1972.

Hardt, J. V. & Kamiya, J. Conflicting results in EEG alpha feedback studies: Why amplitude integration should replace percent time. *Biofeedback and Self-Regulation*, 1976, **1**:1, 63–75.

Hayes, K. J. Wave analyses of tissue noise and muscle action potentials. *Journal of Applied Physiology*, 1960, **15**, 749–752.

Johansson, S., Larsson, L. & Ortengren, R. An automated method for the frequency analysis of myoelectric signals evaluated by an investigation of the spectral changes following strong sustained contractions. *Medical and Biological Engineering*, 1970, **8**, 257–264.

Johnson, L. C. Learned control of brain wave activity. In J. Beatty & H. Legewie (Eds.), *Biofeedback and Behavior*. New York: Plenum Press, 1977, pp. 73–93.

Lang, P. J. Research on the specificity of feedback training: Implications for the use of biofeedback in the treatment of anxiety and fear. In J. Beatty & H. Legewie (Eds.), *Biofeedback and Behavior*. New York: Plenum Press, 1977, 323–329.

Leaf, W. B. & Gaarder, K. R. A simplified electromyographic feedback apparatus for relaxation training. *Journal of Behavior Therapy and Experimental Psychiatry*, 1971, **2**, 39–43.

Lykken, D. T. Properties of electrodes used in electrodermal measurement. *Journal of Comparative and Physiological Psychology*, 1959, **52**: 5, 629–634.

Lykken, D. T., Rose, R., Luther, B. & Maley, M. Correcting psychophysiological measures for individual differences in range. *Psychological Bulletin*, 1966, **66**: 6, 481–484.

Rugh, J. D. Evaluating and selecting biofeedback instrumentation. In J.V. Basmajian & J. Stoyva (Eds.), *Biofeedback Techniques in Clinical Practice vol. 2*. New York: BioMonitoring Applications, 1975.

Rugh, J. D. & Schwitzgebel, R. L. Performance variability in commercial biofeedback instrumentation. *Proceedings of the Association for the Advancement of Medical Instrumentation, 12th annual meeting*, San Francisco, California, 1977b, p. 35.

Rugh, J. D. & Solberg, W. K. The identification of stressful stimuli in natural environments using a portable biofeedback unit. *Proceedings of the Biofeedback Research Society, 5th annual meeting*, Colorado Springs, Colorado, 1974.

Rugh, J. D. & Schwitzgebel, R. L. Variability in commercial electromyographic biofeedback devices. *Behavior Research Methods and Instrumentation*, 1977a, **9**: 3, 281–285.

Schwitzgebel, R. L. & Rugh, J. D. Of bread, circuses, and alpha machines. *American Psychologist*, 1975 **30**, 361–370.

Travis, T. A. Kondo, C. Y. & Knott, J. R. Parameters of eyes-closed alpha enhancement. *Psychophysiology*, 1974, **11**, 674–681.

Chapter 12

Benson, H., Shapiro, D., Tursky, B. & Schwartz, E. Through operant conditioning techniques in patients with essential hypertension. *Science*, 1971, **173**, 740–742.

Blanchard, E. B. & Young, L. D. Clinical applications of biofeedback training. *Archives of General Psychiatry*, 1974, **30**, 573–589.

Brener, J. A general model of voluntary control applied to the phenomena of learned cardiovascular change. In P. A. Obrist; A. H. Black; J. Brener; & L. V. DiCara (Eds.), *Cardiovascular Psychophysiology*. Chicago: Aldine, 1974, pp. 365–391.

Brener, J., Kleinman, R. A. & Goesling, W. J. The effects of different exposure rates to augmented sensory feedback on the control of heart rate. *Psychophysiology*, 1969, **5**, 510–516.

Colgan, M. Effects of binary and proportional feedback on bidirectional control of heart rate. *Psychophysiology*, 1977, **14**, 187–191.

Elmore, A. M. & Tursky, B. The biofeedback hypothesis: An idea in search of a method, submitted for publication.

Engel, B. T., Nikoomanesh, P. & Schuster, M. M. Operant conditioning of rectosphincteric responses in the treatment of fecal incontinence. *New England Journal of Medicine*, 1974, **290**, 646–649.

Furedy, J. & Poulos, J. Heart rate decelerative Pavlovian conditioning with tilt as a UCS. *Biological Psychology*, 1976, **4**, 93–106.

Garcia, J. & Koelling, R. A. Relation of cue to consequence in avoidance learning. *Psychonomic Science*, 1966, **5**, 121–122.

Katkin, E. S. & Murray, E. N. Instrumental conditioning of autonomically mediated behavior. *Psychological Bulletin*, 1968, **70**, 52–68.

Kimmel, H. D. Instrumental conditioning of autonomically mediated behavior. *Psychological Bulletin*, 1967, **67**, 337–345.

Kimmel, H. D. Instrumental conditioning of autonomically mediated responses in human beings. *American Psychologist*, 1974, **29**, 325–335.

Kristt, D. A. & Engel, B. T. Learned control of blood pressure in patients with high blood pressure. *Circulation*, 1975, **51**, 370–378.

Lang, P. J. & Twentyman, C. T. Learning to control heart rate: Binary versus analogue feedback. *Psychophysiology*, 1974, **11**, 616–629.

Miller, N. E. & Dworkin, B. R. Critical issues in therapeutic applications of biofeedback. In G. E. Schwartz and J. Beatty (Eds.), *Biofeedback: Theory and Research*. New York: Academic Press, 1977.

Mulholland, T. B. Biofeedback as scientific method. In G. Schwartz & J. Beatty (Eds.), *Biofeedback: Theory and Research*. New York: Academic Press, 1977.

Noback, C. R. *The human nervous system*. New York: McGraw-Hill, 1967.

Obrist, P. A., Webb, R. A., Sutterer, J. R. & Howard, J. L. The cardiac-somatic relationship: Some reformulations. *Psychophysiology*, 1970, **6**, 569–587.

Schwartz, G. E. Clinical applications of biofeedback: Some theoretical issues. In D. Upper & D. S. Goodenough (Eds.), *Behavior Modification with the Individual Patient: Proceedings of the Third Annual Brockton Symposium on Behavior Therapy*. Nutley, N.J.: Roche, 1972.

Schwartz, G. E. Toward a theory of voluntary control of response patterns in the cardiovascular system. In P. Obrist et al., (Eds.), *Cardiovascular Psychophysiology*. Chicago: Aldine, 1974.

Shapiro, A. K. Contribution to a history of the placebo effect. *Behavioral Science*, 1960, **5**, 109–135.

Shapiro, D., Crider, A. B. & Tursky, B. Differentiation of an autonomic response through operant conditioning. *Psychonomic Science*, 1964, **1**, 147–148.

Shapiro, D., Mainardi, J. A. & Surwit, R. S. Biofeedback and self-regulation in essential hypertension. In G. E. Schwartz & J. Beatty (Eds.), *Biofeedback: Theory and Research*. New York: Academic Press, 1977.

Shapiro, D., Schwartz, G. E. & Tursky, B. Control of diastolic blood pressure in man by feedback and reinforcement. *Psychophysiology*, 1972, **9**, 296–304.

Shapiro, D., Schwartz, G. E. & Tursky, B. Differentiation of heart rate and blood pressure in man by operant conditioning. *Psychosomatic Medicine*, 1970, **32**, 417–423.

Shapiro, D. & Surwit, R. S. Learned control of physiological function and disease. In H. Leitenberg (Ed.), *Handbook of Behavior Modification and Behavior Therapy*. Englewood Cliffs, N.J.: Prentice-Hall, 1976.

Young, L. D. & Blanchard, E. B. Effects of auditory feedback of varying information content on the self-control of heart rate. *Journal of General Psychology*, 1974, **91**, 61–88.

Chapter 13

Blanchard, E. B. & Young, L. D. Clinical applications of biofeedback training. *Archives of General Psychiatry*, 1974, **30**, 573–589.

Brucker, B. S. Learned voluntary control of systolic blood pressure by spinal cord injury patients. Doctoral dissertation, New York University, 1977.

Brucker, B. S. & Ince, L. P. Biofeedback as an experimental treatment for postural hypotension in a patient with a spinal cord lesion. *Archives of Physical Medicine and Rehabilitation*, 1977, **58**, 49–53.

Engel, B. T. & Bleecker, E. R. Application of operant conditioning techniques to the control of the cardiac arrhythmias. In *Cardiovascular Psychophysiology*, P. A. Obrist, A. H. Black, J. Brener, & L. V. DiCara (Eds.), Chicago: Aldine, 1974, pp. 446–476.

Garcia, J. & Koelling, R. A. Relation of cue to consequence in avoidance learning. *Psychonomic Science*, 1966, **4**, 123–124.

Garcia, J., Ervin, F. R. & Koelling, R. A. Learning with prolonged delay of reinforcement. *Psychonomic Science*, 1966, **5**, 121–122.

Harris, A. H., Gilliam, W. J., Findley, J. D. & Brady, J. V. Instrumental conditioning of large-magnitude, daily, 12-hour blood pressure elevations in the baboon. *Science*, 1973, **182**, 175–177.

Kristt, D. A. & Engel, B. T. Learned control of blood pressure in patients with high blood pressure. *Circulation*, 1975, **51**, 370–378.

Luria, A. R. *The Mind of a Mnemonist*, trans. by L. Solotaroff. New York: Basic Books, 1968, pp. 138–143.

Miller, N. E. Liberalization of basic S-R concepts: Extensions to conflict behavior, motivation and social learning. In *Psychology: A Study of a Science*, Study 1, vol. 2, S. Koch (Ed.), New York: McGraw-Hill, 1959, pp. 196–292.

Miller, N. E. Learning of visceral and glandular responses. *Science*, 1969, **163**, 434–445.

Miller, N. E. Learning of visceral and glandular responses: Postscript. In *Current Status of Physiological Psychology: Readings*, D. Singh and C. T. Morgan (Eds.), Monterey: Brooks/Cole, 1972, pp. 245–250.

Miller, N. E. Biofeedback and visceral learning. *Annual Review of Psychology*, 1978, **29**, 373–404.

Miller, N. E. & Brucker, B. S. Learned large increases in blood pressure apparently independent of skeletal responses in patients paralayzed by spinal lesions. In *Biofeedback and Self-Regulation*, N. Birbaumer & H. D. Kimmel (Eds.), Hillside, N.J.: Lawrence Erlbaum Associates, in press.

Miller, N. E. & Dworkin, B. R. Visceral learning: Recent difficulties with curarized rats and significant problems for human research. In *Cardiovascular Psychophysiology*, P. A. Obrist, A. H. Black, J. Brener, & L. V. DiCara (Eds.), Chicago: Aldine, 1974, pp. 312–331.

Miller, N. E. & Dworkin, B. R. Critical issues in therapeutic applications of biofeedback. In *Biofeedback: Theory and Research*, G. E. Schwartz & J. Beatty (Eds.), New York: Academic Press, 1977, pp. 129–162.

Pickering, T. G. & Miller, N. E. Learned voluntary control of heart rate and rhythm in two subjects with premature ventricular contractions. *British Heart Journal*, 1977, **39**, 152–159.

Pickering, T. G., Brucker, B., Frankel, H. L., Mathias, C. J., Dworkin, B. R. & Miller, N. E. Mechanisms of learned vuluntary control of blood pressure in patients with generalized bodily paralysis. In *Biofeedback and Behavior*, J. Beatty & H. Legewie (Eds.), New York: Plenum Press, 1977, pp. 225–234.

Weiss, T. & Engel, B. T. Operant conditioning of heart rate in patients with premature ventricular contractions. *Psychosomatic Medicine*, 1971, **33**, 301–321.

Chapter 14

Brown, B. *New mind, New body: Biofeedback; New Directions for the Mind*. New York: Harper & Row, 1974.

Cuthbert, B. N. & Lang, P. J. Biofeedback and cardiovascular self-control. *Scandinavian Journal of Behavior Therapy*, 1976, **5**, 111–132.

Engel, G. L. The need for a new medical model: A challenge for biomedicine. *Science*, 1977, **196**, 129–136.

Fey, S. G. & Lindholm, E. Biofeedback and progressive relaxation: Effects on diastolic blood pressure and heart rate. *Psychophysiology*, 1978, **15**, 239–247.

Gatchel, R. J. Frequency of feedback and learned heart rate control. *Journal of Experimental Psychology*, 1974, **103**, 274–283.

Hassett, J. *A Primer of Psychophysiology*. San Francisco: Freeman, 1978.

Hatch, J. P. & Gatchel, R. J. Operant modification of human heart rate. Manuscript submitted for publication.

Lachman, S. J. *Psychosomatic disorders: A Behavioristic Interpretation*. New York: Wiley, 1972.

Lang, P. J., Troyer, W. G., Twentyman, C. I. & Gatchel, R. J. Differential effects of heart-rate modification training on college students, older males, and patients with ischemic heart disease. *Psychosomatic Medicine*, 1975, **37**, 429–446.

Lazarus, R. S. A cognitive analysis of biofeedback control. In G. E. Schwartz & J. Beatty (Eds.), *Biofeedback Theory and Research*. New York: Academic Press, 1977.

Lipowski, Z. J. Psychosomatic medicine in the seventies: An overview. *American Journal of Psychiatry*, 1977, **143**, 233–244.

McCanne, T. R. & Sandman, C. A. Determinants of human operant heart rate conditioning: A systematic investigation of several methodological issues. *Journal of Comparative and Physiological Psychology*, 1975, **88**, 609–618.

Miller, N. E. Biofeedback and visceral learning. In M. R. Rosenzweig & L. W. Porter (Eds.), *Annual Review of Psychology*. Palto Alto, Cal.: Annual Reviews, 1978.

Mulholland, T. Can you really turn on with alpha? Paper presented at the meeting of the Massachusetts Psychological Association, 1971.

Price, K. P. The application of behavior therapy to the treatment of psychosomatic disorders. *Psychotherapy: Theory, Research, and Practice*. 1974, **11**, 138–155.

Price, K. P., Gaas-Abrams, E. & Browder, S. Research developments in behavioral intervention with psychophysiological disorders. Paper presented at APA meeting, San Francisco, August, 1977.

Price, K. P. & Tursky, B. Vascular reactivity of migraineurs and nonmigraineurs: A comparison of responses to self-control procedures. *Headache*, 1976, **16**, 210–217.

Schwartz, G. E. Biofeedback as therapy: Some theoretical and practical issues. *American Psychologist*, 1973, **28**, 666–673.

Schwartz, G. E. & Weiss, S. M. What is behavioral medicine? *Psychosomatic Medicine*, 1977, **39**, 377–381.

Shapiro, A. K. Placebo effects in medicine, psychotherapy and psychoanalysis. In A. E. Bergin & S. L. Garfield (Eds.), *Handbook of Psychotherapy and Behavior Change*. New York: Wiley, 1971.

Shapiro, D. & Surwit, R. S. Learned control of physiological function and disease. In H. Leitenberg (Ed.), *Handbook of Behavior Modification and Behavior Therapy*. Englewood Cliffs, N.J.: Prentice-Hall, 1976.

Shapiro, D., Mainardi, J. A. & Surwit, R. S. Biofeedback and self-regulation in essential hypertension. In G. E. Schwartz & J. Beatty (Eds.), *Biofeedback Theory and Research*. New York: Academic Press, 1977.

Shealy, C. N. Letter to the editor. *Headache*. 1977, **17**, 132–133.

Stroebel, C. F. & Glueck, B. C. Biofeedback treatment in medicine and psychiatry: An ultimate placebo? *Seminars in Psychiatry*, 1973, *J*, 379–393.

Tarler-Benlolo, L. The role of relaxation in biofeedback training: A critical review of the literature. *Psychological Bulletin*, 1978, **85**, 7272–755.

Taub, E. Self-regulation of human tissue temperature. In G. E. Schwartz & J. Beatty (Eds.), *Biofeedback Theory and Research*. New York: Academic Press, 1977.

Wallace, R. K., Benson, H. & Wilson, A. F. A wakeful hypometabolic physiological state. *American Journal of Physiology*, 1971, **221**, 795–799.

AUTHOR INDEX

SUBJECT INDEX

Alcoholism, 129
Alpha rhythm, 5, 66, 67, 78, 84, 87, 96, 229
  and addiction, 92
  and anxiety, 159–160, 163, 164, 170
  and headache, 90
  and migraine, 141
  and neurotic symptoms, 91
  and pain, 91
  and relaxation, 87
  instrumentation, 188–189, 191, 201
Anxiety, 15, 21, 85, 127, 148, 230
  measurement of, 149–150, 157, 158, 163
  testing, 162–163, 170
Arrhythmias, cardiac, 32, 42, 46–47, 51, 219
Artifact, 218, 232
Asthma, 127–128
Autogenic training, 87, 135, 228
  and anxiety, 158
  and migraine, 138, 140, 143, 144, 146
  and Raynaud's Disease, 47
  and relaxation, 114
  and tension, 91
Autonomic nervous system, 2, 6, 116, 145,
  212
  and anxiety, 149, 151
  and EMG biofeedback, 120, 122
Aversive conditioning, 151, 159, 161

Behavioral medicine, 216, 233
Bidirectional conditioning, 185, 216
Blepharospasm, 102
Blood flow, 135
Blood pressure, 3, 6, 8, 13, 32, 33, 37, 100,
  109, 179, 223, 224, 228
Blood volume change, 135, 136, 145
Brain, 3
Brain waves, 5
  See also Alpha rhythm; Theta brain waves

Cardiac neurosis, 154
Cardiovascular disease, 28
Case studies
  and anxiety, 152
  and migraine, 140
  and muscular rehabilitation, 106, 114
Central nervous system (CNS), 151
  conditioning, 66
  description of, 3, 10
Cerebral palsy, 103, 104, 109
Cerebrospinal nervous system, 3, 10
  See also Central nervous system
Change, clinically significant, 29
Classical conditioning, 3, 4, 136, 145, 207
Claustrophobic, 156
Cognitive strategies, 56
Cold pressor test, 161
Constant cuff, 36, 37
Contingent feedback, 116, 118
Curare, 8–9

Diabetic, 129
Dopamine-beta-hydroxylase (DBH), 140
Dystonia, 99

EEG. *See* Alpha, Theta
Electrodermal activity, 3, 6, 116
  and anxiety, 154, 156, 159
  instrumentation, 192, 195–197
  skin resistance, 5
  See also GSR
EMG, 229
  and addiction, 92
  and anxiety, 153–154, 156, 157, 158, 163,
  164, 170
  and hypertension, 37, 40
  and insomnia, 95

ABOUT THE EDITORS AND CONTRIBUTORS

Robert J. Gatchel is an Associate Professor of Psychology at the University of Texas at Arlington and Clinical Associate Professor of Psychiatry at the University of Texas Health Science Center at Dallas. He is presently with the Department of Medical Psychology at the U.S. University of the Health Sciences in Bethesda, Maryland. He received his B.A. *Summa Cum Laude* from the State University of New York at Stony Brook in 1969, and his Ph.D. in Clinical Psychology from the University of Wisconsin in 1973. His research in the areas of behavioral medicine and psychophysiology is currently being supported by the National Institutes of Health. He is a reviewer and active contributor to many professional journals such as the *Journal of Abnormal Psychology, Journal of Consulting and Clinical Psychology*, and *Psychophysiology*. He is also co-author of the text *Fundamentals of Abnormal Psychology*.

Kenneth P. Price is an Assistant Professor in the Division of Psychology at the University of Texas Health Science Center at Dallas. He received his B.A. *Magna Cum Laude* from Brandeis University in 1970 and his Ph.D. in Clinical Psychology from the State University of New York at Stony Brook in 1975. His research in the area of stress and psychosomatic disorders has been supported by the National Migraine Foundation, Roche Psychiatric Service Center, and The National Institutes of Health. He has published articles in journals such as *Journal of Abnormal Psychology* and *Psychophysiology*, and has been a reviewer for journals such as *Behavior Therapy* and *Journal of Applied Behavior Analysis* as well as for government agencies. He is co-editor (with John M. Neale and Gerald C. Davison) of *Contemporary Readings in Psychopathology* published by John Wiley and Sons.

A. Barney Alexander (Ph.D., Indiana University) is Head of the Psychophysiology Department at the National Asthma Center in Denver,

Colorado. His current research interests are the psychophysiology of respiration, psychophysiological disorders, in particular asthma, and hormonal concomitants of human learning and memory.

Theodore X. Barber (Ph.D., American University) is Chief Psychologist and Director of Psychological Research at Medfield State Hospital in Medfield, Massachusetts. He is a prominent expert on hypnosis and other altered states of consciousness, as well as psychoactive drugs.

John V. Basmajian (M.D., University of Toronto) is the Director of the Rehabilitation Centre at Chedoke Hospitals in Hamilton, Ontario, Canada. In the early 1960's, he pioneered research on training people to consciously activate individual motor nerve cells in the spinal cord. More recently, he has greatly expanded the use of biofeedback in the treatment of rehabilitation patients with neurological deficits and post-surgical hand problems.

Edward B. Blanchard (Ph.D., Stanford University) is Professor of Psychology and Director of Clinical Training at the State University of New York at Albany. Hs has been active both in basic research on biofeedback processes and in clinical applications of biofeedback to cardiovascular problems, including cardiac arrhythmias and hypertension.

James H. Geer (Ph.D., University of Pittsburgh) is Professor and Chairman of Psychology at the State University of New York at Stony Brook. He has published extensively, principally in the field of human emotion. His most recent work has focused on human sexual behavior.

Steve Goldband (Ph.D., State University of New York at Buffalo) is a post-doctoral research fellow in the Department of Psychology at the State University of New York at Buffalo. His major area of research interest is the psychophysiological assessment of proneness to cardiovascular disorders.

John P. Hatch (Ph.D., University of Texas at Arlington) is a postdoctoral research fellow in the Department of Psychiatry at the State University of New York at Stony Brook. His major research interests are biofeedback and self-regulation techniques, and the psychophysiology of emotion and human sexual arousal.

Bonnie J. Kaplan (Ph.D., Brandeis University) is the Director of the Behavioural Research Unit at the Kinsmen Pediatric Research Centre, Alberta Children's Hospital in Calgary, Alberta, Canada. Her current research interests are in the areas of human psychophysiology and the development of animal models of seizure activity.

Edward S. Katkin (Ph.D., Duke University) is Professor of Psychology at the State University of New York at Buffalo. His major research interest is individual differences in self-control of autonomic responses.

William N. Kuhlman (Ph.D., Yale University) is Associate Investigator at the Neuropsychology Laboratory, V.A. Medical Center, West Haven, Connecticut, and Postdoctoral Associate in Neurology, Yale University School of Medicine. His current areas of research include EEG feedback training in the treatment of seizure disorders and the psychophysiology of the human spontaneous EEG.

Peter J. Lang (Ph.D., University of Buffalo) is Professor of Psychology at the University of Wisconsin. His major research interests are the learned control of cardiovascular responses, cortical and cardiac events in simple information processing, and the psychophysiology of emotional imagery and fear modification.

Neal E. Miller (Ph.D., Yale University) is Professor and Head of a Laboratory of Physiological Psychology at The Rockefeller University. He has made significant contributions to a number of areas of psychology, and sixty-four of his papers have been collected in *Neal E. Miller: Selected Papers*. He has also made some of the earliest and most significant contributions to the field of biofeedback.

John D. Rugh (Ph.D., University of California at Santa Barbara) is an Assistant Professor in the Department of Restorative Dentistry at the University of Texas Health Science Center at San Antonio. His current research is in the areas of stress-related oral disorders and the psychophysiology and learning in the oral cavity.

Deborah Dimmick Smith (M.A., Eastern Kentucky University) is Educational Specialist with the Paraprofessional Training Program at the Northern Nebraska Comprehensive Mental Health Center in Norfolk, Nebraska. One of her major research interests has been electromyographic biofeedback.

Bernard Tursky is Professor of Political Science, Psychology, and Psychiatry at the State University of New York at Stony Brook, and the Director of the Laboratory for Behavioral Research at that institution. His major areas of interest and research are laboratory approaches to the study of pain, cardiovascular biofeedback, and the use of psychophysical and psychophysiological measures in the evaluation of social and political stimuli.

PERGAMON GENERAL PSYCHOLOGY SERIES

Editors: Arnold P. Goldstein, *Syracuse University*
Leonard Krasner, *SUNY, Stony Brook*

TITLES IN THE PERGAMON GENERAL PSYCHOLOGY SERIES
(Added Titles in Back of Volume)

The terms of our inspection copy service apply to all the above books. A complete catalogue of all books in the Pergamon International Library is available on request.

The Publisher will be pleased to receive suggestions for revised editions and new titles.